About the editors

Kim Knott is professor of religious studies at the University of Leeds, UK, and director of Diasporas, Migration and Identities, a programme funded by the Arts and Humanities Research Council (AHRC) that has brought scholars together from all over Britain and from a wide range of disciplines. She has worked on South Asian religious diasporas, particularly British Hindus, and on migration, ethnicity and identity, with publications including *Hindus in Leeds*, *My Sweet Lord: The Hare Krishna Movement*, and *Hinduism: A Very Short Introduction*. In conjunction with government and voluntary sector partners she has researched issues of religious and ethnic diversity and representation. In *The Location of Religion: A Spatial Analysis* and later articles, she has developed a spatial methodology for researching places, bodies and organizations in which controversies occur about matters of sacred concern, whether religious, secular or post-secular.

Seán McLoughlin is senior lecturer in the Department of Theology and Religious Studies at the University of Leeds, UK. Trained in the study of religion, Islam and anthropology, he is an expert on various aspects of South Asian heritage Muslims in Britain and has worked on a number of public projects, as well as giving invited lectures across Europe and in the United States. Co-editor of *European Muslims and the Secular State*, most recently he was principal investigator on an AHRC Diasporas' network, From Diaspora to Multi-Locality: Writing British-Asian Cities (2006–09). A related co-edited volume, *Writing the City in British-Asian Diasporas*, is in preparation, as is a single-authored book, *Representing Muslims: Religion, Diaspora and the Politics of Identity*.

D1600503

DIASPORAS

Concepts, intersections,
identities

edited by Kim Knott and
Seán McLoughlin

Zed Books
LONDON | NEW YORK

February 2012

Diasporas: Concepts, intersections, identities was first published in 2010 by Zed Books Ltd, 7 Cynthia Street, London N1 9JF, UK and Room 400, 175 Fifth Avenue, New York, NY 10010, USA

www.zedbooks.co.uk

FSC
www.fsc.org
MIX
Paper from
responsible sources
FSC® C013604

Set in OurType Arnhem, Monotype Gill Sans Heavy and Elsner+Flake TechnoScript by Ewan Smith, London
Index: ed.emery@thefreeuniversity.net
Cover designed by Rogue Four Design
Printed and bound in Great Britain by CPI Antony Rowe, Chippenham and Eastbourne

Distributed in the USA exclusively by Palgrave Macmillan, a division of St Martin's Press, LLC, 175 Fifth Avenue, New York, NY 10010, USA

A catalogue record for this book is available from the British Library
Library of Congress Cataloging in Publication Data available

ISBN 978 1 84277 947 7 hb
ISBN 978 1 84277 948 4 pb
ISBN 978 1 84813 539 0 eb

Contents

Acknowledgements

We acknowledge the importance of teamwork in the production of this collection of essays, noting the varied and valuable skills that colleagues have brought to the process. Working together as editors has helped us both to endure and at times enjoy the hard work and long hours of planning, commissioning, reading, editing and communicating with authors and the publisher. We thank Katie Roche for her administrative work and for organizing the book symposium, and Mel Prideaux for formatting and cross-checking in fine detail the initial text and bibliography. We acknowledge the thought-provoking and creative work of artists Helen Scalway and Sumi Perera which inspired the book's cover design. The authors did their best to meet our requirements in good spirit, and the collection is a testament to their knowledge, expertise and authority on the subject of diasporas. Ellen Hallsworth at Zed Books was an enthusiastic and engaging commissioning editor; we thank her and Ken Barlow, who took over the role in the later stages. We benefited immensely from the well-informed, positive and helpful comments offered by our expert reader, and have tried to do them justice within the constraints of time and space.

Behind this project lies the momentum and support provided by the 'Diasporas, migration and identities' programme (funded by the UK Arts and Humanities Research Council), particularly by its steering committee, and by the Department of Theology and Religious Studies and the Institute for Colonial and Postcolonial Studies at the University of Leeds.

Our families offered their unconditional love and understanding, particularly over Christmas and New Year when we overworked to get the manuscript to the publisher by the deadline. Love and thanks to John and Anita, Lesley, Thomas and Kate.

Kim Knott and Seán McLoughlin

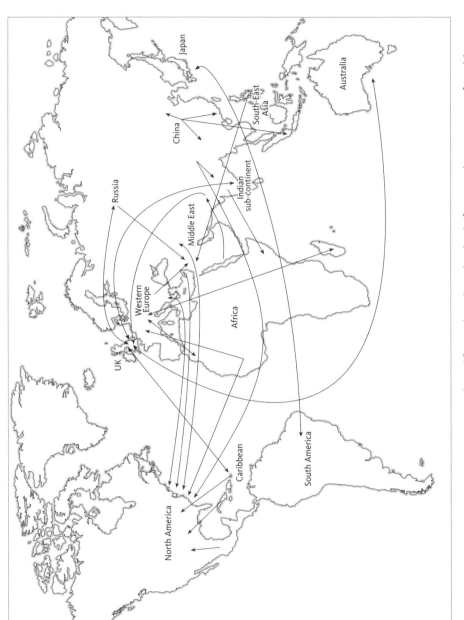

Global diasporic movements in Part Three (© David Appleyard, School of Geography, University of Leeds)

Introduction

Kim Knott and Seán McLoughlin

Diasporic connections; diasporas scholarship

Underground, in the damp darkness, is a network of rooms. They are a testament to three centuries of slavery, when those bought or captured in the African hinterland were incarcerated by European traders and administrators before beginning the second stage of a journey – the middle passage – to the New World. Segregated by sex and length of stay, women and men waited in the dark, crowded into confined and frightening spaces, their health deteriorating, their bodies abused, their senses assaulted. Many died. Others, after months of imprisonment awaiting the arrival of the ships that would take them to the plantations of the Americas, were led into narrow tunnels to exit through the 'door of no return'.

In one room, in the netherworld of Elmina Castle on the coast of Ghana, established by the Portuguese in the 1480s and later administered by the Dutch and finally the British, is a shrine to the memory of the millions who endured the middle passage or died before or during the Atlantic journey. Near by, wreaths have been left by visitors, including the Obamas, who made the pilgrimage in July 2009 as part of the president's first diplomatic visit to Africa (Plate 1). One wreath, 'From diasporas', represents the connection of the African diaspora with this place and many others like it up and down the African coast. It recalls at once a lost and imagined home, a recollection of struggle, survival and death, a revisiting of the experience of confinement and enslavement, and the knowledge of the long journey to freedom, qualified by racism, violence and poverty.

Today, Elmina Castle, with its neighbour at Cape Coast, is a world heritage site, part of a tourist route that takes in the capital, Accra, and the canopy walk in the national park at Kakum. It draws visitors from all over the world, but chief among them are two groups, those from Ghana and neighbouring countries who feel connected to a pan-African history of European enslavement, and those from the Americas and elsewhere whose history places them on a family tree with roots extending back through that netherworld of confinement and slavery. Thus, African 'diasporas' continue to recollect a history and geography of slavery in which Elmina and Ghana's other castles take their place at the outset of a transatlantic passage that, while severing connections and relationships and cutting short many lives, also represents the beginning of a long and complex diasporic journey.

Although some scholars have suggested that 'diaspora' may have become an exhausted concept emptied of meaning by overuse and lack of precise and agreed definition, others have identified it as capturing the very spirit of the age. In a recent panoptical overview, William Safran (2007) has noted that 'diaspora', while once 'an object of suspicion, has [now] become one of fascination', moving from being a 'historically and politically loaded concept' to a neutral and 'catch-all' one. Moreover, the use of the plural form, 'diasporas', has become common only in the last couple of decades. Admittedly an imprecise measure, an all-sites Google search on 11 January 2010 listed some ten million results for the term 'diaspora' globally. Certainly, 'diaspora' continues to have meaning beyond the academy, for diasporans themselves, with copious formal and informal connections being maintained with homelands and with relatives and friends scattered globally. In addition, while diasporas have a long history of political vulnerability, in the contemporary period they have recently become a focus of concern and discussion among government and other public bodies, particularly aid agencies and security departments. In the United States, researchers funded by the Social Science Research Council are examining how members of diasporas and the US government seek to influence one another. It is also the case that many national governments in sending countries – such as India, Mexico, Ukraine and Serbia – have dedicated web pages to their diasporas in recognition of their potential economic and social contribution.

There should be no surprise, then, that diasporas continue to command attention from academics, with Robin Cohen publishing a second edition of *Global Diasporas* in 2008, and with recent books by Braziel (2008), Esman (2009) and Hine et al. (2009). The present volume takes a poly-vocal and multidisciplinary approach, aiming not only to describe the experiences of some diasporic groups, but to chart the varied course of diaspora studies as an interdisciplinary field in which both social scientists and arts and humanities scholars participate. As such, it is expected to fill a gap in the general market for books on the subject in which several key texts (such as Gilroy 1993a; Brah 1996; Cohen 1997/2008; Braziel and Mannur 2003; Kalra et al. 2005) and *Diaspora: A Journal of Transnational Studies* have dominated, and where ethnographic case studies of particular diasporas in specific locations have been the norm.

Diasporas, migration and identities: a research programme

This collection of essays has been compiled in association with a large programme of research on 'Diasporas, migration and identities', funded by the Arts and Humanities Research Council (AHRC) and led by Kim Knott. The newest of the UK's national research councils, the AHRC established this strategic programme in the same year as its own foundation, in 2005. 'Diasporas, migration and identities', a research arena with immense academic interest and support, built on a similar social science initiative several years before, funded by the

Economic and Social Research Council and led by Steven Vertovec, on 'Transnational communities'. The launch of the Diasporas programme took place at the Museum of Immigration and Diversity in London's East End, home to generations of Huguenot, Jewish, Irish and Bangladeshi migrants. At the event, the keynote speaker, Robin Cohen, intimated that social scientific research on migration and transnationalism needed supplementation with work on cultural production, representation, religion, language and human geography in the arts and humanities in order that diasporas be more fully understood and open to analysis. Righting the balance of publicly funded research and making connections across the boundary between the disciplines have been key aspects of the programme.

With a public investment of £6.3 million (in April 2010 the equivalent of $9.7 million or €7 million), it was important that researchers should collaborate with the widest possible range of stakeholders in and beyond the academy and engage the interests of broad publics through innovative forms of dissemination. As such, the programme sought to pursue the following objectives:

1 to stimulate high-quality research on diasporas, migration and identities across the arts and humanities which would draw upon a wide range of disciplinary resources and skills, and encourage interdisciplinary collaboration in and beyond the academy;
2 to make a distinctive contribution to the theoretical, conceptual, thematic, practice-led and empirical study of diasporas, migration and identities by focusing on cultural, historical and linguistic perspectives and creative practice;
3 to develop a body of theory, methods and case studies to enable a comparative analysis of diasporas, migration and their associated identities to be undertaken;
4 to facilitate connection, communication and exchange – at both programme and project level – between researchers and a wide range of individuals and organizations that had an interest in the research and its outcomes, including those in the cultural sector, media, government, public and voluntary bodies, and to contribute to the development of public policy;
5 to contribute to public awareness of arts and humanities research on diasporas, migration and identities;
6 to generate research findings and outcomes of international significance and quality, to disseminate these to an international research audience, and to develop networks of researchers in and beyond the UK;
7 and to develop new connections and approaches that may become embedded in the research agenda and resources of the arts and humanities, and may be built on in future research applications (Diasporas, Migration and Identities 2005).

3

This volume of essays is a response to these objectives, particularly insofar as it stresses the importance of the theoretical and conceptual, the thematic, multidisciplinary and interdisciplinary, as well as the empirical and more metaphorical study of diasporas, and the value of internationalizing such scholarship for a wide audience, including students and members of diasporic communities.

The 'Diasporas, migration and identities' programme comprised three different types of research: small projects focused on individual researchers, large collaborative projects involving between two and eight researchers, and workshops and networks, the first being a series of academic meetings over one year, the latter two-year initiatives to build up national and international groups of scholars focused on a particular research problem, subject or issue. Drawn together and supported by a director (Kim Knott) and administrator (Katie Roche) based at the University of Leeds, forty-nine teams (totalling about 120 investigators and researchers), from universities all over the UK, conducted research on a wide variety of diasporas. Their research addressed six broad themes: (a) migration, settlement and diaspora: modes, stages and forms; (b) representation, performance and discourse; (c) languages and linguistic change; (d) subjectivity, emotion and identity; (e) objects, practices and places; and (f) beliefs, values and laws. Within these themes, projects focused on UK towns and cities (such as Rotherham, Manchester or London's East End) and non-UK locations (the Black Sea ports of Odessa and Istanbul, the refugee camps of Lebanon, or travelling sites of Gypsies), on global movements (e.g. from the Philippines to the Middle East, from the USA and Germany back home to Greece and Cyprus), historical cases (such as Roman migration, Viking identities, nineteenth-century British and South Asian cultural exchange), and comparative studies (e.g. the nature of Jewish and Muslim minority experiences in the USA and Europe, and of legal asylum discourses in France and the UK). Circulating artefacts, food and fashion, as well as cultural exchange and production – in theatre, music, art and reading – were all the subjects of research. Extensive information about the nature, methods, findings and publications associated with these forty-nine projects can be viewed on the programme website, www.diasporas.ac.uk.

Several international conferences were held during the lifetime of the programme, particularly 'Encounters and intersections: religion, diaspora and ethnicities' (in collaboration with research programmes on religion and society, and identities and social action), at the University of Oxford in 2008, and 'Diasporas, migration and identities: crossing boundaries, new directions', held jointly with the Centre for Research on Nationalism, Ethnicity and Multiculturalism at the University of Surrey in 2009, which attracted participants from more than thirty countries. A third event was held, at the University of Leeds in 2008, to review the field and discuss the book's contents, gaps, overlaps and new directions with the volume's contributors. As editors, we are grateful to those who attended for their enthusiasm, ideas and suggestions for improvement, many of which we later incorporated.

About one half of the book's contributors have strong links with the 'Diasporas, migration and identities' programme, as investigators, researchers, steering-committee members or keynote speakers at its major events. Five of the projects – on Greek migration and return, Filipino migrants and sacrality, the diasporic creativity of the BBC World Service, transnational musicians' networks, and diasporic readers and reception – are represented in the third part of the book. The book's co-editor, Seán McLoughlin, was principal investigator on a research network within the programme, 'Writing British Asian cities' (McLoughlin et al. forthcoming). The other half of the book's contributors were selected because they were well-established or emerging international scholars writing with authority on key concepts in diaspora studies, on its principal intersections or exemplary global movements. Residing and working in twelve countries but with roots in many more, the contributors have personal diasporic origins, narratives and connections – in Asia, the global South and the Middle East as well as Europe, North America and Australia – together with in-depth academic knowledge about particular diasporas and diasporas in general. Between them they represent major centres of research related to migration and diasporas – including the Center for Diaspora and Transnational Studies, Toronto, the Sussex Centre for Migration Research in the UK, the Max Planck Institute for the Study of Religious and Ethnic Diversity, Germany, the UK's Wilberforce Institute for the study of slavery and emancipation, the Sociological Institute for Jewish Community Studies at Bar-Ilan in Israel, the Center for Global Studies at George Mason University in the USA, the Danish Institute for International Studies, and COMPAS, the Centre for Migration, Policy and Society at Oxford University. They include scholarly experts on multiculturalism, migration, identity, cosmopolitanism, super-diversity, ethnicity, religion, post-colonialism, creolization, transnationalism, hybridity and identity, as well as diasporas themselves.

Migration and diasporas: global and regional statistics

As global phenomena, with far-reaching histories and multi-located populations, some of which are still in transit, diasporas are impossible to enumerate reliably. Migration statistics are often available for nation-states, showing the extent of movement in and out in any year by people of various ethnicities, religions or countries of birth (e.g. Central Bureau of Statistics, Israel; Office for National Statistics, UK). Often it is scholars with an interest in particular diasporas who have sought out and brought together statistical and other data to present a global empirical overview of one or more populations (e.g. Bozorghmehr and Sabagh 1988; Baines 1991), or groups of scholars contributing collaboratively to develop a global, transnational or regional picture of one or more diasporas (e.g. Ma and Cartier 2003; Gitelman 2003). In terms of global research, however, it is organizations such as the United Nations, the International Migration Organization and the World Bank which carry out or sponsor relevant statistical and demographical research (e.g. United Nations 2008; IOM 2008, 2010; Beine et al. 2009).

According to the UN in 2008, there were some 214 million international migrants globally, about 3 per cent of the world's population (United Nations 2008), and the equivalent of a very large country. With men and women in almost equal number, they were concentrated in relatively few countries, and included some sixteen million refugees (IOM 2008, 2010). The top three sending countries were China, India and the Philippines, with estimated diasporas of 35 million, 20 million and 7 million respectively. In terms of receiving regions, Europe had the highest number of migrants, with nearly 70 million (9.5 per cent of the population), and the USA 50 million (over 14 per cent of the population). Asia and Africa also received large numbers, but these represented less than 2 per cent of their population in each case. Oceania's 6 million migrants, however, constituted nearly 17 per cent of its total population, while, in 2000, international labour migrants constituted over 60 per cent of the population in both Qatar and the United Arab Emirates (IOM 2008, 2010).

In terms of particular diasporas, as Beine et al. suggest,

> [They] constitute invisible nations that reside outside their origin countries. In 2000, there were over 6 million Mexicans working in the United States, more than 1.2 million Turks in Germany and more than 0.5 million Algerians in France. In relative terms, 45 percent of the Surinamese-born were in the Netherlands; about 35 percent of the native-born from Grenada were in the United States; over 25 percent of Samoans were in New Zealand. (2009: 2)

As their work shows, existing diasporas have a very significant impact on future movements of migrants, suggesting that it may be possible to predict – while recognizing local, national and global factors that may inhibit, increase or alter flows – patterns of future migration in terms of sending and receiving societies. Policies and practices of family reunification and other patterns of chain migration are important for understanding the operation and extent of such movements; 'diasporas are by far the most important determinant of migration flows' (ibid.: 33).

Furthermore, as our knowledge of the classic Jewish, African and Armenian diasporas shows, such flows have a long history. In the early modern period, 'some two million settlers crossed the Atlantic from Europe to settle in the Americas [...] [and] nearly eight million Africans were brought to the Americas, most of them in slavery' (Manning 2005: 1), the social, economic and cultural consequences of which were immense. More recent migrations have led to a move from a predominantly rural world to one in which over half its population lives in cities (ibid.: 1). If Beine et al. (2009) are correct, it is not just the call of improved living standards and labour opportunities which drive such migrations, but diasporas themselves, which contribute to sustaining the connections and resources that facilitate migration and telling the stories that encourage others to make the journey. Not least because of advances in communications technology, many generations have a consciousness of diasporic identity and difference that may still be vibrant, with younger and older people seeking to explore their roots and to reconnect with other places and times.

Outlining the book

The rationale for *Diasporas: Concepts, intersections, identities* lies in bringing together within a single volume the fullest possible range of dispersed interests constituting the field, whether in terms of theories, themes or case studies. The majority of essays are contributed by scholars from one or more of the disciplines of religion, history, political science, geography, sociology, anthropology, post-colonial literature and cultural studies. While each discipline reflects a formation within the nation-states of European modernity (or some sort of reaction against this), quite distinctive interests and agendas have emerged historically. Indeed, real differences between disciplines are not at all unknown within diaspora studies (and cognates like migration and ethnic studies). For example, while the study of diaspora, globalization and transnationalism has been pivotal in highlighting the significance of translocal processes, a state-centred 'methodological nationalism' (Glick Schiller and Caglar 2009) has remained evident in many disciplines such as political science and development studies. Similarly, a veritable politics of identity has at times marked out the boundaries, say, between postmodernist anti-essentialism in sociology or cultural studies and a continuing interest in talking (if more dialogically) about groups of people in anthropology.

Nevertheless, diaspora studies today is a broad church characterized by much multi- and interdisciplinary work, especially away from disciplinary rhetoric and at the level of individual/collaborative scholarship. As contributions to all the sections in this book show, there has been much cross-fertilization of ideas, often with a holistic and pragmatic concern to balance the explanatory power of social structure and the insights to be gleaned by recognizing cultural agency. The inclusive approach to diaspora studies adopted here also reflects our own (quite similar) interstitial disciplinary location(s) as two scholars of diaspora who work in a department of theology and religious studies. We have worked as ethnographers of diasporas (British Indian Hindus and British Pakistani Muslims) in the sociological and anthropological traditions, while at the same time being increasingly drawn to and influenced by contemporary social and cultural theory. Our interest in religion, however, makes us especially aware, not only of the continuing pull of tradition (whether ethnic, national or religious), but also of religion's relative neglect in diaspora studies. Too often it has been treated in a cursory and descriptive fashion or its significance simply ignored (Knott 2005b; McLoughlin 2010). Of course things are changing rapidly, as a number of the entries in this volume demonstrate (Martin Baumann, Gerd Baumann, Modood, Vásquez, Johnson et al., McLoughlin). Indeed, we make no special pleading but simply affirm that in this volume, in any number of locations and configurations among diverse and sometimes competing constituencies, religion quietly but visibly takes its place alongside other relevant categories.

All the essays that follow are succinct, two- to three-thousand-word guides to the latest research on, and key contours of, a particular concept, perspective or exemplary case. Significantly, we have not stifled our contributors' particular passions and at times opposed epistemological positions by insisting on a homogenizing template. Each essay offers a more in-depth treatment than a simple dictionary entry, without being painstakingly comprehensive. Thus, as well as conventional academic references, each essay concludes with up to five carefully chosen further readings. There is also a lengthy bibliography at the end of the volume. *Diasporas: Concepts, intersections, identities* is not a textbook in the sense that each contribution is intended to be studied sequentially, from beginning to end. Within a single collection, it offers a reference resource for students, scholars and researchers to dip into; being self-contained, the essays can be read in their own right. Nevertheless, the collection represents much more than the sum of its parts and, as we hope will be evident, its three sections are carefully aligned to narrate the most important and distinctive dimensions of the field, its genesis and exodus. In this regard, the book could undoubtedly be adapted to the needs of a taught course or series of seminars.

As we shall see in the overview that follows, Part One concerns the journeying of diaspora studies with reference to the historical and especially contemporary development of key, and interrelated, *Concepts and theories*. Across thirteen essays, concerning everything from ethnicity to cosmopolitanism, it includes critical reflection on the work of established and emerging theorists, a number of whom are represented among the contributors. Part Two, *Intersections*, brings the subject of diaspora(s) more explicitly into engagement with major cross-cutting disciplinary and intellectual agendas. These include political economy, security and cities, various aspects of social relations such as race, gender and sexuality, as well as forms of cultural production and communication – material, textual, visual and electronic. Part Three, *Empirical and metaphorical diasporas*, examines fifteen historically and geographically significant examples of movement and dwelling, self-consciously seeking to explore such a mapping across the whole globe, while at the same time doing justice to particular translocal circuits and more deterritorialized spaces.

Part One: Concepts and theories As Cohen's (2008) recent periodization suggests, and the essays in Part One demonstrate, it is possible to speak of a number of transformations in the genealogy of diaspora studies (cf. Tölölyan 1991; Baumann 2000). In recent decades, there has been an overall shift from a highly particular sort of scholarship to one that has been sown productively over many borders.

First, as Martin Baumann's essay on 'Exile' shows, there is of course a large volume of historically descriptive studies reflecting the fact that for more or less two thousand years the term diaspora was used mainly in relation to the prototypical Jewish diaspora. He draws out the soteriological nuances of the neologism as it was used in the Septuagint, the Greek translation of the Hebrew scriptures, during the third and second centuries BCE, as well as comparing this with the varied subsequent connotations of diaspora and exile into the contemporary period. Classical Jewish experience testifies to the fact that at the heart of the idea of diaspora is an ideology of separation from, and a longing for return to, the homeland. Stock's essay on 'Home and memory' dwells on the many complex and layered ways in which home is remembered (and forgotten) in strange lands. She argues that, physical or symbolic, one of the strengths of the idea of home is that it is both an emic and an etic category.

From the 1960s and 1970s, usage of the term 'diaspora' came to be extended to other groups with experiences of large-scale scattering due to homeland trauma, including the Armenians, Irish and eventually the Palestinians (see Cohen 1997). At a time of post-colonial independence in Africa, however, and the fight for civil rights in the USA, most notable was the development of African studies, with diaspora becoming associated with the racialized politics of remembering 'Slavery and the black Atlantic', the subject of Richardson's essay. He shows the brutal modern efficiency of this trade in human cargo and yet the pivotal role of Africans in shaping and remaking the Americas after Columbus. While he traces the huge implications of slavery as a 'way of death' for the transmission of fragmented African identities, he also underlines moments of rebellion and great linguistic, cultural and religious creolization.

At the launch of *Diaspora: A Journal of Transnational Studies*, the editor, Khachig Tölölyan (1991), spoke of a further 'decisive shift' in focus for diaspora studies as it also began to encompass those groups hitherto identified as immigrants, ethnic minorities, exiles, expatriates, refugees, guest workers and so on. The social sciences, from political science to anthropology (e.g. Sheffer 1986a; Appadurai 1986), had begun to explore the intersections of diaspora with other aspects of social, spatial and cultural relations. Thus, not all diasporas were necessarily to be seen as the victims of great catastrophes. Moreover, as van Hear's essay on 'Migration' underlines, not all mobility and resettlement leads to homeland consciousness and/or a sense of connection to co-ethnics overseas. Highlighting voluntary as well as forced migration, he sets the former against a picture of clear global inequality, while an increase in the latter since the 1990s followed the break-up of the Soviet Union and ethno-national conflict in the Balkans, Middle East and Africa. Levitt's essay on 'Transnationalism' illuminates the growing impact of globalization theory during the 1990s (cf. especially Appadurai 1996), with contemporary communications technology enabling people, goods, capital and ideas to circulate back and forth between multi-located diasporas, their homelands and beyond as never before. Experiencing the world increasingly as a single space has offered diasporas new possibilities for a life across borders, contesting the idea of the nation-state as the most self-evident unit of society.

At the same time, the national context of settlement still has huge consequences for migrants and diasporas. This can be mapped in terms of the legacy of colonialism; the extent of citizenship rights; the nature of immigration/security legislation; social attitudes to cultural pluralism and levels of protection from discrimination; the status and public recognition of religion; and employment and educational opportunities (McLoughlin 2010). Against this context, Gerd Baumann takes up the complex relationship between 'Nation, ethnicity and community', both in terms of scholars' understanding of all bounded communities of culture as fictive and imagined, and the fact that for their members they continue to feel 'experientially authentic'. Critiquing the continuing ethnicization by plural nation-states of their citizenship, and noting that diasporic leaders are often required by the state to produce a reified account of their difference, Baumann suggests a need for new 'fictions of moral convergence' across borders, valorizing a common faith in human rights particularly. Similarly, Modood's essay on 'Multiculturalism and citizenship' insists that citizens be able to debate the terms of their own public recognition. Reflecting on one of the key issues currently exercising political theorists in the West, he also suggests that religious (especially Muslim) minorities confront particular problems when faced with the 'neutral' secularity of liberal democracy.

For all the shifts in diaspora studies during the 1990s, perhaps the most crucial saw postmodernist, post-colonial and feminist critiques deconstruct, reappropriate (and sometimes eventually reject outright – e.g. Anthias 1998) the necessary relationship between, and scholarly focus upon, ethno-religious communities and their homeland origins. Against the context of such theorizing, more metaphorical and deterritorialized interpretations of diaspora – such as what Brah referred to as 'a homing desire' (1996: 179) – emerged. A period of particular florescence between 1993 and 1997 witnessed the publication of several key texts (e.g. Gilroy 1993a; Bhabha 1994; Brah 1996; Clifford 1997). Reflecting on this work, Huggan's essay on 'Post-coloniality' underlines a desire to escape not only from the outsider exclusions of host-land racisms and nationalisms but also from insider attempts to resist marginalization with nostalgic appeals to cultural purity. Thus, during this period, diaspora also came to be closely associated with the notion of 'Hybridity', which, as Hutnyk shows, celebrated the transgressive intermixtures and impurities of the so-called 'third space'. He maintains, however, that hybridity assumes an 'anterior pure' as well as being readily commodified as exotica by the culture industry. Vertovec's essay on 'Cosmopolitanism', as another theory of cultural encounter, offers a further corrective to ideas about hybridity. Focusing on the extent to which displacement encourages 'social attributes, practices and competencies' supportive of a willingness to engage the other, he traces a shift in understanding from notions of elite rootlessness among exiled intellectuals and artists, to a more vernacular and rooted cosmopolitanism in everyday social structures and relations.

For some scholars, the permissive move beyond the ethno-national marked an unhelpful 'dispersal' of diaspora to encompass literally any far-flung collectivity – gay, deaf, digital, terrorist and so on (Brubaker 2005: 4). Nevertheless, Cohen (2008) now speaks more clearly of a present phase of 'reflective consolidation' in diaspora studies, the field having gone some way to acknowledging the validity of postmodernist/post-colonial critiques and more metaphorical interpretations of home. In this spirit, the final three essays of Part One have a somewhat different tone. Cohen's essay on 'Social identities and creolization' suggests that diaspora is 'an inappropriate tool with which to measure all trajectories of belonging and identification', revisiting especially the idea of creolization (the cross-fertilization of cultural practices as they interact). He puts all his reflections in the broader frame of a five-fold continuum of identity and belonging, however, from sub-national entities such as ethnicity, through nationalism, diasporic identities and creolization, to cosmopolitanism. Werbner's essay on 'Complex diasporas' stresses a consensus in the literature: diasporas are 'hybrid *and* heterogeneous in their own peculiar historically determined ways'; they are 'ethnic-parochial *and* cosmopolitan'. Indeed, complex diasporas of the late modern world need not refer to the same group of people all of the time being segmented by language, culture and religion. Finally, Knott's essay on 'Space and movement' shows how central spatial metaphors have been to the study of diasporas, hinting at a leave-taking from diaspora for other notions such as diaspora space. Revisiting Brah's theorization, she shows how diaspora space is configured by multiple locations of home and abroad and contested relations among and between people with diverse subject positions. Diaspora space is also 'inhabited […] equally by those who are constructed and represented as indigenous' (Brah 1996: 181) and highlights the importance of dwelling as well as travelling – 'the lived experience of a locality' (ibid.: 192).

Part Two: Intersections The *Intersections* explored in the sixteen essays in Part Two can be conveniently seen in terms of three key clusters. These are: (i) the shaping power of social structure and political economy; (ii) the multiple positioning of subjectivities in diasporic space; and (iii) forms of cultural production and expression – material, textual, visual and electronic – both popular and elite.

For all the significance of trade in people for the story of diaspora, Dwyer's essay on 'Diasporas and economies' reminds us that the success of entrepreneurial trading networks, from millionaires to street traders, has often been based on trust between co-ethnics. Indeed, such networks were in many ways the foundation of the global capitalist economy. Lyons and Mandaville's essay on 'Diasporas and politics' reminds us, too, that whatever the nature of their dispersal, host-land governments regulate diasporas' presence through immigration and integration policy, as well as citizenship tests. At the same time, both host-land domestic and foreign policy have become a significant focus for highly organized ethnic/diasporic lobbies which plug readily into translocal activist ethnoscapes.

These themes are extended in Turner's essay on 'Diasporas, conflict and security', with the issue of security especially going to the heart of diaspora space for both diasporas and their new host lands alike. While networks of immigration can clearly also combine with crime and/or terrorism, the 'threat' that diasporas are often said to pose economically, politically, socially or culturally can see attempts to 'protect' the nation-state slide into discourses which 'blame the other' and also repression/violence. Moreover, in political terms, as well as being long-distance 'peace-breakers', diasporas can also be long-distance 'peacemakers'. Tracing more economic and social contributions to the homeland, Page and Mercer's essay on 'Diasporas and development' explores the costs of the 'brain drain' to the global South, as well as the benefits of remittances; in 2007, $25 billion was sent to developing countries from the global North. They also provide an important reminder of South–South as well as North–South migrations, a theme carried forward in Eade's essay on 'Diasporas and cities'. He notes the huge significance of rural-to-urban migration, whether in the North or the South. Underlining that transnationalism does not imply placelessness, he makes clear too that cities are both hubs of 'super-diversity' and new vernacular identities, as well as being sites of ethnic clustering and conflict in particular neighbourhoods.

The second cluster of essays in Part Two explores dominant categorizations and representations of difference, the power relations underlying these and contestation of such hierarchies out of diverse and complex subject positions. Thus, Alexander's essay on 'Diasporas, race and difference' underlines the significance of racially marked groups in the history of diasporas and, for all its disruptive possibilities, problematizes the term's easy appropriation as a polite 'code' for continuing to mark such differences. Indeed, she questions whether the term should be reserved for communities of colour at a time when 'me too-ism' among the privileged means that imperialists can be counted as diasporic too. Similarly, Al-Ali's essay on 'Diasporas and gender' notes that there is still much gender blindness and lip-service in the literature, while women themselves must negotiate 'at least two sets of ideologies of men's privilege'.

Nevertheless, women are key to all processes associated with diaspora(s), including the cultural/biological marking of ethno-nationalism and multiculturalism. Drawing attention to the (androcentric) association of diaspora with the scattering of seed, Kosnick notes in 'Diasporas and sexuality' that queer sexuality has been another marginalized topic, one which troubles 'natural' constructions of the social body in terms of family and kinship. These contributions map the coordinates of hegemonic relations between as well as within 'communities', some of the latter being alleviated, intensified or redefined in the reconfiguring of diaspora space.

While religion has often legitimized the authority of the normative and been enabled by political formations and sponsorship, Vásquez's essay acknowledges the multiplicity of religious subjects' identities and the hybridity of diasporic religious formations more generally. He also underlines, however, the particular saliency of a 'return' to bounded moral communities with a supralocative reference point and authority in the confusing anomie of pluralistic contexts. Language, including sacred language, as Beswick's essay shows, is another key aspect in the sustaining and transmission of heritage, as well as the gradual marking of a loss of connection with homelands as time passes. Language use, like cultural practice, varies from context to context, and different strategies, repertoires and vernaculars evolve, including code-switching and lexical borrowing. Of course, language, religion, sexuality, gender and race must all be seen as intersecting formations. Moreover, each essay in this clustering also engages with the way in which these and other key social positions such as class, generation and disability configure the ascribing and achieving of individual and collective identities.

Crang's essay on 'Diasporas and material culture' examines the circulation of everyday cultural objects and artefacts in diaspora, their production and the ways in which they are received, objectified and consumed, as well as how all this mediates and shapes social relations and values/identity. Of course, diasporic consciousness has also become for some diasporans the impetus for their own creative explorations, reflections and expressions. In this third cluster of essays in Part Two, this is reflected variously in accounts of literature by Kabir, performance by Gilbert and Lo and film and cinema by Berghahn. Forged between 'here' and 'there', creativity in all these aspects of the arts and culture brings new imaginaries to life, as well as novel aesthetics and ritual/performative practices. They further reveal the layering of diasporic subjectivity in terms of memory and nostalgia, experience and inheritance, emotion and the senses. This is true of distinctively private/individual and/or more public/collective cultural productions and both elite and popular forms, although there are still particular problems with the former (or indeed sometimes the latter) being represented or consumed as 'social reality'. Indeed, while some artistic and cultural production is akin to rooted activism, its prosthetic appropriation and commodification by the cultural industries can also fatally exoticize rather than productively engage with the other.

Drawing Part Two to a close, and looping back from issues of creativity into those of social structure and political economy, are the essays by Karim on 'Diasporas and media' and Bernal on 'Diasporas and cyberspace'. Newspapers, radio and television, reflecting both community/public service and more corporate initiatives, have all allowed imagined communities to temporarily 'undo their mobility' and gather again in diaspora. They thus create new spaces for the transmission of language and performance of identity. Indeed, while 'piggybacking' new technology, given the imperatives of their distance from the homeland and co-ethnics overseas, diasporas have often been at the forefront of its take-up and development, e.g. in terms of satellite television. In contrast to broadcasting (or ethnic 'narrowcasting'), cyberspace is relatively inexpensive and interactive, decentralized and democratized, offering freedom to explore social networking and organize counter-publics which offer different ways of seeing the world. Of course, 'we are never all connected to each other' and electronic communities are just as fragmented and segmented as real-time ones. Thus, as suggested by earlier essays in this section, while enabling a more immediate response to distant events, cyberspace is a vehicle for both dialogue and conflict.

Part Three: Empirical and metaphorical diasporas In Part Three, essays trace movements within 'the East/South' as well as to 'the West/North', exploring case studies of conventional territorialized and empirical ethno-national diasporas as well as more deterritorializing linkages and imaginaries, testing the very concept of diaspora to its limits once again. The overall focus here is both modern/contemporary (eighteenth to twenty-first centuries) and ethnographic. Essayists' accounts also often reflect long-standing engagement with diasporic voices over many decades, and from complex insider and outsider positions.

Part Three begins by revisiting exemplary movements within and to the Americas. Stepick et al. reflect upon the complex and dense relations between North and Latin America as well as the Caribbean, underlining the way in which diasporas were created when the USA seized more than half of Mexico in the nineteenth century and by anti-communist policies in the 1960s. Emphasizing the continuing significance of pan-ethnic racial classification systems and immigration law, they discuss real social divisions as well as ethno-national solidarity among Mexicans, Cubans, Haitians and others. Similarly, the story of the so-called 'Great Migration' of 50 million people from 'white' Europe across the Atlantic to North America between 1850 and 1914 is recalled in Christou and King's contribution on the Greeks. While part of their story reflects the standard 'American dream' of hard work and success (e.g. in the ethnic food sector), consciousness of ethno-national difference, as well as a commitment to returning home, still remains remarkably salient.

Another (central/eastern) European group that found its way to the USA during the twentieth century, and especially following the Holocaust and the final collapse of the former Soviet Union in 1991, was the Russian Jews. In her essay Remennick also explores this group's real and symbolic return to Israel, as well as its often very tense relationship with other Israelis. Political circumstances are evident too in the movement of middle-class Iranians to the West, and especially the USA, since the 1970s. Raji dwells upon the impact of the revolution in 1979 and the ambiguous subsequent relationship of exiles in 'Tehrangeles' to a homeland that had become entirely transformed as an Islamic republic. Moving south, and from the 'developed' to the 'developing' world, Lesser highlights the legacy of the end of slavery in Latin America in his account of the Nikkei, the Japanese in Brazil. He reflects on shifts in the pattern of their racialization and the significance of world events such as the Second World War, as well as observing the complexity of being home and away: when in Japan the Nikkei are Brazilian, when in Brazil they are Japanese.

Staying within the East, Christiansen's essay gives an important historical account of regional migrations within the vast space and cultural universe of China, which might be said to include much of South-East Asia. Notably, until 2002, the rural-to-urban migrant workers who powered China's recent economic boom saw their citizenship tied to their homeland localities, thus effectively rendering them a diaspora in their own country. Anand's essay on the Tibetan diaspora is a further, oblique commentary on China's role in creating diasporas. He highlights the former as both a peculiar example of 'positive exoticization' in the Western media's imagination and yet extremely fragile given the symbolic importance given to just one person, Nobel Peace Prize winner the Dalai Lama, who went into exile in 1959. Anand's essay also highlights the diasporic use of religious discourses (associated here with a pacific and universalizing modernist Buddhism). This is a theme which begins to test the idea of diaspora as an essentially ethno-national phenomenon.

Johnson et al.'s essay discusses the experiences of contemporary Filipino women who labour as domestic workers in Israel and Saudi Arabia, and so in close proximity to their sacred homelands as Christians and Muslims respectively. For all their subjects' exploitation and lack of citizenship, the authors stress the sense of reward and empowerment that emerges in these women's creation of congregations, witness to more privileged co-religionists, acquiring of devotional artefacts and enhanced cultural capital back home. McLoughlin's essay further explores the idea of a religious 'homing desire' among Muslim diasporas who often feel 'blocked out' of, or 'in between', a sense of homeland and host-land belonging. Tracing the story of Islam itself as a travelling religion, he examines the salience of the idea of the *umma* (transnational community of believers) for Pakistanis in Britain during various global crises since the Salman Rushdie affair in 1989.

At a distance from the motherland, a further cluster of essays in Part Three interrogates Britain's role as a colonial power in creating diasporas worldwide. The privileged imperial diaspora which benefited from the dispossession of Aboriginal peoples and 'recentred English/Britishness overseas' is the backdrop for Wills's exploration of a post-imperial child migrant's unpublished auto-biographical writing. Lacking mobility and in the context of fading white power in multicultural Australia, as an adult 'Fred' nostalgically seeks wholeness in placed homeland identity. The product of the same world, but an intended dias-poric contact zone and soundscape for Britain's dispersed imperial community rather than a physical location, Gillespie's account of the BBC's Empire/World Service reflects on the challenges of balancing 'corporate cosmopolitanism' and national interest during the colonial and Cold War periods. Its broadcasters were often exiles, refugees and dissident intellectuals, and from 1939 weekly programmes such as *Caribbean Voices* showcased Commonwealth talent, such as the writer V. S. Naipaul. Naipaul's *A Bend in the River* (1979) is the starting point for Quayson's insightful account of how diaspora was tied to British 'colonial space-making' in East and Central Africa. Following the late-nineteenth-century abolition of slavery, indentured labourers from Gujarat and Panjab in India were transported across the hybridizing space of the Indian Ocean, later becoming bankers and then twice-migrants who found their way (back) to Britain and beyond, having been made refugees by Africanization policies in the 1960s.

The relationship between Africa and Europe is documented further by Mein-hof et al., who describe the lives and careers of three different North African and Malagasy musicians, seeing them as empowered transnational individuals rather than as members of diasporas. The networks they are involved in (or seek to bypass) are multiple and dynamic, ethnic and non-ethnic, including the world music 'community'. Stretching the concept of diaspora even farther, through a study of a cyberspatial reading group whose members are dispersed in African and British cities, Procter's essay explores the idea that reading itself is an odyssey 'outside and beyond the self'. He is interested in how 8 million copies of Chinua Achebe's (1958) *Things Fall Apart* have travelled across forty-five languages and, whether in Lagos or London, how eager the readers are to reterri-torialize their readings, and position themselves locally in relation to the text.

Finally, returning us to the story of the Jewish diaspora, Shneer and Aviv question Israel's fear of Jews elsewhere assimilating in a way that challenges the centre–periphery hierarchy between here and there. They celebrate the cosmopolitan rootedness of Jewish diasporas across the globe and reject the tyranny of diaspora as a term when it suggests to them they cannot remake home abroad – indeed, remake home almost anywhere.

PART ONE

Concepts and theories

1 Diasporas wreath, Elmina Castle, Ghana (© Regina Marchi)

Elmina Castle, where many slaves began their journey westwards to the Americas, was established by the Portuguese in the 1480s and later administered by the Dutch and British. Today it is a World Heritage Site. In one of its underground prisons is a shrine to the memory of the millions who endured the Atlantic 'middle passage' or died before or during the journey. Wreaths have been left by visitors, one of which, 'From diasporas', represents the memory and connection of the African diaspora with Elmina and other castles on the African coast.

I | Exile

Martin Baumann

In contemporary discourse, exile and diaspora are often taken to refer to various national, cultural, religious and political groups and peoples. Earlier studies, however, identified the Jewish experience as the paradigm for both exile and diaspora. Such a focus on Jewish communities found its rationale in their capacity to preserve the 'law' outside the 'Holy Land', to live a life according to the commands of the Torah despite strong assimilative pressures from the 'host' society. The terms exile and diaspora have their origins in different linguistic and cultural settings – that of Roman legal terminology and of Jewish theology. Although they need to be distinguished theologically according to Jewish understanding, sociologically they refer to the same socio-political situation of the exiled and diasporized group.

General meaning of exile

The term 'exile' is resonant with ideas of forced emigration, displacement, social and political marginalization of an individual or a group of refugees. It aligns to experiences of loneliness, foreignness, homesickness and an enduring longing to remigrate to the place of origin. The Latin notions *exilium* and *exul* denote a temporary banishment, at times also asylum. During the first millennium BCE, classical oriental empires used mass deportation as a means of punishment and exercise of power, forcing entire nations to leave home and to move into exile.

Generally, people refrain from moving into exile and staying there. Exile is a state forced upon individuals, groups or a nation; they are passive reactors subjected to this state. Exile is rarely sought. At times, though, individuals, entire groups and peoples may actively escape into exile in order to seek refuge and avoid persecution. Once politically secure in exile, these individuals and groups may actively work to support other refugees and to bring about a change in political oppression. Usually, exiles think of their exile as a temporary state and their focus of identification, attention and activities clearly rests with the territory and culture of their former home. Conceived of as transitory, the state of exile may end with repatriation and a radical change of political power back home.

Exile – historical coinage

In Western common knowledge, the notion of exile is predominantly bound to the experience of the Jewish people in the first millennium BCE. Exile is a term used by Jews of that time in both geographical and theological semantics: it refers to a concrete land, far away from Israel-Palestine and Judaea; and it refers to a fourfold theological scheme. According to this, God renders upon the Jewish people banishment into exile as punishment for breaking the law. As such, being forced into exile provides an explanation for the pitiful state. But it carries also advice and admonishment about how to bring exile to an end: to faithfully obey the law again, i.e. the 613 Jewish commandments and prohibitions (Hebrew *mitzvot*).

Jewish experience with exile started in the late eighth century BCE. Assyrian invaders deported members of the ten northern tribes of Israel to upper Mesopotamia. Further displacements to Assyria followed. In 597 BCE, Babylonian king Nebuchadnezzar conquered Judaea and deported large parts of the Judaean upper class. During the second punitive expedition in 587/586 BCE, the Temple of Jerusalem was destroyed. The deported Jews were settled at the 'waters of Babylon' (Psalm 137:1). They built houses and arranged for gardens and gradually integrated into Babylonian society. Religiously, however, Jews warded off assimilation and maintained the tradition of their forefathers. In 538 BCE, the edict of Cyrus ended the banishment and enabled a return to Judaea in 522 BCE. Only a minority returned, however, while the rest arranged for an enduring stay. They formed the nucleus of the later, famous Babylon diaspora (Neusner 1965–70). The completion of the restoration of the Temple in 515 marked the beginning of the era of the Second Temple (ended subsequently in 70 CE).

During the following centuries, Israel-Palestine remained a region of political instability and a war zone contested by Egypt and Persia, before Greece established its supremacy from 333 BCE onwards. Jews emigrated to safer places such as Asia Minor and to existing Jewish communities in Egypt to ply their trade and business. Alexandria in northern Egypt developed into a flourishing Jewish centre of commerce and learning. Here, Jews translated the Hebrew scriptures into Greek, which was their own vernacular and that of the reigning power. The evolved Greek translation, the Septuagint (third/second century BCE), coined the term 'diaspora' to address the various Jewish communities scattered all over the eastern Mediterranean (Barclay 1996; Cohen 1999; Grabbe 2008).

Diaspora as a neologism

The Greek noun *diasporá* derives from the composite verb *dia-* and *speírein*, adopting meanings of 'to scatter, spread, disperse, be separated'. The verb, which became more widely used in the fifth century BCE among classical philosophers and Hellenist writers, had a negative connotation. Epicurus, reported Plutarch, used 'diaspora' in the context of his philosophical treatises to refer to processes of dispersion and decomposition, a dissolution into various parts (e.g. atoms) without any further relation to each other. 'Diaspora' had an adverse, devastating meaning and was not used to imply a geographic place or sociological group. The Alexandrian Jewish-Greek translators of the Hebrew scriptures adopted precisely the disastrous connotations of current philosophical discourse (van Unnik 1993: 86–7).

In the evolved Septuagint, however, the noun *diasporá* and the verb *diaspeírein* were coined as technical terms to interpret Jewish existence far from the 'Promised Land' in light of an encompassing soteriological pattern. As a matter of fact, the Hebrew words for 'exile', 'banishment' and 'deportation', *gôlā* and *galût*, were explicitly not rendered into Greek by the term 'diaspora'. *Gôlā* and *galût* were understood as unique notions for the Babylonian captivity and exile. They were thus translated in the Septuagint by Greek words denoting movement under force (*metoikesía*) and captivity as a result of war (*aìchmalosía*), avoiding any equivalence between *gôlā* and *diasporá*. Jewish–Greek translators of the third and second century BCE intentionally distinguished between *galût* and *diasporá*, adopting a new word to express neologically their situation of living outside Israel-Palestine (Arowele 1977: 46–7; van Unnik 1993: 81–4; Tromp 1998: 23).

Diaspora as part of a soteriological scheme

In retrospect, post-Babylonian Jews interpreted the Babylonian captivity theologically – that is, as God's punishment for their disobedience to the commands of the Torah. With the return to Palestine and Jerusalem, this punishment had come to an end. Living outside the 'Holy Land' subsequently – from the fifth century BCE on – was understood differently. In Egypt, Asia Minor and Greece, many Jews had become secure, established and quite successful. Nevertheless, they still interpreted residing outside Palestine as a transitory, miserable and unfavourable stay. It was understood as a preparation for, an intermediate situation until, the final divine gathering in Jerusalem. Basically, 'diaspora' took on spiritual and soteriological meanings, pointing to the 'gathering of the scattered' by God's grace at the end of time. The term was coined to form an integral part of a pattern constituted by the fourfold course of sin and disobedience, scattering and diaspora, repentance, and finally return and gathering (van Unnik 1993: 113–19; Tromp 1998: 18–19).

In Hellenistic times, Jews from the diaspora were able to travel to Palestine and Jerusalem. The large number of pilgrims gives ample evidence that Jews could have returned to Palestine. Most stayed, however, in the diaspora. Theologically, it was held that the gathering in the 'Holy Land' was not to be brought about by humans, but by God alone. All men and women in the diaspora could do to help usher in such a time was to live wholeheartedly in accordance with the commands of the Torah. In this way, apart from its indissoluble soteriological meaning and context, i.e. the interpretation of history with respect to God's saving grace, the proper term 'diaspora' also takes on meanings of admonition and a reminder to obey the Jewish law. Socioculturally, it appears that quite a number of Jews (certainly not all) fared rather well in cultural centres outside the Holy Land; the Jews of Alexandria and Sardis maintained religious and administrative structures of their own, with synagogues, gymnasia, baths, cemeteries and societies. Many preferred to stay in the diaspora, rather than returning to more or less regularly war-torn Palestine (Eisenstadt 1992; Barclay 1996; Baumann 2003; Gruen 2002).

Ensuing adoption of diaspora

In the first century CE, Christians adopted the term diaspora, but altered its soteriological meaning according to Christian eschatology. The individual writers of the different biblical stories and letters interpreted the early Church 'as a pilgrim, sojourning and dispersed community, in the understanding that it is the eschatological people of God' (Arowele 1977: 476). On earth, dispersed Christians would function as the 'seed' to disseminate the message of Jesus. The Christians' real home, however, was the so-called 'heavenly city Jerusalem', the goal of Christian pilgrimage.

Having become the state religion of the Roman Empire in the late fourth century, the idea of sojourn and diaspora quickly vanished in Christian memory. A millennium later, following the sixteenth-century Reformation and the formation of different Christian confessions, the term came to denote Protestants living in Catholic territory and vice versa. In the nineteenth century, owing to inner state migrations, diaspora became predominantly associated with confessional minorities.

Since the 1960s, with increasing transnational and global migrant movements, 'diaspora' was employed to denote a national, cultural or religious group living in a foreign land. Following African Studies (Harris 1993; Shepperson 1993), which compared the enslavement of sub-Saharan Africans to the expulsion of classical Jews, the term became widely used and popular in various social sciences. The increasing broadening of the term and its at times vague employment were criticized from the mid-1990s onwards, with scholars calling for more theorized and analytically useful usage (Tölölyan 1996; Cohen 1997; Vertovec 1997; Baumann 2000).

Varied connotations of exile

In contrast, the notion of exile did not encounter such popularity and fashionable employment in the twentieth century. During the 1930s and 1940s, many authors, intellectuals, artists, journalists and scientists, chiefly of Jewish birth, fled Nazi Germany for the security of exile in Britain and the USA. There, they initiated and assisted agencies in providing support for refugees, as well as analysing the fascinating power of the 'political religion' of National Socialism (Krohn 1998; Sheppard 2006). During the second half of the twentieth century, many people faced a similar fate, being forced to leave their home countries owing to political pressures and persecution. Among countless examples, the Tibetans, Cubans and Armenians all appeared prominently in the media (Lang 1989; Tweed 1997; Korom 1999). Indeed, Tibetans speak of their central Tibetan administration as a 'government-in-exile', while Edward Said underscores that: 'Modern western culture [...] in large part [is] the work of exiles, émigrés, refugees. In the United States, academic, intellectual and aesthetic thought is what it is today because of refugees from fascism, communism, and other regimes given to the oppression and expulsion of dissidents' (Said 2001: 173). Although exile is, in Said's words, 'the unhealable rift forced between a human being and a native place, between the self and its true home: Its essential sadness can never be surmounted' (ibid.: 173), voices that also value exile positively as a place of freedom and innovation have become widespread. Palestinian, Iranian and African artists, musicians and poets in exile all refer to the possibility of meeting other people, of benefiting from exchange and encounter, and finding inspiration for new ideas. Nevertheless, reference to such voices is not intended to banalize the anguish and predicaments experienced. The memory and longing of the exiled are bound to the former homeland and they interpret their freedom to engage for political change back home.

'Exile', in contrast to diaspora, is seldom associated with religious connotations and semantics. It appears that its use relates more explicitly to political persecution and forced flight caused by a nation-state than does 'diaspora'. The latter, particularly in recent discourse, appears to relate to a state of enduring consciousness of living away from home, adapted to the new social and cultural context. In contrast, contemporary connotations of exile are resonant of a state of sojourn, estrangement and homesickness. The history and experiences of classical Jews, however, do not support such differentiations. The current attributions are rather the result of ongoing intellectual discourses and reasoning, coining the terms anew.

Further reading

Achebe, C. (2000) *Home and Exile*, Oxford: Oxford University Press.

Eisenstadt, S. N. (1992) *Jewish Civilization: The Jewish Historical Experience in a Comparative Perspective*, Albany, NY: State University of New York Press.

Haebich, A. and B. Offord (eds) (2008) *Landscapes of Exile: Once Perilous, Now Safe*, Frankfurt: P. Lang.

Krohn, C. D. (ed.) (1998) *Handbuch der deutschsprachigen Emigration 1933–1945*, Darmstadt: Wiss. Buchgesellschaft.

Said, E. W. (2001) *Reflections on Exile and Other Essays*, 2nd edn, Cambridge, MA: Harvard University Press.

2 | Home and memory

Femke Stock

At the core of the concept of diaspora lies the image of a remembered home that stands at a distance both temporally and spatially. This 'place of origin' may be the focus of a sustained 'ideology of return' (Brah 1996: 180); it can still figure as a home in the present or be seen as belonging entirely to the past. It may have been left recently or generations ago; it may not exist any more or be the destination of regular 'home trips'; it may be a locus of nostalgia and nightmares; it may feel welcoming or strange upon return visits or it may never have been that homey in the first place. Somehow, though, it is imagined, re-created, longed for, remembered in the present through the diasporic imaginary (Anthias 1998: 577; Baumann 2000: 327; Clifford 1994: 310).

Now what significance does such a remembered home have for the lived experience of diaspora? Memories of home are no factual reproductions of a fixed past. Rather they are fluid reconstructions set against the backdrop of the remembering subject's current positionings and conceptualizations of home. As I will suggest below, these conceptualizations are partly shaped by social ascriptions and contestations of home. They encompass both relations to the 'homeland' and feelings of being home; both physical localities and metaphorical symbolizations of belonging (Ghorashi 2003: 189). Adding to the complexity are differences between first-generation migrants, who can relate their diasporic experiences to their own memories of a time before migration, and later generations for whom the 'new land' has never been new and whose memories of the 'homeland' are more fragmented. This layeredness of contemporary perceptions of home resonates in the many complex ways the 'original home' is remembered.

Memories, both personal and collective, form the frame of reference we all use to meaningfully interpret our past and present experiences and orient ourselves towards the future. This means that migrants' perceptions and dreams of home and belonging are fuelled by memories of prior homes, by notions of where 'we' came from (Davidson 2008: 26; Leung 2008: 164). Memory, however, cannot be seen as direct, if partial, knowledge of past experiences. The act of remembering is always contextual, a continuous process of recalling, interpreting and reconstructing the past in terms of the present and in the light of an anticipated future.

What is remembered of a prior home, as well as how it is remembered (whether actively recalled or resurfacing unsought), is thus subject to retrospective teleology (Brockmeier 2000: 60) and evolves in constant dialogue with new memories of other places and changing circumstances, with memories of migration and living in diaspora (Salih 2003: 125). Through complex dynamics of meaning-making, home memories both inform and are informed by the positions individuals and groups occupy in the here and now. Paradoxically, the deep contextuality of diasporic perceptions of a remembered 'original' home, together with its remoteness in time and space as well as the competition from other possible home spaces, makes 'home' a concept that is far from self-evident, while at the same time carrying strong connotations of exactly such a self-evidence. It is this tension which makes home such a compelling notion both for those who study diaspora and for those who live it. This proves to be even more the case if we extend our scope to include a far broader spectrum of meanings of home with which perceptions of a remembered 'original' home are intertwined.

In the study of diasporic groups, the notion of home is referred to and employed in diverging, sometimes contradictory ways. Two rather common areas of enquiry concern the relationship of (descendants of) migrants to an 'originary homeland', and questions of 'feeling at home'. The first might focus on (material or symbolic) transnational ties, myths of migration and dreams of return; while the second might trace the desires and the (im)possibilities of making oneself at home – in the different spaces diasporic subjects inhabit, but mainly in the current place of residence. The question about the relationship between 'homeland ties' and successful homemaking in the 'new home' is one of the more straightforward examples of the interrelatedness between these two uses of home. Although this question partly reproduces a dichotomy between 'homeland as the object of longing [...] and hostland as the object of efforts to belong' (Fortier 2000: 136) that cannot do justice to the complex dynamics of longing for and belonging to multiple places in various ways, it also hints at the layeredness of a notion of home that is not necessarily bound to physical places but may also allude to symbolic spaces of belonging.

There are many discussions of home that try to capture this layeredness. Brah, who also reminds us that the 'homing desire' that is such a potent force in human and especially migrant experience should not be confused with a desire for a homeland (Brah 1996: 180), distinguishes between a 'mythic place of desire in the diasporic imagination' and 'the lived experience of a locality' (ibid.: 92). Other authors make comparable distinctions between home as a physical space one inhabits and as 'the symbolic conceptualization of where one belongs' (Salih 2003: 70), an 'actual place of lived experience and a metaphorical space of personal attachment and identification' (Armbruster 2002: 120), or as a 'conceptual or discursive space of identification and as a nodal point in concrete social relations' (Rapport and Dawson 1998).

It is remarkable how each of these authors distinguishes between a realm of concrete locality and everyday experience on the one hand and a more ideational, symbolic or discursive realm on the other, while at the same time stressing that home entails both. This suggests a certain tension between these realms that is specific to diaspora, or at least far more pronounced in diasporic settings than elsewhere, where these realms are expected to more or less coincide.

While this tension, which seemingly springs from the experience of 'living here relating to a there' (Baumann 2000: 324), can be viewed and is indeed often experienced as problematic, it is also part of what Clifford (1994: 322) calls the 'empowering paradox of diaspora'. The moving between a multiplicity of home spaces, the experience of ambivalently belonging both here and there, can open up new spaces to reflect on and critique essentialist discourses of nation, ethnicity or origin (Anthias 1998: 565; Baumann 2000: 324; Brah 1996: 192; Hall et al. 1999: 10), and to creatively construct new homes and identities that are deemed hybrid, syncretic or fluid. In light of the frequent tendency to discuss the diasporic condition in terms of problems and loss, the celebration of its subversive and creative potential forms an important counterbalance. Yet this celebration has also been criticized for disregarding disparities in power and opportunities between diasporic individuals and groups (Anthias 2008: 570). Moving between contrasting settings may be liberating for some at some times; for others at other times it may mean a disturbing in-betweenness of belonging nowhere.

Clearly social factors play an important role here. Homes can be ascribed or denied to individuals and groups by public opinion and significant others. Collective memories of home and dominant discourses of otherness inform and restrict their options for constructing notions of (non-)home. Despite their attachments to certain places or social constellations both here and there, (descendants of) migrants sometimes feel unable to identify with these as homes because there is no place for them in collective memories or everyday interaction: 'It is quite possible to feel at home in a place and, yet, the experience of social exclusions may inhibit public proclamations of the place as home' (Brah 1996: 193). Diasporic consciousness is produced negatively by such experiences of exclusion. For Clifford the positive shaping of this consciousness takes place 'through identification with world historical cultural/political forces' (1994: 312; Vertovec 1997).

This consciousness gains a different dynamic for later generations, who quite literally do not have the same starting point as those who originally migrated. The places and (imagined) communities their (grand)parents left behind are not forgotten (Levitt and Waters 2002: 2). The remembered 'original home' should not be regarded as a lasting point of primary orientation (Anthias 1998: 568; Fortier 2000: 160). Positive identifications with a 'homeland' may go hand in hand with feelings of estrangement when being ascribed a home one has never lived in, or denied belonging by those still living there. Similarly, the 'new' land can provide both a source of positive identification and of negative experiences of othering.

Later generations have not experienced migration and have no memories of the time before it (Brah 1996: 194). They are the heirs to diasporic memories that are told and retold, reappropriated and reinterpreted in light of the here and now. Throughout their lives they construct their own diasporic narratives of home and belonging out of these memories, together with their own experiences, their 'migration routes and migrant roots' (Kuah-Pearce and Davidson 2008: 2). Often, for descendants of migrants the question 'Where do I belong?' is more pressing, and the meanings they give to home are more complex (Blunt and Dowling 2006: 217).

The point of departure in this contribution was the centrality of the remembered home in conceptions of diaspora. We can now conclude that home is a 'subtext of diaspora' (Brah 1996: 190) in a far broader sense. From this cursory reflection, the concept of home emerges as a highly contextual and ambivalent notion, referring to multiple places and spaces in past, present and future in various ways. Home can be remembered, lived, longed for. Notions of home are fluid and bound to change as one moves in time and space. Rather than referring to one single home, in diasporic settings feelings of belonging can be directed towards both multiple physical places and remembered, imagined and/ or symbolic spaces (Al-Ali and Koser 2002: 8; Salih 2003: 70). At each moment in time, various home spaces may compete, collide or complement each other.

The many different ways in which home is conceptualized and employed in academia lead Mallett to write: 'Is home (a) place(s), (a) space(s), feeling(s), practices, and/or an active state of being in the world? Home is variously described as conflated with or related to house, family, haven, self, gender, and journeying' (2004: 65). In addition to this we have seen that home can be connected to memory and identity, to origin as well as to hybridity. Given this bewildering array of uses, it could be suggested that the concept of home becomes an empty one, one which can mean anything and, in consequence, signifies nothing.

The ongoing relevance of home lies in the fact that it is not only an analytical tool, but an emic term which is highly salient for diasporic subjects themselves. While for them the ambivalence of home is a lived reality, the term continues to *suggest* self-evidence. In the popular imaginary, it is the strong undertones of familiarity, continuity, safety, unproblematic belonging, exclusivity and warm memories which make home so compelling and inform migrants' homing desires (Brah 1996: 180). Although scholarly conceptualizations of home derive from this emic notion, and its meanings continuously feed into our analyses, paradoxically they are also perpetually trying to contradict and deconstruct it, insisting on the complexity, fluidity and ambivalent multiplicity of home. It is the creative tension between the emic notion of 'home is where the heart is' and the openness and layeredness of home as an analytical concept which makes it such a powerful idea in the study of diaspora.

Further reading

Armbruster, H. (2002) 'Homes in crisis: Syrian Orthodox Christians in Turkey and Germany', in N. Al-Ali and K. Koser (eds), *New Approaches to Migration? Transnational Communities and the Transformation of Home*, London: Routledge, pp. 17–33.

Blunt, A. and R. Dowling (2006) *Home*, London: Routledge.

Brah, A. (1996) *Cartographies of Diaspora: Contesting Identities*, London: Routledge.

Mallett, S. (2004) 'Understanding home: a critical review of the literature', *Sociological Review*, 52(1): 62–89.

Rapport, N. and A. Dawson (eds) (1998) *Migrants of Identity: Perceptions of Home in a World of Movement*, Oxford: Berg.

3 | Slavery and the black Atlantic

David Richardson

The peoples of Africa have been on the move from time immemorial. Sub-Saharan Africans, most of them in some form of slavery, helped build the pyramids in Egypt. They helped, with other enslaved peoples, to build the later Greek and Roman civilizations. As trans-Saharan and East African captives they provided an essential labour force for the Ottoman Empire for half a millennium, and as captives within sub-Saharan Africa they were pillars upon which indigenous African empires were built until at least the nineteenth century. The numbers involved in these activities are incalculable; they surely ran into scores of millions. Today, Africans are still on the move, whether through internal displacement or through movement or flight to other continents. Millions have left Africa in the last decade alone. Yet, in the public mind, such movements of Africans pale in significance when compared to the Atlantic slave trade between the early sixteenth and mid-nineteenth centuries.

Indeed, whenever one contemplates slavery, it is the Atlantic slave trade and the chattel slavery that it helped to sustain in the Americas after 1500 which typically spring most readily to mind. The identity of slavery with Africans lies at the heart of Paul Gilroy's (1993a) concept of the black Atlantic and its relationship to the creation of the modern world. Gilroy sought to explore 'the stereophonic, bilingual, or bifocal cultural forms originated by, but no longer the exclusive property of, blacks dispersed within the structures of feeling, producing, communicating, and remembering' that he calls the black Atlantic world (ibid.: 27). Under transatlantic slavery, Africans were the legal property of others, who largely controlled the disposition of their output and dictated their well-being (on definitions of slavery, see Quirk 2009: 23–33). They were also ideologically and socially marginalized, exploitable 'outsiders' condemned in the words of sociologist Orlando Patterson to a status of 'social death' (Patterson 1982). Yet, as Gilroy emphasizes, Africans were more than simply the raw labour on which the post-Columbus Atlantic economy was built; they became actors in shaping the hybrid social and cultural life of an Atlantic world in which they and their descendants found themselves.

The reasons for privileging study of the Atlantic slave trade are not difficult to uncover. It was an activity of exceptional brutality and cost to its victims and their descendants as well as to the continent from which they were taken. It was, according to historian Joseph Miller (1988), 'a way of death'. It left legacies of enormous complexity. On the one hand, it polarized wealth distribution and fostered racial tension, while on the other, as a classic example of what Robin Cohen has labelled 'victim diasporas' (involving traumatic dispersals of people from their homeland, the salience of which remained part of their collective memory and of the creative rebuilding of their identity), it helped to promote the modern world's cultural diversity and multiculturalism (Cohen 2008: 2–6, 39–48). Compared with other migrations, the Atlantic slave trade is also incredibly well documented, as the source fields of a recently published online database attest (www.slavevoyages.com). There is a wealth of official documentation, reflecting the trade's association with Europe's conquest and resettlement of the Americas and European fiscal-military states' preoccupation with bullion, trade balances and 'political arithmetic'. Equally there is an abundance of private data, reflecting the eagerness of such states to subcontract slaving activities to private merchants or organizations. The resulting richness of source materials has allowed historians to track some 35,000 (or at least three-quarters of all) transatlantic slaving voyages between the early sixteenth century and the end of the Atlantic slave trade in 1867. The range of evidence available is wide, ranging from ships and their itineraries to the composition of their 'human cargoes' (see description of fields of information in www.slavevoyages.com). These shipping data are complemented by growing evidence on the ethnicity of victims (for which see 'African names' in the resources section of www.slavevoyages.com). For no other slave trade in history do we have such detailed information.

The broad contours of the Atlantic slave trade are now well established (for the most recent survey, see Eltis and Richardson 2008). In terms of chronology, the numbers of people forced to leave Africa rose from under 5,000 a year in the sixteenth century to 60,000 or more a year in the late eighteenth century. Numbers remained near to this level through 1850. As a result, of the 12.5 million captives estimated to have been taken from Africa to the Americas between 1500 and 1867, three-quarters left their home continent between 1700 and 1850. A testament to human greed and European economic efficiency, the intensity of the African slave trade is one of its defining features (on efficiency, see Eltis, Lewis and Richardson 2005). That intensity, in turn, rested on widening and deepening slave usage in Latin America, especially Brazil, where over four million captives were sold, and the spread of sugar planting after 1640 throughout the Caribbean basin, where the vast majority of the other survivors of the Atlantic crossing disembarked ship. Economics drove the flow of captives across the Atlantic; it also dictated the exceptionally high concentrations of enslaved Africans in those parts of the Americas wedded to cash crop production, notably sugar. Often accounting for more than 75 per cent of the populations of particular islands or colonies, such concentrations of enslaved people were among the highest in human history (Higman 1995). They created both wealth and fear within the small white minorities that comprised the slave-owning class. They were also centres of new transnational and arguably trans-ethnic cultural formations in the Atlantic world, thereby provoking debates then and now about the influence of Africa and Africans on Atlantic history and the legacies of the Atlantic slave trade as a form of African diaspora. The interrelationships between heritage, memory, environment, the market and power have been at the heart of debates around such issues (see, among many, Mintz and Price 1992; Sweet 1996; Morgan 1998; Thornton 1998; Gomez 2004; Hall 2005).

Other demographic evidence, beyond population concentrations of enslaved Africans in the Americas, would seem, prima facie, to underscore the importance of Africans to American societal reformations after Columbus. Before 1820 Africans accounted for three times as many voyagers from the 'Old' to the 'New World' (Eltis 1983). Though concentrated in tropical and subtropical regions, enslaved Africans were found throughout the Americas. It is evident, too, that though American planters favoured male over female slaves as labourers, about two out of five of the captives taken to the Americas were female. Moreover, the ratio of women among captives was particularly high during the seventeenth century as resettlement of the Caribbean was beginning and contrasted with the heavily male-dominated white migration to American plantation regions at that time (Eltis and Engerman 1993). Furthermore, while changes in the scale and direction of the Atlantic slave trade occurred through time, Atlantic winds and ocean currents combined with the emergence of Afro-European commercial networks in Atlantic Africa to foster continuities in flows of peoples between specific African embarkation and American disembarkation centres for captives (Eltis and Richardson 1997, 2010; www.slavevoyages.com). People of Bantu origin, for example, were primarily taken to Brazil, whereas very large proportions of those taken from the Bight of Biafra, commonly labelled Igbo, found themselves in the West Indies, notably Jamaica. Trading patterns and the social composition of the slave trade seem to lend some credibility, therefore, to arguments that emphasize the importance of African heritage and memory embodied in the ethnicity of captives in shaping the emergence of new, or Creole, communities in the Americas (Hall 2005). Some have even suggested that homeland influences reached beyond the cultural lives that diasporic Africans rebuilt and embraced the core working practices of slave plantation societies (Carney 2001; cf. Eltis, Morgan and Richardson 2007). Notwithstanding slavery, African agency was, according to this line of argument, a powerful force in shaping Atlantic history.

Counting by numbers, however, can be an imperfect indicator of African influences on societal formation and the cultural history of the Americas. For one thing, tensions can be discerned between what is sometimes seen as the influence of a specific ethnic group of captives in shaping the cultural institutions of an emerging community and the numerical minority status of that group within the community. In this context, the chronology of slave arrivals and the establishment of a 'charter' generation are sometimes thought to have had a disproportionate influence on later societal practices (Berlin 2003: 23–49). Problems in attaching weight to ethnic groupings are compounded when one explores the derivation, meaning and social content of ethnic labels, whether in Africa or in the diaspora, and the degree to which African notions of belonging were suppressed, reinforced or reshaped in the course of the middle passage (Northrup 2000). They are further compounded by the intermixing of ethnic groups on American plantations and by the emergence of American-born Creole slaves who could learn about their African heritage only second-hand (Burnard 2007). Such forces of fragmentation of potential collective African identities in exile were yet further reinforced by both the low survival and negative reproduction rates of Africans in European and American captivity. This applied particularly to sugar-producing regions in the Caribbean and Brazil, where maintenance of slave populations depended on continuous infusions of new captives from Africa (Eltis and Lachance 2008). Moreover, even where, as in the British colonies that became the United States, slave populations grew by natural reproduction, relocation of African and Creole-born captives through internal slave trades always remained a threat to the stability of interpersonal relationships and community bonds (Tadman 1989; Gudmestad 2003).

The socially destructive elements inherent in transatlantic slavery, however, should not blind us to Africans' capacities to challenge the institution and, if they survived the Atlantic crossing, to both reconstruct meaningful lives and create enduring legacies in the diaspora. The Atlantic slave trade is sometimes depicted as an almost wholly dehumanizing experience, in which traumatized captives were force-marched to the sea, packed 'sardine-like' on board ship, and bought and sold like animals (Smallwood 2007). Visual representations as well as contemporary reports of the slave trade do little to dispel such images. Yet the fact remains that Africans did not accept their fate impassively. They resisted and, at times, fought back – in Africa, on board ship, and in the Americas – and they often found allies in Creole-born captives (Diouf 2003). In resisting they asserted their humanity and their identity. It is estimated that one in ten slave voyages experienced a shipboard revolt in which some loss of life occurred (Richardson 2001). Others claim that Africans fought a two-hundred-year war against their enslavement in the Americas (Beckles 1982). Such acts of resistance rarely brought immediate freedom, but communities of runaway slaves known as Maroons developed (Price 1996; Price and Price 2000). Moreover, slave rebellions in the French colony of Saint-Domingue in 1791 and subsequently in other nations' colonies or territories exposed a sense of shared anger among captives and a collective will to assert their freedom (James 1980 [1938]; Dubois 2004; Matthews 2006). Such acts of defiance and self-liberation helped to undermine transatlantic slavery in the century after 1788 and in doing so helped ideologically to redefine the black Atlantic.

That process involved more than heroic acts of resistance and rebellion. It involved, too, efforts to dismantle the cultural divide upon which transatlantic slavery was built and to identify slavery as an exceptional affront to a common humanity (Davis 2006). British abolitionists within and outside Parliament are typically given centre-stage in such endeavours, but the contribution of former slaves to changing images of Africa and Africans should not be overlooked. In this context, attention tends to focus on the writings and campaigning of liberated Afro-Britons such as Quobna Ottobah Cugoano, Olaudah Equiano and Ignatius Sancho and their American counterparts in shifting perceptions of Africa (Carretta 1998, 1999, 2003). Their endeavours in this regard, however, need to be seen as part of a wider and more complex process of cultural interaction that involved free Africans not only as abolitionists but also as participants on a much broader front in restructuring and redefining the Atlantic world from the late eighteenth century onwards. Notable in this respect was the founding of Sierra Leone as a 'free' colony in 1787, as well as a growing tide of slave narratives and other stories of liberated Africans (Byrd 2008). Reinforcing African humanity, such developments highlighted former captives' understanding of the market and their capacity to participate successfully in a broad range of activities throughout the Atlantic basin during the 'age of revolutions'. Former captives and their descendants were revealed as successful farmers, landholders and land speculators; as business, commercial and shipping entrepreneurs; as publishers and promoters of education and the arts; and as missionaries and church leaders (see, for example, Curtin 1967; Winch 2002; Carretta 2005; Stewart 2010). Central players as slaves in underpinning growth in the Atlantic economy from the sixteenth century onwards, diasporic Africans – through the weight of their presence, the power of their resistance and the example of their achievements – would become important instruments for reconfiguring the Atlantic as a cultural space during the nineteenth century.

Further reading

Berlin, I. (2003) *Generations of Captivity: A History of African-American Slaves*, Cambridge, MA: Harvard University Press.

Eltis, D. and D. Richardson (2010) *Atlas of Transatlantic Slavery*, New Haven, CT: Yale University Press.

Gilroy, P. (1993a) *The Black Atlantic: Modernity and Double Consciousness*, Cambridge, MA/London: Harvard University Press/Verso.

Morgan, P. (1998) *Slave Counterpoint: Black Culture in the Eighteenth Century Chesapeake and Lowcountry*, Chapel Hill: University of North Carolina Press.

Thornton, J. (1998) *Africa and Africans in the Making of the Atlantic World, 1400–1800*, Cambridge: Cambridge University Press.

4 | Migration

Nicholas Van Hear

The notion of diaspora straddles some of the most fundamental and problematic divides in the migration field. Among these is the distinction between so-called '*voluntary*' and '*forced*' migration, or in broad terms between labour or economic migrants and refugees or forced migrants. Another key division is that between analysis of *migration itself* on one hand – the process, experience and dynamics of mobility – and on the other the *outcomes of migration*, such as the integration, assimilation, segregation or exclusion of people of migrant background and the changes in society that may result. These divisions are found both in analysis of migration and in the migration policy field. To some extent the notion of diaspora helps to reconcile these divides in migration discourse, as this essay aims to show.

The emergence of diaspora as a key concept in the migration field may be tracked through a number of streams of cognate scholarship that gathered pace from the 1990s. The current wave of interest can be traced to a number of political scientists who from the 1980s saw the implications of increasing migration for politics and international relations. For those in anthropological and cultural studies who followed them, the focus on migration was less in evidence. The place of migration in the formation, consolidation and unmaking of diasporas was taken up rather by those whose perspective on migration drew on political economy approaches shaped partly by Marxist analyses, tempered by emphasis on human agency (Cohen 1997, 2008; Van Hear 1998). Since then the literature on diaspora and migration has proliferated from various disciplinary perspectives, and the notion of diaspora has been subjected to meticulous and often well-targeted critique (Brubaker 2005). In what follows some of these interwoven threads of scholarship on migration and diaspora are considered in relation to the formation and consolidation of diasporas.

Migration and diaspora formation

Diaspora formation can occur by accretion, as a result of gradual, routine migration, which may be a matter of choice or strategy on the part of households and communities. Alternatively, dispersal may be brought about by crisis and may involve coercion, catastrophe, expulsion or other forcible movement resulting from conflict or persecution. Dispersal may also result from a combination of compulsion and choice, so that diasporas may emerge as a result of both cumulative processes and crises (Van Hear 1998).

Diaspora formation through 'routine' or 'voluntary' migration In a percipient article early on in the development of the diaspora discourse, Weiner (1986) characterized labour migrations as 'incipient diasporas', and noted 'the illusion of impermanence' of 'temporary' labour migrants in North America, Europe and even the Gulf states. This notion was resonant of the often-cited comment 'Nothing is so permanent as a temporary worker'. It also chimed with the observation by Castles and Miller (2009 [1993]) that the temporary migration of the 1960s associated with guest-worker programmes in Europe shifted to more permanent settlement after the downturn of the mid-1970s, as former guest workers settled and brought in dependants who helped to form new ethnic minorities – now commonly characterized as diasporas.

Migration and diaspora scholarship took some time to converge, however. In their book *Worlds in Motion*, Massey et al. (1998) traced approaches to the inception and perpetuation of migration, some of which were applicable to diaspora formation and consolidation, although they were not explicitly cast as such. Their synthesis of migration theories pointed to how explanations of the *initiation* of migration could be found in a number of approaches: in neoclassical economics, which located the drivers of migration in differences in income levels between countries; in what became known as the new economics of (labour) migration; in segmented labour market theory, which held that migration stemmed from labour demand in industrialized societies; and in variants of historical-structural and world systems theories, which sought explanations of migration in the unequal distribution of power worldwide through a political economy approach drawing on Marxist analyses. Explanations of the *perpetuation* of migration could be found in theories about social capital, networks and 'cumulative causation'.

While all of these approaches in different ways could be applied to help explain the inception, formation and consolidation of diasporas, some of them may be identified as being particularly relevant. The new economics of (labour) migration approach was helpful in that it pointed to decision-making not just by individuals, but also by households and sometimes communities, with the object not just of maximizing income, but also spreading risk: this seemed to chime with the behaviour of diasporas in formation, particularly in circumstances of conflict or stress. Notions of social capital and networks are likewise helpful in explaining the formation and reproduction of diasporas by pointing to ways in which social connections can be drawn upon in the migration context – again this accords very much with the behaviour of people in diasporas. Likewise the notion of cumulative causation strikes a chord with diaspora behaviour by highlighting the manner in which each act of migration alters the social context in which subsequent migration decisions are made, often making additional movement more likely (ibid.).

Migration crises and diaspora formation While insights from analysis of so-called 'voluntary' migration in the 1980s and 1990s helped to account for the formation and perpetuation of diasporas, interest in forced migration was gathering pace, partly stimulated by increased numbers of asylum seekers moving from the global South to the global North, but also by the rash of major forced migration crises in the early to mid-1990s onwards. The crises included the break-up of the Soviet Union and the communist bloc after the fall of the Berlin Wall in 1989; subsequent wars and 'unmixing' of formerly ethnically diverse populations in the Caucasus region, Central Asia and other parts of the former Soviet Union, and in the Balkans/former Yugoslavia; the 'Gulf crisis' of 1990/91 and its associated mass exodus of refugees, of Asian and Arab migrant workers, and of Palestinians from Kuwait, Iraq and elsewhere; the genocide, wars and mass refugee movements in Central Africa from 1994; protracted conflict and massive displacement in Palestine, Afghanistan, the Horn of Africa, Sri Lanka, Colombia and elsewhere; and more recently the conflicts and refugee movements associated with the post-September 11 'war on terror' in Afghanistan (from 2001) and in Iraq (from 2003).

Major new diasporas have formed from or been augmented by these conflict-induced population movements over the last two decades. These new or resurgent transnational social formations have consolidated, are enduring, have undertaken new or extended existing forms of transnational activity, and are becoming integrated into the global order, particularly in respect of relations between affluent countries and conflict-ridden societies (Van Hear 2009a).

Not all of those coming from such conflict-ridden countries have been refugees or forced migrants, however. Many have come for economic betterment, study, marriage or other reasons, often against the background of conflict. This points to another thread connecting analyses of migration and diaspora, for both analysts of migration (Richmond 1994; Van Hear 1998) and more recently those who design and implement policy have increasingly recognized the reality and growing salience of what has been called 'mixed migration' – the intersection between so-called 'voluntary' and 'forced' migration alluded to at the start of this chapter. Migration can be 'mixed' in several senses, which to some degree relate to stages of the migratory process: motivations may be mixed at the point of making the decision to move, which almost always involves varying combinations of choice and compulsion; people may travel with others in mixed migratory flows; motivations may change en route; and people may find themselves in mixed communities during their journeys or at their destination. Onward migration may feature similar mixtures of motivation, mixed flows and mixed communities in transit or at the destination (Van Hear 2009b). Diaspora formation can therefore involve diverse forms of migration, which in turn contributes to differentiation within them as they consolidate and establish themselves.

Migration and the durability of diaspora

The notion of diaspora consolidation points to another necessary feature of diaspora – durability – in contrast to the sometimes fleeting nature of migration. Diasporas need to endure before being considered as such – their 'reality is proved in time and tested by time' (Marienstras 1989: 125). Here another analytical current in migration studies has proved useful in considering the consolidation of diasporas – the 'transnational turn'. The notion of transnationalism gathered purchase in migration studies at more or less the same time as the related notion of diaspora took hold in the mid- and later 1990s. The seminal expression of this was the observation by Glick Schiller et al. (1992) that 'a new kind of migrating population is emerging, composed of those whose networks, activities and patterns of life encompass both their host and home societies' (ibid.: 1). While the novelty claimed for this phenomenon has been questioned (Portes and Landholt 1999), it did point to new trends in the formation of social, economic, political, cultural and other relationships among migrants and their networks that spanned several societies (Van Hear 1998). The connected notions of transnationalism and diaspora acknowledged that migrants no longer made a sharp break from their homelands (if indeed they ever did); nor was migration a simple unilinear movement. Rather, links with the homeland continued to be salient, connections that were maintained from afar through remittances and other forms of transfer and exchange, or through return and circular migration (Van Hear 2002, 2006).

Guarnizo (2003) later refined this notion to take account of the growing practice among migrants of 'transnational living', which referred to 'a wide panoply of social, cultural, political and economic cross-border relations that emerge, both wittingly and unwittingly, from migrants' drive to maintain and reproduce their social milieu of origin from afar' (ibid.: 667). In the case of diaspora, the transnational linkages were not only between the host and home societies, but also with other societies in which diaspora members were located. In the case of diasporas formed from displacement resulting from conflict, there were at least three kinds of site among which links developed – the homeland, neighbouring countries of first asylum, and territories farther afield (Van Hear 2006, 2009a).

The recognition of substantial transnational links and ways of transnational living has given rise to a debate about the tension between such transnational connections and integration – in particular whether maintaining transnational ties is compatible with integration in a host society (Snel et al. 2006). In some ways this debate harked back to the earlier 'dual loyalty' debates of the political scientists (Sheffer 1986a). The question is also linked to the issue of the sustainability of diasporas, since if transnational linkages decayed over time, so too might diaspora identity and practices. Currently transnational linkages show little sign of decay and indeed appear to be blossoming. If the current economic crisis undermines migration flows to the global North, however, the diasporas formed over the last twenty or thirty years may be weakened. Equally, however, tomorrow's migrants may well make their way to new destinations in emerging economies and polities, making for new vibrant configurations of diaspora and transnational connections that will continue to shape global society.

Further reading

Cohen, R. (2008) *Global Diasporas: An Introduction*, 2nd edn, London and New York: Routledge.

Massey, D., J. Arango, G. Hugo, A. Kouaouci, A. Pellegrino and J. Taylor (1998) *Worlds in Motion: Understanding International Migration at the End of the Millennium*, Oxford: Clarendon Press.

Safran, W. (1991) 'Diasporas in modern societies: myths of homeland and return', *Diaspora: A Journal of Transnational Studies*, 1(1): 83–99.

Van Hear, N. (1998) *New Diasporas: The Mass Exodus, Dispersal and Regrouping of Migrant Communities*, London: Routledge.

Van Hear, N. (2009a) 'The rise of refugee diasporas', *Current History*, 108(717): 180–85.

5 | Transnationalism

Peggy Levitt

In this essay the aim is to propose a different way of seeing all kinds of cross-border phenomena, including what migrants or members of diasporas do, that more accurately describes these social relations and cultural exchanges and the social geographies within which they take place. What follows is an intellectual framework and gaze, a way of asking questions and a set of assumptions about what constitutes an acceptable answer which I believe allows for a more accurate and insightful analysis of social experience.

A transnational optic

More and more, we live in a world in which people embrace multiple identities and turn to a variety of institutions around the globe to claim them. Social movement activists promote human rights and environmental policies that often conflict with national approaches. Members of global faith communities sometimes privilege religious over national loyalties. Defendants seeking justice turn to international courts when national institutions come up short. And as diaspora scholarship so aptly points out, increasing numbers of migrants maintain ties to the nations that they come from at the same time that they establish roots in the countries where they settle.

Grasping that people earn their livings, participate in election campaigns or raise children across borders is challenging because it is often assumed that the world has been and always will be organized into sovereign nation-states. But such a view turns a blind eye to history. Capitalism, imperial and colonial regimes, anti-slavery and workers' rights campaigns, illegal pirating networks, artistic and cultural forms and religions have always crossed borders. The modern nation-state system did not even exist until after the Treaty of Westphalia in 1648. In the early 1900s, there were barely 130 sovereign states; the remaining 65 per cent of the world's political entities were colonies and protectorates. Three-quarters (about 150) of the countries recognized today came into existence in the last century. Therefore, studying contemporary social life by looking only at relations and processes enacted within or across presumably bounded social units, whether they are localities, regions, nation-states or empires, necessarily comes up short (Khagram and Levitt 2007).

Cross-border dynamics have received a great deal of scholarly attention.

But most of the researchers doing this work do not see themselves as part of the same conversation. They study transnational corporations, migration, religions or social movements in isolation, without looking at what the networks and institutions that characterize these domains share. Because, as it turns out, transnational economic forms and processes have a lot in common with their transnational political and religious counterparts, and these arrangements challenge deeply held notions about citizenship, democracy and identity, my colleague, Sanjeev Khagram, and I (2007) proposed a new Transnational Studies optic, based on different epistemological assumptions and goals, grounded in five intellectual foundations:

1 *Empirical Transnationalism* describes, maps, classifies and quantifies transnational phenomena and dynamics. These transnational processes stand in contrast to bounded and bordered units, actors, structures and processes that are generally associated with the local, regional, global or the nation-state system.

2 *Methodological Transnationalism* involves reclassifying existing data, evidence and historical and ethnographic accounts that take boundedness and borders for granted so that transnational processes and relations come to light. It involves creating and implementing novel research designs and methodologies based on new types of data, evidence and observations that can capture these cross-border realities.

3 *Theoretical Transnationalism* formulates explanations and crafts interpretations that either parallel, complement, supplement or are integrated into existing theoretical frameworks and accounts.

4 *Philosophical Transnationalism* starts from the metaphysical assumption that social worlds and lives are inherently transnational. In other words, transnational phenomena and dynamics are the rule rather than the exception, the underlying reality rather than a derivative by-product.

5 *Public Transnationalism* creates space to imagine and legitimize options for social change and transformation by reframing questions and problems and thereby bringing innovative approaches to light.

In sum, we argue that the global, regional, national and the local can be analysed through transnational methodological, theoretical and epistemological lenses. The terms 'transnational' or 'transnationalism' are misnomers because they imply that we are interested only in dynamics that cross and go beyond or between nations or states. But we mean much more. By transnational, we propose a gaze that begins with a world without borders, empirically examines the boundaries that emerge, and explores their relationship to unbounded arenas and processes. The analysis does not assume a fixed spatial unit of analysis. A transnational perspective is, therefore, a way of understanding the world, a shared set of questions and puzzles, and a different set of assumptions about what constitutes an acceptable answer.

Changing assumptions and expectations

A transnational optic brings to light several aspects of migration obscured by looking only within nation-state borders. I use examples from my own empirical work throughout this section to make my case.

The migration experience is as much about non-migrants as it is about people who move because migrants and non-migrants, although separated by physical distance, often continue to occupy the same socio-political space. Because goods, people, money and social remittances circulate regularly, even individuals who never move are influenced by values and practices from near and far. The social fields within which migration takes place are multilayered as well as multi-sited. The horizontal ties between sending and receiving sites need to be understood within the context of the regional, national and global connections within which they arise.

Seeing migrants and non-migrants as occupying the same social space also challenges the meaning of incorporation. The immigrant experience is not a linear, irreversible journey from one membership to another. Rather, migrants pivot back and forth between sending, receiving and other orientations at different stages of their lives. The more their lives are grounded in legal, healthcare and pension systems on both sides of the border, the more likely it is that they will continue to live transnational lives. Increasing numbers of newcomers will not fully assimilate or remain entirely focused on their homelands but will continue to craft some combination of the two in ways that ebb and flow across the life course. Their lives will be enabled and constrained by multiple cultural repertoires and institutions. Social mobility and inclusion in a new place, therefore, are strongly connected to social status and inclusion in the old one.

There is, however, a difference between ways of being and ways of belonging in a social field (Levitt and Glick Schiller 2004). *Ways of being* refers to the actual social relations and practices that individuals engage in rather than to the identities associated with those actions. Individuals can be embedded in a social field but not identify with any label or cultural politics associated with that field. They may be unaware or reject the 'diaspora' label offered to them by their peers, the academy or sending states or they may actively embrace it. On the other hand, there are people with few or no actual social ties to people in a sending country who assert their identification with a particular group. Because these individuals have some connection to a *way of belonging*, through memory, nostalgia, cultural competency or imagination, they also belong to this social field and express their membership through their actions. If individuals engage in social relations and practices that cross borders as a regular feature of everyday life, then they exhibit a transnational way of being. When people explicitly recognize this and act upon the transnational elements of who they are, then they also express a transnational way of belonging. Clearly, these two experiences do not always go hand in hand.

A transnational lens breaks open what some have called 'groupism' or 'methodological ethnicity' by acknowledging that people construct identities in reference to family, friends and 'others' living all over the social fields they inhabit (Glick Schiller and Caglar 2008). People decide how to 'be' and 'belong' based not only on options in their home or host countries but on their connections to co-ethnics, co-professionals and co-religionists around the world. They traverse multiple pathways towards simultaneous incorporation.

Not taking 'groups' as given also calls attention to the within-group racial, class and ethnic variation. Under the broad 'Indian' umbrella, for example, there are highly skilled and barely literate; light and dark skinned. The same individual is a Gujarati, a Patidar, a Bhaghat, a follower of Ram Kabir and a resident of Vadodara. If she cares little about India or Gujarat, her deep commitment to other Ram Kabir disciples may inspire her to remain active in homeland affairs. That individuals manage such internally diverse identities drives home the analytical risks of taking ethnic communities as monolithic givens or of giving more analytical weight to processes of incorporation over transnational attachments (Levitt 2007).

One way to correct this, suggested by Transnational Studies, is to enter the analysis spatially. Instead of assuming that particular groups exist and that ethnicity is the master organizing identity, researchers should start with context. In the United States, attention to space is normally confined to discussions about contexts of reception. Certain contexts, generally defined in national terms, are more or less conducive to immigrant integration. But contexts of reception are not just national. And culture, history and geography matter. We need to look not only at the circulation of culture, goods, social remittances and people within them but to see circulation and exchange as cultural acts.

For example, some scripts reinforce enduring homeland involvements while others discourage them. One prevailing narrative about Brazil that I heard regularly from migrants from Governador Valadares was that it is a corrupt, dangerous country that is beyond repair. Why would anyone want to continue to be active in homeland affairs? In contrast, Gujarati narratives reinforced homeland ties. In conversation after conversation, parents proclaimed that their primary goal was to train their children in 'Indian *sanskar*' or culture which was firmly rooted in India. Their conversations were peppered with references to how close Indian extended families are compared to families in the United States and to how Indian children take so much better care of their elderly parents. The cultural repository and the indicators used to evaluate how well a family measures up reinforce homeland connections.

Geopolitical position also strongly influences migrant incorporation and enduring homeland ties because it affects the cultural repertoires, economic resources and institutional regimes places bring to bear (Brettell 2005; Bommes and Radtke 1996). Glick Schiller and Caglar (2008) define 'scale' as a city's geopolitical status, shaped by the flow of capital and structures of power that are constituted across regions, states and the globe. Cities are not necessarily contained within a nested hierarchy of regional and national institutions but sidestep the national to compete independently on the global stage. They respond to global institutional forces as well as state policies, which themselves reposition cities within national territories in different ways (Sassen 1991).

Boston, for example, has a long history as a gateway city, welcoming Italians and Irish at the turn of the last century and Latin Americans and Asians at the turn of the new one. Services for non-English speakers are relatively plentiful. The city's economy has always depended on the world beyond, initially through its fishing and manufacturing industries and more recently through health and computers. The city's many institutions of higher learning attract well-educated immigrant professionals. Many of them contributed to the high-tech boom that drove regional economic growth in the 1990s. At the same time, former mill and manufacturing towns, long abandoned by industry, offered empty storefronts and low rents to low-skilled workers who provided the labour that fuelled this expansion. These positive conditions were reinforced by the US national self-concept of a 'nation of immigrants' founded on the principles of religious pluralism.

Finally, analysing social life using a transnational lens calls attention to the role of global culture in shaping simultaneity. While national citizenship still clearly matters, more and more countries allow some kind of dual membership and the expatriate vote. New kinds of governance regimes, operating supranationally, reflect the recognition that shared problems need shared solutions. Different global values packages create and are created in response to these developments. A neoliberal package, promoting democracy, capitalism, human rights, the rule of law, transparency and accountability and gender equity, is widely promulgated by international foundations and financial institutions around the world. A fundamentalist religious package based on gender complementarity, tradition, conservatism and authority is also being spread by conservative religious networks. All of these scripts provide people who move and people who stay behind with the grist from which to imagine transnational communities and construct transnational lives. They are the discursive backdrop against which we can begin to imagine and put into place a social contract that extends beyond the boundaries of the nation-state.

Further reading

Glick Schiller, N., L. Basch and C. Szanton Blanc (1992) 'Transnationalism: a new analytic framework for understanding migration', *Annals of the New York Academy of Sciences*, 645: 1–24.

Khagram, S. and P. Levitt (eds) (2007) *The Transnational Studies Reader*, New York: Routledge.

Levitt, P. (2001) *The Transnational Villagers*, Berkeley: University of California Press.

Levitt, P. and N. Glick Schiller (2004) 'Transnational perspectives on migration: conceptualizing simultaneity', *International Migration Review*, 38(145): 595–629.

Pries, L. (ed.) (2008) *Rethinking Transnationalism*, London and New York: Routledge.

6 | Nation, ethnicity and community

Gerd Baumann

Since there is no nation without a diaspora, let alone any ethnic label or any cultural community not facing, or faced by, serious questions about exclusion or inclusion, let us weigh the three key concepts against each other. They are interconnected, both in history and politics, as in theory and methodology, so that one may easily arrange them as a triangle, with the problematic concept of identity placed as the interactive question in the middle.

The term nation, originally taken from international student jargon of the thirteenth century, refers to commonalities of birthplace, in present-day words almost congruently translatable as ethnicity. The cultural and political sea-change happened much later – namely, with the invention of the accursed hyphenated beast, the nation-state. Early states had discovered a threefold patent recipe: to centralize territorial sovereignty (if need be by divine kingship), to enforce a state monopoly on legitimizing means and measures of coercion, and to organize economic and ecological redistribution. These states, importantly, were not nation-states, but multi-ethnic empires, whether emerging independently in the Middle East or South America, East Asia or, as pocket editions, in environmentally troublesome bits of Europe. Europe around 1500, however, invented the hyphen that transformed the state into a so-called nation-state, thus translating an efficient form of multi-ethnic organization into a purportedly cultural identity, and hence starting up entirely new, and often self-destructive, mechanisms of civic and cultural inclusion and exclusion. The transient colonial victory, from 1500 to 1960, of European nation-states over the world of 'the people without history' would have been an aberrant episode, were it not for the legacy of colonialism (Wolf 1982; Giddens 2006). Almost all state elites now think that their states should be one-nation states, and all but a handful have taken over the recipes that failed and ruined their colonial ex-masters.

The lure of the nation-state promises the nation as a state, sells the state as a moral ethnos, and advertises that false congruence as a core cultural identity and community. In times of globalization, this error in thought and deed has quickly turned from counterproductive to self-defeating, so it is worth rethinking the other two corners of the triangle.

Ethnicity describes at once the scientifically vaguest and the subjectively most recognizable corner of the conceptual triangle. By commonsense perceptions of ethnicity, we somehow 'recognize it when we see it', but we really do not know what it is. In that sense, it is like the fictional and scientifically content-free cipher of 'race'. The human and social value and anti-value of such terms must not be discredited; but, as I have suggested elsewhere (Baumann 1999), there are no identities, only identifications in changing and opaque contexts. Still, ethnicity as a criterion of (self- or other-)identifications does not go away just because it is unscientific. First, most political and economic structures, as well as most social and even cultural hierarchies, still bear annoying family resemblances to ethnic categorizations. To illustrate it somewhat provocatively, prison statistics and unemployment rates reverberate with rap and Britney, boardrooms and univer- sities resound with remixed Bach pops. Second, people desire a sense of ethnic commonality, whether to rely on in daily praxis, to cherish by feeling, or even to transgress by an act of personal agency. These ethnic bonds are not primordial, as if given by nature or biology; yet like kindred and indeed whole kinship systems, even a knowledge of their social constructedness and contextuality does not stop them from 'feeling' primordial, even when one negates them by an act of rebellion or individuation, depending on context or conviction.

What, then, is cultural community, and how can we rethink this concept to get us out of the fix between 'scientifically false but experientially authentic'? Here, we go to the essence of a non-essentialist understanding of culture. Most good ethnographers of the past twenty years have seen the problem in precisely those terms, and diaspora studies had a lot to do with it. When we study diasporas – a word one may critique, but which we use as an obvious shorthand – we usually study people negotiating different cultural commonalities with the utmost flexibility in the most divergent circumstances. Thinking of cultural commonalities either given or demanded by my nation-state of residence, I must take account of some of these conventions, in order to communicate effectively. Sometimes, these demands are naive, sometimes downright fascist. Let me therefore contrast the oldest trend, the selective de-ethnicization of citizenship, with an intervening one, the racist re-ethnicization of citizenship, with the newest one, the current ethicalization of citizenship.

Most successful European nation-states began their sixteenth- to nineteenth-century nation-building by de-ethnicizing citizenship, at least within their state borders. Whether a citizen of France was an ethnic Breton or an ethnic Corsican, or a Spaniard was Castilian or Basque, the ticket to active civil rights and successful participation was a process that Schiffauer et al. (2004) call 'civil enculturation'. Condensed into its core demands, this was to leave your ethnic or religious community identity at home before you entered the public sphere, to learn a self-standardizing national language and the corresponding hegemonic values, and then to compete with all others admitted as fellow neo-nationals. Metropolitan cities from Amsterdam to St Petersburg selectively stretched this recipe beyond national boundaries, attracting foreign immigrants who offered either special, and often transnational, social capital or exceptionally cheap labour. The nineteenth century saw, in all but some backwater states of Europe, a radical expansion of this de-ethnicization by means of nation-state schooling, universal military conscription and national and nationalist cults tailored to the many, the latter even including women in national public life. The classic example, the nineteenth-century state project of converting 'Peasants into Frenchmen' (Weber 1976), was path-breaking in its methods, but soon paralleled in most other successful nation-states with comparable methods. This selective de-ethnicization of national citizenship as an 'imagined community' and cultural identity (Anderson 1983) almost always stopped short of what were thought to be 'racial' boundaries, and nationalism rightly became the byword for the racism that it still remains.

Misguided ideas about 'race' indeed spelled an opposite trend after a concatenation of nation-state world wars and in the course of global decolonization. National identity as a cultural identity and a supra-ethnic community was re-ethnicized systematically almost everywhere, leaving aside a handful of hesitant exceptions such as population-hungry Canada and Australia, rich Malaysia and poor Surinam. Almost everywhere else, nationalist efforts to control an unprecedented global flow of worldwide labour migrations re-ethnicized citizenship to the point of racial regimes. 'Fortress Europe' is but one of the slogans, but arguably the most critical one. Since post-1950s Europe depended on labour and capital immigrations from overseas, old racisms and new re-ethnicizations of citizenship closed ranks in blatantly racist populisms (Gingrich and Banks 2006) and even EU-wide repressive directives and laws. The policies of a 'Fortress Europe' did not work, since they were neither enforceable nor intelligent. On the contrary, their brute forces of xenophobic exclusion predictably provoked counter-forces of non-state ethnic community-building, be it in the *banlieues* of France, the inner cities of Britain or the putatively dreaded *Parallelgesellschaften* in Germany, Austria and Switzerland. The latter three, as well as the Netherlands, are prime examples of a third process that may be called the ethicalization of citizenship.

The best examples of this tongue-twisting mind-bender are the increasingly widespread citizenship tests. These test a person's ability to transcend or simply deny their ethnic community loyalties and bonds, in order to prove their 'integration into', not 'integration with', a nation-state as a pseudo-ethical imagined community. The difference of prepositions masks two moral universes. 'Integration into' means submitting to a predefined whole: you fit in, or you go home, since this nation could gladly remain without you. 'Integration with' would be a dialogic process of mutual adjustment between hegemonics and diasporics. Ironically, dialogue takes place as it must in states with democratic and cosmopolitan claims, but witness the following exchange in a legally mandatory citizenship test class, mid-2006 in the Netherlands:

Teacher: Do the Dutch watch their pennies?

Students (delighted they know): Yes, they do!

Teacher: But think of the tsunami! Didn't we show the greatest generosity?

Students (hesitantly): Yes, they/we did ...

Teacher: So do the Dutch watch their pennies, or are they generous?

Students (now enculturated): Yes, the Dutch people are generous!

Despite the real-life farce, which I owe to one of my students, Feia Tol, the point is serious. After selective de-ethnicization of citizenship and racist re-ethnicization of citizenship, and after the countervailing reinforcements of ethnic or religious community solidarities, even secularist liberal states turn to an ethicalization of citizenship, in order to integrate people with previously full legal entitlements 'into', not 'with', a nation-state advertising itself as a supreme moral community. Are these states haunted by the spectre of disloyal diasporics with multiple identifications, or do they doubt their own democratic credentials?

Transposing this question on to a more abstract level of debate, one can recognize the two core problems of the nation-state, though now with a special emphasis on diasporic dynamics amid runaway globalization. One, the states that most humans want to live in, and be in as diasporics, are more or less secularist about religion, but never secular about themselves. The post-nation-state must still manage to project itself as a meta-religious moral community. Otherwise, it would face a breakdown not only of taxpaying morale, but of daily civility. Since religious riots at home or abroad are expensive beyond calculation, civil religion must be revived by state-running elites, if this time without systemic rhetorics of religious exclusion. Second, the nineteenth-century remnants of the state as an ethno-national self-fulfilment are discredited, but far from dead. They are revitalized especially by the losers of globalization, both among 'natives' and diasporics, sometimes pitching one against the other, and often helplessly echoed by the winners of globalization who want to console their voters or just to keep the populace or their investors in check. At the same time, however, community remains a problematic idea. The ethno-national state promised 'community' at its peril, only to bury it in the burning ruins of self-inflicted wars. Ethnic and religious 'cultural communities' are no better, supervised as they are by random selections of gatekeepers, power-hungry 'righteous advocates', and sometimes the benighted – much like states.

Must we then take leave of all three guiding notions at once: nation as community, ethnicity as community, and religion as community? Different disciplines take different views. The best political scientists have long argued we must (Young 1990), yet the best alter-globalization economists argue now that we must not (Stiglitz 2002; Mander and Goldsmith 2003). As anthropologists, and indeed as citizens, we stand between these and must weigh them up. It may seem odd, but when locality is no longer an independent variable by which to analyse or shape the world we inhabit (Gupta and Ferguson 1992), there may be wisdom yet in the oldest form of human sociality that we know: hunters and gatherers. Metaphorically, we are all hunters and gatherers, running after life chances and relativizing community pleasures as the world economic environment dictates. Historically, hunters and gatherers are of course the people whom we sacrificed to territorial and, later, nation states. Philosophically, however, they managed three things that we are all searching for anew: one, an intuition or a *conscience collective* (Durkheim 1971 [1915]) of moral community combined with personal agency. Second, we seek trustworthy networks across vast territorial distances and even unpredictable intervals between contact times – as we practise them by email and web every day in this 'information age' (Castells 1996). Third, we secretly desire a fiction (and reflexively, that would be enough) of moral convergence across nation-state borders, such as we celebrate in our converging faiths in human rights (Dembour 2006). Clearly, we are not hunter-gatherers in any literal sense; but in those three senses, we are all diasporics now.

Further reading

Anderson, B. (1983) *Imagined Communities. Reflections on the Origin and Spread of Nationalism*, London: Verso.

Baumann, G. (1996) *Contesting Culture: Discourses of Identity in Multi-Ethnic London*, Cambridge: Cambridge University Press.

— (1999) *The Multicultural Riddle: Re-thinking National, Ethnic and Religious Identities*, New York: Routledge.

Gingrich, A. and M. Banks (eds) (2006) *Neo-Nationalism in Western Europe and Beyond: Perspectives from Social Anthropology*, London: Berghahn.

Schiffauer, W., G. Baumann, R. Kastoryano and S. Vertovec (eds) (2004) *Civil Enculturation: Nation-State, School and Ethnic Difference in Four European Countries*, Oxford: Berghahn.

7 | Multiculturalism and citizenship

Tariq Modood

The emergence of multiculturalist politics

The term 'multiculturalism' emerged in the 1960s and 1970s in countries like Canada and Australia, and to a lesser extent Britain and the USA (all Anglophone countries with histories of immigration) (Goldberg 1994). In Canada and Australia the set of issues covered by the term originally centred on indigenous people and historic minorities, in particular francophone Quebec, though such groups prefer to be considered as 'nations' rather than 'cultures' (Kymlicka 1996), and so the term 'multiculturalism' has come to mean the accommodation of ethno-religious groups formed by immigration in the last fifty years or so. The policy focus was initially on schooling and the children of Asian/black/Hispanic post-/neocolonial immigrants, and multiculturalism meant the extension of the school, both in terms of curriculum and as an institution, to include features such as 'mother-tongue' teaching, non-Christian religions and holidays, halal food, Asian dress and so on. From such a starting point, the perspective developed into the accommodation of cultural requirements in other or even all social spheres and the empowering of marginalized groups.

The ethnic assertiveness associated with multiculturalism has been part of a wider political current of 'identity politics' which first germinated in the 1960s and which transformed the idea of equality as sameness to equality as difference (Young 1990); or, in a related conceptualization, adding the concept of respect or 'recognition' to the older concept of equality between individuals (Taylor 1994). Black power, feminist and gay pride movements challenged the ideal of equality as assimilation and contended that a liberatory politics required allowing groups to assert their difference and not to have to conform to dominant cultural norms. Indeed, the attack on colour-blind, culture-neutral political concepts such as equality and citizenship, with the critique that ethnicity and culture cannot be confined to some so-called private sphere but shape political and opportunity structures in all societies, is one of the most fundamental claims made by multiculturalism and the politics of difference. It is the theoretical basis for the conclusion that allegedly 'neutral' liberal democracies are part of a hegemonic culture that systematically de-ethnicizes or marginalizes minorities. Hence, the claim that minority cultures, norms and symbols have as much right as their hegemonic counterparts to state provision and to be in the public space, to be recognized as groups and not just as culturally neutered individuals.

One of the most fundamental divisions among scholars concerns the validity of 'cultural groups' as a point of reference for multiculturalism. The dominant view in sociocultural studies has become that groups always have internal differences, including hierarchies, gender inequality and dissent, and culture is always fluid and subject to varied influences, mixtures and change. To think otherwise is to 'essentialize' groups such as blacks, Muslims, Asians and so on. Political theorists, on the other hand, continue to think of cultural groups as socio-political actors who may bear rights and have needs that should be institutionally accommodated. This approach challenges the view of culture as radically unstable and primarily expressive by putting moral communities at the centre of a definition of 'culture' (Parekh 2000). Empirical studies, however, suggest that both these views have some substance. For while many young people, from majority and minority backgrounds, do not wish to be defined by a singular ethnicity but wish to actively mix and share several heritages, there is simultaneously a development of distinct communities, usually ethno-religious, and sometimes seeking corporate representation.

Since '9/11' and its aftermath it is Muslims who have become the focus of discourse about minorities in the West. This is partly an issue of security, but more generally is accompanied by a rhetoric of 'multiculturalism is dead'. This has led to, or reinforced, policy reversals in many countries, even pioneering ones such as the Netherlands, and is most marked by the fact that a new assimilationism is espoused not just on the political right but also on the centre-left and by erstwhile supporters of multiculturalism. Muslims in western Europe, it is argued, are disloyal to European states, prefer segregation and sociocultural separatism to integration; they are illiberal on a range of issues, most notably on the personal freedom of women and on homosexuality; and they are challenging the secular character of European political culture by thrusting religious identities and communalism into the public space. The last charge marks the most serious theoretical reversal of multiculturalism, as the non-privatization of minority identities is one of the core ideas of multiculturalism (Modood 2007). Yet the emergence of Muslim political mobilization has led some multiculturalists to argue that religion is a feature of plural societies that it is uniquely legitimate to confine to the private sphere. This prohibiting of Muslim identity in public space has so far been taken farthest in France, where in 2004 parliament passed, with little debate but an overwhelming majority, a ban on the wearing of 'ostentatious' religious symbols (primarily the hijab or headscarf) in public schools.

Civic multiculturalism

In my own work, as a response to the contemporary critique of political multi-culturalism, I restate how I conceive the relationship between multiculturalism and citizenship.

The ideal of multicultural citizenship is a critique of the cultural assimilation traditionally demanded by nation-states of migrants and minorities, as well as of that liberal individualism that has no space for groups. Nevertheless, it is clearly grounded in and is a development out of the ideas of individual equality and democratic citizenship. It is not about pre-democratic arrangements such as the Ottoman accommodation of minorities through the *millet* system. It seeks to pluralize, and hence adapt, not undermine, the unity and equality of citizenship and national identity.

The concepts of equality and of citizenship that are being appealed to can be sketched further by noting that when we talk about equality in the context of race, sex, ethnicity and so on, we are appealing to two different albeit related concepts which, slightly altering Taylor's (1994) nomenclature, I will call *equal dignity* and *equal respect*. Equal dignity appeals to people's humanity or to some specific membership such as citizenship and applies to all members in a relatively uniform way. We appeal to this idea in relation to anti-discrimination policies where we appeal to the principle that everybody should be treated the same. But Taylor, and other theorists in differing ways, also posit the idea of equal respect. If equal dignity focuses on what people have in common and so is gender-blind, colour-blind and so on, equal respect is based on an understanding that difference is also important in conceptualizing and institutionalizing equal relations between individuals.

This is because individuals have group identities and these may be the ground of existing and long-standing inequalities such as racism, for example, and the ways in which some people have conceived and treated others as inferior, less rational and culturally backward. While those conceptions persist they will affect the dignity of non-white people, above all where they share a social life with white people, which is steeped in negative images of non-white peoples. The negative conceptions will lead to direct and indirect acts of discrimination – they will eat away at the possibilities of equal dignity. They will affect the self-understanding of those who seek to be equal participants in a culture in which ideas of their inferiority, or even just of their invisibility, are pervasive. They will stand in need of self-respect and the respect of others, of the dominant group; the latter will be crucial for it is the source of their damaged self-respect and it is where the power for change lies. The imperative for equal respect, the turning of negative group identities into positive ones, then, flows out of a commitment to equal dignity.

Multicultural citizenship is based on the idea that citizens have individual rights but they are not uniform and their citizenship contours itself around specific groups of people with specific cultures and histories. Citizenship is not a monistic identity that is completely apart from or transcends other identities important to citizens. These group identities are ever present and each group has a right to be a part of the civic whole and to speak up for itself and for its vision of the whole. Hence citizenship is a continuous dialogue. As the parties to these dialogues are many, not just two, the process may be described as multi-logical. The multilogues allow for views to qualify each other, overlap, synthesize, for one to modify one's own view in the light of having to coexist with that of others', hybridize, allow new adjustments to be made, new conversations to take place. Such modulations and contestations – along with other practical struggles for resources – are part of the internal, evolutionary, work-in-progress dynamic of citizenship.

In any national context, citizenship consists of a framework of rights and practices of participation but also discourses and symbols of belonging, ways of imagining and remaking ourselves as a country and expressing our sense of commonalities, as well as differences in ways in which these identities qualify each other and create inclusive public spaces. Change and reform do not all have to be brought about by state action, laws, regulation and prohibitions, but may also occur through public debate, discursive contestations, pressure-group mobilizations, and the varied and (semi-)autonomous institutions of civil society. Citizenship, then, is not confined to the state but dispersed across society, compatible with the multiple forms of contemporary groupness and sustained through dialogue, plural forms of representation that do not take one group as the model to which all others have to conform, and new, reformed national identities.

Multicultural accommodation, then, like 'integration', is a two-way process, but differs from the latter in that it recognizes the social reality of groups (not just of individuals and organizations). This reality can be of different kinds: for example, a sense of solidarity with people of similar origins or faith or mother tongue, including those in a country of origin or a diaspora. Such feelings might be an act of imagination but may also be rooted in lived experience and embodied in formal organizations dedicated to fostering group identity and keeping it alive. This form of accommodation would also allow group-based cultural and religious practices to be fitted into existing, majoritarian ways of doing things. These identities and practices would not be regarded as immutable, but neither would there be pressure either to change them (unless a major issue of principle, legality or security was at stake) or to confine them to a limited community or private space. Multicultural accommodation works simultaneously on two levels: creating new forms of belonging to citizenship and country, and helping sustain origins and diasporas.

There is, then, deep resonance between citizenship and multicultural recognition. Not only do both presuppose complementary notions of unity and plurality, and of equality and difference, but the idea of respect for those group self-identities that citizens value is central to citizenship. Moreover, seeing citizenship as a work in progress and as partly constituted, and certainly extended, by critical, ongoing dialogues and novel demands for due recognition, as circumstances shift, means that citizenship can be understood as conversations and renegotiations, not just about who is to be recognized but about what recognition is, about the terms of citizenship itself. At one point, it is the injuries of class which demand civic attention; at another there is a plea for dropping a self-deluding 'colour-blindness' and of addressing racialized statuses through citizenship. Civic inclusion does not consist of an uncritical acceptance of an existing conception of citizenship, of 'the rules of the game', and a one-sided 'fitting-in' of new entrants or new equals (the ex-subordinates, largely of the colonial experience). To be a citizen, no less than to have just become a citizen, is to have a right to not just be recognized but to debate the terms of recognition.

Further reading

Goldberg, D. T. (ed.) (1994) *Multiculturalism: A Critical Reader*, Oxford and Malden, MA: Blackwell.

Kymlicka, W. (1996) *Multicultural Citizenship: A Liberal Theory of Minority Rights*, Oxford: Oxford University Press.

Modood, T. (2007) *Multiculturalism: A Civic Idea*, Cambridge: Polity Press.

Parekh, B. (2000) *Rethinking Multiculturalism: Cultural Diversity and Political Theory*, London/Cambridge, MA: Macmillan/Harvard University Press.

Taylor, C. (1994) 'Multiculturalism and "the politics of recognition"', in A. Gutmann (ed.), *Multiculturalism and the Politics of Recognition*, Princeton, NJ: Princeton University Press.

8 | Post-coloniality

Graham Huggan

The mass relocation, either voluntary or forced, of people from their own home-lands to new regions – probably still the most common understanding of the increasingly multivalent term 'diaspora' – has been a central feature in historical processes of colonization, not least because colonialism itself can be seen as a 'radically diasporic movement, involving the temporary or permanent dispersion and settlement of millions of Europeans over the entire world' (Ashcroft et al. 1998: 69). Ashcroft et al. distinguish broadly between three kinds of diaspora that have historically obtained under colonial/post-colonial conditions. First, there were those (white) diasporas of *settlement* that took Europeans, across a vast spectrum of social, political and economic circumstances, to a series of 'new' countries that they then proceeded to fashion in their own self-image, with highly varying degrees of individual success and equally varying amounts of institutional support. Very different from these were those (non-white) diasporas of *slavery* and *indenture* that emerged out of the need to supply cheap labour in colonial plantation economies, principally though by no means exclusively in the Americas, and which have resulted in large minority, even majority, populations of blacks and Asians in much of the formerly colonized world today. Finally, and more recently, there are those (both white and non-white) diasporas of *casualization* which, loosely bracketed under the Jamaican poet Louise Bennett's sarcastic term 'reverse colonization', are formed by groups of people who have moved, usually by choice but often under duress, from economically exploited and/or marginalized regions to metropolitan centres, either in direct response to labour demands or, more generally, in search of a better life (ibid.: 69–70; cf. Bennett 1964).

It is arguably the second and third categories of diaspora which have received the most attention from post-colonial critics, reinforcing the standard view of diasporas as emerging out of collective experiences of suffering as well as the equally conventional understanding that diasporas are self-affirming, revolu-tionizing even, in the face of historical displacement and devastating loss. Not that some of the earlier, agonistic models of diaspora, particularly the Zionist model, are necessarily adhered to; on the contrary, these are often explicitly challenged. A good example here is Stuart Hall's wide-ranging 1990 essay 'Cul-tural identity and diaspora', which summarily rejects the nostalgia bound up in those reactionary forms of diasporic consciousness (and Hall leaves us in no doubt as to the particular form he is talking about) through which the identity of scattered tribes 'can only be secured in relation to some sacred homeland to which they must at all costs return, even if it means pushing other people into the sea' (Hall 1994 [1990]: 401; for a more recent essay which also critiques the Zionist paradigm of diaspora, see Shohat 2006). This, asserts Hall, is 'the old, the imperializing, the hegemonizing form of ethnicity', and over and against it he puts the notion of diaspora experience as being defined, 'not by essence or purity, but by the recognition of a necessary heterogeneity and diversity; by a conception of identity which lives with and through, not despite, difference; by hybridity' (ibid.: 401–2). 'Diaspora identities', he concludes, 'are those which are constantly producing and reproducing themselves anew, through transformation and difference' (ibid.: 402; cf. Gilroy 1993a).

This 'new', self-consciously secular understanding of diaspora, which is perhaps less fully removed than it imagines from the earlier models it ostensibly opposes, should also be seen in relation to contemporary globalization processes, and to the increasingly accepted view that *hypermobility* (of capital, ideas and goods, if not necessarily people) is the overriding condition of the modern world (see, for example, Appadurai 1996; Clifford 1997). As Arjun Appadurai claims in *Modernity at Large*, 'diaspora is the [new] order of things' (Appadurai 1996: 172); and while she is rightly suspicious of such all-encompassing rhetoric, Diana Brydon concedes the need to distinguish between older notions of diaspora that 'implied the persistence of a homeland through the scattering of its peoples' and newer, implicitly utopian notions that 'stress transnational circulations, multidirectional flows, and the capacity to occupy multiple locations' (Brydon 2004: 701; for a further distinction between 'old' and 'new' diasporas, see also Mishra 1996). In part-response to the generalizing tendency to see 'diaspora' as a descriptive figure for global modernity in its late-capitalist moment, Brydon emphasizes the need to differentiate between alternative kinds of diasporic experience, and to push against the temptation to use the term as a master trope (Brydon 2004: 701; see also Clifford 1997, Cohen 1997). As she admits, however, 'diaspora' continues to be used in precisely this way, often interchangeably with 'hybridity', with both terms being subject to an uncritical appreciation of creolized patterns of cross-cultural location and exchange in a putatively decentred modern world (Brydon 2004: 701; cf. Spivak 1999, on hybridity and subalterneity).

Current studies of diaspora, both theoretically and historically oriented, are usually committed to practising some form or other of internal differentiation, be it between 'victim' and 'labour' diasporas (Cohen 1997), 'trade' and 'imperial' diasporas (Urry 2000), or diaspora as a 'mode of cultural production, a type of consciousness [...] and a social form' (Brydon 2004; cf. Vertovec and Cohen 1999). Perhaps the most obvious differentiation, however, is that between 'good' (socially beneficial) and 'bad' (morally reprehensible) diasporas, with post-colonial critics – for understandable reasons – being more likely to give their attention to the former kind. As Kanishka Goonewardena points out in a challenging essay, post-colonial critics, by and large, have subscribed to the theoretical orthodoxy of diasporas as affirmative countercultures marked both by haunting memories of displacement and by the capacity to convert these memories into self-enabling forms of resistance to current globalizing norms (Goonewardena 2004: 659–60; see also Ashcroft et al. 1998). This view of diaspora is in line, as Goonewardena suggests, with post-colonialism's self-consciously utopian social tendencies, its self-given mission both to trace histories of colonial exploitation and oppression and to gesture towards a more equitable future in which today's conspicuously uneven social relations may be productively transformed.

Very different views, however, can be seen to emerge out of a similarly utopian, if more narrowly partisan, perspective. One such view sets up a correspondence between diaspora consciousness and what Benedict Anderson calls 'long-distance nationalism', which, while not necessarily destructively extremist in its intention, is often politically reactionary in its predominant ideology and social form (Anderson 1994; see also Sivanandan 1990). As Goonewardena tellingly asks, 'What is it in a diaspora that enables it to be a [countercultural] form of resistance to globalization [...] as opposed to lapsing into a virulently ethnocentric communalism or even neofascism?' (Goonewardena 2004: 665). To clinch his point, Goonewardena cites Anderson:

> Not least as a result of the ethnicization of political life in the wealthy, post-industrial states, what one can call long-distance nationalism is visibly emerging. This type of politics, directed mainly towards the former Second and Third Worlds, pries open the classical nation-state project [...] Many of the most uncompromising, fanatical adherents of an independent Khalistan do not live in the Punjab but have prosperous businesses in Melbourne and Chicago. The [Tamil] Tigers in Jaffna are stiffened in their violent struggles by Tamil communities in Toronto, London and elsewhere, all linked on the computer by Tamilnet. Consider the malign role of Croats not only in Germany but also in Australia and North America in financing and arming Franco Tudjman's breakaway state and pushing Germany and Austria into a fateful, premature recognition. (Anderson 1994: 326–7, also quoted in Goonewardena 2004: 665)

Anderson is quite right to point out the contradictions of a 'transnational imaginary' (Appadurai 1996; Wilson and Dissanayake 1996) made paradoxically to serve the most partisan of *nationalist* interests, and to suggest that the ideal of the global networked community – the type of electronically connected diaspora praised so lavishly, for example, in the work of Arjun Appadurai – is sometimes very far from matching the cause of global citizenship, and is just as likely instead to be associated with regionally divisive interests and concerns. As Goonewardena points out, 'long-distance nationalism' is a subject on which post-colonial criticism, noisy as it is with tributes to the liberating potential of diasporic interconnection, has been strangely muted, although perhaps not quite as silent as his sweeping criticism attests (see, for example, Brydon 2004; also Natarajan 1993). In fact, most post-colonial critics would heartily agree with his conclusion: that diasporas need to be more carefully analysed in the twin contexts of (a) their historically unstable terms and frames of reference, and (b) their often extreme degree of political volatility, a volatility highly likely to be connected with the linked narratives of colonialism/imperialism and global capitalism that necessarily inform most understandings of the word 'diaspora' today. His general objection is still valid, however: that post-colonialism's approach to diaspora – its constitutive entanglement with diaspora – has been largely 'culturalist' in orientation, thus running the risk of failing to engage sufficiently with the raft of political, economic and historical factors that might help explain how people match their expectations of dwelling to their experiences of displacement, and how the particular, historical forms of diaspora consciousness that mediate between them might help explain how and why they move the way they do (Goonewardena 2004: 667). This objection needs to be borne in mind more than ever today, as post-colonial criticism struggles to keep pace with new experiences of migration (and the increasingly inflammatory nationalist rhetorics arraigned against them), by no means all of which can be bracketed under the category of 'diaspora', and which are often more likely to be mystified than measured, still less controlled, by that seductive category's explanatory power.

Further reading

Ashcroft, B., G. Griffiths and H. Tiffin (eds) (1998) *Key Concepts in Post-Colonial Studies*, London: Routledge.

Brydon, D. (2004) 'Post-colonialism now: autonomy, cosmopolitanism, and diaspora', *University of Toronto Quarterly*, 73(2): 691–706.

Goonewardena, K. (2004) 'Post-colonialism and diaspora: a contribution to the critique of nationalist ideology and historiography in the age of globalization and neoliberalism', *University of Toronto Quarterly*, 73(2): 657–90.

Hall, S. (1994 [1990]) 'Cultural identity and diaspora', in P. Williams and L. Chrisman (eds), *Colonial Discourse and Post-Colonial Theory: A Reader*, New York: Columbia University Press, pp. 392–403.

Shohat, E. (2006) 'Taboo memories, diasporic visions', in E. Shohat, *Taboo Memories, Diasporic Visions*, Durham, NC: Duke University Press, Durham, pp. 201–32.

9 | Hybridity[1]

John Hutnyk

It is by now established that authors writing on diaspora very often engage with the mixed notion of hybridity. We will see that this term also offers much for debate, and that this debate in turn offers material that elaborates, and may further complicate, the cultures and politics of diaspora. This essay explores this uneven terrain and presents a kind of topographical survey of the uses and misuses of hybridity, and its synonyms.

In its most recent descriptive and realist usage, hybridity appears as a convenient category at 'the edge' or contact point of diaspora, describing cultural mixture where the diasporized meets the host in the scene of migration. Nikos Papastergiadis makes this link when he mentions the 'twin processes of globalization and migration' (Papastergiadis 2000: 3). He outlines a development that moves from the assimilation and integration of migrants into the host society of the nation-state towards something more complex in the metropolitan societies of today (cf. Kraidy 2005). Speaking primarily of Europe, the Americas and Australia, Papastergiadis argues that as some members of migrant communities came to prominence 'within the cultural and political circles of the dominant society', they 'began to argue in favour of new models of representing the process of cultural interaction, and to demonstrate the negative consequences of insisting upon the denial of the emergent forms of cultural identity' (Papastergiadis 2000: 3). Hybridity has been a key part of this new modelling, and so it is logically entwined within the coordinates of migrant identity and difference, same or not same, host and guest.

The career of the term hybridity as a new cultural politics in the context of diaspora should be examined carefully. The cultural here points to the claim that hybridity has been rescued – or has it? – from a convoluted past to do duty for an articulation of rights and assertions of autonomy against the force of essential identities. The hybrid is a usefully slippery category, purposefully contested and deployed to claim change. With such loose boundaries, it is curious that the term can be so productive: from its origins in biology, its interlude as syncretism to its reclamation in work on diaspora by authors as different as Paul Gilroy, Stuart Hall, Iain Chambers, Homi Bhabha and James Clifford. It is in the dialogue between these works especially that hybridity has come to

---

1 This essay is a revised version of Kalra et al. (2005: ch. 4).

mean all sorts of things to do with mixing and combination in the moment of cultural exchange. Gilroy, for example, finds it helpful in the field of cultural production, where he notes that 'the musical components of hip hop are a hybrid form nurtured by the social relations of the South Bronx where Jamaican sound system culture was transplanted during the 1970s' (Gilroy 1993a: 33). Hall, as we will see in more detail presently, suggests hybridity is transforming British life (Hall 1995: 18), while Chambers finds talk of tradition displaced by 'traffic' in the 'sights, sounds and languages of hybridity' (Chambers 1994: 82). Bhabha uses hybridity as an 'in-between' term, referring to a 'third space', and to ambivalence and mimicry, especially in the context of what might, uneasily, be called the colonial cultural interface. Clifford uses the word to describe 'a discourse that is travelling or hybridizing in new global conditions', and he stresses 'travel trajectories' and 'flow' (Clifford 1994: 304–6). Worrying that assertions of identity and difference are celebrated too quickly as resistance, in either the nostalgic form of 'traditional survivals' or mixed in a 'new world of hybrid forms' (Clifford 2000: 103), he sets up an opposition (tradition/hybrid) that will become central to our critique of the terms.

There is much more that hybridity seems to contain: 'A quick glance at the history of hybridity reveals a bizarre array of ideas' (Papastergiadis 2000: 169; cf. Burke 2009). In addition to the general positions set out above, hybridity is an evocative term for the formation of identity; it is used to describe innovations of language (Creole, patois, pidgin, travellers' argot, etc.); it is code for creativity and for translation. In Bhabha's terms 'hybridity is camouflage' (1994: 193) and, provocatively, he offers 'hybridity as heresy' (ibid.: 226), as a disruptive and productive category. It is 'how newness enters the world' (ibid.: 227) and it is bound up with a 'process of translating and transvaluing cultural differences' (ibid.: 252). For others, hybridity is the key organizing feature of the cyborg, the wo-man/machine interface (Haraway 1997). It invokes mixed technological innovations, multiple trackings of influence, and is acclaimed as the origin of creative expression in culture industry production. With relation to diaspora, the most conventional accounts assert hybridity as the process of cultural mixing where the diasporic arrivals adopt aspects of the host culture and rework, reform and reconfigure this in production of a new hybrid culture or 'hybrid identities' (Chambers 1996: 50). Whether talk of such identities is coherent or not, hybridity is better conceived of as a process rather than a description. Kobena Mercer writes of 'the hybridized terrain of diasporic culture' (Mercer 1994: 254) and of how even the older terminologies of syncretism and mixture evoke the movement of 'hybridization' rather than stress fixed identity. Brah and Coombs's millennium volume, *Hybridity and Its Discontents*, is able to describe hybridity as: 'a term for a wide range of social and cultural phenomenon involving "mixing", [it] has become a key concept within cultural criticism and post-colonial theory' (2000: cover); and Kraidy follows this five years on, in his work on hybridity and globalization, with an endorsement of its conceptual and disciplinary reach (2005: 1–2).

The idea of borrowing is sometimes taken to imply a weakening of a supposedly once pure culture. It is this myth of purity which belongs to the essentialist nationalisms and chauvinisms that are arraigned against the hybrid, the diasporic and the migrant. It is to combat this rationale that so many writers insist that affirmations of hybridity are useful in the arena of cultural politics. Such affirmations are proclaimed precisely because the varieties of cultural borrowing that are thereby entertained undermine the case of a pure culture. These claims may be more important than the philosophical incoherence of the terms, but this incoherence has to be considered. A key question would be: to what degree does the assertion of hybridity rely on the positing of an anterior 'pure' that precedes mixture? Even as a process in translation or in formation, the idea of 'hybrid identities' (Chambers 1996: 50) relies upon the proposition of non-hybridity or some kind of normative insurance. The main concern here is the specific manner in which notions of purity are related to the biological antecedents of hybridity. Hybridity theorists have had to grapple with this problem and have done so with a revealing degree of agitation. Gilroy, for example, has moved away from an allegiance to hybridity and declared: 'Who the fuck wants purity? [...] the idea of hybridity, of intermixture, presupposes two anterior purities [...] I think there isn't any purity; there isn't any anterior purity [...] that's why I try not to use the word hybrid [...] Cultural production is not like mixing cocktails' (Gilroy 1994: 54–5).

The latitudes of sexuality fester in the earthy connotations of this quote as Gilroy knowingly references the less reputable anxieties at stake. It was probably work like that of Robert Young's *Colonial Desire: Hybridity in Theory, Culture and Race* (1995) which provoked the outburst. Numerous scholars have examined the biological parameters of hybridity, but the matter is perhaps best exemplified in Young's historical investigation, which traced the provenance of the term hybridity in the racialized discourse of nineteenth-century evolutionism. The Latin roots of the word are revealed as referring to the progeny of a tame sow and a wild boar (ibid.: 6). Is this old usage relevant to the diversity of cultural hybridities claimed today? In the sciences of agriculture and horticulture, hybridity is used with little alarm: the best-known hybrid being the mule, a mixture of a horse and donkey, though significantly this is a sterile or non-productive mix. In the world of plants, hybrid combinations are productively made by grafting one plant or fruit to another. Although in this field such graftings may seem legitimate, only a mildly imprudent jump is needed to move from notions of horticulture and biology to discussions of human 'races' as distinct species that, upon mixing, produce hybrids.

Both Gilroy and Hall have made efforts to distinguish their use of hybridity from its dubious biological precedents. Gilroy clearly recognizes the problem of purity when he laments 'the lack of a means of adequately describing, let alone theorizing, intermixture, fusion and syncretism without suggesting the existence of anterior "uncontaminated" purities' (Gilroy 2000: 250). He is correct that the descriptive use of hybridity evokes, counterfactually, a stable and prior non-mixed position, to which 'presumably it might one day be possible to return' (ibid.: 250). 'Who wants to return?' is a good question. But equally, can a focusing and tightening of descriptive terminology, or the even farther-off 'theorizing', be adequate to the redress that is required? Does it disentangle the range of sexual, cultural and economic anxieties race mixture provokes? Gilroy continues, this time with the arguments of Young firmly in his sights:

> Whether the process of mixture is presented as fatal or redemptive, we must be prepared to give up the illusion that cultural and ethnic purity has ever existed, let alone provided a foundation for civil society. The absence of an adequate conceptual and critical language is undermined and complicated by the absurd charge that attempts to employ the concept of hybridity are completely undone by the active residues of that term's articulation within the technical vocabularies of nineteenth-century racial science. (Ibid.: 250–51)

It is difficult to agree with the view that scholarship should avoid examining the antecedents of emergent critical terminologies. Hall also reacts, naming Young, admittedly in defence against an even more sweeping condemnation of post-colonial theory, yet significantly with the penultimate words of a volume entitled *The Post-Colonial Question*, where he writes: 'a very similar line of argument is to be found [...] [in] the inexplicably simplistic charge in Robert Young's *Colonial Desire* [...] that the post-colonial critics are "complicit" with Victorian racial theory *because both sets of writers deploy the same term – hybridity – in their discourse!*' (Hall 1996: 259, emphasis in original).

It is absolutely imperative that the uses and usefulness of hybridity as descriptive term, as political diagnostic and as strategy be evaluated without recourse to petty common-room squabbles. That the use of a term can be condemned because of one sort of association or another remains problematic unless the consequences of that association can be demonstrated to have unacceptable consequences. As hybridity appears in several guises, it is important to look at what it achieves, what contexts its use might obscure, and what it leaves aside.

Further reading

Brah, A. and A. Coombs (2000) *Hybridity and Its Discontents*, London: Routledge.

Burke, P. (2009) *Cultural Hybridity*, Cambridge and Malden, MA: Polity Press.

Kraidy, M. M. (2005) *Hybridity or the Cultural Logic of Globalization*, Philadephia, PA: Temple University Press.

Papastergiadis, N. (2000) *The Turbulence of Migration*, Cambridge: Polity Press.

Young, R. (1995) *Colonial Desire: Hybridity in Theory, Culture and Race*, London: Routledge.

10 | Cosmopolitanism

Steven Vertovec

As a growing set of recent literature demonstrates, cosmopolitanism has be-come a topic of considerable attention, particularly in light of globalization, new modes of transnational interconnectedness and increasing ethnic diver-sity. Much interest in cosmopolitanism concerns its ethical or philosophical dimensions, especially regarding questions of how to live as a 'citizen of the world'. Other dimensions concern normative political issues that are deemed cosmopolitan, such as global governance structures or forms of international intervention. With reference to general notions of diaspora (considered here as an imagined community living away from a professed place of origin), how-ever, it is the sociological dimensions of cosmopolitanism which are perhaps of most relevance. Hence this essay addresses the question: What is the nature of 'cosmopolitan' social attributes arising from conditions of diaspora?

In the nineteenth century, cosmopolitan traits were largely associated with rootlessness, characterizing individuals (particularly Jews) who – owing to their tendencies to be mobile, to speak several languages and to have open political views – were believed to belong not really anywhere. In an age of consolida-ting national identities, therefore, cosmopolitans were often rather suspect and unwelcome.

By the middle of the twentieth century, cosmopolitan attributes were associ-ated with an elite class (or jet set, following the introduction of commercial jet aircraft in the 1950s). These were people whose wealth, social activities and leisure pursuits took them to exotic locations where they interacted with people of similar socio-economic standing drawn from a variety of cultural backgrounds. Consequently cosmopolitans were often characterized by well-travelled experience, sophisticated style and *savoir faire*.

Today this sort of elite cosmopolitanism might best be characterized by international business-class professionals. Since the 1990s, however, and con-comitant with the growth of studies concerning diasporas and transnational communities, social scientists have increasingly drawn attention to charac-teristics of 'working-class cosmopolitans' such as labour migrants and other non-elites spread throughout global diasporas (see Werbner 1999a). This is what some scholars also point to by way of modes of 'actually existing cosmo-politanism' (Robbins 1998), 'everyday cosmopolitanism' (Ang et al. 2002) and 'tactical cosmopolitanism' (Landau and Haupt 2007). Elite or not, of what does such contemporary cosmopolitanism consist? Drawing on a range of literature, it is suggested that we might understand cosmopolitanism as comprising a combination of attitudes, practices and abilities gathered from experiences of travel or displacement, transnational contact and diasporic identification.

Attitude or orientation

Most writers on the topic would agree that fundamental to cosmopolitanism is a kind of personal stance towards cultural difference. As Ulf Hannerz (1996: 103) has put it, cosmopolitanism is based on 'an orientation, a willingness to engage with the other [...] an intellectual and aesthetic openness toward divergent cultural experiences'. This could be described as a kind of xenophilia, or penchant for diversity. The experience of living in conditions of diaspora, or in fact engaging in transnational life spread across two or more global settings, exposes individuals to cultural differences that may give rise to such cosmopolitan views.

In a unique study, Mau et al. (2008) have researched the relationship between transnational ties and broad cosmopolitan attitudes. With surveys designed to test whether cross-border social ties and activities have an impact on people's attitudes and worldviews, Mau and colleagues measured key attitudinal traits such as openness towards difference and the capacity to reason from the point of view of others. Finding a positive correlation between the transnationalization of life worlds and the cosmopolitanization of attitudes and values, Mau et al. suggest that:

> People with cosmopolitan attitudes and values are characterized by their recognition of others because of their value and integrity as human beings, quite independently of their national affiliations. They share an open and tolerant world view that is not bound by national categories but is based on an awareness of our increasing economic, political and cultural interconnectedness, which they perceive as enriching rather than threatening. (Ibid.: 5)

Consequently, we might say, being a member of a diaspora or transnational community doesn't automatically produce cosmopolitan attitudes, but certainly the potential for this is high.

Practices or skills

Individuals and communities in diaspora have always been faced with the challenge of simultaneously adapting and maintaining traditions, practices and identities – what Martin Sökefeld (2000: 23) calls the 'diasporic duality of continuity and change'. While selectively sustaining or indeed enhancing their own particular cultural practices and institutions, people in diaspora also adopt and transform cultural phenomena drawn from others around them. Much of this arises through the simple strategy of 'When in Rome, do as the Romans do': eating like, dressing like, talking like and conforming to the behavioural norms of a 'host' society. The motivations for doing so might entail pleasure, ease of interaction, better understanding, social or economic advantage, social distinction or sheer survival.

One model for adopting others' cultural practices is the 'wolf in sheep's clothing', whose implementation entails a conscious act, based on specific knowledge of the right thing to do in the right circumstances and undertaken purposefully for some kind of advantage. This is in contrast to the cultural chameleon, who assumes others' ways non-consciously with subtle communication cues to signal commonality or to attempt shared meaning.

What are the mechanisms – conscious or non-conscious – by which cosmopolitans develop and utilize such multiple cultural competence, or ability to draw from various cultural registers? Various approaches to this question are possible. One is represented by script theory (e.g. Schank and Abelson 1977). This examines structures of knowledge or the organization of memory through reference to 'scripts', conceived as sets of pattern recognition or causal chains of thought and behaviour obtained through frequently experienced events (such as acquaintance with the sequence of events and behaviour in going to a restaurant, based on previous visits to restaurants). In this way a cosmopolitan would acquire and use appropriate cultural knowledge and practice through gathering, recognizing and applying cross-cultural scripts.

Echoing Bourdieu's concept of *habitus*, another approach is through considering culture as a kind of 'toolkit'. Here cultural attributes drawn from a number of sources throughout one's life are understood as a set of resources from which one can construct diverse strategies of action, situation by situation. This means, according to Ann Swidler (1986: 281), that people engage in their everyday activities by 'selecting certain cultural elements (both such tacit culture as attitudes and styles and, sometimes, such explicit cultural materials as rituals and beliefs) and investing them with particular meanings in concrete life circumstances'. The cosmopolitan accumulates such a repertoire from an array of cultural influences and appropriately enacts selected elements as the circumstances require.

Yet another approach arises through linguistic analogy. In this way cosmopolitanism might be understood as akin to bi- or multilingualism. Aspects of culture can be conceived as similar to modes of linguistic communication, including grammars, syntaxes and lexicons. With the skill to strategically or inadvertently use the right cultural expressions, cosmopolitans are adept at what linguists call code-switching (Rampton 1995). Ballard (1994: 31) underlines the analogy between cultural and linguistic practice, emphasizing that 'Just as individuals can be bilingual, so they can also be multicultural, with the competence to behave appropriately in a number of different arenas, and to switch codes as appropriate.'

These are just a few ways in which the mechanisms of cosmopolitan practice can be assessed. It should be recognized, however, that the uses of cultural markers, drawn from a range of sources through individual diasporic or transnational experience, are not unbounded. As stressed by Ayse Caglar,

> [T]he debris of our past experiences are not immediately usable, since they are already embedded in structures in which they have meanings. These limit their immediate use in producing new arrangements [...] Moreover, these juxtapositions and bricolage are not random, nor do they represent a chaotic jumble of signs. In their hybridity, they still tell a story. They have an organizing principle or principles. The objective is then first to identify the conditions that enable this drastic uprooting of elements and practices from very different sources, and second to explain the organizing principle(s) of their recombination and resetting [...] (1994: 34)

Caglar's points provide a significant corrective to perspectives towards hybridity, cosmopolitanism, multiple identities and similar concepts, which often suggest an unbridled horizon of cultural appropriation and enactment. She importantly reminds us that social actors' actions are embedded in a constellation of relations and structures, and that actions of transnational actors are, indeed, multiply embedded. Hence to gain a fuller comprehension of cosmopolitan practices, in every case we need to ask: what is the 'package' of meaning-carrying traits that has to be read, engaged, performed, and how is it embedded in class, locality, gender, religion, age, sexuality, 'subculture' and other configurations of social meaning?

Abilities or competences

In addition to attitudes and practices, cosmopolitanism is also said to entail 'a personal ability to make one's way into other cultures through listening, looking, intuiting and reflecting' (Hannerz 1990: 239) and a kind of cultural competence, 'a built-up skill in manoeuvring more or less expertly with a particular system of meanings and meaningful forms' (ibid.: 239). Koehn and Rosenau (2002: 114) have sought to elaborate just what kind of skills or competences are acquired through transnational experiences that enable individuals to 'participate effectively in activities that cut across two or more national boundaries'. Grouped under a series of types, their list includes:

Analytic competence
- Understanding of the central beliefs, values, practices and paradoxes of counterpart cultures and societies – including political and ethnic awareness;
- assessment of the number and complexity of alternative cultural paths;
- ability to discern effective transnational strategies and to learn from past successes and failure.

Emotional competence
- Motivation and ability to open oneself up continuously to divergent cultural influences and experiences;
- ability to assume genuine interest in, and to maintain respect for, different (especially counterpart) values, traditions, experiences and challenges;
- ability to manage multiple identities.

Creative/imaginative competence
- Ability to foresee the synergistic potential of diverse cultural perspectives in problem-solving;
- ability to envision viable mutually acceptable alternatives;
- ability to tap into diverse cultural sources for inspiration.

Behavioural competence – communicative facility
- Proficiency in and use of counterparts' spoken/written language;
- proficiency in and relaxed use of inter-culturally appropriate non-verbal cues and codes;
- ability to listen to and discern different cultural messages;
- ability to avoid and resolve communication misunderstandings across diverse communication styles.

Of course, not all of these attributes are developed or utilized at once; rather, 'actors possess components of the several skills in varying degrees and in different mixes' (ibid.: 114). Each of these kinds of cosmopolitan competences might best be understood along a continuum from incapable to proficient.

With regard to the persons who acquire and develop such competences, the notion of cosmopolitan cultural competences produced by diasporic and transnational lives resonates with the range of concepts that researchers in sociology and cultural studies have invoked to convey better a sense of mutability in the cultural practices of migrants and ethnic minorities. These include notions of (cultural) translation, creolization, crossover, cut 'n' mix, hyphenated identity, bricolage, hybridity, syncretism, third space, multiculture, inter-culturalism and transculturation.

This essay has outlined features of attitudes, practices and abilities that can be associated with experiences of travel or displacement, transnational contact and diasporic identification. This gives rise to a significant question: Can cosmopolitan attributes be taught, fostered or instilled in people who themselves don't have such diasporic or transnational experience? In part at least, this seems to be the objective of multicultural education, 'inter-cultural competence' courses, diversity management initiatives within corporate and public sectors, events and spaces created for cross-cultural contact, and a range of public campaigns promoting tolerance and the valuing of diversity.

Not all diasporas entail open acceptance of diversity and willingness to engage with others. To be sure, many diasporas often include hardened identities, reified cultures and reactionary nationalisms (Vertovec 2006). Yet the modes and expressions of inter-cultural engagement evident among many members of diasporas certainly have much to teach us all, both in terms of social scientific understanding of the way culture works and in terms of practical living-with-difference.

Further reading

Appiah, K. A. (2006) *Cosmopolitanism: Ethics in a World of Strangers*, New York: Norton.

Beck, U. (2006) *The Cosmopolitan Vision*, Cambridge: Polity Press.

Cheah, P. and B. Robbins (eds) (1998) *Cosmopolitics*, Minneapolis: University of Minnesota.

Vertovec, S. and R. Cohen (eds) (2003) *Conceiving Cosmopolitanism: Theory, Context and Practice*, Oxford: Oxford University Press.

Werbner, P. (ed.) (2008) *Anthropology and the New Cosmopolitanism: Rooted, Feminist and Vernacular Perspectives*, Oxford: Berg.

11 | Social identities and creolization

Robin Cohen

In general, interest in social identities has dramatically enlarged over the last thirty years – to such a degree, indeed, that it has become a dominant theme in anthropological and sociological studies. Historically, this is somewhat surprising in that most of the grand figures in these disciplines (luminaries like Weber, Marx, Durkheim and Malinowski) managed perfectly well without recourse to the idea of social identity. Of course, none of these scholars was so naive as to assume that ethnicity, nation, community, class or religion ('gender' was rarely used) were fixed and unyielding social categories. It took a fundamental change in outlook, however – a paradigm shift, to use an overused expression – to propel social identity to the centre of the social scientific stage.

While the work of many other scholars could also be cited, there are three accounts that are emblematic of this shift. First, Erik Erikson (1963 [1950]) moved the study of identity from the ego and personality adjusting over a lifespan (the traditional domain of psychology) to the social roles individuals were called upon to play. The idea that there might be a tension between these processes was vital to his notion of 'identity crisis'. The sociological aspects of his analysis were picked up and diffused by numerous other social scientists. Second, an influential work by Peter L. Berger and Thomas Luckmann (1967) generated a conviction in social constructivism that almost became an article of religious faith among some social scientists. Their work fed a radical anti-essentialism that questioned any given historical fact or material entity, let alone the contours of any group identity. Reality itself could be constructed, destroyed or reconstructed by the work of representation, imagination and social action. Third, given such a radical programme, it was perhaps a modest enough claim to suggest, as Benedict Anderson (1983) did in his famous account, that the nation, not to mention any sub-national identities, was also an imagined community.

The effect of these and many lesser interventions was to shatter any notion of fixed social identities. The social world became a world of boundary formation and deformation, frontier zones, blurring, uncertainty, hybridity and mixtures rather than one marked by purity, homogeneity, timelessness and bounded entities. This new emphasis on fluidity also resonated with many aspects of an increasingly globalized world. Improved connectivity had brought many cultures into eye contact, sometimes into collision. Increased resistance to neoliberal versions of global capitalism reactivated old religious beliefs and new social movements alike. Greater levels of international migration meant that alien ways appeared not only on television screens but as lived realities in local communities. For the radical social constructivists, this was all grist to the mill. Modernity, with its attempt to integrate differences through ideology, citizenship and the nation-state, had to yield to the ambiguous and fuzzy world of postmodernity, where grand narratives explained nothing. Reality was reduced to the caprices of contingency.

With the near-collapse of the global financial system in September and October 2008 the wheel has turned again. Nationalism has resurfaced – in an ugly xenophobic form in Russia, South Africa, China and Israel and in a determined reassertion of the modernist project (integration through citizenship) in Europe, Canada, Australia, Japan and many other places. Protectionism and anti-foreigner sentiment led by threatened national working classes have emerged from under apparently tranquil transnational surfaces. Even the Obama phenomenon, which looked so promising to a world battered by the simplicities of the neoconservative nostrums of unilateralism and militarism, is marked by evocations of Lincoln, a swelling patriotism in the USA and a determined attempt to reconstruct a new *unum* from the new *pluribus*.

Diaspora

The ancient concept of diaspora re-emerged before the latest reaffirmations of national consciousness and was very much part of the transnational and anti-essentialist turn in the study of social identities. It served many functions but, in particular, it spoke to the ways in which we could understand old minorities that had never fully integrated, and new migrants who wanted to, or had been forced to, maintain their cultural and social ties to their countries of origin. It captured and still captures a world on the move, a world of belonging and alienation, of home and away, of political inclusion and social exclusion. Using the notion of 'new diasporas', it provided a prism through which the displacement and exodus of millions could be viewed (Van Hear 1998). Though its universality was always disputed, in a welter of studies of international migration and ethnic relations, 'diaspora' became the keyword to explain the hitherto seemingly inexplicable flows and counter-flows of migrants and refugees. Beyond the world of the social scientists, cultural, literary and post-colonial studies rapidly incorporated the idea of diaspora, with Chariandy (2006), for example, arguing that the concept of diaspora could be used to illuminate contemporary forms of progressive cultural politics.

A weighty intellectual and political agenda was thus assigned to the notion of diaspora and, arguably, it was always an error to load so much on to a single concept. When the inevitable doubts set in about the utility of the concept, the opposite danger of over-scepticism arose. As described earlier, diaspora works as an insightful way of understanding many aspects of migration and an important trajectory of social identity construction, one marked by incomplete subordination to a single national identity. It is an inappropriate tool, however, with which to measure all other trajectories of social assertion and belonging.

Creolization

One contrasting form of identity formation is the idea of creolization, which centres on the cross-fertilization between different cultures as they interact. Unlike diaspora, the expression is not ancient but modern, and was first manifested in the fifteenth century when Portuguese and African cultures interacted on Santiago, one of the islands of Cape Verde. It later spread across the Atlantic to the New World and many other places. When creolization occurs, participants select particular elements from incoming or inherited cultures, endow these with meanings different from those they possessed in the original culture, and then creatively merge these to create totally new varieties that supersede the prior forms. Creolization is thus a 'here and now' sensibility that erodes old roots and stresses fresh and creative beginnings in a novel place of identification. A diasporic consciousness, by contrast, generally reflects a degree of unease with cultural identities in the current place of residence. In evoking diaspora, a homeland or a looser notion of 'home' is reconstructed and revalorized through fabulation, recovered historical memory and social organization. The past provides a continuing pole of attraction and identification.

Any full account of creolization would have to include discussion of creolized popular cultural practices (especially in food, carnivals, music and dancing), syncretic religions and Creole languages. Whereas these have been studied for decades, new understandings of creolization have emerged more recently in sociology, anthropology and the study and practice of cultural politics. This has led to a renewed interest in recognized Creole societies in countries as diverse as Sierra Leone, Nicaragua, the Guyanas, Cape Verde, the Caribbean islands and coastal zones on the edge of the Caribbean, Réunion, Mauritius, the Seychelles, Liberia and Nigeria. More ambitiously, the substantial mixed-heritage populations in Brazil, South Africa and the USA have been re-examined using the lenses of creolization. And beyond these countries, the Swedish social anthropologist Ulf Hannerz (1987) has provocatively suggested that we all live in a 'creolizing world'.

Interestingly, some of the same forces that have been used to underwrite the concept of diaspora are used to legitimize creolization. Mobile, transnational groups are seen to practise what has been described as 'everyday cosmopolitanism'; while dominant, formerly monochromatic, cultures have become criss-crossed and sometimes deeply subverted by hybridization and creolization. It is this last quality which lends credence to the notion that cultures are no longer as bounded or autonomous as they once were and that complex and asymmetrical flows have reshaped inherited social identities in new ways (Cohen 2007).

While it is true to assert that creolization had its *locus classicus* in the context of colonial settlement, imported black labour and often a plantation and island setting, by indicating that there are other pathways for creolization, I want to signal the potentially general applicability of the term. To be a Creole is no longer a mimetic, derivative stance. Rather it describes a position interposed between two or more cultures, selectively appropriating some elements, rejecting others, and creating new possibilities that transgress and supersede parent cultures, which themselves are increasingly recognized as fluid.

Conclusion

I have briefly sketched the heuristic limits and possibilities of the expressions diaspora and creolization. Both have provided a space for many people to create a new sense of home, a locus from which to express their uniqueness in the face of cultural fundamentalisms and imperialism. Behind the strident assertions of nationalism, 'old ethnicities' and religious certainties is an increasing volume of cultural interactions, interconnections and interdependencies and a challenge to the solidity of ethnic and racial categories. If this is indeed happening on a significant scale (and not merely imagined or constructed in the minds of scholars), we need to recast much traditional social theory concerning race and ethnic relations, multiculturalism, nation-state formation and the like – for we can no longer assume the stability and continuing force of the ethnic segments that supposedly make up nation-states. Accepting the force of diaspora and creolization is also to accept that humankind is refashioning the basic building blocks of organized cultures and societies in a fundamental and wide-ranging way.

Starting from a more general discussion of social identity, however, I would argue that diasporic and creolized identities are but two among several possible outcomes for those seeking to define or redefine their self-conceptions, cultural identities or political trajectories in the face of the challenges arising from globalization, international migration and other rapid social changes. The five major possibilities are:

1 a reaffirmation of felt (that is collectively invented) loyalties to *sub-national entities* like clan, tribe, ethnicity, region or locality which are often wrongly described as primordial;
2 a revival of *nationalism*, particularly in the wake of the break-up of the Soviet Union, the fragmentation of the Balkans and the appeals to national solidarity after recent terrorist incidents and in response to the current global financial crisis;
3 a recasting of *diasporic identities* and other supranational and transnational identities such as world religions (for example, the *umma* or global Catholicism) and world language groups (for example, *francophonie*);

4 a linking and blending with other groups through a process of *creolization*;

5 and the development of a universal spirit that transcends any particularities and simply stresses the quality of being human, that is the *cosmopolitan* possibility.

I have focused here on diaspora and creolization without explicating the remaining possibilities. I can make two brief general points about the numbered list, however. First, my five possibilities are arranged on a spectrum starting from the narrowest forms of social identity and ending with the most aspirational forms of human identification. Second, these are not watertight and mutually exclusive alternatives. Situational and life-course changes allow movement between the categories and overlaps.

Finally, while diaspora and creolization do tend in opposite directions, the one to a recovery of a past identity in reconstituting an old transnational link, the other to a severance of past identities in the interests of establishing a new cultural and social identity, 'Creolistas' and 'diasporists' also probably share something less tangible and more idealistic. They probably both believe that global justice requires that people's languages, religions, attitudes, behaviour and social conventions are respected and given space to develop but, crucially, without excluding others. Where there is no self and group expression, we have only poverty of the creative impulse and of the imagination. Expanded uses of diaspora, and certainly creolization, demonstrate that people thrive not by getting stuck in fixed quasi-racial identities, but at the nodes and connection points where original ideas and bold inventiveness are nurtured and fashioned.

Further reading

Cohen, R. (2008) *Global Diasporas: An Introduction*, 2nd edn, London and New York: Routledge.

Cohen, R. and P. Toninato (2009) *The Creolization Reader: Studies in Mixed Identities and Cultures*, London: Routledge.

Jenkins, R. (1996) *Social Identity*, London: Routledge.

Song, M. (2003) *Choosing Ethnic Identity*, Cambridge: Polity Press.

Stewart, C. (ed.) (2007) *Creolization: History, Ethnography, Theory*, Walnut Creek, CA: Left Coast Press.

12 | Complex diasporas

Pnina Werbner

The limits of the diaspora concept

The prising open of a familiar concept inaugurates new directions for research. It also leads to a proliferation of definitions and typologies as the concept comes over time to be reworked from different disciplinary vantage points, and reinterpolated into widely divergent ethnographic accounts. This complex, often dialectical process of thinking through a concept anew is not simply linear; it loops back on itself in creative tension with earlier theoretical insights.

So too with diaspora: as the concept has travelled, certain new generalizations have come to be widely accepted and often repeatedly rediscovered. For example, early discussions of diasporic cultural hybridity are countered by a stress on the *social heterogeneity* of diasporas: not just symbolic *fusion* of discourses but a *multiplicity* of discourses, some intersecting, some mutually clashing and contradictory, are recognized to underpin the dynamics of late modern diaspora.

A second emergent consensus recognizes that diasporas are historical formations *in process*; changing and responsive to the different political and social contexts; reconstructed and reinvented imaginatively and socially in new places or as political circumstances change in their place of settlement. Paradoxically, however, they develop in similar, predictable ways – *chaordically* – wherever they settle (Werbner 2002a): they are *both* hybrid *and* heterogeneous in their own peculiar, historically determined, ways.

Third, a growing consensus recognizes the *dual* orientation of diasporas: to fight for citizenship and equal rights in the place of settlement, often alongside other ethnic groups, while simultaneously continuing to foster transnational relations and to live with a sense of displacement and loyalty to other places and groups beyond the country of settlement.

This points to a fourth emergent understanding that many diasporas are deeply implicated both ideologically and materially in the nationalist projects of their homelands (Basch et al. 1994; Tölölyan 1996). While these are often emancipatory and democratic, by the same token diasporics often feel free to endorse and actively support ethnicist, nationalistic and exclusionary movements. They engage in 'long distance nationalism' without accountability (Anderson 1994); they support the IRA, Hindu nationalist movements (Gopinath 1995), Greek Cypriot separatism (Anthias 1998) or religious zealotry in Israel. With regard to this, the ability of diasporas to actively participate and intervene in the politics of the homeland has been greatly enhanced and facilitated by the spectacular development of global media and communication technologies. Although transnationalism is by no means a new phenomenon, today sending societies often encourage such participation while receiving societies range from those which refuse to assimilate newcomers to those, such as Britain and the USA, which tolerate cultural pluralism, dual citizenship and transnational activism as never before (Foner 1997).

This highlights one of the dilemmas which the new concept of diaspora has thrown up. The powerful attraction of diaspora for post-colonial theorists was that, as transnational social formations, diasporas challenged the hegemony and boundedness of the nation-state and, indeed, of any pure imaginaries of nationhood (Gilroy 1993a; Clifford 1994; Hall 1990). The creative work of diasporic intellectuals on the margins is celebrated for transgressing hegemonic constructions of national homogeneity (Bhabha 1994). The more recent scholarly riposte to this view has highlighted the continued imbrication of diasporas in nationalist rhetoric, and critiqued the celebration of rootlessness as ahistorical and apolitical (Fabricant 1998). Again, the new postmodern interpretation challenged simplistic paradigms of diasporas as scattered communities yearning for a lost national homeland, whether real or imaginary (Hall 1990; Boyarin and Boyarin 1993; Ghosh 1989). The growing consensus is, by contrast, that such imagined attachments to a place of origin and/or collective historical trauma are still powerfully implicated in the late modern organization of diasporas. Diasporas, it seems, are both ethnic-parochial *and* cosmopolitan. The challenge remains, however, to disclose how the tension between these two tendencies is played out in actual situations. Transnational loyalties, like struggles for citizenship, are never finally settled. They are the stuff of debate in the diasporic public sphere.

In a sense, we may say that those who deny the saliency of a homeland are both correct and incorrect. The orientation to 'home' may not necessarily be to a *national* home. In the present essay I want to address this possibility by exploring the contours of late modern *complex diasporas.* Complex diasporas have arisen in response to the emergence of regional mass popular cultural production centres in various parts of the world and the mass migration from these regions which has created new diasporas. To understand such complex diasporas in the late twentieth and early twenty-first centuries requires, I propose, a reconceptualization of what we mean by diaspora.

Complex diasporas

Complex diasporas defy any neat typological theorizations of diaspora that look to national historical origins exclusively as determining the groups that may be defined as diasporas. In this type of typologizing the Jewish diaspora assumes paradigmatic status and its central features are taken as the starting point in formulating the fundamental parameters of diaspora (see Safran 1999). This is partly, of course, because the colloquial use of the term diaspora has historically been with reference to the Jewish dispersion. The question thus becomes how far can a diaspora community deviate from the original prototype and still be called a diaspora?

Complex or segmented diasporas reflect the fact that similar cultural preoccupations, tastes, cuisines, music, sport, poetry, fashion and popular cinema are widely enjoyed across vast geographical regions encompassing several postcolonial nation-states in a globalizing world. This points to a key feature of late modern diasporas (and indeed of some earlier ones) which has remained so far untheorized in the scholarly literature and which cannot easily be incorporated by the archetypical Jewish model of diaspora. That model starts from the fact that Jewish religion, culture and national political orientation to Zion *coincide* despite geographical dispersion and despite internal religious or political disagreements. This coincidence is true also of the Armenian and Greek diasporas. But where vast cultural regions of consumption do *not* simply coincide with either religion or national homelands, as is true for South Asians, Middle Easterners, Latin Americans, Africans, Afro-Caribbeans and Chinese, we may talk of complex or *segmented diasporas.* In such complex diasporas the fact that people from a particular region share a rich material culture of consumption, both high cultural and popular, and often a dominant religion (e.g. Islam, Catholicism), creates public arenas and economic channels for cooperation and communal enjoyment, *which cut across the national origins or religious beliefs of performers and participants.*

An example of such a complex diaspora is the South Asian one, which includes five nation-states (India, Pakistan, Bangladesh, Sri Lanka and Nepal) and at least five world religions (Islam, Hinduism, Buddhism, Sikhism and Christianity). The South Asian diaspora, seen as a regional diaspora of cultural consumption (Ghosh calls it a diaspora of the 'imagination'), in no way determines either political loyalties and commitments or more focused exilic yearnings for a lost homeland. It is quite possible for people from a single cultural region to be locked in bitter national or religious conflicts as they are in South Asia. In the diaspora, however, the sharing of a regional culture can create cross-cutting ties and the potential for transcendent coalitions and alliances which mitigate such conflicts.

The pluralization of the public sphere

The notion of a unified (national) public sphere has been subjected to scrutiny by feminist and diaspora theorists, who argued for the need to conceptualize the pluralization and complexity of the public sphere. Reconsidering Habermas's concept, Fraser argues that women and other marginalized groups historically created a counter-civil society to the official, hegemonic public sphere. A truly functioning democracy, she proposes, requires such 'subaltern counterpublics' in which oppositional interpretations of 'identities, interests, and needs' are formulated (1992: 123). The increasing porousness and complexity of the public sphere allow women and other marginalized groups to set new agendas (Benhabib 1992: 94). The point made by feminist theorists is that, rather than a single public arena, such separate and diverse spaces are essential for subalterns to thrash out their own perspectives on public policies and the public good.

If the public good, according to Habermas, was defined through public debate between rational citizens, later conceptualizations took account of its aesthetic and affective dimensions as well (for an overview see Dahlberg 2005). Paul Gilroy, for example, spoke of a black 'alternative' public sphere of 'story-telling and music-making' (1993a: 200). Fraser stressed that 'public spheres are not only arenas for the formation of discursive opinion. In addition, as arenas for the formation and enactment of identities' (1992: 125), they are in some sense a 'theatre' (ibid.: 110). In Alberto Melucci's (1997) terms, the work of identity is one of first discovering and then negotiating shared identities. Such views reflect the fact that 'meaning is always in excess of what can be understood discursively, spilling over beyond the symbolic' (Dahlberg 2005: 115, citing Young 1987). In her theorization of public arenas in India, Sandra Freitag argued that processions and public rituals encompass both the 'political' and 'religious', the formal and informal, elite and popular concerns (Freitag 1989: 14). My study of the local Pakistani diasporic public sphere similarly highlighted its poetics – the way that political passion and rhetoric allow speakers to reach out persuasively to their audiences (Werbner 2002b).

A recognition of the pluralized nature of the diasporic public sphere allows for a theorization of diaspora, community and culture not as homogeneous, unified, monolithic, harmonious forms of sociality but as heterogeneous and conflictual.

Conclusion

Some contemporary new diasporas still appear to remain confined to a single nationality – the Japanese spring to mind. But the vast new diasporas of the late modern post-colonial world – such as the South Asian diaspora – are complex in new ways: culturally, linguistically, religiously, politically. Their borders are porous, their identities multiple, intersecting and in constant flux, shifting situationally. Nevertheless, they do not simply assimilate. Instead, they retain passionate attachments to aesthetic, religious and national modes of living in the world. At the same time, however, the 'worlds' they inhabit are not defined or limited to the same groups of people, all the time.

Further reading

Safran, W. (1999) 'Comparing diasporas: a review essay', *Diaspora*, 8(3): 255–91.

Tölölyan, K. (1996) 'Rethinking *diaspora*(s): stateless power in the transnational moment', *Diaspora*, 5(1): 3–36.

Werbner, P. (2002a) 'The place which is diaspora: citizenship, religion and gender in the making of chaordic transnationalism', *Journal of Ethnic and Migration Studies*, 28(1): 119–33.

— (2002b) *Imagined Diasporas among Manchester Muslims*, London: James Currey.

— (2004) 'Theorising complex diasporas: purity and hybridity in the diasporic public sphere', *Journal of Ethnic and Migration Studies*, 30(5): 895–911.

13 | Space and movement

Kim Knott

As is often noted, 'diaspora' is both a spatial and a biological term, in the original Greek meaning to sow, scatter, distribute or disperse. As such it conveys a sense of the movement of people from a centre outwards, of their dispersal from the place of origin into new territories. And, as James Clifford suggested, it is, by implication, 'a travelling term' (1994: 302), one that carries the entwined concepts of 'root' and 'route'. Its academic popularity reflects a move from a scholarly interest in the 'old localizing strategies' (ibid.: 303) of community, culture, nation, centre and continuity to strategies of movement and discontinuity, circulation and contact zone. In addition to the explicit geographical treatment of migration and transnationalism, of the border and the homeland, much of the discussion of diasporas in the social sciences and humanities unwittingly reflects the idea that 'diaspora' is an inherently spatial and travelling notion as a result of either literal or metaphorical reference to people on the move, home, exile, return, circulation, border-crossing, social and cultural boundaries, place of origin, displacement, settlement and multi-locality. The lure of such language for the representation of diasporas and the diasporic imaginary and its consequences for their scholarly construction has yet to be analysed, however.

Spatial theory and metaphor in diaspora studies

Like 'migration' and 'transnationalism', 'diaspora' invites us to hold together in creative tension notions of 'home' and 'away' while, at the same time, unsettling and questioning both. In distinguishing the three, however, Vertovec and Cohen (1999) stress the centrality for diasporic groups of self-consciousness, of the capacity to imagine as well as to enact – both physically and socially – geographies of displacement and multi-location. It is necessary, then, for scholars of diaspora to adopt and work with a multidimensional understanding of space and movement that does not restrict it to actual physical migration but makes room also for imagined, discursive, material, cultural, virtual and socially networked places and travels. This call explains in part why several scholars have drawn on Henri Lefebvre's conception of space to devise new analytical strategies for examining diasporic and post-colonial experience and relations (e.g. Rogoff 2000; Knott 2005a, 2005b; Tweed 2006; Quayson 2010). Calling for a reunification of disparate fields of enquiry, he draws together the physical, mental and social in an investigation of 'the space of social practice, the space occupied by sensory phenomena, including products of the imagination such as projects and projections, symbols and utopias' (Lefebvre 1991 [1974]: 12).

Although Paul Gilroy did not take Lefebvrian social space as his starting point, his adoption of 'the Atlantic as one single complex unit of analysis' in the development of 'an explicitly transnational and inter-cultural perspective' has much in common with it (1993a: 15). His selection of a physical space – the middle passage – repeatedly crossed by the movements and struggles of black people, is given focus by his choice of the ship as a central organizing symbol for discussing 'the various projects for redemptive return to an African homeland [...] the circulation of ideas and activists as well as movement of key cultural and political artefacts: tracts, books, gramophone records, and choirs' (ibid.: 4).

In the mid-1990s, Gilroy, like Homi Bhabha in *The Location of Culture* (1994: 1–9, 212–23), made explicit use of spatial references to theorize cultural inter-mixing and the history of the African diaspora. Avtar Brah, in the same period, was setting out an agenda for thinking about diasporas that has become a touchstone for scholars in this field. In *Cartographies of Diaspora* (1996), in which she brought together earlier articles, Brah developed 'an innovative theoretical framework for the study of "difference", "diversity" and "commonality" which link[ed] them to the analyses of "diaspora", "border" and "location"' (ibid.: back cover). It is from Brah, in particular, that we inherit a host of spatial terms with potential for analysing diasporas, including 'cartographies of intersectionality', 'the homing of diaspora, the diasporizing of home' and, of course, 'diaspora space' itself, to which I shall return in the final section.

Brah's starting point is autobiographical, 'the historical entanglement of a multitude of biographies in the crucible of the British Empire' (ibid.: 1). She wrestles with the intersection of personal narrative and intellectual labour (ibid.: 10), establishing her own 'political coordinates' in context (ibid.: 9). Like a number of other black British, Asian and African-American scholars (as well as feminist and queer) at this time, she uses spatial language to explore her diasporic subjectivity. Like hooks (1992), Hall (1990), Gilroy (1993a) and Bhabha (1994), she employs concepts of location, situation, position, margin, in-between, intersection and border, as well as diaspora itself, in the formation of a politics of cultural difference.

Geographical movement and settlement

In a warning to those employing spatial metaphors to theorize the politics of location, the geographers Smith and Katz noted that 'the spaces and spatial practices that serve current metaphors in social, cultural and political theory are neither so fixed nor so unproblematic as their employment as metaphor would suggest' (1993: 71). A disciplinary awareness of the complex spaces from which such metaphors derived led them to sound a note of caution. This loss of geographical mooring, in which terms float free from their physical and social context, may also have led several years later to calls for the regrounding, rematerialization and re-embodiment of theory (e.g. Jackson 2000). Such calls had relevance for the areas of diaspora, race and identity, as well as gender and body.

It would be disingenuous, then, to focus exclusively on spaces of identity and the imagination at the expense of the actual geographical migrations of which diasporas, transnational relations, diasporic experience and creativity are entailments. Conceptions of diaspora – whether held by migrants and settlers themselves (emic) or by the scholars who research and write about them (etic) – are in general contingent upon a historical migration, recent or in the distant past. This may have been a forced exile or voluntary migration in pursuit of employment, trade or mission. The details of that journey may or may not now be known or recorded; they will certainly have been inscribed with imagined recollections and, often, overladen with feelings of loss and hope, tradition and solidarity. Researching the geography not only of such population diffusion but also of return, heritage tourism and pilgrimage has been an important aspect of diaspora studies. Settlement as well as migration has been experienced and represented spatially with reference to borders, ghettos, enclaves, as well as – in policy discourse – to integration, assimilation and cohesion.

Diasporic spatialities

Global movements and journeys, then – whether real or imagined – are not the sole focus of attention for geographers of diaspora and other scholars who focus on space and circulation. As Jackson et al. have argued,

> Different diasporas are characterized by different geographies that go beyond simple oppositions between the national and the transnational, the rooted and the routed, the territorial and the deterritorialized. Diaspora is not only an inherently spatial term. Its particular historical forms evidence particular and distinctive spatialities. (2004: 2)

Every diaspora – whether recent or of long standing, whether caused by exile or movement for trade, whether multi-sited or settled in a single place – has its 'distinctive spatiality', informed by actual journeys past and present, the particular forms and distribution of its settlements, its demography, the nature and extent of its social networks (intra-, inter- and transnational), the characteristic circulations of its members, goods, culture and religion, its local inflections (social, linguistic, cultural), and its distinctive imagined, historical and present geography.

It is to ethnographic studies that are attentive to geographical and spatial movements, patterns and scales that we must look for accounts of particular diasporic spatialities. Ma and Cartier's (2003) edited collection on the Chinese diaspora is a valuable example not only in its explicit focus on geographical rather than metaphorical diasporic space, but in offering cases from a variety of national contexts, historical periods, ethnic groups, trade and social networks, thus illustrating the idea that 'a diaspora is a space of places' (Ma 2003: 9). With different scholars contributing accounts of the Chinese in Taiwan, Hong Kong, Singapore, Vietnam, Thailand, Malaysia, the Caribbean, Latin America, Honolulu, Canada, Germany, Australia and New Zealand, a picture of the complex differences of place, settlement, social interaction and mobility emerges, with the editors focusing on the interconnections between places and the diasporic regions – of origin and settlement – that become visible once so many particular ethnographies are brought together. For the Chinese,

> diasporic spaces are not so much 'ungrounded' and 'deterritorialized' structures of economic domination across the Asia Pacific [...] as they are place-centered and network-based spaces with porous boundaries whose real extents are changeable in association with intra-diasporic contexts and events. (Ibid.: 9)

Discussions of the nature and dynamics of other diasporic spatialities include Muslim spaces in North America and Europe (Metcalf 1996), the South Asian diaspora (Rai and Reeves 2008) and black geographies (McKittrick and Woods 2007).

Diaspora space: place, dwelling and living together

What these and other ethnographies show is how diasporic communities, cultures and identities localize yet continue to respond to global processes including continued migration and return, transnational relations and politics, and the demands of multi-locality. Recent research on 'writing British Asian cities' (McLoughlin et al., forthcoming) illustrates how, within a single national context, different urban localities emerge as distinctive not only as a result of their demographic, economic and environmental characteristics, but also through the cultural work of Asian individuals and communities and those who produce them through fiction, anthropological and sociological texts, journalism, civic discourses, oral history, music, dance and religious practice. The British Asian cities of Manchester, Bradford, Birmingham, Leicester and London's East End were found to be particular in both their constitution and representation (www.leeds.ac.uk/writingbritishasiancities).

Such cities are not only produced at the point of intersection between their local history, regional and national situation and simultaneous global interconnections, but by the jostling together of individuals and groups both indigenous and diasporic (cf. Eade 1997; Massey 2007; Knott 2009). Avtar Brah referred to this as 'diaspora space' – that is,

> [...] the intersectionality of diaspora, border, and dis/location as a point of con-

fluence of economic, political, cultural and psychic processes [...] Diaspora space as a conceptual category is 'inhabited' not only by those who have migrated and their descendants but equally by those who are constructed and represented as indigenous. In other words, the concept of *diaspora space* (as opposed to that of diaspora) includes the entanglement of genealogies of dispersion with those of 'staying put'. (1996: 181)

These genealogical and spatial entanglements and their various social, cultural and practical entailments, despite being placed by Brah on the agenda of diaspora studies some fourteen years ago, have yet to be fully examined, though increasingly scholars take seriously one facet of her argument, the importance of locally situated configurations.

I began by referring to Clifford's reference to 'diaspora' as 'a travelling term', reflecting the importance in diaspora studies of movement and circulation; let me end with James Procter's reminder that dwelling, 'travel's Other', reflects the idea that diaspora is 'to deposit' as well as 'to sow' (2003: 14; cf. Tweed 2006). Evoking the motif of the travel bag, he notes that 'while such baggage signals movement and migration, it also anticipates arrival, settlement, home' (Procter 2003: 207), carrying with it 'the burden of dwelling' (ibid.: 209). A key challenge for diaspora studies is to engage with the realities of settlement, the political contingencies and relationships of diaspora space, as well as the narratives of travel and circulation, and the location of diasporic subjectivity. Arguably, a refocusing on the metaphor of 'place', on the actual spaces and spatial practices of social diversity around borders, residential and working environments and cultural venues, even on 'the old localising strategies' (Clifford 1994: 303), would help diasporas scholarship to tighten its geographical moorings and resist the criticism that its spatial turn has been more poetics than politics.

Further reading

Brah, A. (1996) *Cartographies of Diaspora: Contesting Identities*, London: Routledge.

Gilroy, P. (1993a) *The Black Atlantic: Modernity and Double Consciousness*, Cambridge, MA/London: Harvard University Press/Verso.

Jackson, P., P. Crang and C. Dwyer (eds) (2004) *Transnational Spaces*, London and New York: Routledge.

Ma, L. J. C. and C. Cartier (eds) (2003) *The Chinese Diaspora: Space, Place, Mobility and Identity*, Lanham, MD, and Oxford: Rowman and Littlefield.

Procter, J. (2003) *Dwelling Places: Postwar Black British Writing*, Manchester and New York: Manchester University Press.

PART TWO

Intersections

2 House Textile 1 (© Helen Scalway)

Helen Scalway's collage is part of a series entitled 'Moving Patterns', produced in association with 'Fashioning Diaspora Space', a research project examining textiles and cultural exchange between Britain and South Asia. In House Textile 1, in which she explores different worlds touching, she places two sources in juxtaposition, a nineteenth-century London house and a pattern from the South Asian Textile Collection at the V&A museum.

14 | Diasporas and economies

Claire Dwyer

Some critics of mainstream post-colonial and diaspora studies have argued that insufficient attention is given to the question of economies (Parry 2004). In this essay I explore the effects of foregrounding economies in studying diasporas. My starting point is to evoke Artemis Leontis (1997) writing about the Greek diaspora, who distinguishes between two topographies of the Mediterranean, based on the notions of *diaspora* and *emporium*. While etymologically diaspora suggests the notion of a scattered people, *emporium* translates literally as 'commerce' and suggests ideas of 'motion', 'traffic' and 'passage' through the verb *poreuo* ('to set in motion, make crossing, secure passage'). Leontis uses these ideas to contrast a diasporic imagination which is based on land-based scatterings with a more fluid maritime space, a 'counter-topoi' (ibid.: 192; cf. Crang et al. 2003) which emphasizes circulation, motion – and commerce.

In his classic, if sometimes disputed, typology of diasporas, Cohen (1997) includes what he defines as 'trade diasporas', citing as examples Chinese traders in the European colonies of South-East Asia and the Lebanese in the Caribbean and West Africa. More recent scholarship (Baghdiantz-McCabe et al. 2005) explores the role of 'diaspora entrepreneurial networks' – merchant families and their extended regional networks with others of the same ethnic origin – focusing particularly on Armenians, Jews and Greeks. These organized groups of diaspora merchants were able to carry out 'cross-cultural' trade, mainly in the Eurasian continent in the early modern period, particularly working across a Christian–Islamic divide. While such diaspora trade networks are often characterized as 'brokers' between 'East' and 'West', Baghdiantz-McCabe et al. (ibid.: xiv) argue for a more complex understanding of the interrelationship between ethnic trading diasporas and national trading networks. Thus there is evidence of the participation of Sephardic Jews in the Dutch East India Company or Armenians in the French Royal East India Company. In the nineteenth century, with the consolidation of Western capitalism, the multinational activities of trade diasporas adapted to play an important role in the services sector – notably trade, shipping and finance – and were involved not only in trade but also in production of key commodities including silk, cotton, grain and jute. Jones (2000), for example, describes accounts and letters in scripts other than the Latin alphabet as a means by which flows of information were controlled. Analysis of the success of diasporic entrepreneurial networks suggests the importance of the evolution of a common commercial culture, transmitted generationally, which is not narrowly reduced to attributes of ethnicity, but nonetheless relies on closed networks of trust (on diasporas, trade and trust, see Trivellato 2009).

What emerges from these historical accounts is the significant role played by diaspora entrepreneurial and trading networks in the foundation of Western capitalist economies in the colonial era. Similarly in the post-colonial context the activities of diasporic networks of trade and commerce, or transnational commodity cultures (Jackson et al. 2004), have been described as a form of 'globalization from below' (Portes 1996) and integral to the making of contemporary transnational urbanism (Smith 2001). This dynamic framing of diaspora economies emerges from an earlier stream of scholarship which focused more narrowly on ethnic economies or immigrant entrepreneurship. The traditional focus of work on ethnic economies has been to recognize the ways in which the process of immigration shaped economic survival in particular ways. Highlighted is the significance of self-employment, and the employment of co-ethnic workers often in the provision of goods and services for other members of a co-ethnic group (Light and Bhachu 1993). Studies of 'ethnic economies' in post-colonial contexts might include the emergence of Chinatowns (Lin 1998) or the study of garment districts founded on immigrant labour (Rath 2001; Waldinger 1986; Werbner 1984). Analysis of ethnic economies has often centred on the extent to which they are separate 'ethnic enclaves' more or less connected with the 'formal' economy. So, for example, studies of immigrant labour in the garment industry emphasize the ways in which home working and subcontracting provide an 'informal' often invisible sub-economy to the more formal, more regulated 'mainstream' economy, raising important questions about exploitation and safety. Analysts have often focused on how immigrant businesses can 'break into' the mainstream economy, measured by extending their markets to providing services beyond the 'co-ethnic' market (Ram and Hillin 1994; Rath 2000). At the same time recent comparative work points to the dynamic ways in which the so-called 'ethnic economy' can transform urban and increasingly suburban landscapes in Europe, North America and Australia (Kaplan and Li 2006).

Jan Lin's account of the history of New York's Chinatown (Lin 1998) begins by tracing its role as an 'ethnic enclave' central in the provision of sweated labour for the restaurant and garment industry. Alongside this version of an ethnic economy is the emergence since the 1980s of Chinatown as a 'mini-finance centre', the site of transnational investment of overseas Chinese capital in real estate development in Chinatown and beyond. Lin's account ends with reflections on Chinatown's contemporary role as a site of tourism via a 'sanitized ethnic tourist village' (ibid.: 203). This is set alongside the emergence of newer suburban 'satellite Chinatowns' which include both new, upwardly mobile, residential ethnic enclaves, supported by transnational Chinese investment, such as Flushing, Queens, and new suburban ethnic enclaves of sweated labour, in Sunset Park, Brooklyn. This account thus nicely encapsulates some of the dynamics of diaspora economies in post-colonial contexts.

Lin's discussion of the significance of the transnational activities of overseas Chinese investors is echoed in work on the role of Chinese transnational capital in the Pacific Rim (Ong and Nomini 1997; Ley 2010). Tracing the transnational flows of migrants and capital between China and the west coasts of the USA and Canada, these studies emphasize a complex geography of flows and connections through 'diaspora space' (Brah 1996). These are diaspora economies which are shaped not only by migrants who live transnational lives operating across continents and with transnational families (Waters 2006), but also migrants who have been enticed by migration regimes that prize both 'skilled migrants' and entrepreneurship and business capital (Wong 2003). In this transnational framing of diasporas and economies migrant entrepreneurs are integral to the workings of regional, national and transnational economies and also involved in reshaping local and national forms of governance (Ley 2010).

Understanding the transnational dynamics of diasporic economies involves transnational scholarship – an anthropology that 'follows the thing' (Jackson 1999; Cook 2004). Lesley Rabine's (2002) ethnography of the global circulation of African fashion provides a fascinating account of the informal global networks that underpin the dynamic African fashion industry, which links together Synovia, designing children's clothes in California from fabrics from Senegal and Côte d'Ivoire, Wairimu, returning from Los Angeles to Kenya to sell vests made from West African fabrics alongside baseball caps and sneakers, and Oumou, based in Dakar, a celebrated designer for the Senegalese cultural elite who also exports her clothes to boutiques in France. Rabine traces both the 'suitcase economies' that characterize the informal networks of commerce underpinning the ethnic clothing industry (see also Bhachu 2004; Dwyer 2004) and the creative cross-cultural linkages that produce new understandings of 'African fashion'. The discussions that Rabine has with her informants about what constitutes 'African' fashion and contested constructions of origins, craftsmanship and 'authenticity' are shaped in part by the diverse transnational markets she traces. Consumers of African fashion include those within Africa, members of the African diaspora, but also a much broader constituency in search of 'ethnic' fashion (see also Dwyer and Jackson 2003).

It is this commodification of ethnicity through the expansion of new markets, beyond the narrow co-ethnic market of the 'ethnic enclave', which might characterize much analysis of contemporary diaspora economies. The new landscapes of the ethnic economy (Kaplan and Li 2006), whether London's 'Banglatown' (Mavrommatis 2006), New York's 'Chinatown', Sydney's 'Little Italy' (Collins 2006) or Manchester's Curry Mile (Barrett and McEvoy 2006) are sites of consumption not only for diaspora populations but increasingly for a wider range of different consumers seeking a more touristic experience. Indeed, within the city's 'symbolic economy' (Zukin 1995) municipal boosterism is increasingly oriented towards the production of commodified experiences within which ethnic enclaves are often central (McEwan et al. 2005; Halter 2000). While critics invariably frame such encounters as exoticism (hooks 1992; Hutnyk 2000), and there are clearly questions about how different groups are positioned in the negotiations of corporate opportunities and municipal politics (Keith 2005), they also offer possibilities for creating new 'diaspora spaces' (Crang et al. 2003; Dwyer and Crang 2002). Further possibilities for what might be termed a 'postcolonial political economy' (Pollard and Sammers 2007) can be traced through analysis of the rapid growth of Islamic banking and finance services. While co-ethnic services such as banking may often have been important to the success of diaspora economies, the emergence of Islamic banking offers possibilities for seeing how diaspora economies might reconfigure or '"provincialize" our understandings of normative, hegemonic economic practices and knowledge' (ibid.: 313).

The relationship between diasporas and economies is complex, diverse and multifaceted. I have offered a reflection on the different ways in which we might frame diaspora economies which clearly operate across many different scales and in many different contexts. My argument has been that diaspora economies, although they may often operate 'under the radar' of conventional economic flows of goods or capital, should be understood as both integral to, and parallel to, normative accounts of transnational global economies. While the 'millionaire migrants' (Ley 2010) from Hong Kong and Taiwan to Vancouver are obvious examples, street traders from Niger on the streets of Harlem (Coombe and Stoller 1994) or from Bangladesh and Senegal in Barcelona (Kothari 2008) are also examples of 'migrant cosmopolitanisms'.

Further reading

Baghdiantz-McCabe, I., G. Harlaftis and I. P. Minoglou (eds) (2005) *Diaspora Entrepreneurial Networks*, Oxford: Berg.

Crang, P., C. Dwyer and P. Jackson (2003) 'Transnationalism and the spaces of commodity culture', *Progress in Human Geography*, 27(4): 438–56.

Dwyer, C. and P. Crang (2002) 'Fashioning ethnicities: the commercial spaces of multiculture', *Ethnicities*, 2(3): 410–30.

Kaplan, D. and W. Li (2006) *Landscapes of the Ethnic Economy*, Lanham, MD: Rowman and Littlefield.

Rabine, L. (2002) *The Global Circulation of African Fashion*, Oxford: Berg.

15 | Diasporas and politics

Terrence Lyons and
Peter Mandaville

Diasporas and politics have long been conjoined. Many of the forced expulsions of peoples that gave rise to historical diasporas – one thinks immediately of the classic example of the Jews – were precipitated by politics. Modern forms of nationalism – such as the Irish – initially were incubated among exiles. Notions of exile and dissidence, often political in nature, are inextricably entwined with the phenomenon of diaspora. Over the last century, increased human mobility on a global scale has given rise to new modes of political activism by immigrant groups while simultaneously challenging conventional notions of political identity – including the theory and practice of citizenship. Where contemporary globalization has often seemed to empower the political efficacy of diasporas, recent violent conflicts have also reminded us of the horrors of human displacement on a mass scale.

Much of the literature on diasporas and politics has focused on three issues: (1) governance by the nation-state of non-citizen populations residing within its territory (e.g. immigration policy); (2) the role of diaspora groups as political actors and lobbying forces in the domestic and international politics of the countries in which they reside (e.g. ethnic lobbying); and (3) consideration of the challenges and opportunities posed by diasporas to theories and models of political community (e.g. post-national and multicultural citizenship). More recently, scholars have begun to consider the possibility that diasporas today are able to leverage the effects of globalization – e.g. ease of communication and travel – in order to become directly involved in homeland politics, sometimes bypassing nation-state 'gatekeepers'. Simultaneously, nation-states have become increasingly aware of the fact that their nationals residing abroad represent new challenges and opportunities and consequently work to co-opt or limit their political influence.

The presence of non-citizen populations within the boundaries of the nation-state has always been a source of political contention. This same effect has also at times spread to members of ethno-national or religious minorities who hold citizenship, with some of the more extreme examples involving the US internment of peoples of Japanese descent during the Second World War or Idi Amin's expulsion from Uganda of that country's South Asian citizenry in the

1970s. While much of the recent debate in European and North American settings has focused on the politics of social integration and cultural assimilation of immigrant groups (Hoskin 1991), at the level of policy issues surrounding the legal status and rights of non-citizens have been paramount. In the United States in recent years, for example, labour demographics have shifted such that much of the country's unskilled workforce is composed of Mexicans and other Latin Americans without formal status or work authorization. While their labour is badly needed and the conditions they face often border on exploitative, some groups have politicized this population, accusing them of leaching employment from the citizen workforce. Others have gone even farther, suggesting that the new Latin American diaspora in the United States threatens to undermine the very basis of American society (Huntington 2005). Countervailing voices, however, welcome the social, cultural and linguistic diversity that such communities engender, arguing that such diasporas strengthen American society (Smelser and Alexander 1999). In both Europe and North America, the changing demographic equations produced by regional and global migration have ensured that immigration reform and the question of diasporas remain central issues on the political landscape.

Another trend within the literature has highlighted the role of diasporas in seeking to influence the policies of the governments in which they reside, particularly in the realm of foreign policy (Ambrosio 2002; Haney and Vanderbush 1999). Such activism by diaspora groups – sometimes termed an 'ethnic lobby' or 'ethnic interest group' – is often aimed at influencing politics and conflicts in their homelands (Armstrong 1976). Much of this analysis has focused on the role of the Jewish, Cuban and Armenian groups in lobbying the United States government, although other scholars have pointed to similar phenomena in other Western nations (Werbner and Anwar 1991).

Beyond the issues of immigration policy, political economy and diasporic lobbying discussed above, another group of scholars has sought to explore the ways in which diaspora communities challenge conventional notions central to political science, such as identity and the limits of the nation-state as a model of political community. Much of the debate on multiculturalism (Taylor 1994; Benhabib 1996) developed as a response to the increased presence of ethnonational minorities and diaspora groups in Western nation-states. This literature regards the presence of immigrants as an invitation to reimagine the meaning and remit of citizenship via various models of differentiated or flexible rightsholding (Kymlicka 1996) within the territorial nation-state. Others see in the position and experience of diaspora the expression of a form of politics that is disjunct with the territorial – and, as some see it, the Eurocentric – logic of the nation-state. Figures in cultural studies, such as Homi Bhabha (1994), equate diaspora with a 'third space' of political identity: one that resists prevailing framings of identity and belonging in both host and homeland settings. This is an approach that seeks to figure hyphenated and hybrid identities as em-powering and explicitly critical of categories and limits of political modernity. As James Clifford (1994: 328) suggests:

> Viewed in this perspective, the diaspora discourse and history currently in the air would be about recovering non-Western, or *not-only-Western*, models for cosmopolitan life, non-aligned transnationalities struggling within and against nation-states, global technologies, and market – resources for a fraught co-existence.

A major advance in our understanding of the political dimensions of dias-poras was offered by another anthropologist, Arjun Appadurai (1996), who theorized this experience in terms of *translocality*. For Appadurai, translocal-ity captures the idea that the nation-state has been displaced as the exclusive mediator of connectivity across and between disparate political communities. It now becomes possible, indeed in some respects already quite mundane, to claim that certain villages in Bangladesh are more intimately connected with suburbs of Bradford in northern England than with other population centres in Bangladesh itself – an experience of the 'international' in which the nation-state is merely one actor among many. Appadurai's translocality is nicely concretized by ethnographies such as those by Olwig (1993) and Levitt (2001), which pro-vide rich accounts of the ways in which immigrant lives today are frequently configured in relation to multiple settings simultaneously. Other authors have focused on the dispersed structuring of sociocultural practices across multiple, diverse and often geographically distant settings. Basch et al. (1994), for example, address this phenomenon through their work on transmigration. Challenging the traditional framings in immigration studies of distinct 'host' and 'homeland' societies, these authors argue instead that human mobility today must be viewed in terms of the continuity of social relations across space rather than through abrupt ruptures between 'here' and 'there'. Some scholars have figured this as an effort to move beyond what they see as the 'methodological nationalism' present in much contemporary social theory (Wimmer and Schiller 2003).

Appadurai (1996) also gestures more specifically towards the globalization of politics by introducing the notion of *ethnoscape* – a deterritorialization of communalist affiliation which suggests that, under globalizing conditions, ethno-nationalist projects are constituted across a broad terrain (both spatial and imagined) rather than within the exclusive jurisdiction of a single polity. The hyphen that links nation and state, he argues, 'is now less an icon of con-juncture than an index of disjuncture' (ibid.: 160). Aihwa Ong's (1999) work on Chinese transnationalism in East/South-East Asia picks up on similar themes, identifying the presence in contemporary global politics of new formations of 'flexible citizenship' that allow the nation-state and its *ethnie* to coexist in mutually profitable tension. In his most recent period of work, Appadurai (2006) pushes the political analysis even farther by explaining how, through the good offices of globalization, minority groups in various nation-state contexts are able to reconstitute themselves as a global *majority* by reaching out to co-religionists/ ethnics abroad. For Appadurai, this explains, in part, recent increases in violence prosecuted in the name of communal identity groups.

In some cases, as Lyons (2006) argues, transnational politics remains intensely territorial in its focus and goals even if deterritorialized in terms of actors and processes. Many conflict-generated diaspora groups such as the Tamils, Irish, Croatians, Armenians and Eritreans conceptualize politics in territorial terms – the liberation of a symbolically important piece of land (Hockenos 2003). Rather than seeking to build a deterrorialized transnational community, some diaspora groups retain and amplify attachment to their identity's territorial aspect even if they are physically distant or unlikely to travel to that territory. A sense of solidarity and attachment to a particular locality can generate a common identity without propinquity, where territorially defined community and spatial proximity are decoupled without diminishing the salience of territoriality. Geographical detachment shifts the territorial concept from the 'concrete to the metaphysical realm and from one that has relatively clear boundaries to one that is unbounded and abstract' (Newman 1999: 13).

Much of the most recent literature on global migration and politics also starts from a dichotomized framework of 'here' and 'there' that attaches political activity to one of two specific spaces – the sending or receiving societies – with the assumption of a correspondingly bifurcated political orientation on the part of immigrants. Alejandro Portes's (Portes et al. 2003) work emphasizes that transnationalism is state-bounded – for example, from a specific country in Latin America to the United States – and that political transnational ties, activism and involvement are socially bounded by territorial jurisdictions as well as pre-existing power asymmetries. While migration scholars are recognizing that enduring transnational ties are compatible with assimilation, they also argue that the numbers engaging in transnational political activities are often small and limited to the first generation (Levitt and Schiller 2004; Portes et al. 2003; Bauböck 2003). One group of migration scholars questions these binaries, however, developing an alternative theory of serial migration that accounts for people who move from place to place, 'appear[ing] at home everywhere but belong[ing] nowhere' (Ossman 2004: 111). A number of scholars today are also beginning to pay more attention to transnational political networks and practices, defined as 'forms of cross border participation in the politics of [countries] of origin by both migrants and refugees, as well as their indirect participation via the political institutions of the host country' (Østergaard-Nielsen 2003a: 762). In this work, which marks the most recent phase of scholarship on diasporas and politics, we see the emergence of an explicit interest in the ways in which globalization and transnationalism permit diasporas to become directly involved in politics and conflicts beyond the territories in which they reside – and often without, unlike in the example of 'ethnic lobbying' cited above, the mediating hand of the host nation-state.

Working in this vein, Fiona Adamson (2005) explores how 'political entrepreneurs' are affecting transnational political mobilization and creating networks that do not necessarily include the state. She recognizes that there is an increased blurring of the distinction between internal and external affairs of state – meaning that the rise of these transnational practices has implications for politicized identities and national policies as well as the international system. Eva Østergaard-Nielsen's (2003b) research on Kurds and Turks in Europe also explores the consequences of migrant engagement in transnational political practices. She finds that migrant organizations and networks are influenced by global norms and yet remain embedded in local discourses, playing a serious and significant role in local, national and international political processes. This approach is also to be found in Mandaville's (2001) work on Muslim networks in Europe and their impact on political discourse in the wider Muslim world, and in Lyons's (2006) study of diasporas and homeland conflicts.

A second dimension to the more recent work on diasporas and politics focuses on the extension of citizenship privileges and concomitant political rights (e.g. voting) across borders. This literature (Laguerre 1998; Hansen and Weil 2002; Fitzgerald 2006; Faist and Kivisto 2008) explores the conditions under which certain states (or sub-national units within the state) reconfigure the boundaries of belonging and political participation to more readily accommodate dual or multiple citizenship-holding, or even to grant voting rights to non-citizens who reside permanently abroad but who have historical family ties to the nation. The motivation on the part of the state here often concerns a desire to ensure that those living abroad – with relatively high levels of social mobility, affluence and education – remain at least partially tethered to the nation and in some sense continue to be material stakeholders in its well-being. Hence countries that are net exporters of migrant labour feel the need to ensure that their distantiated populations remain objects of governance. For their own part, migrants living outside the nation-state, well aware of the economic importance of the remittances they send home, may use this clout to demand some measure of extraterritorial representation in local or national legislative bodies.

In the work of these various authors one can begin to discern the first impulses of a distinctive approach to global migration and transnational politics that permits us to understand how political processes are increasingly spread *between* multiple localities today. The agendas and goals are still often defined in territorial and normatively particularist terms, but the modes of organization and activism increasingly defy state sovereignty and physical borders.

Further reading

Al-Ali, N. and K. Koser (eds) (2002) *New Approaches to Migration? Transnational Communities and the Transformation of Home*, London: Routledge.

Koslowski, R. (ed.) (2005) *International Migration and the Globalization of Domestic Politics*, London: Routledge.

Sheffer, G. (ed) (1986a) *Modern Diasporas in International Politics*, London: Croom Helm.

— (2003) *Diaspora Politics: At Home Abroad*, Cambridge: Cambridge University Press.

Shain, Y. (2008) *Kinship and Diasporas in International Affairs*, Ann Arbor: University of Michigan Press.

16 | Diasporas, conflict and security

Simon Turner

Diaspora is a deterritorializing and subversive phenomenon; it is simultaneously about fixing and stabilizing identities – often in relation to particular places/nations. Owing to this ambiguity, the ways in which diasporas have been conceptualized in studies of security and conflict – to the extent that they have been conceptualized at all – have also been ambiguous. In this essay I outline three lines of thought, stemming from three different traditions, not only in research but also in politics and public debate.

Migration and security

Didier Bigo was the first to talk of the securitization of migration in Europe, arguing that migration has increasingly been articulated as a security issue in Europe – both at state and EU level (Bigo 2002). Owing to migrants' position as neither here nor there, they have often created fear and uncertainty in host societies. This objectless fear is hard to deal with as it creates ontological insecurity or angst; it is translated in public discourse into manageable and concrete threats such as unemployment, crime, national culture and the environment. Putting the blame on migrants transforms diffuse fears of globalization into issues upon which governments can act in order to protect 'their' citizens. This is the main mechanism of what has been termed 'securitization' by the post-structuralist 'Copenhagen school' of international relations. They argue that states (or other actors) can articulate a particular phenomenon as a security threat to the survival of the community. This need not necessarily be physical survival, as the issue of security has spread from traditional security to all walks of life – from culture to environment and health. Their point is that once something has been defined as a security issue, all means are allowed to be used in order to counter this risk. Normal politics is suspended and extraordinary action may be taken.

With the fall of the Berlin Wall, the bipolar security picture associated with the Cold War shattered and security threats became diffuse, global and transnational. The link between drug smuggling, international terrorism and irregular migration was easily made. In the words of Thomas Faist, 'diasporas have become the quintessential expression of globalization' (Faist 2005: 7). The fact that migration has been 'securitized' can be seen not only in the emergence of populist anti-immigrant parties across Europe, but also in the laws and institutions that have been established in order to control immigration, international crime and terrorism – implicitly linking the three as part of a common security threat. Despite the limited effects of these laws in terms of curbing migration, it has become pertinent for states all over the world to invest heavily in controlling borders, thus demonstrating that the state is ready to act firmly in the name of its citizens.

Whereas the securitization of migration has become a common argument among scholars exploring European policies and practices, none has explored this issue in relation to diasporas. It may be argued that diasporas pose a specific 'security problem', as they are already inside the host states and therefore cannot be controlled by the usual migration control means. Meanwhile, having a foot in two countries, they are perceived to have dubious loyalties. In other words, their position inside the nation – probably with citizenship rights – while showing emotional and political loyalties to another nation, combined with the fact that they are often more or less organized, politically or culturally, makes diasporas appear as an even greater security threat than the amorphous flows of unorganized migrants at the borders.

This fear of diasporic groups has been nourished in recent years by the post-9/11 war on terror and an increased focus on what have been dubbed 'home-grown terrorists', in particular in Britain and other European countries (this has been less of an issue in the USA). Diasporic networks of disgruntled young Muslim men have caught the public eye and are perceived as the new threat to national security, which illustrates very well the uneasiness caused among the public by diasporas. These young men are at once in our midst and alien to us; at once a product of British or German society and part of a global Muslim diaspora, their dual allegiances create a sense of fear and unease among a sedentary population. Whether these young men actually are a threat or not is beside the point here. They have come under scrutiny as a 'security problem', and this problem is increasingly seen as linked to diaspora. Apart from the concrete threat that a tiny fragment of them pose in terms of planting bombs, they are perceived as a threat because they defy the 'national order of things' by polluting the nation from within.

While state authorities have cast 'Islamic fundamentalism' as a security issue to be cracked down on by all means, critical voices in academia and civil society have called for a more holistic understanding of the context for these actions, arguing that radicalization is due to marginalization and lack of integration into European society; the solution therefore being to assist these groups with education and jobs. Meanwhile, the realization that most of these young men are relatively 'successful' in their countries of residence invalidates this line of reasoning. The fact that they function well in their country of residence – according to mainstream society's standards of integration – only makes them more disturbing, as their actions cannot be explained away as 'failed integration', 'identity problems', 'uprootedness', etc. Despite the allegedly multicultural, pro-migrant position of these claims, they still reconfirm the trinity of state-nation-citizenship by seeing mobility as the source of the problem rather than accepting that global terrorism is truly global and diasporic in its nature and cannot be boiled down to integration issues in any one country.

Long-distance nationalism

While much of this discussion has been focused on the security concerns of the country of residence, the example above illustrates that diaspora engagements go far beyond the place where members of the diaspora live. A number of issues and a separate literature deal with the ways in which diaspora populations affect violent conflict in their 'homeland'. Basically, there are two tendencies in this literature, either to see diasporas as peacemakers or as peace-breakers, to paraphrase Smith and Stares's (2007) catchy title on this theme. The former, which we will come to in due course, takes its point of departure in the lives of the diasporas themselves and emphasizes transnational practices of engagement with the homeland. The latter takes its point of departure in conflict and security issues in the sending country and tends to perceive the diaspora as unaccountable troublemakers.

Benedict Anderson coined the term 'long-distance nationalism' in a ground-breaking article in *New Left Review* in 1992. His basic argument was that:

> While technically a citizen of the state in which he comfortably lives, but to which he may feel little attachment, he finds it tempting to play identity politics by participating (via propaganda, money, weapons, any way but voting) in the conflicts of his imagined Heimat – now only fax time away. But this citizenless participation is inevitably non-responsible – our hero will not have to answer for, or pay the price of, the long-distance politics he undertakes. (Anderson 1992: 3–13)

Writing in the short era of fax machines and the nascent years of the World Wide Web, Anderson was contemplating the effects of the growing inter-connectedness of the world. He was worried by the fact that diasporic longing for a Heimat might take on new shapes, as these long-distance nationalists might contribute to conflict 'at home' while being unaccountable for their deeds. Protected by their new passports, they did not run the risk of prison, torture, violence or simply losing their livelihoods owing to conflict, and could therefore be more uncompromising than others, as is often the case with con-flict-generated diasporas (Lyons 2007; Turner 2008a).

These worries have been taken up by a number of scholars who see diaspora populations as a determining risk factor in civil wars. Proponents of the New Wars hypothesis (Duffield 2001; Kaldor 2001) argue that the dynamics of war and conflict have changed and become more transnational since the end of the Cold War. The many New Wars can be seen 'as a form of non-territorial network war that works through and around states' (Duffield 2001). While the wars produce large refugee populations, these populations play important roles in the ongoing conflicts, politically and economically. It is argued that diasporas play an important role in these conflicts and that the strong ties between homeland and diasporas have led to a 'transnationalization' of domestic wars, providing the warring parties with access to shadow economies such as illegal trafficking of drugs and arms.

Using statistical data, World Bank economist Paul Collier has argued that diasporas contribute money and weapons to rebel groups and therefore 'substantially increase the risk of conflict renewal' (Collier and Hoeffler 2004: 588). The case of the Tamil diaspora's role in the Liberation Tigers of Tamil Eelam (LTTE) in Sri Lanka has often been mentioned as an example in this 'alarmist' literature (Wayland 2004). The LTTE is heavily organized in the diaspora and systematically 'taxes' Tamils living outside Sri Lanka in order to support the war effort. Apart from supporting rebel groups financially and ideologically, diaspora groups may lobby host societies – governments, NGOs, civil society organizations – in order to gain support for their cause. While a weakness of this 'alarmist' literature in international relations has been its lack of in-depth empirical knowledge of diaspora communities, a handful of researchers from anthropology, human geography, sociology and political science have carried out more thorough analyses of particular diasporas and demonstrated the complexity of long-distance nationalism in relation to conflict (Fuglerud 1999; Koser 2001; Lyons 2007; Skrbis 1999; Tölölyan 2007; Østergaard-Nielsen 2003b). They argue that diasporas may well contribute to conflict, but they may equally contribute to resolving it, depending on the concrete context.

Transnationalism and peace-building

We have so far seen how diasporas are often perceived as liabilities both in the countries where they reside and in the 'home country'. Living across nation-states, belonging as it were to more than one nation-state, they challenge hegemonic perceptions of belonging and ideas of loyalty, which makes them a threat to national and ontological security. Other perceptions of diaspora exist parallel to these, however, both in public opinion and in academia: perceptions of diasporas as tolerant, democratic cosmopolitans that can help put an end to violent identity politics. While policy-makers on the one hand associate migration with insecurity, they also tend to assume that diasporas in the West have been subject to democratic culture and therefore can contribute to peace and democracy in their country of origin. With the support of the international community, prominent members of the diaspora are therefore given important government positions in post-conflict states such as Liberia, Afghanistan, Iraq, Burundi and South Africa, just as international NGOs encourage diaspora involvement in reconciliation and peace-building efforts.

The notion of transnationalism has been used to demonstrate the great potentials of migrants – both for sending and receiving societies – as they continue to maintain attachments to more than one nation-state by, for instance, sending remittances home. Recently, the positive effects of diasporas on sending societies have been measured not only in terms of money but also in terms of 'social remittances' (Levitt 2001), which include ideas and values. This generally positive picture of transnational migrant groups tends to assume that transnational belonging is unproblematic and that it is a contribution to society, if only societies are open to understanding and making the best of this potential. In this line of thought, conflict and oppression are associated with states and immobility while mobility is perceived to be emancipating; diasporas are seen as cosmopolitans who may help end conflict.

In sum, there are multiple nexuses between diaspora, security and conflict, depending on the point of departure, with international relations theory focusing on conflict, transnational studies on peace-building, and diaspora studies attentive to both.

Further reading

Bigo, D. (2002) 'Security and immigration: towards a critique of the governmentality of unease', *Alternatives*, 27: 63–92.

Faist, T. (2005) *The Migration–Security Nexus: International Migration and Security before and after 9/11*, Bielefeld: Centre on Migration, Citizenship and Development.

Skrbis, Z. (1999) *Long-distance Nationalism: Diasporas, Homelands and Identities*, Aldershot: Ashgate.

Smith, H. and P. Stares (eds) (2007) *Diasporas in Conflict: Peace-makers or Peace-wreckers?*, Tokyo, New York and Paris: United Nations University Press.

Van Munster, R. (2009) *Securitizing Immigration: The Politics of Risk in the EU*, London: Palgrave Macmillan.

17 | Diasporas and development

Ben Page and Claire Mercer

In September 2006 the United Nations inaugurated the first High Level Dialogue on Migration and Development in New York (Global Commission on International Migration 2005). The meeting was attended by over ninety government ministers as well as influential civil servants, think tanks, research units and NGOs. At the end of the meeting the delegates resolved to create a Global Forum on Migration and Development, which has held further ministerial level meetings in Belgium in 2007 and the Philippines in 2008. In the five-page final summary issued at the end of the New York meeting the word 'migration' was used fifty-eight times and the word 'migrants' appeared thirty-two times, but the word 'diaspora' was not used once. As a result of this international policy interest, analysing the links between migration and development has rapidly become one of the most fashionable topics for academics in development studies. Yet the way that ideas about diasporas have been incorporated into that debate has been piecemeal, laboured and peripheral. As often as not when the term 'diaspora' appears in the literature on the 'migration–development nexus' (or indeed in associated policy documents) there is a sense that it is being used as a synonym for migrants for a bit of variety or merely to signal a group of migrants. As a result the ways in which the concept of diaspora could be used to interrogate some of the assumptions at the heart of development studies is being missed.

Why are development policy-makers interested in migration?

Development in the global South, seen as economic growth, has always relied on the movement of people. Labour migration to the mines and plantations in the colonial era was essential to the expansion of colonial economies, while migration to urban industries was regarded as key to economic growth in the post-colonial period. Most interest at the current time, however, concerns the development implications of international migration. Highly skilled professionals, such as engineers, medical and IT workers, migrate to the global North, taking advantage of the opportunities provided by global labour markets. For sending country governments, however, this global mobility is often perceived in terms of 'brain drain', which impedes development by depleting the pool of national talent in which governments invest. Meanwhile less skilled and unskilled workers (often encouraged by their governments) migrate out of the global South more speculatively in the hope of securing employment or education elsewhere as an alternative to underemployment at home. Such individuals walk in to a controversy in destination countries where there is a debate as to whether their presence is in the national economic interest, framed around the quality of public services, welfare systems and race relations. Current aspirations to pursue managed migration policies in Europe and North America are premised on a desire to reduce immigration of unskilled workers and to boost return migration. Both goals are believed to be fostered by increasing economic growth to accelerate development in the global South, thereby reducing the incentive to migrate. Thus development in the global South has become integral to managing migration from the perspective of governments in the global North. In this discourse, development is no longer justified as a goal in itself, but as a means of protecting wealthy regions from a perceived invasion by unwanted immigrants.

'Brain drain' is increasingly justified in the global North by reference to the development impact of the remittances which flow 'home' to the global South. Such remittances might take the form of capital or commodities. The World Bank estimates that, in 2007, migrants sent $251 billion in remittances to developing countries (Ratha et al. 2008). The claim is that the benefits of remittances outweigh the costs of lost human resources. The precise mechanism by which remittances translate into 'development' remains opaque, however, and the uneven social and spatial distribution of remittances also adds complexity to this assumption (Adams and Page 2005; de Haas 2005). The search for policies that maximize the development benefits of remittances remains the central task for the Global Forum on Migration and Development.

More recently scholarship has drawn attention to the fact that migrants remit more than just money and goods. The idea of 'brain circulation' has been introduced to represent the benefits of temporary or permanent returns to home by migrants and the term 'social remittances' has been introduced to describe the transfer of knowledge, ideas and values across space by migrants. These might include ideas about a renewed commitment to democracy, advocacy of good government, the rejection of patriarchy, and the questioning of 'tradition'. Such arguments often rest on the assumption that the ideas, knowledge and values that flow out of the North will accelerate development in the South. This assumption reveals a deeply entrenched and largely untroubled Eurocentrism within much of this discourse. Again, the process of creating policies that convert social remittances into national economic growth remains in an exploratory phase.

Why does development studies privilege migration over diaspora?

The policy interest in remittances and managed migration as well as the limited knowledge base on the contemporary relationship between development and migration have undoubtedly been to the benefit of researchers in development studies, for whom a new field has been opened. Throughout this analysis both policy-makers and researchers have tended to talk about 'migration' rather than 'diaspora'. When the term 'diaspora' is used it generally means little more than 'a group of migrants' who might cooperate to send remittances en masse, or who might mobilize collectively to intervene politically in their 'home' country. The effective reduction of the meaning of diaspora to 'groups of migrants' reflects the fact that the analysis of migration in development studies has generally worked within an economistic framework, which has privileged and measured the rational acts of individuals. Thus quantitative research methods seek to enumerate stocks and flows of migrants within migration systems usually understood in terms of economic imperatives and incentives. Other studies measure the volume and distribution of remittances, which are explained using ideas of altruism or economic self-interest. Even when the analysis considers movement within family networks those families are still conceptualized in corporate terms. Furthermore, the main goal of analysis has been to understand the economic, social and political impacts of migrants on the bounded spaces of some developed and some underdeveloped nation-states – an imagined geography that is anathema to cartographies of diasporic space.

How might development studies benefit from taking diaspora studies more seriously?

We take it as axiomatic that a diaspora is more than a group of migrants. What, then, is that 'more than'? There are, of course, many ways in which diasporas are 'more than' simply migrants, but for our purposes, the central distinction arises from the shared commitment of a diaspora to a home place, somewhere other than where they reside (Mercer et al. 2009). That commitment to a home place, however, does not imply a failure to 'integrate' or 'assimilate'. Ethnographic studies have shown that it is a common experience for diasporas to be simultaneously deeply imbricated in the place where they live as well as being continuously engaged with another place which also holds meaning for them (Werbner 2002b). The problem, then, is with the concepts of 'assimilation' and 'integration' (so central to the discourse of international migration) and the imagined geography of separate, bounded territories they imply. The intellectual value of 'thinking with' diasporas is that it reveals the contradictions and partisan histories of the existing concepts and language of migration. Diasporas disrupt the categories into which 'knowledge' has been divided.

Development studies is underpinned by the same imagined geography of disconnected spaces. It is based on a map that separates the world into 'underdeveloped' and 'developed', or 'modern' spaces. In other words, it is a geography that never moves beyond a notion of absolute, or Cartesian, space, whereas a development studies cognizant of 'diaspora' would necessarily have to consider space in relational terms (Massey 2005; Harvey 2006). Diaspora space is not an unchanging container that can be simply treated as mappable distances or coherent bounded territories; rather it is in a dynamic process of becoming, produced through ongoing historical social relationships between groups of people. From the perspective of diaspora studies it is impossible to forget that the process of development in western Europe cannot be separated from a history of slave labour and the global trade of commodities, which were central to imperial expansion. Yet the fact that the resulting economic growth was most visible within western Europe meant that the idea of modernity became synonymous with that space, while the history of the role of other people and places in western Europe's development was forgotten. This process of forgetting is neither accidental nor disinterested. By disconnecting the history of the development of Europe from the history of the production of poverty elsewhere, those in Europe absolve themselves of responsibility for it. So, it is in the interests of those who write the story of global development to operate with an imagined geography of discrete bounded spaces. Yet such a geography cannot be sustained from a diaspora perspective. Just as thinking about diasporas reveals the ideology of assimilation, so it also reveals the ideology of space inherent in orthodox development studies. Development studies should take diasporas more seriously because they provide a possible mechanism for its decolonization.

Decolonizing development studies is a grandiose aspiration, and as always, operationalizing such aspirations is a challenge. Giles Mohan (2002) gives a useful first attempt at a typology for thinking about the ways in which diasporas currently contribute to development. He distinguishes between development *in*, development *by* and development *through* the diaspora, which is particularly useful because it refuses to locate development in the 'developing world'. Development *in* the diaspora refers to benefits that accrue to the place where diasporas currently live. Such benefits are independent of the fact that these workers are members of a diaspora and relate simply to their function as labourers who propel economic growth. On the other hand development *through* the diaspora refers to the additional benefits experienced in the place where diasporas live but which emerge from the ongoing transnational connections that are a particular feature of diaspora groups. For example, the presence of a diaspora creates new markets for cultural commodities (Mohan 2006).

Finally, development *by* the diaspora refers to benefits that diasporic communities bring to their countries of origin. Research has shown that diasporas undertake a range of ventures at home, including house-building, support for education and training, fund-raising and charitable donations, trading with and investing in businesses at home, paying taxes, and transferring technology and knowledge (Vertovec and Cohen 1999; Al-Ali et al. 2001; Newland and Patrick 2004; Vertovec 2004a, 2006). The development impact of return migration and 'brain drain' has also attracted interest (Ammassari 2004; Germenji and Gedeshi 2008). China, India and Mexico are often portrayed as archetypal 'success stories' in that their diasporas have made astute use of knowledge and technology transfers in the case of China and India, and remittances in the case of Mexico (Bolt 1996; Orozco 2002, 2004; Davies 2007; de Haas 2007). Research has also explored how diasporas engage with development collectively. For example, some Africans in Britain organize themselves into 'home associations' in which most members have some affinity with a particular village or area in Africa. Among many other activities the associations collect money which is sent to the village to support development projects, such as health and education facilities (Mercer et al. 2009; see also Orozco 2004; Mazzucato et al. 2006; Portes et al. 2007; Kleist 2008).

Diasporas are central to the project of the decolonization of development studies for two further reasons. First, diasporas can define development differently. Throughout this chapter we have left the idea that 'development' equals economic growth unchallenged. Some diaspora groups do indeed prioritize investment opportunities and responsibilities. Diasporas are also concerned with other dimensions of development, however, such as personal well-being and security, and the reproduction or improvement of the 'culture' (such as ceremonial life or language) associated with home. Second, although diasporas are often interested in development, we should nevertheless question the policy assumptions underlying renewed interest in their interrelationship. Why should diasporas take on particular responsibilities for the burden of unequal global development? (Herbert et al. 2008; Raghuram 2009a).

Further reading

Castles, S. and R. Delgado Wise (eds) (2008) *Migration and Development: Perspectives from the South*, Geneva: International Organization for Migration.

Faist, T. (2008) 'Migrants as transnational development agents: an inquiry into the newest round of the migration–development nexus', *Population, Space and Place*, 14(1): 21–42.

Mercer, C., B. Page and M. Evans (2009) *Development and the African Diaspora: Place and the Politics of Home*, London: Zed Books.

Mohan, G. (2002) 'Diaspora and development', in J. Robinson (ed.), *Development and Displacement*, Oxford: Oxford University Press, pp. 77–140.

Raghuram, P. (2009b) 'Which migration, what development? Unsettling the edifice of migration and development', *Population, Place and Space*, 15(2): 103–17.

18 | Diasporas and cities

John Eade

Global migration and the importance of cities

Although the flows of people, capital, materials, information and images across national borders are not new, a crucial distinction has to be made between international and global flows, between internationalization and globalization. As Scholte points out, despite the criticisms directed towards globalization, what distinguishes recent flows is their 'supraterritorial' character. While territory 'still matters in our globalizing world, it no longer constitutes the whole of our geography' (Scholte 2000: 46) – place is no longer so restricted by territorial boundaries. As debates concerning transnationalism and translocality have pointed out, however (Basch et al. 1994; Smith and Guarnizo 1998; Vertovec 1999; Favell 2003), we must be careful not to overemphasize placelessness. Nation-states still shape global flows and attachments to place are still powerful. What has emerged is a complex interweaving of transnational, national and translocal processes where local and global engage across an uneven terrain of changing inequalities and structural constraints (Massey 1994; Robertson 1995; Levitt 2001).

The issue of place and placelessness is important for any discussion of cities, of course. They are undoubtedly physical places shaped by social, economic and political forces, but we also know them through the process of imaginary construction such as in texts, films and pictures. Moreover, we can look beyond them to a wider world through global communications where space and time are shrunk. Research on diasporas illustrates the issue of place and placelessness, since it refers to the links between countries of origin and destination established in many cases by those migrating from the countryside to urban areas in other countries, and to cities in particular. This mobility has to be set in the context of a rapidly expanding global population, which is predicted to rise from 6 to 8 billion by 2030. In 2008 for the first time in human history over half the world's population was located in urban centres and it is claimed that the urban population of Africa and Asia 'will double between 2000 and 2030', by which date 'the towns and cities of the developing world will make up 81 per cent of urban humanity' (UNPA 2007: 1). Cities and their surrounding regions have become major hubs where global flows are concentrated and are crucial exemplars of the ways in which place and placelessness operate in the twenty-first century.

Globalizing cities and cultural diversity

During the nineteenth and twentieth centuries cities played a key role as sites for the political and cultural construction of nations and state institutions. This process of construction frequently involved conflicts between different sections of emerging national societies and struggles against imperial and colonial domination. With the rapid break-up of Western colonization during the second half of the twentieth century, cities in Asia and Africa, in particular, became sites where regional, national, international and globalizing forces intersected. While 'global cities' in the North, such as London, Frankfurt, New York and Los Angeles, have dominated the global expansion of the service sector, especially banking and finance, they are facing increasing competition from other globalizing cities within their own regions and across the globe (see Sassen 1991; Marcuse and Van Kampen 2000). The recent downturn in the global economy has highlighted the ways in which cities are now intimately linked through global flows of capital, people, information and goods and the limited but still significant room for manoeuvre possessed by nation-states to control those flows. These flows have produced a mixture of old and new modes of social and economic inequality infused by increasing cultural diversity and, in some cases, stiffening national and local resistance to such diversity (Eade 1997; Fincher and Jacobs 2000).

The empirical study of these developments has been deeply influenced by the 'Chicago School' of the 1920s. Chicago, as the archetypal modern industrial city, was shaped by both international migration and the movement of black Americans from the Southern states after the American Civil War. Diasporic communities with links to Poland, Germany and Italy, for example, had emerged and were particularly associated with certain zones of the city. According to Robert E. Park (1950), these communities interacted with one another through a process of 'race relations' where initial contact was followed by competition, accommodation and finally assimilation. As groups settled their members typically moved out from the poorer inner zone to the more desirable suburbs. Pioneering ethnographic research undertaken by the Chicago School also shows how the issue of race relations was associated with the wider and continuing debate about cities as the site for 'social problems' – slums, gangs, ghettos and homelessness, for example (see Anderson and Council of Social Agencies of Chicago 1923; Thrasher 1927; Wirth 1928; Zorbaugh 1929).

While subsequent research has drawn heavily on these and other key propositions developed by the Chicago School, the changing character of global flows over the last eighty years has inevitably produced new economic, social and cultural formations. North American and western European cities have been caught up in a process of deindustrialization which has resulted in some cities emerging as post-industrial centres dependent on the service sector, while others have slowly declined as their industrial base weakens. New migrants from less wealthy regions of the globe have understandably sought opportunities in these post-industrial cities, while settled minorities in the declining industrial centres face stiffer competition for scarce local resources. Some migrants can decide to stay or move again – to the post-industrial cities of the West or other areas of the globe where they may have an economic, social or cultural advantage.

How have these economic changes affected cities in other areas of the globe, and what have been the implications for cultural diversity? Economically, one obvious feature has been the emergence of certain global cities such as Mumbai, Bangalore, Hong Kong, Shanghai and Singapore as key competitors to those at the topmost reaches of the global urban hierarchy. This process has been driven in some cases by rapid industrialization at the national level. It has also entailed, however, the growth of services and the marketing of these cities as attractive locations for globally mobile transnational elites (see Sklair 2001) and even those from Western diasporas who are able to return, such as wealthy Non-Resident Indians from the USA. The expansion of the service sector in these cities has likewise involved the growth of migrant workers at the lower levels of the socio-economic ladder, such as domestic servants, who come not just from the national hinterland but from abroad. Other less prosperous cities in the South have been drawn into this global urban network and the strain on their resources has been increased by the influx of refugees and illegal immigrants from other countries. The growth of cultural diversity in this context may entail bitter local resistance and violence, reminding us, if needed, of the darker sides to global migration and urban cultural diversity (Palmary et al. 2003; Landau 2006; Drieskens et al. 2007).

Diasporas and contemporary British cities

The influence of the Chicago School can still be seen in empirical research on how these processes outlined above are changing urban societies around the world. In Britain, for example, John Rex's collaborative studies of how post-Second World War immigration was changing the social, political and cultural life of Birmingham, a quintessential industrial city, drew heavily on the model of zones, relations between racial and ethnic groups, and movement out to the suburbs (Rex and Moore 1967; Rex and Tomlinson 1979). The changing nature of global flows during the last thirty years, however, has directed attention to other social phenomena. There is a greater awareness of how diasporas are connected to their countries of origin, not only physically by return visits or relatives and friends coming to stay, for example, but even more importantly through virtual communication by mobile phone, Internet, letter, radio and television. Villages and cities in the countries of origin become connected to globalizing cities through this process and encourage the diasporas within them to develop attachments to multiple homes, contributing to emergent 'new ethnicities' and contestations over traditions shaped by gender, sexuality, generation, religion and class (Hall 1992; Baumann 1996; Anthias 2001; Werbner 2002a). These imaginings are reflected in a variety of hybrid cultural forms created in British cities through films, music, novels, poetry and plays (cf. Sharma et al. 1996; Procter 2003).

Nation-states struggle to contain these globalizing cities and the cities connected with them, as well as their diasporas. Urban competition between different ethnic and racial groups over local resources, for example, involves a complex power geometry shaped by transnational connections between places in the countries of origin and destination. This complexity is made more intense in the western European region through the changing character of immigration. The multicultural diversity created in British cities, for example, after the Second World War by migration from colonies and ex-colonies has been followed by the arrival of refugees and asylum seekers, mainly during the 1990s, and a very rapid influx of migrants from eastern and central Europe after the expansion of the European Union in 2004. Relatively well-organized and established 'black and ethnic minority' communities from former colonies are now part of a more complex situation 'distinguished by a dynamic interplay of new, small and scattered, multiple-origin, transnationally connected, socio-economically differentiated and legally stratified immigrants' (Vertovec 2007: 1).

This has also been accompanied by a restructuring of the post-1945 welfare state system, which has led to the shrinking of state involvement and new forms of governmentality characterized by a 'more complex cartography of political power' involving consumer 'choice' and new institutional forms of local participation (Back et al. 2009: 3). Not surprisingly, these changes have emerged through the interweaving of global and local processes whereby diasporas engage with others across space and time and generate new understandings of place at multiple levels. At the same time those who define themselves as 'the real locals' may resist the physical and imagined changes of place wrought by global migration through formal and informal means. This resistance involves not just secular conflicts over scarce material resources but also increasingly religious institutions as new churches, mosques and temples, used by diasporic groups, change the local landscape in European cities (Metcalf 1996; Hüwelmeier and Krause 2009).

Conclusion

Clearly, cities play a key role in the development of diasporic ties and identities across the world. Since they vary in size and magnetic power, this development has been most striking in rapidly globalizing cities and certain regions, such as western Europe and North America. Connections between diasporas and their countries of origin are maintained through virtual means which shrink the distance between space and time. At the same time the placelessness associated with global connectivity is accompanied by the production of new forms of living in, understanding and governing local place, which have been usefully described in terms of transnationalism, translocalism, superdiversity and more complex modes of governmentality. Yet nation-states still deploy long-established notions of territory and place in their engagement with transnational migration. Furthermore, those with a long-established presence in a particular nation or urban locality may resist the changes produced by global migration in various ways, including formal and informal modes of exclusion and even violence.

So there is an important engagement between established and emergent modes of discourse and practice at work. Analysis of how this engagement is developing in cities across the world requires an understanding of both historical continuities and discontinuities. It requires attention to the specificities of globalizing places, the changing role of nation-state institutions and the dynamic links between diasporas and their countries of origin, and the relationship between diasporic and other forms of social identification, as well as different expressions of consumerism and local participation around the world, in the cities of the global South as well as the North.

Further reading

Baumann, G. (1996) *Contesting Culture: Discourses of Identity in Multi-Ethnic London*, Cambridge: Cambridge University Press.

Eade, J. (ed.) (1997) *Living the Global City: Globalization as a Local Process*, London and New York: Routledge.

Marcuse, P. and R. Van Kampen (eds) (2000) *Globalizing Cities: A New Spatial Order?*, Oxford: Blackwell.

Smith, M. P. and L. Guarnizo (eds) (1998) *Transnationalism from Below: Cities, Migrations and Identities*, New Brunswick, NJ: Transaction.

Vertovec, S. (2007) 'Super-diversity and its implications', *Ethnic and Racial Studies*, 30(6): 1024–54.

19 | Diasporas, race and difference

Claire Alexander

In the wake of the rapidly transforming patterns of migration and settlement of recent times, the concept of diaspora has been central to understanding the changing ethnoscapes of Western societies (Appadurai 2003), and to rethinking race and ethnicity in the past two decades (Gilroy 2002 [1987]; Donald and Rattansi 1992; Solomos and Wrench 1995). This essay explores how 'diaspora' has been thought of in social theory, focusing on the sister disciplines of sociology and cultural studies (Alexander 2010). It considers first the association of diaspora with particular raced and ethnic movements and experiences, and as a synonym for racial and cultural 'difference'. Next, an emphasis on 'empirical diasporas', which invokes a more bounded, transhistorical category, is contrasted with the idea of 'metaphorical diasporas' (*pace* Hall 1990), highlighting processes or practices through which notions of ethnicity and difference are contested and remade. The essay concludes by considering some of the critiques of diaspora theory and its future possibilities.

Race-ing diaspora

As Brah has argued, while 'at the heart of the notion of diaspora is the image of a journey [...] not every journey can be understood as diaspora' (1996: 182). Rather, she continues, attention must be paid to the historical, socio-economic, political and cultural conditions of movement and settlement: 'The question is not simply about *who travels*, but *when, how, and under what circumstances*' (ibid.: 182, original emphasis). Contesting the expansion and conceptual thinning of the concept – the emergence of diaspora-lite – other theorists have insisted on a more exclusive definition that retains the historical provenance of the term, most particularly its focus on the circumstances of movement and the productive tension between the invocation of shared origin and germination in new and unfamiliar places. Paul Gilroy has defined diaspora as

> A network of people, scattered in a process of non-voluntary displacement, usually created by violence or under threat of violence or death. Diaspora consciousness highlights the tensions between common bonds created by shared origins and other ties arising from the process of dispersal and the obligation to remember a life prior to flight or kidnap. (1997: 328)

Here the emphasis is on diaspora as inseparable from forced movement, exile, loss and longing, on the one hand, and the forging of new identities in the places of arrival, on the other. The recognition of the unequal and often traumatic circumstances of migration and dispersal, along with the minoritization, marginalization and exclusion of diaspora peoples in the 'host' societies, and the power of the 'myth of return', are defining features (Safran 1991) that set diaspora theory apart from more politically neutral, elite or casually celebratory versions of social and cultural encounters across national borders. It is hardly accidental, then, that the 'classic diasporas' – Jewish and African (Cohen 2008; Safran 1991) – are those defined through racial and ethnic minority status and difference, conflict and exclusion. For this reason, perhaps, 'diaspora' has often come to substitute for other marginalized statuses such as 'immigrant', 'refugee', 'guest worker', 'exile' or as a semantic code for racial or ethnic minorities more generally (Brah 1996; Brubaker 2005; Kalra et al. 2005). One might argue, indeed, that 'diaspora' is most usually reserved for communities of colour, for the marginalized and the dispossessed – although some recent theorists have claimed the word for diasporas of privilege ('the white diaspora' or 'the British diaspora'), this has met with limited success to date (Knowles 2004).

'Diaspora' remains, then, a label most closely associated in social theory with marginalized and socially excluded racial and ethnic minority communities in the global cities of the West and the North (Kalra et al. 2005). As such, it has been criticized both for overlooking or erasing the far greater movements of displaced peoples within the South itself (Chatterji 2009), and for positioning diasporic communities as permanent strangers in their new homelands – what James Clifford has termed being '"not here" to stay' (1997). At the same time, however, diaspora has been used by racialized minority ethnic communities, artists and theorists as a form of claims-staking and place-making in often highly localized sub-national spaces, levering open 'diaspora spaces' (Brah 1996) or 'third spaces' (Bhabha 1990a) that unsettle and contest the boundaries and narratives of the post-imperial nations. The focus here is on migration and settlement 'from below', with a more people-centred, subjective and occasionally 'messy' approach that provides a critical (in both senses) alternative to reified notions of identity, difference and belonging.

The questions of origins, shared history and present solidarity that lie at the heart of 'diaspora' render the term deeply ambivalent and problematic – it can be seen to reinscribe and champion essentialized notions of racial and ethnic difference, as well as contest and fracture them. This tension can be traced in the dual approaches to diaspora, what Brubaker has termed the distinction between diaspora as an 'entity' and as a 'stance' (2005), or between diaspora as a descriptive tool or as a process – what I have chosen to term here 'the empirical' and 'the metaphorical' diasporas.

Empirical and metaphorical diasporas

It can be argued that, with the emphasis on shared origins, histories and consciousness that define the 'classic diaspora', the term is inseparable from the idea of boundaries, being and belonging, often rooted in organicist metaphors of cultural reproduction, blood and nation (Tölölyan 1996). Far from fracturing notions of ethnic belonging, diaspora potentially reproduces ethnicity as its foundational moment; how indeed can we speak of 'the Jewish diaspora' or 'the Bengali diaspora' without evoking the myths of ethnic origin? How can we speak of 'the black diaspora' or 'the African diaspora' without conjuring notions of 'race'? Furthermore, it is often in this sense of solidarity, of shared trauma and identity, that its attraction and its power lie for marginalized groups (Anthias 1998).

Certainly, key definitional features and clear boundaries make for easier social categorization and investigation, and it is perhaps unsurprising that the search for diaspora in social research begins with the establishment of what Safran terms 'ideal type' diasporas (see also Cohen 2008; DuFoix 2008). What these ideal-type diasporas comprise, however, varies among theorists; Robin Cohen (2008), for example, notes that the 'classical' use of the term was expanded from the 1980s to include additional features and groups, most particularly around the reasons for dispersal and the weakening of territorial identification. Cohen himself adds four additional categories to the classic 'victim' diaspora, to include labour, trade, imperial and cultural forms of diaspora. Brubaker (2005), by contrast, distils the key features of diaspora into three core elements: dispersion, homeland orientation and boundary maintenance, with the last feature crucial in signalling difference and enabling the political and social mobilization of diasporic 'communities' in the place of arrival. Central to each of these classifications is the issue of relationship to the place of origin – for example, DuFoix (2008) develops a fourfold typology of diaspora – 'centroperipheral', 'enclaved', 'atopic' or 'antagonistic' – in which the variation of relationship to the homeland is the defining feature. As Brubaker acknowledges, however, this version of diaspora as a form of categorization or classification runs the risk of creating 'entities' that emphasize coherence and objectivist measurement which can be empirically quantified, measured and counted (Sheffer 2003) and which emphasizes historical continuity over contemporary change and differentiation – a process of homogenization, condensation and reduction that privileges a backward-looking relationship to 'ancestral' homelands over the politics of settlement, and 'roots' over 'routes'.

The 1990s saw a shift in the theorization of diaspora, towards what Cohen (2008) terms 'social constructionist critiques', aimed at contesting and fracturing the ideas of 'homeland' and 'ethnic community' at the heart of empirical approaches to diaspora. This deconstructive turn, heralded by Stuart Hall's seminal article on 'Cultural identity and diaspora' (1990), has been championed by a number of prominent post-colonial and minority ethnic scholars, particularly in Britain, and is marked by a shift in disciplinary alliance from sociology to cultural studies, and in focus from social configurations towards questions of culture and identity (Kalra et al. 2005). Diaspora here appears not as a bounded entity or object of empirical knowledge, but as a process or stance, a form of engagement whose primary motif is that of the journey – perhaps most poignantly captured in the image of the slave ships of the black Atlantic (Gilroy 1993a). Hall argues that diaspora is to be thought of 'metaphorically as well as literally' (1990: 228), as capturing the complex cultural imaginings, experiences and positionings of post-colonial migrants and settlers in ways that transcend and contest simplistic and essentialized narratives of displacement, arrival and identity. Thus he writes:

> Diaspora does not refer to those scattered tribes whose identity can only be secured in relation to some sacred homeland to which they must at all costs return [...] The diaspora experience as I intend it here is defined, not by essence or purity, but by a recognition of a necessary heterogeneity and diversity; by a conception of 'identity' which lives with and through, not despite, difference. (Ibid.: 235)

For Hall, the productive tension of diaspora resides in a process of translation of histories, cultures and representations, where 'cultural identity is a matter of "becoming" as well as of "being"' (ibid.: 225), and where old identities take on new formations:

> Cultural identities come from somewhere, have histories. But, like everything else which is historical, they undergo constant transformation [...] Diaspora identities are those which are constantly producing and reproducing themselves anew, through transformation and difference. (Ibid.: 225, 235)

This version of diaspora emphasizes the place of arrival rather than the place of origin – a shift from the idealization of 'homeland' to the multiple and fractured process of 'homing' (Brah 1996). For Hall, the tensions between history *and* culture, power *and* representation, similarity *and* difference, being *and* becoming provide the framework in which diaspora identities take shape and are contested. The primary concern, however, is with the ways in which diaspora is used to open up spaces and imaginative possibilities in the place of settlement – it is a mode of engagement rather than an assertion of separateness and distinction. The shift is from borders and boundaries to border/boundary crossings, from continuity to disjuncture, tradition to translation, 'roots' to 'routes'. As Gilroy captures it: 'It ain't where you're from, it's where you're at' (1993b).

If the metaphorical diaspora is more concerned with 'here' than 'there', it is similarly focused on the present and the future, rather than the past – or perhaps more accurately, the past is imagined and narrated as a way of positioning the present and addressing the future. Brubaker thus argues that: 'We should think of diaspora in the first instance as a category of practice [...] used to make claims, to articulate projects, to formulate expectations, to mobilize energies, to appeal to loyalties [...] It does not so much describe the world as seek to remake it' (2005: 12).

As such, it challenges fixed ways of thinking about racial, ethnic and national identity, citizenship and belonging, placing an emphasis instead on 'contingency, indeterminacy and conflict' (Gilroy 1997: 334). Diaspora here constitutes not an entity but a field of interaction, externally porous and internally differentiated. Brah, in particular, pays close attention to the internal fissures of imagined diasporic communities, notably those of gender, sexuality and class, as well as the fusions and power relations operating across the porous boundaries of diasporas within contested political, social and cultural terrains. She notes that diasporas 'reference a politics of location' (1996: 204), and she points to the significance of 'diaspora space' as the site where diaspora, border and dis/location intersect – the conceptual place, indeed, where diaspora theory overlaps with ideas of multiculturalism, hybridity and 'conviviality' (Gilroy 2004a; Kalra et al. 2005).

Conclusion

It is perhaps true, however, that the optimism with which diaspora theory was greeted by social science in the 1990s has been severely challenged in the new millennium by the resurgence of neo-nationalist ideologies and the threat of religio-cultural conflict. Kalra et al. thus note, rather gloomily, that 'If words could change the world, then "diaspora" is one of those terms that promised much and delivered little' (2005: 8), its progressive potential swept away in the wake of the war on terror globally and the pursuit of citizenship and security at home. Certainly, there are grounds for caution: the ambivalent nature of diaspora can be used to reify ethnic and racial boundaries and underpin absolutist and reactionary nationalist politics as much as contest them; the celebration of difference, of multiplicity and fragmentation, can erase both internal inequalities of power (around gender, sexuality and class) and continued social injustice and violence; there has been insufficient attention to the historical and cultural specificities of diaspora experiences; and a mistaking of cultural practice as a solution to structural problems.

Cohen has recently claimed (2008) that a new, fourth 'consolidation' phase in diaspora studies is emerging, one which seeks to combine the critical insights of the 'social constructionist' (or metaphorical) diaspora theorists with the emotional, social and historical insights of empirical approaches to diaspora – what we could perhaps term 'critical diaspora studies'. Such an approach suggests a space where the historical and lived experiences of diasporas intersect with an anti-racist and materialist politics of engagement with the contemporary local, national and global context – as Brah has argued, 'Diasporas are [...] potentially the sites of hope and new beginnings' (1996: 193).

Further reading

Alexander, C. (2010) 'Diaspora and hybridity', in P. H. Collins and J. Solomos (eds), *Handbook of Race and Ethnic Studies*, London: Sage.

Brah, A. (1996) *Cartographies of Diaspora: Contesting Identities*, London: Routledge.

Donald, J. and A. Rattansi (eds) (1992) *'Race', Culture and Difference*, London: Sage.

Gilroy, P. (2002 [1987]) *There Ain't No Black in the Union Jack: The Cultural Politics of Race and Nation*, London and New York: Routledge.

Hall, S. (1990) 'Cultural identity and diaspora', in J. Rutherford (ed.), *Identity: Community, Culture, Difference*, London: Lawrence and Wishart, pp. 222–37.

20 | Diasporas and gender

Nadje Al-Ali

The study of diasporas has greatly influenced the expanding and evolving field of gender studies through theoretical and political affinities around notions of marginalization, subversion, fluidity, hybridity and transgression. Simultaneously, changes and developments within the theorizing of gender and its underlying feminist politics have impacted significantly on the way many scholars understand and approach diasporas. As in other fields of study, however, large segments of diaspora studies continue to either pay only limited attention to frequently narrow conceptualizations of gender or even display complete gender blindness. In this essay, I will explore the intersections of diaspora and gender by addressing conceptualizations of difference, the centrality of gender within diasporic imaginations of home, nation, community and citizenship, the shift from a focus on women to 'gendering' processes and, finally, the significance of political economies within performative aspects of gender and diasporas.

Women's experiences

The women's movement associated with second-wave feminism in the 1960s and 1970s struggled to challenge the hitherto systematic exclusion of women and the naturalization of gender ideologies within hegemonic knowledge productions. The impact of this project on diaspora studies started to be recognizable in the 1980s and 1990s when a gendered perspective started to be translated into interrogating depictions of diasporas in homogeneous and essentialized terms by 1) including the experiences of women, and 2) exploring the multifarious ways women might experience and contribute to diaspora formations differently from men. More specifically, feminist scholars have tried to document and analyse diasporic processes related to migration and mobility (Anthias and Lazaridis 2000; Buijs 1993; George 2005; Sweetman 1998), labour force participation (Fikes 2008; Kofman et al. 2000; Parreñas 2001; Phizacklea 1983; Thomas 2008), conceptualizations of home (Al-Ali and Koser 2002; Armbruster 2002; Salih 2003), transmissions of cultural traditions and norms (Anthias and Yuval-Davis 1989), cultural productions (Gopinath 2003, 2005), as well as political mobilization (Al-Ali 2007; Fabos 2002; Mojab and Gorman 2007; Werbner 1996, 1999b, 2000).

These wide-ranging studies shed light on the significance of prevailing gender ideologies, i.e. the normative attitudes and systems of thought which naturalize and legitimize predominant social hierarchies that tend to privilege men as a group, and gender relations, i.e. the way a culture or society defines and organizes rights, responsibilities, access to resources, decision-making processes, and the division of labour of men and women in relation to one another.

One underlying issue which has interested feminist scholars of different disciplinary backgrounds is the question of whether diasporas provide enabling contexts in which previous gender norms can be challenged or whether they reproduce and possibly even harden existing gender ideologies and relations. The existing literature provides evidence for both scenarios: it points to the potential to challenge traditional gender ideologies and relations in those contexts where the prevailing gender norms in the receiving country are more liberal and progressive than in the country of origin and where members of diasporic communities have access to political and economic resources and rights. But even then, there is a real risk of hardening of notions pertaining to 'cultural authenticity' and 'traditions', depending on the specific circumstances of the diaspora within the new country of settlement. In both scenarios, feminist scholars have been careful to avoid simplistic depictions of women as passive victims and have articulated various degrees of agency, ranging from choice with respect to migration, involvement in decision-making processes within the household but also larger communities, participation in formal and informal economic activities and cultural productions, as well as political mobilization.

The emphasis on difference

Early feminist scholarship on diasporas focused on women as a distinct group from men, who have to negotiate two sets of gender ideologies and relations – those of the country of origin and within the country of residence. This soon gave way to an emphasis on difference that has stressed the intersectionality of gender, class, race and sexuality. The convergence of black and post-colonial feminist critiques towards naive notions of sisterhood and the wider postmodern shift towards multiplicity, positionality and fragmentation have led to a concern with difference within the category of women. Here the following key question emerged: How do gender, class, race and sexuality intersect and constitute each other in specific contexts and within processes related to diaspora formations, mobilizations and cultural productions?

Yet, rather than offering a mere recognition of diversity, feminist scholars have approached difference in terms of inequities, asymmetries and power hierarchies. Gender not only denotes the social and cultural construction of what it means to be a woman and a man but it also refers to relationships characterized by power differences. An intersectional analysis has been integral to the move away from conceptualizations of gender as social and cultural constructions of 'female' and 'male', and, in more abstract terms, a state of being, to an analysis of 'gendering' in terms of processes in which hierarchies are established, re-produced and challenged (Al-Ali and Pratt 2009).

Common to a wide range of feminist gender analyses is the view that the differentiation and relative positioning of women and men is an important ordering principle that 'is seen to shape the dynamics of every site of human interaction, from the household to the international arena' (Cockburn 1999: 3). Gender also has expression in prevailing laws, in citizenship rights, in political dynamics and struggles, in economics and, of course, in the social and cultural norms around sexuality (Al-Ali 2007: 39–40) – all aspects crucial to the multiple layers and aspects of analysing diasporas.

Ethnicity, nation and citizenship

The control of women's bodies and sexualities is key in the context of con-structions of ethnic and national communities, especially when in flux. Case studies of women in a variety of geographical and political contexts substanti-ate the theoretical model sketched out by Anthias and Yuval-Davis (1989: 7) to describe the various ways in which women can and do participate in ethnic and national processes: 1) as biological reproducers of members of ethnic collec-tivities; 2) as reproducers of the boundaries of ethnic and national groups; 3) as actors in the ideological reproduction of the collectivity and as transmitters of its culture; 4) as signifiers of ethnic and national groups; and 5) as participants in national, economic, political and military struggles.

Within diasporas, the most 'naturalized' way in which women participate in national and ethnic processes is the 'biological reproduction of the nation' (Yuval-Davis 1997: 66). Gender relations, however, are also at the centre of diasporic cultural constructions of social identities and collectivities where women tend to constitute their symbolic 'border guards'. Specific codes and regulations around women's dress codes, mobility, general comportment and sexuality delineate 'proper women', constructed as carriers of the diasporic community's 'honour' and the inter-generational reproducers of its culture, and 'proper men' (ibid.: 67).

The study of women and gender has been central to countering the prevalent notion that diasporic communities are inherently challenging the significance of nation-states and transgressing national homogeneity. The celebration of counter-hegemonic cultural practices has been disrupted not least by gender-sensitive analyses which have uncovered the various ways diasporic commun-ities, groups and actors are deeply implicated ideologically and materially in the nationalist projects of their homelands, as seen among the South Asian diaspora in Britain (Werbner 2002a), and that women and gender are central to these transnational nationalist projects and processes, as has been documented in the contexts of Bosnia and Iraq, for example (Al-Ali 2007). Paradoxically, however, women are both key to nationalist projects and sentiments and also often excluded from them.

State citizenship as a criterion for membership in the national collectivity could potentially be 'the most inclusive mode of joining a collectivity, because in principle anybody – of whatever origin or culture – might be able to join' (Yuval-Davis 1997: 24). But in reality, state citizenship is also exclusive and tends to favour those with socio-economic resources. Gender is one of the many factors (others are ethnicity, class, sexuality, ability and place of residence) that affect people's citizenship and the distribution of resources. Within any given nation-state, women tend to be subjected to specific laws and regulations, despite being included in the general body of the citizens (Al-Ali 2007: 45).

In the context of diasporas, unequal citizenship rights for men and women might hold true in the context of both the country of origin and the country of residence. The gendered concept of citizenship women embody and the status they are accorded in the host country forge or impede their activities and movements while in the diaspora. Women's activities might be conditioned by regulations based upon hegemonic interpretations of gender roles within both their country of settlement and that of origin (but see George 2005). For example, women are assigned duties and responsibilities in the reproductive spheres which they are expected to carry out while being in their country of origin and in the diaspora. The obstacles posed by social customs and normative rules might prevent them from keeping up links with what is perceived to be 'back home', as has been shown in relation to Iraqi, Bosnian and Moroccan diasporas (Al-Ali 2007; Salih 2003).

Limitations of the performative nexus

Post-structuralist approaches to gender, particularly those foregrounding discursive and representative dimensions, have been increasingly influential within the study of diasporas. Queer studies, in particular, has not only opened up new approaches and understandings of the relationships between gender, sexuality and desire, but the queer subject and the diasporic subject are often constructed as theoretical twins (Wesling 2008: 90). Queerness is perceived as a mobile resistance to the boundaries and limits imposed on gender, which is seen as similar to the migrant's movement through national and cultural borders. In other words, queerness is constructed to disrupt gender normativity as globalization and transnational diaspora activities and practices disrupt national sovereignty.

As Meg Wesling (ibid.) eloquently argues, however, while the queer subject is often used to symbolize the age of globalization and transgressivity, we tend to lose sight of real material conditions related to forced mobility, the commodification of desire, new policies of surveillance and prevailing norms of heterosexuality. Her contribution is part of a wider important cutting-edge theoretical and political intervention (Campt and Thomas 2008) that has adopted a transnational feminist analytic by successfully articulating feminist transnationalism with feminist scholarship on the African diaspora.

Diasporas are frequently described and analysed as embodiments of cultural, political, social and sentimental performances. Yet, beyond the imaginary, textual and visual representations and cultural practices and performances, diasporas also exist through material flows of goods and money (Werbner 2002a). Indeed, as Campt and Thomas as well as their various contributors show (2008), both the sexual and international division of labour, global capital flows and political economies are central in shaping diasporic and gendered subjectivities, mobilities and performativities. It is within this tension of recognizing the performative nexus of gender and diaspora and the significance of political economies and labour relations that some of the most inspiring and exciting research and writings can be found.

Further reading

Al-Ali, N. (2007) 'Gender, diasporas and post-Cold War conflict', in H. Smith and P. Stares (eds), *Diasporas and Post-Cold War Conflict*, Washington, DC: United States Institute for Peace and United Nations University, pp. 39–62.

Anthias, F. (1998) 'Evaluating diaspora: beyond ethnicity?', *Sociology*, 32(3): 557–80.

Campt, T. and D. Thomas (eds) (2008) 'gendering diasporas', *Feminist Review*, 90.

Osirim, M. J. (2008) 'African women in the new diaspora: transnationalism and the (re) creation of home', *African and Asian Studies*, 7(4): 367–94.

Salih, R. (2003) *Gender in Transnationalism: Home, Longing and Belonging among Moroccan Migrant Women*, London and New York: Routledge.

21 | Diasporas and sexuality

Kira Kosnick

Can sexuality be more than an afterthought in diaspora research? Are the two concepts external to each other, to be brought into conversation only via the route of specialist interest? The aim of this essay is to explore the complex issues that open up when trying to think of these two concepts together. I will show how sexuality occupies different, albeit usually implicit, places in constructions of diaspora, and suggest how 'queer' perspectives on sexuality, or rather *sexualities*, might open up productive new avenues for diaspora research.

Eroticism, alliances or procreation?

Linking the dispersal of erstwhile territorially bound, unilocal human populations to the 'scattering or sowing of seeds' (*diaspora*) forges a strong tie between migration and human reproduction, one that is profoundly androcentric in its metaphorical emphasis on active male procreation and patrilineal descent (Delaney 1991). The image of the mobile seed is often complemented by that of the former homeland as immobile soil, as the botanical metaphor for the native place of true territorial belonging and fertility (Malkki 1992).

But what do we mean by sexuality? Do we mean erotic practices, the set of affiliations or lineages between people that are assumed to be a result of sexual practices, or are we considering mechanisms for the biological reproduction of the human species? Once we recognize that sexuality is not 'naturally' linked to kinship and other forms of alliance-building, a different question emerges: How is and has knowledge about sexuality been institutionalized and produced in different locations or circuits that bear upon diasporas?

Sexuality and trans-state formations

Could technologies of power related to sexuality be of relevance in the study of populations that are by definition dispersed over different state territories? And does the transformation and potential weakening of nation-states in the wake of globalization render such technologies less important? With regard to the first question, the anthropologist Stoler (1995) has drawn attention to Michel Foucault's (1978) failure to consider that the very nation-states he was referring to in his history of sexuality were simultaneously engaged in imperial projects that went far beyond the confines of a single population. The colonial management of sexuality was a key site in the production of racialized bodies, and Stoler has suggested that the alleged libidinal energies of the 'savage' or the colonized functioned as racialized erotic objects of knowledge in dominant Western discourses on sexuality. Stoler's critique of Foucault allows us to see sexuality and 'race' as intimately coupled, so to speak. She draws attention to the fact that neither state territory nor citizenship has historically marked the limits of interest in controlling sexuality, and that different historical formations of racism have been closely linked to projections and injunctions concerning sexuality.

Both insights are crucial for any consideration of how diasporas might be thought of in conjunction with sexualities. Diasporas, particularly those that have emerged in the wake of colonial projects, have had to contend with racialized politics of sexuality in different ways. Racial and ethnic categories have been in use to subject potential and actual immigrants to differential policies of family reunification, marriage and moral control (Cruz-Malavé and Manalansan 2002). Modern immigration regimes have generally used hetero-normative standards of sexuality to regulate the entry and settlement of non-citizens (Luibhéid and Cantú 2005). Not only are those suspected of harbouring homosexual or other 'perverse' and 'immoral' tendencies sometimes explicitly barred from legal immigration (e.g. in the USA until 1990), but heterosexual marriage and 'family' reunification continue to be among the most promising avenues for legal migration around the globe, with 'family' usually defined as the 'nuclear' unit of a heterosexual couple and its biological children. Controlling immigration has thus been crucially linked to state projects of managing and regulating the normative sexuality and reproductive behaviour of citizens (Manalansan 2006).

Contemporary work on the transformations of technologies of state power in the wake of globalization certainly undermines the assumption that it is possible to speak of states as singular, unified actors that represent and enforce the will of sovereign governments (Burchell et al. 1991). Agents of nation-states and supra-state agencies, however, continue to shape the constitution and movement of diasporas as they regulate immigration and conditions of residence, and reach out beyond geopolitical borders to citizens and nationals abroad. The 'manufacture of citizenship normativized within the prism of heterosexuality' (Alexander 2005: 181) that characterizes many state formations around the globe cannot be assumed to lose its power just because the social formations in question might no longer be firmly tied to the sovereign space of a single nation-state. Any hopes that migrants might escape the hegemonic grip of nation-states are quick to evaporate in light of both the deterritorialized powers of many contemporary states and the neocolonial projects that are tied to corporate interests beyond state borders (Basch et al. 1994).

For many theorists, the at least symbolic ties to an original homeland constitute a prerequisite in order to categorize particular social groups as diasporic

(Safran 1991). While the most prominent analysis of the nation as an imagined community did not pursue issues of kinship and genealogy much beyond the 'fraternal spirit' among (male) co-nationals (Anderson 1991), earlier academic work had already exposed the crucial role of normative ideas about the nuclear heterosexual family, as the nucleus of national community and gendered bearer of differential obligations with regard to its well-being and future. In his study of middle-class morality and sexual norms in modern Europe, Mosse (1985) revealed how central hetero-normative and androcentric understandings of sexuality were to nationalist ideologies and politics, points that have been similarly and more complexly elaborated by post-colonial and feminist theorists for other state and imperialist projects (Anthias and Yuval-Davis 1989; Mohanty and Alexander 1997; Stoler 1995). There is no reason to assume that the territorial 'scattering' of diaspora as an imagined community would not continue similar concerns (Gilroy 2004b). Quite the contrary – diasporic anxieties around issues of preservation and temporal continuity often focus on cultural-biological reproduction, and are linked to this by a need to control sexuality, particularly the sexualities (practices and desires) of women.

The implicit bias in migration studies

What are the assumptions with regard to the work of reproduction that are involved in sustaining the diasporic 'community', a concept that has become the default setting and placeholder for the actual complexities of social relations that might constitute diasporic practice and imagination? Just as the early German sociologist Ferdinand Tönnies (1912) once influentially posited the hetero-normative family as a reproductive unit that formed the centre of community development, diaspora research has tended to regard diasporas as 'exemplary communities of the transnational moment' (Tölölyan 1991: 4–5), a language rife with implications of heterosexual kinship and family relations.

Hetero-normative assumptions and principles have not just shaped the fields that research on diasporas and migration has addressed, they have also implicitly structured many of the research perspectives themselves. As Martin F. Manalansan (2006) has pointed out in his critique of sexuality and gender in migration studies, heterosexual partnerships and 'biological' parenthood provide the primary models for thinking about migrant families, genealogies and networks of care that span across different localities. Researching migration and diaspora in implicitly hetero-normative terms runs the risk of unwittingly underwriting gendered and sexualized assumptions about women as 'natural nurturers' (ibid.: 239). It thus becomes difficult to consider the importance of differential sexual desires and non-normative family formations in migration processes and diasporic life.

Hetero-normative and gendered assumptions have also left their imprints on those seemingly neutral theoretical accounts that have proved highly influential in contextualizing diaspora research within processes of globalization and formations of late capitalist (post)modernity. As Halberstam (2005: 5) has argued, influential theorists such as David Harvey, Frederic Jameson, Edward Soja and others have dismissed sexuality as a negligible category of analysis, only to reinstate normative suppositions related to sexuality when it comes to examining the production of contemporary spaces and temporalities in the context of globalization. Relegating issues of sexuality to the realm of the personal and local also prevents any examination of how struggles around sexualities contribute to place-making practices and mobilities at different scales and across different localities, a crucial issue for diasporic subjects whose capacities for place-making are often shaped and constrained by histories of racialization, deprivation and forced migrations.

The productivity of 'queer'

What, then, could be the benefit of 'queering' diaspora research? It will seem easy enough to move towards a reformulation of the title of this essay that pluralizes also its second term: diasporas and *sexualities*. For sexuality research in the arts, humanities and social sciences over the last two decades has emphasized, if anything, the complex and dynamic qualities of both sexual identities and practices. To quickly pluralize the term, however, runs the danger of skimming over the fact that thinking of sexuality in the singular has long been linked to normative models of heterosexuality within which non-normative practices and identities have been positioned as deviant. The very impetus for queer studies, as a disciplinary field and intellectual as well as political agenda, has been the attempt to disrupt the mainstream of social and cultural theory that remains stubbornly unaware of its binary gender assumptions and hetero-normative underpinnings: in its descriptions of society, of reproduction, of the family, but also in seemingly quite unrelated areas (Warner 1993: ix). The ambition and strength of queer theory has thus not just been to add 'other' sexualities to the picture, but to render both hetero-normativity and gender binarisms explicit and point out the need for radical revision and rethinking of theoretical traditions in different fields.

In turn, the thesis of geographically dispersed 'queer subjects' themselves constituting diasporic communities, not on the basis of ethno-national origin but on that of queer solidarities and shared identifications, can help to unsettle some of the assumptions of community as based on biological and biologized kinship (Fortier 2002). Fortier, Manalansan and others, however, have also pointed out that the assumption of a queer solidarity that spreads from the West to non-Western locations and subjects usually carries with it a highly problematic teleological vision of white, male gayness as the most advanced stage of queer identity and life forms. The ways in which and degrees to which queer solidarities and imagined and practised forms of community can actually emerge in and across different locations thus have to be concretely examined, just as much as the facile claims to such unity have to be interrogated as to their implications.

Comparative research into sexual practices and identifications in non-Western locations points to a wide variety of forms that cannot be dismissed as 'lagging behind' the development of queer subjectivities in the West. While persecution of homosexual acts and/or identifications can be a forceful motive for migration, this neither implies that it is always the same queer subject with identical desires and visions of the 'good life' who seeks refuge abroad, nor means that the place of refuge will be a safe haven. Indeed, the very 'impossibility' of queer female diasporic subjectivity is examined by Gopinath (2005) in her study of South Asian queer cultures.

Once we reveal the strong hetero-normative underpinnings of diasporic formations in their ethno-national sense, we can ask about those practices and diasporic subjects that 'queer' their hetero-normativity. For same-sex sexual practices and identifications that potentially disrupt it constitute anything but 'irregular' moments of diasporic sexualities. While the claims to a certain homosexual identity and its decriminalization and de-demonization have been most prominently politicized in the West, non-heterosexual practices, desires and identifications have been well documented as constituting part of non-Western modernities and traditions in different parts of the world.

Further reading

Cruz-Malavé, A. and M. Manalansan IV (eds) (2002) *Queer Globalizations: Citizenship and the Afterlife of Colonialism*, New York and London: New York University Press.

Fortier, A. (2002) 'Queer diasporas', in D. Richardson and S. Seidman (eds), *Handbook of Lesbian and Gay Studies*, London: Sage, pp. 183–97.

Luibhéid, E. and L. Cantú, Jr (eds) (2005) *Queer Migrations: Sexuality, US Citizenship, and Border Crossings*, Minneapolis: University of Minnesota Press.

Manalansan, M. (2006) 'Queer intersections: sexuality and gender in migration studies', *International Migration Review*, 40(1): 224–49.

Patton, C. and B. Sánchez-Eppler (eds) (2000) *Queer Diasporas*, Durham, NC, and London: Duke University Press.

22 | Diasporas and religion

Manuel A. Vásquez

The notion of diaspora bears a close elective affinity with religion. Like diasporic consciousness, which involves rememorializing and the longing for the lost homeland, often understood as a mythical place, religion is also, as Mircea Eliade (1982: 128) argues, about the quest to return to pristine origins and to experience the cosmos in *illo tempore*, at the beginning of time, before humanity fell into the 'terrors of history'. Moreover, diasporic livelihood entails a strong sense of community, a community that, although forcibly dispersed and immersed in hostile host societies, imagines and feels itself as a unified ethnos. In a similar fashion, religion is, according to sociologist Emile Durkheim (1971 [1915]), essentially social solidarity distilled, expressed in collective representations and powerful shared rituals that create and sustain a moral community and protect the individual against the centrifugal forces of anomie. In other words, because religion and diaspora operate in similar ways in the management of time and space and in the articulation of individual and collective identities, they have historically been closely intertwined, often buttressing and reinforcing each other.

One of the foundational uses of the notion of diaspora is *galût*, a term that describes the formation of scattered Jewish colonies outside of Palestine as a result of the Babylonian exile, beginning in 586 BCE. With the destruction in Jerusalem (in 70 CE) of the Second Temple, which was the centre of Jewish politico-religious life, and the violent defeat of the Bar Kokhba revolt (133–35 CE), hope for a return to the homeland all but vanished, forcing Jews to make their identities and culture portable and flexible, while maintaining connections with their ancestors and each other. Here religion played a central role, simultaneously reaffirming tradition and crafting new creative ways of relocating the self and community.

In exile, Jews confronted what religion scholar K. Brown (1999: 82) has called the 'cosmo-logistical problem' – the problem of how to practise a religion that is intimately connected with a particular place when one is dislocated and when travel to that place is impossible or extremely difficult. The search for solutions to this problem was the driving force behind the emergence of portable sacred texts as the new pivot of Jewish religious life. While the texts preserve the wisdom of the elders, they are open to the interpretation of locally based rabbis linked in an ongoing conversation through polycentric networks with key nodes in places as diverse as Amsterdam, Cordoba, Cairo, Vilna and Recife (Boyarin and Boyarin 2002: 11).

The approximately ten million African slaves who were forcibly brought to the Americas from the late 1530s to the 1850s also faced a difficult cosmo-logistical problem. Although violently uprooted and severely repressed, controlled and divided by their colonial masters, the slaves still managed to construct a myriad of individual and collective religious identities in the Americas, blending diverse elements of African religions, such as the cult of the ancestors and divination, with Christianity, particularly the Catholic devotion to saints and the Virgin Mary, and indigenous practices like shamanism, spirit incorporation and ritual sacrifice. The result was the emergence of a diasporic zone of transculturation which Gilroy (1993a) has termed 'the black Atlantic'. This zone linked the Americas, Europe and Africa, serving as the crucible for the rise of many African-based religions, such as Regla Lukumí, popularly known as Santería (in Cuba, Puerto Rico, the Dominican Republic and more recently in New York and Florida), Candomblé (in Bahia and Rio de Janeiro, Brazil), Vodou (in Haiti, Cuba, the Dominican Republic, Louisiana, New York and Florida), Obeah (in Surinam and the English-speaking Caribbean) and 'Afro-Protestantism' (Matory 2005; Sensbach 2005).

Religion is also visible in the other historically paradigmatic understanding of the term diaspora: *diaspeírein* in Greek (*tefutzot* in Hebrew), meaning simply dispersion, 'to scatter about', without the loss of a political and religious centre and the traumatic feeling of severe homelessness that characterizes *galût*. *Diaspeírein* aptly describes the dynamics of Greek colonization of Asia Minor through migration, trade and conquest in 800–600 BCE. Greek trade and migratory diasporas produced interconnected cosmopolitan enclaves throughout the Mediterranean, zones of encounters where not only goods and money were exchanged but also religious ideas and practices, leading to great cultural creativity and hybridity. Thus, religion and *diaspeírein* are connected by the dynamics of syncretism, literally 'with Crete' or 'bringing together in the manner of the cities of Crete', a key entrepôt in the Mediterranean world where cultures interacted to produce new religious constellations.

To say that religion and diaspora are closely connected does not mean that all religions are equally diasporic or diasporic in the same way. Some religions have explicitly universal, translocal horizons. This is the case of Christianity, for example, which, in the wake of the Apostles' baptism by fire during Pentecost, followed the 'Great Commission', the injunction 'to go and make disciples of all nations' (Matt. 28:16–20). The same is true of Buddhism, since Siddhartha Gautama saw the *dharma* as a pragmatic response to humanity's existential predicaments. The Buddha is purported to have said: 'Go ye now, O Bhikkhus, and wander, for the gain of the many, out of compassion for the world, for the good, for the gain, and for the welfare of gods and men. Let not two of you go in the same way' (*Mahāvagga* 1.11.1). Because of its strong emphasis on monotheism, Islam also construed itself as the religion of an all-encompassing *umma*, a righteous community of believers not restricted by kinship ties or territorialized political units (see McLoughlin, this volume).

For these three so-called world religions, their diaspora, their spread, was facilitated by specific political formations, as was the case with Constantine's Roman Empire (306–37 CE) and the Spanish and Portuguese crowns for Christianity, Ashoka's empire (273–232 BCE) for Buddhism, and the Umayyads (610–750 CE) and especially the Abbasids (750–1258) for Islam. Among other things, these empires hired missionaries, built many religious institutions, including temples, monuments, schools, monasteries and nunneries, sponsored translocal conclaves and councils to settle doctrine, and supported the translation of various circulating texts. Movement across territories followed well-established land routes, such as the Silk Road, connecting China and India with Asia Minor, the Mediterranean and North Africa, and transcontinental sea trade circuits.

In contrast to the religions with an explicit global *imaginaire*, other religions were initially more closely connected with a particular people or place, as in the case of Judaism, Hinduism and African-based religions like Vodou and Candomblé. The tight connection to peoples and places did not impede the movement of these religions. As practitioners moved, either as voluntary migrants, merchants, refugees, slaves or indentured labourers, they brought their religions with them to the new places of settlement. Once there, practitioners invariably sought to re-create their religious and cultural lives, carving sacred landscapes through architecture and other embodied practices such as theatre, music and dance. This re-creation, however, was not a mere reproduction of practices and institutions in the homeland. Rather, it often incorporated cultural and religious dimensions of the host society. As the case of the African diaspora and slavery in the Americas shows, hybridization is always accompanied by power relations, by the attempt to impose orthodoxy and erase past traditions and to resist through heterodoxy and creative redeployment. This is why Gilroy uses the 'middle passage', the traumatic but seminal journey of slave ships between Africa and the Americas, as the central metaphor to characterize the black Atlantic, as a diasporic, 'rhizomorphic, fractal [...] [and] transcultural, international formation' (1993a: 4).

The distinction between universalistic and particularistic religions is necessarily heuristic (see McLoughlin 2010). The time–space compression and distantiation that accompany globalization are constantly deterritorializing and reterritorializing religions in ways that undermine simplistic dualistic categories. For example, Santería, a Yoruban-derived religion that was once closely associated with the descendants of African slaves in Cuba (down to their imagined diasporic community as a *Lukumí nación*), is now a global religion that often interacts with shamanism, Wicca and neopaganism, as part of what are nebu-lously described as New Age religions or alternative spiritualities. Despite this hybridization, a drive to authenticity persists, with many practitioners seeking to recover the roots of Santería in Cuba and West Africa.

Conversely, as the centre of gravity of 'universalistic' Christianity shifts to the southern hemisphere, it has become particularized in new independent and indigenous churches in Africa and Latin America. Such is the case of the Church of Jesus Christ on Earth by the Prophet Kimbangu, founded in the 1920s by prophet and miracle worker Simon Kimbangu in what is now the Democratic Republic of Congo. While this church carries Christianity's global *imaginaire*, it images the Bakongo, particularly the holy city of Nkamba, where Kimbangu was born, as the sacred centre of the world, as the New Jerusalem, where all human tribes will eventually converge.

The examples of Santería and the Kimbangu church demonstrate that re-ligious universality and particularity are not mutually exclusive. Instead, the diasporic experience is marked by the interplay between the universal and the particular and between the global and the local. To study this interplay, religion scholars have developed some useful theoretical and methodological tools. Thomas Tweed (1997) draws from the work of religion scholar Jonathan Z. Smith and of humanistic geographers Tuan Yi-Fu and Henri Lefebvre to characterize the narratives and practices of Cubans who live in exile in Miami in the wake of the 1959 revolution. According to Tweed, diasporic religion operates at three levels: the locative, the translocative and the supralocative. Diasporic Cubans draw from their religious tradition to recentre themselves in Miami, inscribing their portable visions of the sacred in the local landscape. Thus, they have built a shrine to Our Lady of Charity, the patroness of Cuba. This shrine, however, is not only locative, providing a home for a particular brand of lived Cuban Catholicism in the midst of a Protestant host nation. The shrine was deliberately constructed to face Cuba, barely ninety miles across the water. Moreover, the internal space of the shrine is dominated by a large mural depict-ing the history of Cuba, minus the traumatic events that led to exile. Religion, then, is translocative, because it links the diaspora with the imagined homeland across space and time. Finally, beyond the horizontal links to the homeland, the shrine connects the Cuban people in Miami vertically with God, making their sufferings in exile part of a cosmic struggle between good and evil, part of a sacred narrative of redemption that hopes for the restoration of a God-fearing pre-revolutionary Cuba.

Cosmization – the irruption of the absolute time and space of the sacred into history and geography – represents one of the most distinctive and significant contributions of religion to the diasporic experience. While nationalism and religion have played similar roles throughout history in forging enduring dias-poric communities of feeling, alternatively reinforcing each other or holding each other in tension, what makes religion unique is the dimension of supra-historical or trans-historical transcendence. Very often, religion adds a powerful utopian, millenarian and even apocalyptic dimension to diasporas, imagining a radical, perhaps even violent, inversion of the present, a rectification of all the traumas and unfulfilled longings in being homeless, and a return to a time-less state of grace. In that sense, the 'powers of [religious] diasporas are not necessarily benign, whether directed outward or inward. An investigation of the powers of diaspora is thus vitiated by a hasty assumption that such powers are only creative or progressive' (Boyarin and Boyarin 2002: 8).

Elsewhere, Johnson (2007) stresses the material dimensions that support the work of religion in diaspora. Artefacts that have been brought from the homeland become supercharged with nostalgia, desire, hope and the power to awe. When these objects are not present, practitioners sacralize other artefacts in the new place of settlement. This selection and sacralization operate through what Johnson calls 'metaphoric, metonymic, and synecdochic hooking' (ibid.: 55). New ritual objects and sacred sites are selected because they are similar to those in the homeland, or because they bear associations with buried memories, or because an element of them condenses all previous religious significations.

In recent years, the study of the intersection between religion and diaspora has also become cross-fertilized with works on globalization, transnational migration and media studies. For instance, there are promising studies of the role the Internet has played in the deployment of a 'long-distance nationalism' (Anderson 1983: 12; Glick Schiller 2005: 570–80), which is often buttressed by religious discourses and practices. Indians in the USA and the UK have not only bankrolled Hindu nationalist organizations in India but have used their generally high digital literacy to spread their message across the Hindu diaspora through the Internet. In different circumstances, given its persecution by the Chinese government, the Falun Gong movement has been able to spread via the Internet despite the existence of the 'Great Firewall of China', maintaining a loose connection with its leader exiled in the USA, as well as organizing large public demonstrations. As such cases show, future study of the intersection between religion and diaspora will have to pay close attention to the impact of virtuality and the explosive growth of global mass media and the culture industry in the construction of religiously inflected diasporic memories, desires, experiences, artefacts and identities. This construction is likely to involve the rearticulation of old and the emergence of new forms of religious embodi-ment and emplacement – that is, new understandings of self, space, time and materiality.

Further reading

Boyarin, J. and D. Boyarin (2002) *The Powers of Diaspora: Two Essays on the Relevance of Jewish Culture*, Berkeley: University of California Press.

Johnson, P. (2007) *Diaspora Conversions: Black Carib Religion and the Recovery of Africa*, Berkeley: University of California Press.

Matory, J. L. (2005) *Black Atlantic Religion: Tradition, Transnationalism, and Matriarchy in Afro-Brazilian Candomblé*, Princeton, NJ: Princeton University Press.

McLoughlin, S. (2010) 'Religion and diaspora', in J. Hinnells (ed.), *Routledge Companion to the Study of Religion*, 2nd edn, London and New York: Routledge, pp. 558–80.

Tweed, T. A. (1997) *Our Lady of the Exile: Diaspora Religion at a Cuban Catholic Shrine in Miami*, New York: Oxford University Press.

23 | Diasporas and language

Jaine Beswick

Key to our understanding of the relationship between language and diaspora is that each scenario is often one of language contact between the heritage language and the host language. Furthermore, the language of the diaspora is regularly more than just a pragmatic tool of interpersonal communication. Rather, as we shall see, languages frequently embrace extralinguistic characteristics and play important sociolinguistic, sociocultural and even sociopolitical roles in the conceptualization of diaspora group interfaces.

Of course, language choice has not always been feasible within the diaspora. Central to the essentialized character of eighteenth-century nation-states was the promulgation of linguistic homogeneity as the marker of a single identification strategy, aimed at minimizing linguistic, social and cultural differences within minoritized, ethnic groups, including diasporas. These 'one-nation, one-state, one-language' ideologies continued to resonate throughout the twentieth century (Beswick 2007: 27–51). In the former Yugoslavia, for example, the imposition of a common language, Serbo-Croat, was an attempt to enforce a total correlation between ethnic group and nation in order 'to homogenize within, and heterogenize outwardly' (Bugarski 2001: 73). Similarly, the rise of anti-Semitism led to heritage language repression in the Jewish diaspora. There have been examples of 'tolerance', however, and even encouragement of linguistic multiculturalism too, as in Canada (especially Quebec).

Cohen (1997) and Safran's (1991) initial conceptualizations of diasporas as victims of circumstance reinforced the idea that all diasporas struggled against prejudice and marginalization, even if they were willing to accept the host's social, cultural and linguistic norms. Safran's dual territory approach (ibid.) also considered fundamental the relationship that the group maintained with the homeland. Diasporas were thus portrayed as existing in some kind of 'no man's land' (Mishra 2006), displaced through migration and exile from the homeland yet not belonging to the host land. It was suggested that, for many migrants, the transition between the rural homeland and the urban host land could be eased by their shared ethnicity, encompassing shared memories and shared history, which provided the cohesive force to support them until their projected return home. Furthermore, it was often through the heritage language that such nostalgic evocations were transmitted and maintained. Indeed, during

Salazar's dictatorship the transition for rural Portuguese migrants to the cities of other European countries was problematical, but by clustering together in particular neighbourhoods, they were able to maintain their sociolinguistic and sociocultural identification practices through the use of Portuguese. In this way, the heritage language upheld the diaspora's own sense of legitimacy and authenticity within an alien environment, reinforcing the sense of historical and cultural difference, as well as being a pragmatic communication tool (Beswick 2010a).

Postmodern conceptualizations of diaspora move away from their portrayal as victims, seeking instead to highlight more positive aspects of their experiences and emphasizing that diaspora can be proactive and should be seen as truly 'authentic' (see Hall 1991a, 1993). Previous assumptions regarding relationships between diasporas and host societies tended to be too focused on the notion of shared ethnicity, yet diasporas are not homogeneous elements, since the experiences and identification practices of individual members are often far too disparate to characterize the whole group. Here, time is a key factor. Diasporas are no longer simply viewed as striving for the past, since they are also confronting the future to establish a new sense of place, belonging and role. Across generations, new strategies are developed to confront and adapt to disparate situations, which influence the contextualization and usage of language in intra- and inter-group interfaces and demonstrate the potential for the heritage language to be used as a prestigious, solidarity-enhancing and even politically charged tool of identity/ies.

This individualization of diasporas is now fundamental to our appreciation of their differing trajectories. Irrespective of geographical and territorial constraints, the globalized movement of people creates contemporary transnational spaces in which contact with the homeland through the use of the heritage language, and the heritage language itself, may be maintained through email, the Internet and satellite television, as well as through more conventional modes of communication, such as the mass media. Thus, diasporas may effectively negotiate a new level of adaptation to host societies on the one hand as well as the continued maintenance of relations with the home country on the other. A good example is that of Kurdish refugees in Sweden and the Netherlands, who have established strong transnational networks linked to the Kurdish movement in the Middle East, while benefiting from liberal multicultural integration strategies in the country of residence (Faist 2004: 12–13). In analogous circumstances, heritage language loyalty may be a good indication of the host society's tolerance of linguistic pluralism, although linguistic pluralism does not always enhance such loyalty, as in Clyne's accounts of certain ethnolinguistic groups in Australia (1991, 2003).

Of course, contextual language selection may be for essentially pragmatic reasons: effective communication with the host society may be the primary motivating factor for the use of its language. Conversely, the maintenance of transnational relationships and 'counter-diasporic' return objectives, as well as the itinerant nature of some diasporas such as the Bangladeshis (Khondker 2008), may as a corollary necessitate the maintenance of the heritage language for intra-group communication purposes. As we have seen, however, in a multilingual setting language selection often also embraces extralinguistic, social, cultural or even political motivation: it may thus be discriminate, with each speech act manifesting one of a range of strategies, as evidenced for migratory groups by Pavlenko (2006: 27).

This brings us back to the issue of heterogeneity, since diasporic identities, like the cultures, societies and individuals they represent, are not homogeneous but hybrid, and particularly in subsequent generations of migrants they often comprise a 'layering' of features and traits, some retained from the autochthonous community, others acquired from the host society (Gilroy 1993a). Thus, migrants may choose to reinforce particular identification practices in order to ally themselves more closely either to the host society (use of the out-group language to mark enhanced status), such as occurs with Galicians in Guildford, UK (Beswick 2010b), or to their own diasporic group (use of the in-group language to mark associated solidarity and non-integration), such as occurs with the Portuguese on Jersey (Beswick 2005).

So again, attitudinal factors may impact on how much the diaspora acculturates to the host society, as well as on whether a diasporic community holds on to its heritage language in contexts of potential language shift – see Weinreich's (1966 [1953]: 68) original characterization of such and Fishman's (1964) further development of the term in the following decade. They may find, for example, that speaking their heritage language in out-group contexts provokes xenophobic reactions; a case in point is the Serb diaspora (see Pavlinic 1993). Alternatively, acquisition of the host language may be perceived as financially advantageous; many members of the Portuguese diaspora in Venezuela have forgone their heritage language in their efforts to achieve economic and political power. Other diasporas may draw upon what they deem to be the positive aspects of multilingualism, so that language use may be demarcated according to some form of functional distribution, where each language conveys discrete social meanings. Schiff (2002: 214–15) discusses language use by the Hasidic and Ultra-Orthodox Jewish diaspora in New York, in which Hebrew is their 'internal' language, strictly reserved for prayer, study and ritual observance; Yiddish is the daily vernacular for in-group communication; and English is the language of out-group business activities. Hence, language shift may predominate as the outcome of language contact in a migration context, but language maintenance is also possible.

In order to appreciate the issues surrounding linguistic form in diasporic settings we now examine some potential outcomes. Lexical borrowing, for example, defined as 'the incorporation of foreign features into a group's native language by speakers of that language' by Thomason and Kaufman in their early framework of language change (1988: 21), is often a feature of adult second-language acquisition where no formal teaching is in evidence. Diaspora speakers may incorporate host language loanwords for new terminology and concepts into their repertoires which in the initial stages do not undergo adaptation to the phonological and morphological systems of the heritage language, since speakers are often less concerned with the correctness of their linguistic output than with achieving a successful communication. Their eventual structural adaptation, however, means that loanwords are generally considered to be long-term additions to the recipient language (Lehiste 1988: 2–13).

Code-switching is a strategic and eminently controllable communicative device, in which speakers choose to switch between the languages of their repertoire within a particular speech event for identity-reinforcing reasons, or for other reasons such as topic of conversation, interlocutor status, stylistic nuance and so on. The adoption and integration of the structural characteristics of either language are often not in evidence (Poplack and Meechan 1998) and code-switching is generally considered to be a short-term effect of language contact (see Clyne 2003: 70–76), which may lead to the loss of one of the language varieties, typically that of the diaspora.

Once again, key to such scenarios is inter-generational shift over time. In migration contexts in which heritage language maintenance is not possible or desired, language shift often occurs over three generations, depending on the education of the children and grandchildren in the host language. Thus, the general use of the heritage language in all contexts by the first generation gives way to the functional distribution of heritage language in the home and the host language elsewhere in the second generation, to the potential domination of the host language in all contexts in the third generation. In some diasporas, though, the heritage language may be maintained in some intra-group interactions; Li (1998), for instance, examines the use of Cantonese in such contexts in the Chinese communities of Newcastle-upon-Tyne, UK.

The example of Spanglish in New York demonstrates how code-switching and lexical borrowing may occur simultaneously. As the host language of status and power, and owing in no small part to multilingual intolerance in some quarters, English exerts a substantial lexical influence on the Spanish spoken by the Hispanic diaspora. In particular, loanwords representing new or unfamiliar American cultural realities are adopted in cross-cultural and social exchanges, but competent bilinguals also use code-switched sentences as a significant discourse strategy (Zentella 2002: 179–80). Thus, Spanglish is often cited as a mixed or even 'hybrid' language variety. In such varieties, the linguistic structures of both parent languages are drawn upon (Clyne 2003: 70–76), often resulting in unusual linguistic combinations. Ultimately, this may lead to the creation of a unique language variety deemed appropriate for expressing the multiple identities of speakers (Coulmas 2005: 120–21; see also R. Jacobson 1998), although this depends on how contact takes place, on its intensity and, importantly, on who the agents are and their level of communicative and linguistic competence. Historically, this occurred in the Jewish diaspora, where so-called 'diaspora languages' emerged (Judaeo-Arabic, Judaeo-Spanish, Judaeo-Persian) as a result of mixing phenomena (Goldsmith 1976: 27).

Finally, it should be noted that pidgins – structurally simplified trade languages based largely on lexical interpretation – and Creoles – pidgins that are structurally more complex and used in more wide-ranging communication contexts – are often considered to be mixed or hybrid language varieties. These too are the result of (historical) language contact, such as that between colonizing and autochthonous language varieties, as, for example, on the islands of the Caribbean and the Indian Ocean (cf. Le Page and Tabouret-Keller 1985; Thomason and Kaufman 1988; Matras and Bakker 2003). A good example is that of Mauritian Creole (Nallatamby 1995).

Further reading

Garcia, O. and J. A. Fishman (eds) (2002) *The Multilingual Apple: Languages in New York City*, 2nd edn, New York: Mouton de Gruyter.

Jacobson, R. (ed.) (1998) *Codeswitching Worldwide*, Berlin and New York: Mouton de Gruyter.

Matras, Y. and P. Bakker (eds) (2003) *The Mixed Language Debate. Theoretical and Empirical Advances*, Berlin: Mouton de Gruyter.

Pavlenko, A. and A. Blackledge (eds) (2004) *Negotiation of Identities in Multilingual Contexts*, Clevedon: Multilingual Matters.

Winford, D. (2003) *An Introduction to Contact Linguistics*, Oxford: Blackwell.

24 | Diasporas and material culture

Philip Crang

This essay is concerned with the stuff of diaspora. In exploring the relations between diaspora scholarship and the interdisciplinary field of material culture studies, it considers how diasporic identities and processes are forged through the production, circulation and consumption of material things and spaces. Long apparent within the human sciences that most directly work with material forms, such as archaeology, design history and certain strands of anthropology and geography, a focus on material culture has become much more widely influential over the last fifteen years, as epitomized in the launch (1996) and subsequent fertility of the interdisciplinary *Journal of Material Culture*. Driven forward by debates and research within anthropology in particular, these material culture studies have emphasized the role of the material world in objectifying, mediating and shaping social relations, identities and differences. This emphasis on the mutual constitution of material objects and sociocultural processes has also chimed with other theoretical inspirations to take the agencies of material 'stuff' more seriously, including those from Science and Technology Studies, Actor-Network Theory and a wider post-humanism (see Miller 2005).

Here, such theoretical lineages are left somewhat implicit, in favour of an emphasis on substantive engagements. In that spirit, let us introduce the essay's themes via a particular materialization of diaspora, the 'Indian' grocery store in America. In Mankekar's fascinating study, these stores are cast as 'a crucial node in the transnational circulation of texts, images and commodities between India and the diaspora' (2005 [2002]: 197). Rather than simply being functional commercial spaces, or repositories of mundane objects, for her these stores illustrate the 'mutual entanglement of things, values and social relations' (ibid.: 202). Focusing especially on detailed ethnographic research in the Bay Area of San Francisco, Mankekar draws out three sets of diasporic experiences to which these retail spaces are central. First, performing 'diasporic memories', their tastes and smells connect to personal and social memories of India. The foods they provide are implicated in the reproduction of Indian identities, in particular with regard to what is cast as women's role in domestic eating and the ongoing production of a domestic Indian culture. Their localized, niche marketing strategies and product-line provision, attuned to the specific demographics of their customers, enact a diasporic Indian culture of unity in diversity.

Second, it is apparent how specific product brands – Maggi Noodles, Haman soap, Brahmi Amla hair oil, Glucose biscuits, Amul butter – afford powerful affective responses, notably a rich and complex range of nostalgias. And third, these stores are significant social spaces, providing diasporic sociality (in mundane togetherness and proximity), visibility (in the wider urban landscape) and indeed forms of communal surveillance (in particular, a number of women spoke of the role of the shops in policing their identities and behaviour). These stores raise wider research questions, then, about the relations between diaspora, commerce and the commodity form; things and diasporic homemaking; and the diasporic materials of public culture. These are the themes that organize the remainder of this essay.

Commodifying diaspora

A commodity is a thing that is being turned to commercial advantage. Not all things are commodities, and things that are commodities do not always remain unequivocally so (just think of products that others may have bought as gifts to you, but that you would now be very uneasy about reselling). But in a world dominated by capitalist modes of production, commodities are ubiquitous and central to our material cultures. They certainly feature strongly in diaspora studies, for example in accounts of 'ethnic entrepreneurship' and the cultural industries and creativity (for example Westwood and Bhachu 1988; Bhachu 2004). For some, the predominance of the commodity form renders the materialization of diaspora deeply problematic. For example, Kalra et al. write passionately about the consequent tendency for the dilution of resistant, diasporic cultural forms, such as rap, into 'neatly packaged units for mass consumption', serving a 'culture industry feasting upon plurality and difference' and with the result that 'expression, creative exchange, and the possibility of political struggle are left to putrefy in the rest-stop of smorgasbord culture' (2005: 40, 93; see also Hutnyk 2000). At stake here is how commodified diasporic materials can operate as media of decontextualization, becoming thin signifiers of difference that can be made, circulated and consumed in ways that sidestep any significant cultural recognition, dialogue or rethinking in favour of the satiating of desires for an easily engaged and untroubling diversity (hooks 1992; Root 1996).

Material culture studies are more agnostic about commodity cultures. In emphasizing the 'social life of things' (Appadurai 1986), they emphasize how things transport and transform cultural meanings, values and practices as they move in space and time. Such movements involve processes of appropriation, but the politics surrounding these, in terms of both the powers of the different actors involved and the implications of this cultural traffic, are not inherent, but a matter for substantive scrutiny. This can be undertaken through detailed investigation of specific things and their transnational spaces (Crang and Ashmore 2009; Spooner 1986), particular negotiations of diasporic expression and commerce (Dwyer and Crang 2002) and wider cultural surveys and histories of particular commodity genres and the multicultural imaginaries in which they are implicated (see Cook 2008; Cook et al. 1999; Parker 2000).

The case of the bagel in the USA is illustrative (Balinska 2008; Gabaccia 1998). Brought to north-eastern cities in the late nineteenth century as a mundane foodstuff by Jewish immigrants from eastern Europe, the bagel became marked as Jewish once its bakeries were frequented by Gentile urban neighbours. Accompanied by cream cheese, introduced to the continent in the eighteenth century by the English Quakers of the Delaware Valley and Philadelphia, the bagel then became a crucial ingredient of 'New York deli' cuisine. In the twentieth century the bagel's Jewish bakers participated in wider trends in the industrialization of American food production, and sought to extend their markets across the nation. Most famously, this saw a baker such as Lender's transformed from a bakery in New Haven employing six family members and with a capacity of 2,400 bagels per day in the mid-1940s to having confrontations with unions over craft production, to its purchase by Kraft (1984) and the opening of its non-unionized plant in the 'corn and bean country' of Mattoon, Illinois, producing over one million bagels per day (Balinska 2008: 176). Meanwhile, the now American bagel was being imported to Israel by New Yorker Gary Heller, and distributed via deals with a supermarket chain and Dunkin Donuts (Gabaccia 1998: 2), as well as featuring with cream cheese and lox as a signature menu item on El Al flights (Balinska 2008: 166–8). For Gabaccia, this is a story of diasporic material culture that goes well beyond singular narratives of 'corporate hegemony', 'ethnic fragmentation' or 'postmodern decadence' (1998: 5).

The stuff of diasporic homemaking

Things also play a vital role in processes of diasporic homemaking. To ease the narrative flow, we will continue with the focus on foods for a while. There is now a substantial body of research on the culinary practices of diasporic populations. For some, what is at stake in the domestic diets within diasporas is the desire of migrant populations for familiar foods that, if available, allow for the continuation of established culinary competencies (Collins 2008; Mannan and Boucher 2002). For Petridou (2001), in her study of Greek students in London, England, familiar food operates more as a marker of difference and as a reaction to feelings of displacement, in this case through an opposition between tasty, real and nurturing Greek food and tasteless, superficial and uncaring English food/culture. Sutton emphasizes the relations between food and memory in his account of movements of food from Kalymnos, Greece, to other parts of the world (2001: 73–102). He is provoked by the testimonies of Kalymnians abroad of the importance of foods brought with them or sent from 'home'. For Sutton, food sent or sourced from Kalymnos provides the displaced with a (literal) sense of wholeness, as tastes and smells and textures provoke memories and feelings of connection to, indeed presence in, variously located senses of home (the family home, a home town, a Greek national belonging). Of course, in all these cases there are important counter-cases, where food 'from home' is resisted, or at least seen in the context of a wider array of options and adaptations (see Panayi 2008).

Studies of material culture have also paid particular attention to other domestic objects, considering in particular the role of 'belongings in belonging' (Walsh 2006: 123). This has included an interest in the (differential) mobilities of objects, and their potential to construct translocal domestic environments through their portability from one domestic location to another (see ibid. on British expatriates in Dubai). Focusing on the collections of objects that make up domestic *mandirs* (places of worship), Tolia-Kelly's research with Hindu South Asian women in north London argues that they 'activate a connection biographically and spiritually [...] trigger[ing] re-memories of sites of spiritual well-being' (2004: 321). Furthermore, decorative curios, craft objects and landscape images of Africa in the homes of 'twice migrant' East African Asians, once 'replaced, and replanted in the UK [...] are imbued with different values and meanings'. Once kitsch, they are now 'treasures' that enact past residence and reform the cultural landscape of residence in England (ibid.: 324, 325). In both cases, these domestic objects are prismatic, refracting other times and places into the here and now through their sensory prompts. They help to constitute a diasporic home that complicates and enriches senses of residential location.

Homemaking is not a purely private matter, but an articulation of private and public spaces. Clarke (2001), for example, narrating the case of the Santoses – relatively recent migrants from Chile to London, and of late moved from a house multiply occupied by Chileans to owner-occupation of a three-bedroom flat – examines the emphasis placed on the redecoration of the children's bedrooms and the bathroom, in comparison to the as yet undecorated living room. Her interpretation is that this prioritization, and the 'modern European style' adopted in the decorated rooms, represents 'the material context for an envisaged aim [...] a carefully managed syncretism [...] easing the way of [...] first-generation British-Chilean children into their new social worlds' (ibid.: 39). Other work emphasizes disjunctures between private and public spaces. David Ley has highlighted the struggles over residential urban space in the Shaughnessy Heights neighbourhood of Vancouver, as Anglophiliac landscapes of settler culture are challenged by Chinese 'millionaire migrants' and their desire to remodel this heritage and build what became derogatively known as new 'monster homes' (Ley 1995, 2010). Lisa Law considers the experiences of Filipino domestic workers in Hong Kong, living under tight regulation in their employers' domestic spaces, but every Sunday using their day off to participate in 'a spectacular gathering [...] in and around Central Hong Kong of more than 100,000 Filipino women [...] eat[ing] Filipino food, read[ing] Filipino newspapers/magazines and consum[ing] products from an abundant number of Filipino speciality shops' and stalls (Law 2001: 265–6). For Law, these materials remake Hong Kong's sense-scapes, transforming the visual iconography of Central's architecture to a 'Little Manila' composed of tastes, smells and sounds that here become Filipino.

Diasporic collections

I have been arguing, then, that things, their arrays and sensory engagements with them are an arena within which diasporic belongings can be fashioned, and through which more bounded and territorialized cultural maps may be unsettled. But studies of material culture also have long-standing interests in movements, collections and sensings of objects that have traditionally been more distanced from diasporic subjects. A notable case is work on the relations between 'empire, material culture and the museum' (Barringer and Flynn 1998). It is with this work that I want to conclude.

In a fascinating recent project, Pahl and colleagues started from the proposition that 'every object tells a story', and then used domestic artefacts from five families of Pakistani origin from Rotherham, South Yorkshire, to prompt both recorded narratives and to curate a museum-style exhibition at the local Rotherham Arts Centre (Pahl and Pollard 2008). One could view this project as a critical intervention into an arena of public culture in which other subject positions have traditionally been given a leading role. Metropolitan museums are stuffed with objects from other times and places, but represent a disjuncture between diasporas of objects and people. As colonial institutions they had the power to collect objects, while the people these objects resided with were either left *in situ* or mobilized as temporary, travelling exhibits themselves (Mathur 2007). In the contemporary moment, museum collections thus have an ambivalent post-colonial potential: to engage with diasporic subjectivities, to enact forms of diaspora space through their created congeries of objects and people, and to respond imaginatively to the complex politics, possibilities and problems of object 'repatriation' (Edwards et al. 2006; Poovaya-Smith 1998).

Museums and their collections also prompt wider questions about what the intersection of diaspora and material culture studies achieves. First, diaspora studies alert us to other agencies at work in the movement and constellating of things, beyond the more commonly recognized energies of corporate capital or metropolitan institutions. Attending to these neglected agencies remains a fertile area for further work. Second, material culture studies pose a challenge to how we conceive diaspora, asking to what degree diaspora studies can and should extend beyond a focus on human populations and movements. It is at least arguable, in my view, that a more-than-human purview is an important resource against the reduction of diaspora to a 'descriptive tool' applied in the fixing and minoritization of identifiable communities (Kalra et al. 2005: 3).

Instead diaspora is rendered as a field in which movements and settlements of people, things, ideas, feelings and so forth (dis)connect in politically charged ways (Crang et al. 2003). Third, and finally, one could cast the substantive preoccupations of material culture studies as a welcome 'grounding' of diaspora studies, an antidote to diaspora becoming a free-floating cultural-political sensibility. But crucially, through the emphasis in material culture studies upon how things mediate, circulate and enact culture in motion, and have done for millennia, this is a grounding that complicates the ground itself, refusing simply to locate diasporic processes, but instead suggesting the exploration of the complicated material geographies of locations themselves.

Further reading

Law, L. (2001) 'Home cooking: Filipino women and geographies of the senses in Hong Kong', *Cultural Geographies*, 8(3): 264–83.

Ley, D. (1995) 'Between Europe and Asia: the case of the missing sequoias', *Ecumene*, 2(2): 185–210.

Mankekar, P. (2005 [2002]) 'India shopping: Indian grocery stores and transnational configurations of belonging', in J. L. Watson and M. L. Caldwell (eds), *The Cultural Politics of Food and Eating: A Reader*, Oxford: Blackwell, pp. 197–214.

Parker, D. (2000) 'The Chinese takeaway and the diasporic habitus: space, time and power geometries', in B. Hesse (ed.), *Un/settled Multiculturalisms: Diasporas, Entanglements, Transruptions*, London: Zed Books, pp. 73–95.

Tolia-Kelly, D. (2004) 'Locating processes of identification: studying the precipitates of re-memory through artefacts in the British Asian home', *Transactions of the Institute of British Geographers*, New Series, 29(3): 314–29.

25 | Diasporas, literature and literary studies

Ananya Jahanara Kabir

> I have crossed an ocean
> I have lost my tongue
> And from the old root
> A new one's sprung.
>
> Grace Nichols, 'Epilogue', *The Fat Black Woman's Poems*

The phenomenon of diaspora gives rise to population displacements and cultural disorientations that, in turn, catalyse creative expression as the means to grapple with, evaluate and transcend diaspora's material consequences. As Hanif Kureishi, British Asian author, said while reading from his novels at Cambridge, UK, in 2000, 'the only way I could make sense of my confused world was to write'. The epigraph above, by Nichols, a British poet of Guyanese origin, succinctly and memorably presents these losses and gains of diaspora in terms of 'tongues', old and new (2003: 64). While drawing on the colloquial metonymy of 'tongue' and 'language', the mention of 'root' returns to that commonplace idiomatic substitution a powerful sense of the bodily, the fleshly. The balance sheet of diaspora, this little poem seems to suggest, is inscribed on the very body of the diasporic subject.

This body is seen as inhabiting several times and spaces simultaneously: does it belong to the Guyanese poet who has crossed the Atlantic in an aeroplane to make a new life in Britain, or is it the body of her ancestor, who had been uprooted from Africa and forced to cross the Atlantic in a ship to work in the plantations of the New World? The pun on root/route, which in turn draws attention to the poem as oral artefact, insists on its inhabitation by the memory of the 'Middle Passage', or the crossing made by thousands of Africans in their passage from freedom to slavery during the height of European expansionism and empire. The organic connectedness of 'old' and 'new' tongues – not one of mere grafting, but a springing forth – complicates temporality further. Linear time is here first split, then braided into a genealogy that brings together the movement of peoples and the formulation of personal histories.

Nichols's 'Epilogue' provides us with a useful starting point for this essay. It foregrounds the major topics that are implicated within a consideration of how diaspora impacts on literature and the study of literature: the relationship between cultural loss effected through the diasporic displacement of peoples and subsequent cultural production, particularly as seen in the realm of creative writing; the interpenetration of literary with other forms of cultural production (here, oral forms of poetic and lyric expression) that diaspora makes visible and urgent; the multiplicity and tenacity of diasporic experiences, including the layering of colonial and post-colonial diasporic movements of people; and the ways in which the experience of the traumas induced by diaspora are remembered and memorialized in literature. This overview of the ways in which diaspora and literature intersect will also engage with modes of analysing diasporic forms of creative expression that have arisen largely within the academic domains of post-colonial literary studies and cultural studies; under scrutiny, too, will be the fact that these models of studying diasporic cultural production have been largely formulated by scholars who are themselves the products of various diasporas.

Diaspora, trauma and literature

Even in cases where historical circumstances of coercion, force or violence have become relatively uncontested in the public sphere (such as the facts surrounding slavery and indentured labour), diaspora consistently opens up spaces for individual reflection on the divergence between official histories and private traumas, including traumas that have been transmitted through generations. For the creative intellectual, both the moment of departure and the moment of arrival have immense emotional significance and commemorative potential as nodes when histories of individuals and families intersect with larger historical processes. The diasporic subject, conscious always of a slippage between origin, belonging and location, seems best placed to respond to the questions that have vivified modern literature: Who am I, and what has formed me? Hence the richness and variety of creative responses to diasporic existences and histories particularly in two genres of literature that have evolved in modernity: the novel and the lyric poem. V. S. Naipaul, Derek Walcott, Lorna Goodison, Wilson Harris, Salman Rushdie, Hanif Kureishi, Michael Ondaatje, Amitav Ghosh, Jhumpa Lahiri: any roll-call of novelists and poets who speak from diasporic subject positions and explore the psychic terrain of diaspora will include both literary giants and emergent voices whose names bear international currency.

This international prominence of authors writing from and on diaspora is in part because of the optimal combination of cultural prestige and commercial capital that the publishing industry has garnered worldwide through the twentieth and twenty-first centuries. Yet this explication cannot be the whole story: rather, it is the deep sense of 'unhomeliness' (Bhabha 1994) precipitated by diaspora and crystallized in literary reflections on it which has made these latter resonate with the endemic alienation and fragmentation of subjectivity precipitated by, and understood as, modernity. There is, nevertheless, an uneasy tension here between universalism and particularity. Is the diasporic literary text, in all senses of the term, emblematic of the general malaise of modernity?

Should we read it as evidence of a response to specific historical conditions and events that have formed the diasporic subject? A third option: is the diasporic literary text written from a particularist position, but typically read to yield a universalist message? When V. S. Naipaul writes of an Indo-Trinidadian family in *A House for Mr Biswas* (1961), is he writing a petty-bourgeois family drama in the European realist tradition, which just happens to be set in the Caribbean, or is he giving expression to the trauma of forced migration that has created the Trinidadian of Indian origin – Mr Naipaul as much as Mr Biswas?

As counter-intuitive as it may seem, literary scholarship on as high profile a 'diasporic author' as Naipaul has, until very recently, focused on matters of his – admittedly very fine – literary style, rather than his relationship to the 'old' Indian diaspora caused by indentured labour: the migration of people from the Indian heartlands to work on plantations across the British Empire, in the Caribbean, Mauritius and Fiji, which urgently required an infusion of human capital after the abolition of slavery (Torabully and Carter 2002; Mishra 2007). This odd lacuna may be attributed to the fact that Naipaul wrote about migrancy before migrancy became fashionable, as it were; during the 1960s and the 1970s, the study of literature was largely focused on relationships between form and content, between style and structure. The reception of Guyanese author Wilson Harris, who uses pre-Columbian tradition to refashion post-diasporic Caribbean subjectivity, is, likewise, centred on the idea of the author as 'genius' (and, latterly, 'post-colonial' genius) rather than the author as voicing a particularist diasporic consciousness (*pace* Durrant 2004). And while Derek Walcott is recognized as the most magisterial lyric articulator of the division of the self caused by the slavery-dependent plantation economies of the Caribbean that still traumatizes its inheritors (cf. Thieme 1999), critical readings of his poetry have not yielded a broad theoretical model for the analysis of diasporic literary and cultural production.

Diaspora as the generator of cultural 'newness'

It would be inaccurate to state that the work of Caribbean authors such as Walcott and Harris has not been taken up in theoretical considerations of the relationship between diaspora and literary production. Their work has fruitfully intersected with that of eminent Caribbean theorists, Antonio Benitez-Rojo (1996) and Édouard Glissant (1997), writing from hispanophone and francophone scholarly traditions respectively. They have used the Caribbean Sea to conceptualize forms of historical and social commingling between differently displaced and transplanted population groups. Through terms such as 'supersyncretism' and 'creolization', they have bestowed a utopian dimension on debilitating and traumatizing phenomena, by pointing instead to the infinite possibilities of new and unexpected forms of cultural production that the African diaspora to the New World, in conjunction with European cultural forms also carried thence, made possible. These models of understanding diasporic cultural production, which take important cues particularly from Afro-Caribbean music and dance, were disseminated across the anglophone world through the theorizations of Stuart Hall (1990) and Paul Gilroy (1993a). Yet the usefulness of 'creolization' as a general model for the study of diasporic cultural production was restricted by the necessity, in all these scholars, to anchor analysis to the trauma of the Middle Passage, as expressed in Gilroy's powerful formulation, the 'black Atlantic'.

The model that did emerge as the standard one for examining diaspora was that formulated by theorist Homi Bhabha, himself a product of a new Indian diaspora – the post-colonial movement of intellectuals from India to the West – and given a fillip by its partnership with the writing of Salman Rushdie, another product of that diasporic wave (Assayag and Benei 2003). Bhabha's theory of 'hybridity', the product of the 'interstice' or the 'third space' that exists between restrictive binaries, including that of 'homeland' and 'diasporic location', was formulated within his seminal collection of essays *The Location of Culture* (1994) with overt reference to writers and scenarios of diaspora. Its most productive linkage, however, was Bhabha's citation of the questions Rushdie poses early on in his controversial novel *The Satanic Verses* (1988: 8): 'How does newness enter the world? Of what fusions, translations, conjoinings, is it made? How does it survive, extreme and dangerous as it is? [...] Is birth always a fall?'

Explicitly drawing on Rushdie's celebration of the danger and exhilaration of 'newness', Bhabha's espousal of 'hybridity' was not restricted to a discussion of diasporic subjectivities; like Rushdie's novel, however, it did privilege 'in-between-ness' as an ideal position from which to posit a liberating and powerful destabilization of binaries. Themselves embodying the fuzzy boundary between migrancy and diaspora, their view of hybridity and newness encompassed all manner of subject positions interstitially placed between cultures and allegiances. The person in diaspora, the migrant, the refugee, the intellectual in exile – all were collapsed under the sign of 'hybridity', which rapidly became the most influential model for considering the productive capacity of diasporic existence, including that which manifested itself in literature.

Thus, while the Afro-Caribbean specificity of 'creolization' held it back from becoming a dominant literary and cultural studies model for studying diasporas, the nexus between Bhabha's theory of 'hybridity' and Rushdie's dramatization of 'newness' had, thanks to its celebratory anti-essentialism, the ability to appeal across the board to the examination of diverse diasporic situations. Bhabha's belief in the liberating and productive potential of the in-between position came at a time when new waves of economic migration caused by globalization fused with emergent articulations of cultural and social dissatisfaction by younger generations of diasporic communities in the developed world. The consequent contestations around the concepts and practices of multiculturalism, pluralism and liberalism in Western public spheres thus sat in uneasy tension with the academy's eager espousal of 'hybridity': an eagerness that either reflected naive optimism or was symptomatic of its wilful blindness to social realities.

The euphoric reception and understanding of hybridity as the exemplary model for the study of diasporic literary and cultural production (the theme has been extended to the consideration of films, art and music alongside literature; see, for instance, Sharma et al. 1996) has been balanced by scholarly scepticism towards the easy appeal of 'hybridity' as a heuristic paradigm. Nevertheless, 'hybridity' as a tool to unpack a range of minoritarian subjectivities, including the diasporic, is here to stay. The concept, and the attendant emphasis on its potential to destabilize national and cultural hegemonies through the generation of newness, has become a cornerstone of Post-Colonial Studies (McLeod 2000). Because of Bhabha's own disciplinary location within a department of English literature, its impact on the latter has been immense and, in turn, it has made the study of diasporic literary production a vital aspect of literary scholarship. Tropes related to diasporic preoccupations and foregrounded by the focus on hybridity have become standard axes of scholarly examination and scrutiny: the idea and location of home; the relationship between home and homeland; the post-colonial, multicultural city as the space where the diasporic subject can remake the self and add further to the mosaic of its urban texture.

Looking ahead

Today, technology, the Internet and continued movements of people across political boundaries, whether it be out of seeming choice, economic necessity or political persecution, have both made the world smaller and culture more particularist. When a Cuban rapper with an Indian-sounding name now resident in Barcelona collaborates with a Spanish rock group to produce a song that starts unmistakably with sounds of the tabla (Kumar 2009) it is difficult to know whether to classify this as the 'creolization' of the Caribbean theorists, the 'hybridity' of Bhabha, or something else altogether. On the one hand, Bhabha himself has tried to regain a toehold for cultural particularism by musing on the possibilities of a 'vernacular cosmopolitanism' that, appearing unexpectedly in metropolitan sites, has the 'uncanny' capacity to 'domesticate' the universal (Bhabha 1996). On the other, studies of the 'brown Atlantic' and 'Southernization' processes in the Indian Ocean (Shaffer 2002 [1994]) muddy the oceanic waters with new ways of thinking about sea routes and diasporic movements (Niranjana 2006).

These new approaches may well bring together the Atlantic, Indian and possibly even the Pacific Oceans in a fruitful reconsideration of the productive and traumatic capacities of diaspora: the Ibis trilogy by Amitav Ghosh, of which the first part has been published as *The Sea of Poppies* (2008), traces precisely such a movement through the story of a slave ship that is redeployed to transport

Indian indentured labour to Mauritius; subsequent parts promise to take us farther afield to China. In the meanwhile, that the elegiac strand present in literary studies of diasporic cultural production remains visible owes a debt above all to the work of the late Edward Said, whose extensive writings on the Palestinian diaspora, be they journalistic, academic or autobiographical, together with his towering stature as a cultural critic, have not let us forget the human cost of displacement (Said 1998). This awareness, together with a necessary celebration of human resilience and creativity through traumatic memories and inheritances, is, arguably, the most valuable contribution diaspora has made to literature and literary studies.

Further reading

Benitez-Rojo, A. (1996) *The Repeating Island: The Caribbean and the Postmodern Perspective*, 2nd edn, Durham, NC: Duke University Press.

Bhabha, H. (1994) *The Location of Culture*, London and New York: Routledge.

Gilroy, P. (1993a) *The Black Atlantic: Modernity and Double Consciousness*, Cambridge, MA/London: Harvard University Press/Verso.

Hall, S. (1990) 'Cultural identity and diaspora', in J. Rutherford (ed.), *Identity: Community, Culture, Difference*, London: Lawrence and Wishart, pp. 222–37.

Said, E. (1998) *Where Do the Birds Fly after the Last Sky: Palestinian Lives*, New York: Columbia University Press.

26 | Diasporas and performance

Helen Gilbert and Jacqueline Lo

If diaspora is best understood as 'an interpretive frame for analysing the eco-nomic, political and cultural modalities of historically specific forms of migrancy' (Brah 1996: 16), theatrical performance offers a distinctive window on the lived experience of crossing cultures and the multiple forms of dislocation, affiliation and belonging that typically characterize this process. Theatre, in Yan Haiping's terms, 'is a humanly animated site where living community and live performance are mutually engendered and the lifeworld at large is writ small with human materiality' (2005: 226). In this dynamic space, it is possible to trace the cultural impacts of global mobility as well as the embodied practices and complex emotional lives of diasporic subjects and communities.

As an aesthetic practice, theatre focuses attention on the ways in which dias-pora is embodied, spatialized and temporalized through performance rather than simply inhering in sentiment or consciousness. As a social practice, theatre performs and activates a wide range of links with homelands and host lands, situating diaspora within specific cultural, political, geographical and historical contexts. These complementary levels of materiality may be discerned in the thematic concerns, linguistic cadences, representational styles, kinetic scores and scenographic choices of given performances, ranging, for example, from narratives of first-generation migration struggles in realist dramas to anti-racist agit-prop theatre, to postmodern multimedia works. Diasporic connections may also be evident in remnant or reinvented aesthetic forms (for instance, the Kathak-influenced work of high-profile British Asian dancer/choreographer Akram Khan) and in the structures of production and reception that embed particular cultural ventures in specific communities. One company that has harnessed this community-based mode of diasporic performance is the Los Angeles-based East West Players, enabling it to play a pioneering role in the establishment of Asian American theatre. While some aesthetic practices are aimed specifically at cultural preservation, they are inevitably transformed in their migrations across time and space. The Notting Hill Carnival demonstrates this dynamic tension between tradition and innovation in the street theatre of black British communities in London.

Notwithstanding these examples of theatre's capacity to demonstrate the interconnectivity of diaspora, our intention here is less to analyse specific forms of expressive practice than to consider the ways in which performance, as both concept and praxis, might extend current understandings of diaspora. To this end, we focus on three areas where diaspora and performance studies can productively intersect: space, bodies and affect. Our aim is to outline some of the ways in which performance – through its capacity to hold together, in the one iteration, the physical and the material with the abstract and the affective – usefully enlarges and complicates empirically based views of living with, and in, diaspora.

Diaspora space

Avtar Brah helpfully puts forward the notion of *diaspora space* as a concept that captures the intricate connections between translocated and indigenous populations in a globalizing world. In her terms, this conceptual space is marked by 'the entanglement of genealogies of dispersion with those of "staying put"' (1996: 181) where staying put encompasses communities linked to sites of arrival as well as origin. Diaspora is thus a relational space, a zone of interaction that is inflected by memory and imagination as well as the materialities of migration. Such relationality has long been taken as a fundamental aspect of space in theatre, which encompasses complex interactions between the material site(s) of a performance and the locations it may conjure. In this respect, perform-ance brings space into being as a dynamic cultural entity that is situated and temporalized at any given moment to convey distinct but flexible meanings to an audience. These meanings, like the spaces constructed, may be multiple, ambiguous and contradictory. Michel Foucault captures the malleability of performative space when he includes theatre among his list of 'heterotopias', sites that are 'capable of juxtaposing in a single real place several [incompat-ible] spaces' (1986: 25). Understood thus, theatrical space lends itself well to the imaginative (re)mapping that tends to characterize diasporic expressions of subjectivity.

In particular, performance has become a resonant means by which to trace processes of displacement as a seminal motif of diaspora. Across disparate social groupings in translocated communities, there are abundant examples of per-formances that bring to life specific places of origin or transit and their associ-ated memories, whether through scenographic hooks, flashback techniques or evident spatial connections, to name just a few common strategies for registering the loss of place and belonging that migrancy entails. Renowned French director Ariane Mnouchkine extends the reach of such strategies to make visible the intrinsic link between forced mobility and dislocation in her epic collage of refugee and asylum seeker stories, *Le Dernier caravansérail* (2002), fashioned from verbatim interviews across three continents. As well as juxtaposing sites of the (unwilling) travellers' dispersal and arrival in various parts of the world, the seven-hour performance conveys the impossibility of emplacement for its refugee protagonists by staging all their actions, including entrances and exits, on small mobile platforms set adrift on a vast stage. This technique, whereby the characters literally never set foot in any given locale, captures in spatial terms something of the instability of refugee subjectivity.

Refugees bring the border into focus as another aspect of diasporic experience that can be analysed through performance. Sophie Nield argues that international borders function as theatricalized spaces where asylum seekers are required to represent themselves as particular (disenfranchised) subjects in order to claim the legal/juridical rights and freedoms they seek (2008: 138–9). This performative moment is re-enacted in numerous refugee plays as well as in tribunals across the Western world where asylum may be granted or withheld according to the effectiveness of self-representation. The arbitrariness of the border in determining who does/does not belong likewise animates the work of migration activists such as Guillermo Gómez-Peña, whose transgressive border performances are designed to challenge the geopolitics of transnational mobility between Mexico and the United States. Such performance operates as a locating agent by reworking, through an embodied occupation of prohibited space, the prescribed links between place, territory and national identity. Dramatized expressions of relocation and border-crossing can be similarly empowering for diasporic subjects insofar as theatrical performance allows under-represented groups to enact personal and cultural histories and to rehearse new forms of being 'in place'.

Bodies

Human embodiment is integral to the fundamental relationality of space in diaspora. As de Certeau reminds us, the visceral presence of the body 'is what indefinitely organizes a *here* in relation to an *abroad*, a "familiarity" in relation to a "foreignness"' (1984: 130). In diaspora contexts, embodiment communicates the full sensuousness of native speech and gives cultural nuances to second languages through tone, rhythm and gesture, actualizing polyphony in ways that signify multiple sites of language acquisition and practice. Specific movement and mapping patterns can likewise be expressed through choreographic choices that highlight mobility as a form of socially produced movement. Yet despite an increasing attentiveness to the everyday practices of making diaspora, the corporeal specificities of diasporic subjects often disappear from view, particularly in empirical studies of migration that are inclined to assume the material givenness of the body. Performance offers ways of thinking about agency and subjectivity within certain demographics by suggesting how specific power/knowledge mechanisms produce different kinds of diasporic bodies and how these bodies respond somatically to such forces.

The primacy of the body as the most visible and dynamic signifier in performance not only draws attention to the ways in which diasporic subjects carry markings of their particular histories of ethno-racialization, but also enables the strategic use of bodies as prime sites for political intervention and resignification. A performance framework prompts us to be attentive to strategies of embodied self-representation – including mimicry, passing, black/yellow-facing, parody, drag and intentional hybridity – employed within and beyond the theatre to exercise diasporic subjectivity. With *Chinese Take Away* (1997), Australian artist Anna Yen demonstrates hybridity in process in a monodrama that harnesses different languages and aesthetic forms to transmit the experiences of three generations of women in her family. Offsetting the losses of transnational migration is Yen's recuperation of agency through the evocation of transgressive female figures in Chinese history – the warrior woman and the marriage resistors. The performance opens with Yen as warrior woman furiously striking at invisible enemies, an image that undermines Western stereotypes of the Asian woman as submissive. The physical and mental discipline necessary to perform these dangerous martial arts movements counters the disciplinary techniques (both Western and Chinese) that produce normative gender practices. Multiple histories are inscribed on and through the solo performer to effect an embodied hybridity that is both a locus of power/knowledge and a site for the articulation of difference and resistance. Yen's capacity to morph between different identities frustrates the spectator's impulse to fetishize the body onstage and points to ways by which racialized diasporic subjects can perform new iconic possibilities beyond those imposed by the dominant culture.

The concept of performativity helps to theorize an embodied agency that remains grounded in the social and material. As Judith Butler explains, performativity turns on 'a process of iterability, a regularized and constrained repetition of norms' that 'is not performed *by* a subject' but rather 'enables a subject and constitutes [its] temporal condition' (1993: 95). In other words, performative acts repeat and recite, thereby calling into being that which is being acted out. Among diaspora subjects, performativity encompasses the repetition of stylized bodily acts that gives substance to notions of a bio-racialized identity, thereby suggesting that identity is not genetically determined but rather socially activated. This is not to say that performances of race are entirely voluntary: Butler specifies that bodily acts are determined by the disciplinary regimes in which the subject is located and that their iterability is what produces specific identities as a taken-for-granted materiality (ibid.: 35). Performativity thus offers an effective theoretical challenge to concepts of racial purity and cultural authenticity and undermines notions of diaspora as the contaminated parts of either/both homeland and host-land cultures. Repetition in theatricalized performance, with all its attendant possibilities of appropriation and hybridization, can offer a consciously crafted iterability to counter the constraining agendas of aggressive nationalism.

Affect

While highlighting the body's responsiveness to its environment, performance also gives access to the complex register of emotions shaping the ways in which individuals and communities make sense of themselves and their place in the world. Emotionally dense experiences such as a longing for homelands or the trauma of forced migration are readily communicated in theatre as embodied dimensions of translocation. In this respect, theatre activates diaspora space not only as a site of polycultural exchange but also as a zone of heightened affect where, in David Chariandy's (2006) terms, 'irrepressible desires, imagined pasts, [and] projected futures' can be expressed.

China (2007), by third-generation Chinese-Australian artist William Yang, demonstrates the complexities of affect in a deceptively simple performance that combines Yang's own narration with digital still and video images. The show enacts a journey through emotional landscapes of intimacy, recognition and alienation evoking the diasporic subject's uneasy association with a 'homeland' he is visiting as an outsider. Chineseness, which Yang says he experienced as 'a curse' when growing up in Australia, proves difficult to define between moments of affinity or 'feeling yellow' – despite his lack of access to a language he does not share – and moments of dis-identification when he is acutely aware of his difference within the communities he visits. Such moments shift the claims of identification away from Chineseness as a stable identity to a relational process of *becoming* Chinese. By staging the contradictions and anxieties attached to Yang's homing desire (his desire to find belonging in diaspora space), *China* demonstrates that ethnicity is not necessarily innate but responsive to context and partly determined by praxis. In this sense, belonging can be understood as socially constituted between people who recognize, in each other, a need to connect in spite of difference.

The rich emotional tapestries characteristic of diasporic theatre are part of its efficaciousness as an artistic practice that can speak across cultures and generations. Affect is fundamental to what Jill Dolan has termed 'utopian performatives', those 'small but profound moments in which performance calls the attention of the audience in a way that lifts everyone slightly above the present, into a hopeful feeling of what the world might be like if every moment of our lives were as emotionally voluminous, generous, aesthetically striking, and intersubjectively intense' (2005: 5). In Dolan's formulation, utopia is processual, an index to the possible rather than a vision of what should be. The utopian performative is not 'a program for social action because it's most effective as a *feeling*' (ibid.: 19), but it does have a politics in so far as it rallies spectators to *hope* for the possibility of improving social relations (ibid.: 14).

Understood as a critical frame as well as an artistic form, performance reveals ways in which diasporic subjects insert themselves into social relations and cultural practices. Thinking about diaspora through performance and the different kinds of communities thereby engendered helps us to disaggregate the various global diasporas and to be aware of their cultural and geographical specificities. In this sense, diasporas are neither discrete nor preformed but function as historically and politically produced formations that are emplaced, embodied, interactive and performative.

Further reading

Clifford, J. (1994) 'Diasporas', *Cultural Anthropology*, 9(3): 302–38.

Gilbert, H. and J. Lo (2007) *Performance and Cosmopolitics: Cross Cultural Transactions in Australasia*, London: Palgrave Macmillan.

Taylor, D. (2003) *The Archive and the Repertoire: Performing Cultural Memory in the Americas*, Durham, NC, and London: Duke University Press.

Um, H. (ed.) (2005) *Diasporas and Interculturalism in Asian Performing Arts*, Oxford: Routledge.

27 | Diasporas, film and cinema

Daniela Berghahn

Since the 1990s film studies has witnessed a surge of publications on diasporic cinema, film and media cultures. These studies are based on the premise that the collective experience of displacement and dispersion inherent in the concept of diaspora is the most important creative impetus behind a variety of cinemas (e.g. Martin 1995; Naficy 2001; Desai 2004; Marchetti 2006; Berghahn and Sternberg 2010). In addition, there are studies exploring the contribution of diasporic film-makers to particular national cinemas, notably Maghrebi French (Tarr 2005), and contemporary black and Asian British film-makers (Mercer 1988; Pines 1991; Korte and Sternberg 2004).

The growing attention that has recently been paid to the work of directors with a migratory background goes hand in hand with a more general shift from national to transnational film studies. In the era of globalization, hitherto prevalent critical approaches probing the relationship between the cinemas of particular nation-states and national identity no longer correspond with the reality of film production and circulation. The majority of films nowadays are multinational co-productions, involve a transnationally mobile crew, and circulate transnationally or globally. According to Andrew Higson (2000), a transnational film is simply a film whose national and cultural provenance is no longer discernible because its creation is shaped by the confluence of many different cultural identities. Its typically bland aesthetics and lack of cultural specificity are programmatic since a transnational film is intended to be of universal appeal.

In response to these shifting mediascapes (Appadurai 1996), the critical paradigm of 'national cinema' is becoming rapidly superseded by transnational approaches which conceive of 'the cycle of film production, dissemination and reception as a dynamic process that transcends national borders and reflects the mobility of human existence in the global age' (Iordanova 2007: 508; cf. Ezra and Rowden 2006). It needs to be stressed, however, that diasporic and transnational cinema are not one and the same. While both transcend the boundaries of the nation-state, they do so in different ways. Arguably, transnational cinema is part and parcel of the McDonaldization of culture, the product of cultural imperialism, 'Hollywoodization' and various other homogenizing forces of hegemonic Western cultures. Diasporic cinema, by contrast, resists the homogenizing forces of globalization and is centrally concerned with issues of identity and identity politics, making the experience of ethnic minorities and other marginalized groups its central concern. The standardized variety of transnational cinema emulates the universal appeal of Hollywood and is conceived at supra-state level by powerful media magnates of global media corporations. By contrast, the creative origin of migrant and diasporic cinema is located at sub-state level, inasmuch as diasporic subjects are often excluded from the social fabric of the host society, yet at the same time are no longer fully partaking in the customs and traditions of their or their parents' country of origin (Elsaesser 1999: 118). Diasporic cinema is more specific in its address. It targets primarily audiences in the film-makers' 'home' and 'host' countries and the far-flung diasporic networks to which the film-makers belong. But it also enjoys a considerable following among cosmopolitan cinephiles with an interest in world cinema and 'exotic' film cultures.

Even though diasporic cinema has only relatively recently attracted scholarly attention, partly in response to the boom in migration, diaspora and post-colonial studies, it is actually almost as old as cinema itself – only previously different scholarly perspectives and terminologies have prevailed. For example, the cinemas of the Jewish diaspora, identified by Cohen (2008), Safran (1991) and other leading diaspora scholars as the 'ideal' or 'prototypical' diaspora, have been considered in terms of their linguistic and ethnic specificities and in terms of the artistic trajectories of outstanding creative individuals. Yiddish cinema, which 'flourished in eastern and central Europe throughout the silent era and into the 1930s' as well as among the 'Jewish diaspora in the United States, Mexico, Argentina, and elsewhere in the New World' (Hendrowski and Hendrowski 1997: 174), has been defined first and foremost by the use of the Yiddish language and its roots in Jewish theatre and popular culture. Yet Hoberman refers to it as an example of a 'national cinema without a nation-state' (1991: 5), which suggests a diasporic perspective.

An entirely different type of diasporic film culture is associated with Jewish exile and émigré directors, actors and actresses, scriptwriters and producers, many of whom fled Germany when the National Socialists came to power in 1933, seeking refuge in Paris, London and eventually Hollywood. Even though these dispersed film professionals were part of the Jewish diaspora, they are usually not conceptualized in those terms by film historians – for three reasons: first, Jewish exiled film-makers are generally referred to as 'European émigrés', a term that obliterates their Jewish ethnicity; second, most studies on European émigrés are devoted to tracing the artistic trajectories of outstanding *auteurs* and other creative *individuals* and the contribution they made to Hollywood cinema. In contrast with the terms 'exile' and 'émigré' that can refer to collectives as well as individuals, the term 'diaspora' inevitably implies a group affiliation. Third, according to Thomas Elsaesser, 'foreigners in Hollywood' had the choice either to '[disavow] their own homeland and heritage' or to 'assimilate and become 110 per cent American or be European and exotic, but also 110 per cent!' (Elsaesser 2005: 99). The latter strategy was more likely to be pursued by actors and actresses, who were often cast on account of their exotic allure and foreign accents (see Phillips and Vincendeau 2006). Certainly, the majority of European émigré directors who played important roles in the studio system downplayed their ethnicity and cultural origins. In order to succeed, they promoted core American values, while at the same time engaging in 'various performative strategies of camouflage in their films and self-fashioning in their lives' (Naficy 2001: 8). Thus, different terminologies such as 'émigré film-makers' or 'European exiles in Hollywood' on the one hand, and 'diasporic film-makers' on the other, point towards different agendas: for most Jewish émigré film-makers in Hollywood cultural assimilation was the key strategy of artistic survival; for contemporary diasporic film-makers – as will be illustrated below – a self-conscious engagement with difference is the preferred and expected strategy.

Over the past twenty-five years, European cinema has undergone an enormous transformation as a result of the increased visibility of film-makers with a migratory background. These film-makers, their parents or grandparents came to Europe as part of post-colonial migrations to the imperial 'mother countries' or as part of labour migration which affected virtually all northern and western European countries, irrespective of their colonial past. Others came after the end of the Cold War, when global migration, in particular from the East to the West, intensified and when other migratory flows that followed a more random logic and direction occurred. Yet time has to pass before one can establish with certainty whether these migrants will settle or embark on further, secondary migrations. In fact, many of these film-makers may not be 'diasporic' at all but merely 'transnationally mobile', going wherever the best funding and production opportunities arise.

Recent examples of cinemas associated with more established diasporas in Europe, such as Turkish German, black and Asian British and Maghrebi French cinema, have won considerable acclaim and have, occasionally, even captured mainstream audiences. Witness the international, mainstream appeal of British Asian girl-power movie *Bend It Like Beckham* (2002, dir. Gurinder Chadha), the critical success of Fatih Akin's Turkish German melodrama *Gegen die Wand/ Head-On*, the first German film in eighteen years to win the Golden Bear at the International Berlin Film Festival in 2004, or the cult following of *La Haine/ Hate* (1995, dir. Mathieu Kassovitz), which depicts a 'black-*blanc-beur*' (black-white-Arab/Maghrebian) trio of disenfranchised young men living on the urban periphery of Paris.

Inscribed in these films is the collective memory or 'postmemory' of the migratory experience, which has had a profound impact on the cultural identity and the aesthetic sensibilities of migrant and diasporic film-makers. Migrant film-makers are first-generation immigrants who have themselves experienced migration, leaving their country of birth in search of better economic conditions, a more stable socio-political environment or for any number of other reasons, and moving to the old Europe. Diasporic film-makers, by contrast, are second- or subsequent-generation settlers, born and raised in the destination country. They have no personal recollection of migration and often little familiarity with their parents' country of origin. They access their families' histories of migration and dispersal through oral history, family photos and home videos. Marianne Hirsch coined the term 'postmemory' for this process, which 'is distinguished from memory by generational distance and from history by deep personal connection' (Hirsch 1997: 22).

Yet how can we accommodate the many films about the experience of migration and diaspora made by film-makers of the hegemonic host societies that lack this deep personal investment? To bridge this apparent gap Brah's concept of 'diaspora space' provides a useful framework, since it disavows the significance of any essentialist notions of origin or of the history of displacement as prerequisites for participating in the diasporic experience:

> Diaspora space as a conceptual category is 'inhabited', not only by those who have migrated and their descendants, but equally by those who are constructed and represented as indigenous. In other words, the concept of *diaspora space* (as opposed to that of diaspora) includes the entanglement, the intertwining of genealogies of dispersion with those of 'staying put'. (1996: 209)

Those films authored by film-makers belonging to the majority culture are based on what Landsberg calls 'prosthetic memory'. Mediated through film, television and other mass media, it is a commodified type of memory which allows non-diasporic film-makers to articulate a collective memory that is not their own and, in doing so, 'to make possible alliances across racial, class and other chasms of difference' (Landsberg 2003: 156).

Migrant and diasporic cinema is characterized by a distinctive aesthetic approach, which reflects the 'double occupancy' (Elsaesser 2005), the 'double consciousness' (Gilroy 1993a) and 'diasporic optic' (Moorti 2003) of its creators. This particular 'way of seeing [...] underscores the interstice, the spaces that are and fall between the cracks of the national and the transnational as well as other social formations' (ibid.: 359). Diasporic aesthetics reflect a 'subject position that lays claim to and negotiates between multiple affiliations [...] [and that] seeks to reveal [a] desire for multiple homes through specific representational strategies' (ibid.: 359). Thus, diasporic cinema is an aesthetically hybrid cinema that juxtaposes and fuses stylistic templates, generic conventions, narrative and musical traditions, languages and performance styles from more than one (film) culture.

As a 'cinema of displacement' (Ghosh and Sarkar 1995/96), migrant and diasporic cinema is characterized by 'a heightened sense of spatial activity', a preponderance of liminal spaces and journeys of quest. The films' distinctive spatiality signals a thematic concern with identities in flux. The numerous claustrophobic interiors and a predilection for locations on the urban periphery draw attention to the social exclusion or marginalization experienced by the migrant or diasporic subjects in these films.

Being by definition a cinema that originates from marginalized collectivities that are negotiating their place in the social fabric of hegemonic host societies, migrant and diasporic cinema is centrally concerned with identity politics and the 'other'. It probes difference along the multiple coordinates of race, colour, ethnicity, nationality, gender, religion, generation, class and sexuality. It is a cinema in which spatio-temporal (e.g. the chronotope of the homeland or nostalgic home-bound journeys) and spatio-racial modalities (e.g. the black and the brown Atlantic) coalesce and converge and whose strategic agenda is the relocation of the margins to the centre, the valorization and, ultimately, 'the redemption of the marginal' (Stam 2003: 35).

Further reading

Berghahn, D. and C. Sternberg (eds) (2010) *European Cinema in Motion: Migrant and Diasporic Film in Contemporary Europe*, Basingstoke: Palgrave Macmillan.

Desai, J. (2004) *Beyond Bollywood: The Cultural Politics of South Asian Diasporic Film*, London and New York: Routledge.

Martin, M. T. (ed.) (1995) *Cinemas of the Black Diaspora: Diversity, Dependence and Oppositionality*, Detroit, MI: Wayne State University Press.

Naficy, H. (2001) *An Accented Cinema: Exilic and Diasporic Filmmaking*, Princeton, NJ, and Oxford: Princeton University Press.

Shohat, E. and R. Stam (1994) *Unthinking Eurocentrism: Multiculturalism and the Media*, London and New York: Routledge.

28 | Diasporas and media

Karim H. Karim

This essay reviews the print, broadcast and Internet-based operations of diasporic groups. The media of immigrants and ethnic minorities have been treated
for almost a century as a marginal form of communication activity within
nations. The study of diasporas during the last few decades, however, has drawn
attention to the substantial rise in the quantity and scope of ethnic media (Naficy
1993; Gillespie 1995; Hargreaves and McKinney 1997; Cunningham and Sinclair
2002; Sun 2002; Karim 2003; Browne 2005). Diasporas are using increasingly
sophisticated communications technologies to produce media that operate
within countries and across them. The relative prominence of these communication flows has come about owing to a combination of factors, including the
growing wealth of minority communities, the rising acceptance of ethnic media
among receiving societies and the increasing technological possibilities for
'narrowcasting'.

Ethnic media are no longer confined within borders of nations but have transnational audiences. The dispersed nature of settlement patterns has encouraged
immigrants to adopt cutting-edge media technologies in order to develop links
between their fellows, who are spread in several locations. In some cases, live
or same-day television programming is available from the homeland for its diasporas. People who previously lived in the same neighbourhood and have migrated
to different parts of the world are also able to reassemble in cyberspace. But
whereas the new technologies are becoming prevalent around the globe, diasporic
individuals living in developing countries have less access to them than their
Western counterparts. The increasing corporatization of what were previously
community-run ethnic media is also leading in many cases to the commercialization of their content. Nevertheless, diasporic media do provide an alternative to
the long-standing Western dominance of international media flows.

The nature of the mass media is such that their operation and often their
viability depend on drawing large readerships and audiences. Therefore, they
usually strive to serve the needs of the largest demographic groups and exclude
the cultural expressions of smaller ones. This is one of the main reasons why
migrant groups establish distinct media organs to serve their members. Park
(1922), one of the first scholars to conduct a serious study of ethnic media,
noted that they serve two primary purposes – cultural maintenance and ethnic

cohesion, as well as integration into wider society. These observations have been repeated in more recent studies (Riggins 1992; Husband 1994; and Browne 2005).

Newspapers are the oldest form of migrant media and are widely found in countries with a large diasporic presence. They are usually published in the language of the ethnic group that produces and consumes them, but some also appear in the dominant languages of the country of settlement. There are large variations in the form, quality, finances and frequency of ethnic print media. Some are well-staffed, established dailies that compete with mainstream papers; these media usually have large-scale production facilities and strong advertising revenues. At the opposite end are small publications run by dedicated individuals out of their homes – such operations have fairly irregular production cycles and tend to be transitory. They appear and disappear rapidly, to be replaced by other similarly short-lived ventures. Ethnic groups also publish directories and speciality magazines, some of which have high production values and are distributed to transnational diasporic readerships.

The usually strict regulation of broadcasting by authorities has generally made it more difficult for migrant groups to produce and distribute radio and television programming.

When ethnic broadcasters manage to obtain small time slots on the schedules of existing stations, it is often at the most inconvenient times for their potential audiences. Vernacular services of government broadcasters in Africa have allowed for some inclusion of migrant programming. Radio, television and Internet content is distributed by the publicly owned Special Broadcasting Services of Australia in some seventy languages. In the UK, Channel 4's public service remit includes the dissemination of programming which appeals to a culturally diverse society.

Community and campus stations in Canada and the USA have tended to be accommodating, but minorities are also making major inroads into commercial broadcasting. Operating within multiculturalism policies, some broadcast authorities have taken significant initiatives to ensure the presence of the cultures of minorities on the airwaves. The Canadian Radio-Television and Telecommunications Commission has provided an enabling environment for the growth of radio and television programming for minority communities. Its ethnic broadcasting policy specifies the conditions for the dissemination of commercial multilingual programming. The largest Hispanic US television network has hundreds of affiliates and is available to the vast majority of Spanish-speaking households in the United States. Niche marketers in many countries are looking upon advertising on ethnic electronic media as a way to access their growing minority populations in a time of fragmenting audiences. Dávila (2001) has conducted a critical examination of these developments. Diasporas also tune in to state-supported multilingual broadcasters with an international reach, such as the BBC World Service (Gillespie, this volume) and Germany's Radio Multikulti.

The dispersed characteristics of migrant communities have encouraged diasporic media to seek out the most efficient and cost-effective means of communication. Technologies that allow for narrowcasting to target specific audiences rather than those that provide the means for mass communications tend to be favoured. Ethnic media have frequently been at the cutting edge of technology adoption owing to the particular challenges they face in reaching their audiences. Digital broadcasting satellites are providing remarkable opportunities for diasporic communities. Ethnic broadcasters, previously having limited access to space on the electromagnetic spectrum in Western countries, are finding much greater options opening up for them through digital broadcasting satellites. For example, when France's main broadcast authority excluded Arabic stations from licensed cable networks in the 1990s, a significant number of Maghrebi immigrant families began to subscribe to digital broadcasting satellite services, which provided them with programming from North African countries (Hargreaves and Mahdjoub 1997).

Diasporic broadcasters were the early adopters of this technology, well ahead of many mass media operations. The Arab-owned and -operated Orbit TV in Rome had begun by 1994 to provide extensive programming via digital broadcasting satellites to Arab communities in Europe and the Middle East, even as mainstream networks in Europe were making plans to introduce digital broadcasting. Several Kurdish satellite television stations serve a diaspora within and without the divided homeland. This form of communication has become key to dispersed Kurdish communities which are attempting to establish links between themselves for the first time in history. Univisión and Telemundo, the two largest Spanish-language networks in the USA, have been more successful than mainstream American ones in exporting programming to Central and South America, standing as other examples of 'reverse flows' of programming to home countries. Strong South Asian diasporic subscriber bases exist for competing channels carrying material from Bollywood and other centres of production in the region. Cable and satellite television services in Western countries have realized the viability of ethnic channels and are making them an integral part of their offerings.

Internet-based media seem especially suited to the needs of diasporic communities in being able to support ongoing communication among widely separated transnational groups. They provide relatively inexpensive, decentralized, interactive and easy-to-operate technologies in contrast to broadcasting's highly regulated, linear and capital-intensive operations characteristics. In addition to extensively using online media such as email, Usenet, Listserv and the World Wide Web, diasporic groups are also publishing content on offline digital media such as CD-ROMs. Recent migrants separated from family and friends are placing notices on news groups and social networks giving particulars of individuals with whom they want to re-establish contact or to search for marriage partners.

A number of websites have established global directories of community members that include categorization under alumni of colleges, professionals and businesses. The medical necessity to find human marrow donors from one's own ethnic group for the treatment of more than sixty blood-related diseases has extended these searches into cyberspace.

Community online networks provide a small but important counterweight to the massive production and export capacities of the cultural industries of developed countries by facilitating global accessibility to Asian, Latin American and African views of the world. This becomes a way to mitigate the effects of cultural imperialism and to foster global cultural diversity. A primary motivation for migrant communities to go online seems to be survival in the face of the overwhelming output of dominant cultures and the limitations of immigrants' access to the cultural industries in their countries of settlement. Isolated members of diasporas using online media can participate to some extent in cultural production rather than merely consume media content. Information about reunions, festivals and worldwide locations of community institutions facilitates the physical gathering of diasporic individuals. Current events and new publications of materials relating to the transnational group are regularly discussed in online forums. Diasporas are increasingly turning to blogs to contribute to discussions on contemporary political and cultural issues as well as on developments in their respective communities. Social networking sites such as My Space and Facebook are also providing for diasporic community members to form cyber-groups whose members remain in constant touch.

Worldwide dispersions from home countries over several generations are seemingly reversed by bringing together disparate members of ethnic groups to interact in electronic 'chat rooms'. These include online services catering to Sindhis, a South Asian ethnic group whose members were dispersed by the partition of colonial India and by migration patterns outside the sub-continent. Cooperative arrangements between students and professionals of recent Chinese origins working in high-technology sectors in Canada, the United States and the United Kingdom have led to the emergence of online magazines that express their particular concerns. These new arrivals feel that their information needs are not met by the content of the thriving print and broadcast Chinese ethnic media, which is produced largely by older groups of immigrants from China. The restrictions of national borders therefore appear to be partially overcome in this alternative form of globalization. From the perspective of immigrant-receiving governments, the process of integrating newcomers into receiving societies has become more challenging as the recent arrivals remain in regular touch with their homelands.

A number of diasporic websites are designed to challenge misperceptions by outsiders and to mobilize external political support. Several groups also use online media to challenge hate propaganda and to carry out polemics against other websites. Some anti-government organizations have taken even more strong action with the use of electronic technology. Diasporic supporters of al-Qaeda-like groups routinely coordinate their activities through the Internet (Bunt 2000, 2009). One Tamil group electronically disabled the websites of several Sri Lankan embassies that it viewed as disseminating propaganda. The speed of simultaneous, worldwide demonstrations in March 1999 by Kurdish protesters, who reacted immediately to the capture of a guerrilla leader by Turkish forces, was the result of the Internet links maintained by that global community.

Restrictions are beginning to appear on diasporic communication flows. The ability of global communities to maintain and extend effective electronic links is being affected by the controls that governments are exerting over online networks. Additionally, as national borders are sealed more tightly in order to prevent terrorism, transnational communication is becoming increasingly difficult for diasporas. The extensive presence of the media conglomerates that are increasingly buying up diasporic print and broadcast media and the growing commercialization of online operations are also having an effect on the kinds of material that they carry. Whereas the improvements in infrastructure and software may benefit transnational groups, commercial contingencies may overwhelm community considerations in the organization of communication networks and in the production and distribution of content. Participation by members of global diasporas in communication networks is far from equal. Migrant communities living in wealthier parts of the world have considerably more access to media technologies than their counterparts in developing countries. Nevertheless, it is clear that diasporic connections have become integral to the networks of transnational communication. Even as diasporic media are piggybacking on the communications infrastructures established and maintained by states and corporations, they are also engaging in the further development of the means of global communication.

Further reading

Bailey, O. G., M. Georgiou and R. Harindranath (eds) (2007) *Transnational Lives and the Media: Re-imagining Diasporas*, Basingstoke: Palgrave Macmillan.

Brinkerhoff, J. (2009) *Digital Diasporas: Identity and Transnational Engagement*, Cambridge: Cambridge University Press.

Bunt, G. (2009) *iMuslims: Rewiring the House of Islam*, London: C. Hurst and Co.

Hirji, F. (forthcoming) *Beyond Resistance: Canadian Youth, Indian Cinema, and Identity Construction*, Vancouver: University of British Columbia Press.

Karim, K. H. (2007) 'Nation and diaspora: rethinking multiculturalism in a transnational context', *International Journal of Media and Cultural Politics*, 2(3): 267–82.

29 | Diasporas and cyberspace

Victoria Bernal

Key tropes of cyberspace have been speed, mobility, connectivity, unbounded-ness, information, access, escape from everyday reality, from the body and from identity, decontextualization and deterritorialization, all of which have been understood as kinds of freedom (Castells 2001; Haraway 1991; Bell 2006). In con-trast, members of diasporas have been deterritorialized and decontextualized, but they may experience this not so much as liberation, but rather as dislocation and displacement. Therefore, they tend to use the Internet in part to undo the effects of their mobility rather than to enhance mobility. They may seek, through their online practices, to recontextualize themselves, and in some sense even to reterritorialize themselves through cyberspace. They do so by creating or visiting online versions of 'home', through connecting to others like themselves in diaspora, and by connecting with their homeland through a transnational field of communication facilitated by (but never limited to) the Internet. Thus, for example, in the case of diasporic Trinidadians, 'the major reason for being on the Internet in the first place: [is] to make contact with Trinis, talk about Trini things and also do Trini things online' (Miller and Slater 2006: 106), while Kurds in diaspora use 'the deterritorialized space of the Internet [to] express territorial claims for Kurdistan' (Georgiou 2006: 138). And the longest-running website used by Eritreans in diaspora for exchanging news and views for many years displayed the subtitle 'Eritrea Online' on its home page, suggesting that the website served as a virtual Eritrea.

Many scholars have focused on the possibilities that cyberspace offers for escaping the body and transcending identity. People in diaspora, however, are often concerned not with escaping their identities, but, on the contrary, with how to maintain their identity in new contexts. One way of doing this is through creating websites, blogs and email lists where their identity can be publicly asserted and performed. Moreover, through the interactivity of the Internet, iden-tities can be socially constructed in dialogue, and sometimes even in conflict, with others. The social construction of identity online is particularly significant for diasporas because their everyday lived social reality may be one of being assimilated into a dominant society or being rendered culturally, ethnically and religiously invisible, or possibly stigmatized.

Scholars have highlighted the global scale of the Internet and its rendering insignificant of borders. The very concept of the 'World Wide Web' suggests we are all globally connected to each other all the time. People in diaspora seem drawn to the Web for very different reasons, however. Diasporas tend to use the Internet to undo mobility, to reterritorialize, to retain rather than to escape their identity, and to connect, not with a vast larger world without borders, but to other members of their own diaspora or their homeland (see Burrell and Anderson 2008 for a contrasting case). As I like to say about Eritreans in diaspora in relation to cyberspace: Eritreans may have entered the global village, but it is a distinctly Eritrean village.

Despite this, English is used by a surprising number of diasporas online, such as Haitians, Tamils and Eritreans. For some, it may reflect their location in English-speaking North America or the UK; for others, the language of their advanced education or a lingua franca that bridges linguistic diversity. For some groups whose languages use different writing systems, the use of English rather than a language of the homeland may reflect the computer keyboard available. The Eritrean case suggests that, as software for various other writing systems becomes available and as more people from the homeland access cyberspace, online language usage will become more diverse.

For members of diasporas, their lived reality is fragmented as they often find themselves located in a dominant social milieu that does not share their perspectives or interest in their homeland. The Internet allows diasporas to create and to access media that speak to them as a primary audience, something they may not be able to get anywhere else and certainly not as cheaply. The interactivity of the Internet may be its key feature in this regard. Users can create content, by blogging, posting comments, having a home page, creating a website, and so on. But equally significant is that users also actively construct their own media world through their routine patterns of online practices – checking or posting to particular sites regularly, reading particular blogs, or participating in particular email lists. Even the silent reader, or so-called 'lurker', is partaking of this form of interactivity because of all possible websites and activities in cyberspace they are selecting particular ones to visit.

In this regard it is interesting to contrast cyberspace with satellite television, that other important media of diasporas. The availability of satellite TV allows immigrants and diasporas to see television broadcasts from their home countries. But satellite TV has all the limits of any broadcast medium. It is highly centralized, often censored, and one size fits all. Moreover, it is often controlled by the government, by a dominant ethnic group or by an elite class, and may therefore be narrow in perspective, unrepresentative and regarded by the diaspora as an unreliable source for news and analysis.

Cyberspace allows the expression and development of diversity because almost anyone can express themselves online. It allows for experimentation and pushing the boundaries of official or acceptable views. There are no editors or censors in control. Counter-publics thus can flourish, bringing alternative perspectives to light. This aspect of cyberspace has been important for the Eritrean diaspora, for example, because there is no free press or civil society within Eritrea. Open debate and dissenting views cannot be openly articulated there, but such views can be expressed and explored online. In cyberspace, as sometimes happens offline in diaspora where distances between people may shrink in comparison to those around them who share none of their culture and history, interlocutors from very different social categories come to engage with each other. Thus, debates that occur online may have no counterpart in offline social interactions where people tend to congregate with those of similar class, age and religious and ethnic backgrounds. Diasporas' engagement with cyberspace may thus allow the bridging of some social divides that cannot easily be crossed in the home territory or elsewhere offline. Furthermore, the spaces of diaspora and cyberspace both offer possibilities for freedom of expression not available in other places. Thus, for example, 'The role of the Burundian diaspora has long been to express what was impossible to say inside the country for fear of political retribution by the regime in place' (Turner 2008b: 1161). Cyberspace as a non-physical location offers particular safety. While people may engage in conflict online, expressing anger or hatred towards those with opposing perspectives, the protagonists in such fights are often far removed from one another and can be further insulated by the anonymity of screen names or pseudonyms, and thus remain safe from the kinds of violent reprisals for which they might otherwise be at risk. The significance of cyberspace as a place where conflicts can be waged passionately but without actual violence has not been adequately recognized by scholars, who have focused to a large extent on Western users to define what cyberspace is and what cyberspace means to human society.

Diasporas have long been associated with information flows across distances and borders. Diasporas constitute a social World Wide Web of sorts, already socially connected across different territories. Diasporas may be attracted to the Internet because they are already engaged in dispersed social networks. But new information technologies do more than simply speed up or facilitate existing social networks. The characteristics of the Internet as a medium allow new possibilities for and dimensions of communication. One aspect is the immediacy of response to distant events allowed by the speed of the Internet. Far-flung members of a diaspora can respond quickly to breaking news, and they can do so as a group, coordinating their efforts, and pooling new information easily. On the Internet every receiver of information can easily be a transmitter, furthering the spread of messages. It is important to recognize that what is taking place here is not simply the circulation of information, however, but opinion formation, mobilization, organization and the building of social momentum. What may make diasporas particularly effective in using the Internet in these ways is that they are also connected to transnational networks in various ways offline. Diasporas may be exceptionally well positioned to translate between and across diverse media and to translate between online and offline communities, between the local and the international, and between communication and action. This highlights the significance of context for understanding the impact of the Internet, in terms both of the larger media world with which people engage, and the offline communities and networks that connect people.

The fact that diasporas use new information technologies tells us very little about them or about the significance of these new media in their lives. The Internet may be one kind of media or one kind of technology, but it is not a singular social phenomenon. Its very flexibility and interactivity make it different things for different people. Cyberspace may appear to operate outside of everyday time and space. To understand who is using it to communicate what to whom for what purpose, however, and to understand the meaning and context of what people post in cyberspace, requires broader contextualization. For diasporas that context includes the histories of their homelands, the reasons for their displacement or migration, and the new social locations in which they find themselves.

The Internet may be changing the experience of diaspora by offering a third space – neither here nor there – which may be particularly useful for diasporas who feel themselves in two or more places at once or live with a sense of dislocation. This third space also offers new opportunities for collaboration and co-production between diasporas and compatriots in the home country. Journalism appears to be a particular forefront in this respect as indicated by the examples of Tamil.net, where reporters in the field contribute news stories that are then translated in diaspora and posted online, and Cameroon's online newspaper, which draws on the Cameroonian diaspora for technological expertise and dissemination (Ndangam 2008).

While many scholars have focused on the connectivity offered by cyberspace, far fewer have considered how cyberspace simultaneously fosters fragmentation. To conceptualize the World Wide Web as open lines of global connection is an idealization or a potential that does not reflect how people engage with the technology in practice. We are never all connected to each other. In fact, the Internet is quite segmented because people connect selectively. Furthermore, while some scholars imagine an information highway characterized by open access and transparency, what happens in cyberspace is to a large degree hidden. For example, while Tamil.net reportedly got 3 million hits a month, and many Tamils in diaspora checked it daily, I never even knew it existed until I read Whitaker's (2004) article. The global scale of the Internet and the sameness of the technology people use to access it obscure how varied and fragmented our media worlds in cyberspace are. This relates to fundamental questions about the nature of globalization and technological progress: are they connecting us or dividing us, are they homogenizing or contributing to diversity, are they facilitating democratization or reinforcing hierarchies and exclusions? There are, in fact, movements in both directions, there are sites of struggle, and forms of resistance and creativity. The ways various people in diaspora have adopted the Internet for their own needs and purposes, though the technologies were not developed with them in mind, is one example of such processes.

Further reading

Bernal, V. (2005) 'Eritrea on-line: diaspora, cyberspace, and the public sphere', *American Ethnologist*, 32(4): 661–76.

Dahan, M. and G. Sheffer (2001) 'Ethnic groups and distance shrinking communication technologies', *Nationalism and Ethnic Politics*, 7(1): 85–107.

Georgiou, M. (2006) 'Diasporic communities online', in K. Sarkakis and D. Thussu (eds), *Ideologies of the Internet*, Cresskill, NJ: Hampton Press, pp. 131–46.

Panagakos, A. and H. Horst (2006) 'Return to Cyberia: technology and the social worlds of transnational migrants', *Global Networks*, 6(2): 109–24.

Whitaker, M. (2004) 'Tamilnet.com: some reflections on popular anthropology, nationalism, and the Internet', *Anthropological Quarterly*, 77(3): 469–98.

PART THREE

Empirical and metaphorical diasporas

3 Cross-diasporic contact zones at the BBC's Bush House, 1940 (© British Broadcasting Authority)

Voice, the monthly radio magazine programme, broadcast modern poetry to English-speaking India in the Eastern Service of the BBC. From left to right seated: Venu Chitale, a member of the BBC Indian Section; M. J. Tambimuttu, a Tamil from Ceylon, editor of *Poetry* (London); T. S. Eliot, British poet; Una Marson, BBC West Indian Programme Organizer; Mulk Raj Anand, Indian novelist; Christopher Pemberton, a member of the BBC staff; Narayana Menon, Indian writer. From left to right standing: George Orwell, author and producer of *Voice*; Nancy Parratt, secretary to George Orwell, William Empson, British poet and critic.

30 | South/North relations in the Americas

Alex Stepick, Carol Dutton Stepick and
Patricia Vanderkooy

More people from Latin America and the Caribbean have settled in the United States and Canada than from any other region of the world. In 2007, 47.5 per cent of US foreign-born residents reported Hispanic or Latino origins. Every single nation of Latin America and the Caribbean can be described as having a significant diaspora in North America. Mexican-born migrants are by far the largest migrant group, accounting for 30.8 per cent of all foreign-born residents of the USA in 2007. Roughly 10 per cent of Mexico's population of about 107 million now lives in the USA. Canada has proportionately more migrants from the Caribbean, particularly the English-speaking islands. Because the overall population of Canada is only one tenth that of the USA and its migrant population is even smaller, this essay focuses primarily on migrants in the USA.

Popular discourse explains these diasporas as a result of uneven development in which people from the developing South seek better economic opportunities in the more developed North. While there is some truth in this, it ignores how the USA, rather than individuals in the various southern countries, initiated or expanded many of these diasporas. This essay focuses on the role of the economically more powerful receiving countries in creating both the geographic dispersion from the South to the North in the Americas, and the consciousness of diaspora among these migrants. It specifically examines the role of foreign policy, use of migrant labour, and the racialized categories and policies applied to migrants along with the migrants' agency in responding to discrimination.

The particular mix of politics and economics in the USA played a critical role in making the Mexican diaspora. In the middle of the nineteenth century, the USA seized more than half of the nation of Mexico, annexing what later became the states of Texas, New Mexico, Arizona and Colorado. The Mexicans then living in those areas thus formed part of an involuntary diaspora without having migrated. They were also subjected to racialized discrimination, policies and practices, experiences shared by a majority of migrants to the USA from Latin America and the Caribbean.

In the twentieth century, US desires for low-wage labour, particularly in agriculture, led US firms to recruit and transport Mexican workers. Formal recruitment ended in the 1960s, but by then Mexicans were transporting themselves to satisfy US employers' needs. More recently, the evolution of the US economy from manufacturing to services and commerce has created a split labour market, one with a powerful demand for both high- and low-skilled workers. In major urban areas and increasingly throughout the USA, low-skilled jobs are filled by the diasporas from the South, primarily Mexico, but also the rest of Latin America and the Caribbean.

Beginning in the 1960s, US anti-communist policies also created diasporic refugee flows from the South, first from Cuba and then Central America. While US policies only indirectly produced Cuba's 1959 revolution, which catapulted Fidel Castro to power, the US response did directly contribute to the creation of a Cuban diaspora. After the failure of the 1961 US-sponsored Bay of Pigs invasion which attempted to dislodge Castro, the USA encouraged Cubans to flee their homeland by offering early Cuban refugees an extraordinary bundle of benefits that included automatic legal immigration status (Stepick and Grenier 1993).

During the late 1970s and 1980s, Central American struggles against the US-supported military regimes and dictators, particularly in Guatemala, El Salvador and Nicaragua, led to thousands of refugees fleeing their homelands, generally passing through Mexico to subsequently settle in the USA. Treating them differently from Cubans, the USA generally denied legal status while attempting to return them to their homelands. Yet they had significant civil society support, especially in the religiously based sanctuary movement, and were able to establish communities in the USA in spite of government efforts to deport them to their homelands (Hondagneu-Sotelo 2008).

Canada's geopolitics and associated role in diaspora creation contrast with those of the USA. The USA, for example, supported the 1973 military coup that toppled democratically elected, but leftist, Chilean president Salvador Allende. Subsequently, the USA did not welcome those fleeing persecution in Chile, but Canada did, along with Mexico and some other South American nations. Accordingly, the Latino diasporas in Canada are more likely to be politically left-leaning in contrast to the primarily more apolitical working-class nature of the Latino diasporas in the USA.

The forces that form a diaspora also affect the diaspora's relationship to those remaining in the homeland. Working-class diasporas in the USA, such as those from Mexico, Central America and much of the Caribbean, contribute tremendous resources to the economies of their home nations, primarily through remittances sent back to relatives. Typically arriving in small monthly transfers of $100 and $200, remittances to Latin America and the Caribbean almost equal the US foreign aid budget for the entire world. For the homeland nations of most current large diasporas, remittances are the greatest source of foreign exchange and generally exceed lending by multilateral development agencies and foreign direct investment combined (Orozco 2009).

Diasporic remittances have become such a significant form of cash assistance that home-country governments have reconsidered their relationship to their diasporas. In the past many nations considered those who left as unpatriotic or even traitors, and correspondingly created barriers to retaining ties with the homeland. As the diaspora's economic contribution has become increasingly important, home-country governments have worked to reincorporate the diaspora. Mexico has created a special programme for rural development that matches diaspora contributions for particular projects such as building a school. The Haitian government of former president Jean-Bertrand Aristide created a cabinet-level ministry for the diaspora. Numerous countries in Latin America and the Caribbean now invite members of their diasporas to vote in national elections, and presidential candidates from these countries often visit diaspora communities in the USA during election campaigns. One president of the Dominican Republic, Leonel Fernández, even spent a considerable part of his youth in New York City, the site of the Dominican Republic's largest diaspora community.

As migrant populations grow and gain citizenship their political influence may also grow. The US Jewish Israeli lobby is the prime example that other diasporas seek to emulate. Within the Americas, the Cuban diaspora in the USA has been the most politically successful. It convinced the US government to continue Cold War anti-communist polices against Castro's Cuba, and influenced policies against other leftist movements in Latin America and the Caribbean for more than twenty years after the fall of the Soviet Union.

The USA has always raised barriers to entry, particularly to those from less wealthy nations and especially to those from modest backgrounds in less wealthy nations. In the wake of the terrorist attacks on New York City on 11 September 2001, those barriers have become even higher. An ironic consequence of reinforcing the border between Mexico and the USA has been that more Mexicans have remained in the USA rather than engaging in circular migration. They still have available to them all the modern electronic communication means that have made diaspora relationships so much more intense than they were 100 years ago. But it has become much more difficult for individuals to cross the border to maintain the face-to-face social relationships that concretely embody the diaspora. Villages in some parts of Mexico have become sparsely populated and have difficulty remaining 'traditional', with too few residents to fill local political and ritual roles. In some cases this has increased tensions between those who are dispersed and those who have remained in the ancestral village (Stephen 2007).

Migrants from Latin America and the Caribbean to the USA are confronted with an ethnic and racial classification system of pan-ethnic categories, such as black and Latino or Hispanic, which most find alien, but which still affects how they self-label and the associated sense of being part of a diaspora. Migrants from the English-speaking Caribbean, for example, often comment, 'I did not know that I was black until I came to the USA.' They are being only slightly disingenuous. People in the Caribbean are certainly aware of colour, which is often associated with class. Disregarding the gradual gradations of colour and intermediary categories such as mixed or mulatto, the USA reduces individuals with any visible African heritage into a single group, black. Given the history of segregation in the USA and the continuance of racism and prejudice towards African-Americans, most first-generation migrants from the Caribbean reject the label black and prefer to emphasize their national origins (see, for example, Vickerman 1998).

For those from Spanish-speaking nations and Portuguese-speaking Brazil, migrants confront a social category and labels that emerged from the civil rights struggles of the 1960s. While African-Americans were the primary focus of these struggles, other racialized minorities both participated and were affected. A 'Brown Power' movement (parallel to Black Power) arose to champion the rights of those of Mexican descent who lived primarily in the west and south-western USA. Activists adopted the label 'Chicano', a word that was originally derogatory until appropriated and valorized by 'Brown Power' activists. Parallel to the activism from within the community, the US government created its own label when the US Census Bureau used the term 'Hispanic' to describe people of 'Spanish origin or descent' within the United States. Activists with roots in the USA, such as Chicanos and Puerto Ricans, found 'Hispanic' to be an imposed term and suggested 'Latino', since it came from Spanish, the language that the group purportedly shared. Correspondingly, many universities created programmes in Latino Studies, although a few still maintained separate Chicano or Mexican-American Studies. Among the educated and politically active, and with the exception of South Florida, Latino has become the preferred term over Hispanic (O'Brien 2008).

Migrants from Central and South America often reject any overarching label as they argue that it obscures their vital diversity on such dimensions as national origin, social class, ethnicity, race and length of stay in the USA. The most political critiques argue that the label is: 'a state-imposed hegemonic project that culturalizes economic exploitation and political oppression [...] These populations [...] are where they are, politically and economically, not because of their "Hispanic" or "Latin" culture but because of their class location' (Gimenez 1998). Overarching and racialized categorizations also create misleading perceptions of minority progress.

Little national or pan-ethnic solidarity exists across the diasporas from Latin America and the Caribbean. Many diaspora members identify much more with their village or ethnic group than with the nation from which they came. For example, Smith (2006) describes the home-town associations and identifications that Mexicans in New York have with their village of origin in the state of Puebla. While they may use a Mexican passport to be able to visit their homeland, their primary sense of identification remains with their village and with New York. In this sense, these migrants are translocal, rather than transnational.

Yet there are forces that can create a new sense of diasporic consciousness. When those with power identify and discriminate against another group, even if the discriminated group did not previously feel a sense of solidarity, they are likely to coalesce in response to discrimination. Bedolla (2005), for example, found that Mexicans and Mexican-Americans in Los Angeles, who had previously differentiated between themselves and maintained a social distance, found solidarity in response to anti-immigrant political initiatives in California in the 1990s. On the West Coast of the USA, particularly in California, politicized ethnic organizations have also emerged that focus on human and labour rights for some of Mexico's indigenous diasporas (Velasco Ortiz 2005). In South Florida, Latin American migrants, who often expressed frustration and resentment at how well Cubans were treated by the US government, supported the local Cuban community when the federal government returned to Cuba a young child, Elian Gonzalez, whose mother drowned attempting to bring him to Miami on a raft. Cubans in Miami argued that the boy should remain with relatives in Miami rather than be returned to his father in communist Cuba. After numerous delays and demonstrations, armed US officers stormed the Miami house where the child was and returned him. Latin American migrants discovered a new solidarity; as one Miami-Nicaraguan youth expressed it: 'The Americans [meaning non-Hispanic whites], it's like this is their country and we're not part of this' (Stepick and Dutton Stepick 2009). The diverse Latin American diasporas, at least for that moment, felt a sense of pan-ethnic Hispanic or Latino unity based in perceived discrimination and being an 'other' through the application of US immigration law.

Consciousness of solidarity is frequently riven by class and racialized ethnic divisions within diaspora groups. While most public discourse focuses on working-class migrants, particularly those labelled as 'illegal' or 'undocumented', the USA welcomes elites from Latin America and the Caribbean, who also tend to be of European descent. When they come to the USA, elites arrive under far different circumstances and seldom express solidarity with non-elites. Able to hire legal assistance, they have fewer difficulties obtaining a legal immigration status. They bring economic and human capital resources that allow them to establish themselves relatively easily. They live in neighbourhoods with few poor people and may even bring servants with them or hire new ones from their country's working-class migrants. They thus often find it easy to re-establish in the USA the class relations they enjoyed at home. Indeed, much of Miami's high-end real estate has been created for these elites, who are looking for political and economic stability to protect their capital. Similarly, elite Mexicans often have homes in Los Angeles, Houston or other cities. In the migrants' homelands, class is one of the most pervasive and important social and economic distinctions.

Although seldom part of public discourse, class divisions are present among all Latin American and Caribbean diasporas (see, for example, Postero and Zamosc 2004).

Haitians, for example, have suffered more prejudice and discrimination than any other contemporary immigrant group in the USA (Stepick 1998). Middle- and upper-class Haitians in South Florida often distance themselves from the 'boat people', those whom they think provoke this prejudice because they are poor. Only once did all Haitians demonstrate cross-class solidarity. In the late 1980s the organization responsible for overseeing the collection and distribution of blood donations in the USA, the federal Food and Drug Administration (FDA), banned the acceptance of blood from individuals of Haitian descent. There was no scientific basis for this ban. The policy appeared racist and particularly anti-Haitian; and it discriminated against all Haitians, not solely those who were poor (Farmer 1990). For those few months of protest, there was a Haitian diaspora consciousness that incorporated all Haitians regardless of their class background. Subsequently, some elite Haitians maintained this consciousness and instrumentally employed it, for example by standing for municipal office and campaigning as representatives of Haitians in South Florida. Other elite Haitians established charities and non-governmental organizations directed at helping the Haitian diaspora, while others returned to their previous position in which class differences between them and other Haitians were more important than diaspora solidarity.

This brief review of diasporas within the Americas exemplifies how the creation of and consciousness within diaspora groups arise dynamically from the interaction between members of the diasporas and the actions of those with power who may discriminate against or favour particular groups.

Further reading

Levitt, P. (2007) *God Needs No Passport: Immigrants and the Changing American Religious Landscape*, New York: New Press.

Smith, R. C. (2006) *Mexican New York: Transnational Lives of New Immigrants*, Berkeley: University of California Press.

Spickard, P. (2007) *Almost All Aliens: Immigration, Race, and Colonialism in American History and Identity*, New York: Routledge.

Stephen, L. (2007) *Transborder Lives: Indigenous Oaxacans in Mexico, California, and Oregon*, Durham, NC: Duke University Press.

Stepick, A., G. Grenier, M. Castro and M. Dunn (2003) *This Land Is Our Land: Immigrants and Power in Miami*, Berkeley: University of California Press.

31 | Movements between 'white' Europe and America: Greek migration to the United States

Anastasia Christou and Russell King

The setting

West-bound transatlantic migration during the nineteenth and early twentieth centuries is known simply as the 'Great Migration' (King 1996: 32). The largest intercontinental mass migration ever seen, an estimated fifty million 'white' Europeans, migrated across the Atlantic between 1850 and 1914, most of them bound for the United States (Baines 1991: 7–9). Arriving at New York harbour and overlooked by the iconic Statue of Liberty, they were part of the 'American Dream' – a rags-to-riches mythology of the proletarian huddled masses, entering the 'golden door' of the 'land of the free'. They not only 'made' America, but in the process 'became' Americans. In this cliché-saturated self-narrative of the USA as a country of immigration, settlement, success and assimilation, there was little space for countervailing notions of transnationalism, diaspora or return migration. Yet, as the Greek-American experience shows, all such notions were to become important, since the Greeks, more than most, displayed a strong loyalty to their homeland and its culture, and had high rates of return (Cohen 1995: 77–9; see also Jusdanis 1991; Lambropoulos 1997; Gourgouris 2004; Anagnostou 2003, 2008).

During the first half of the nineteenth century the settler influx mainly came from northern Europe – Britain, Germany, Scandinavia and, especially after the 1845–49 potato famine, Ireland. At the end of the century and into the next, the centre of gravity of emigration shifted south-east – to Poland, Russia, Italy and Greece. While the northern Europeans were welcomed because they conformed to the enduring self-image of the USA as a white, Anglo-dominated Protestant society, the southern Europeans were seen as somehow 'less white' and as culturally different; they also had a lesser tendency to migrate *en famille* and they generally settled in major cities rather than as rural homesteaders. Among the southern Europeans, the quantitatively dominant Italian migration to the Americas has been well documented (see, notably, Gabaccia 2000), the Greek much less so.

Greeks in America: two waves, and some return

In the long history of mobility of the Greeks from ancient to modern times, two important waves of mass emigration took place after the formation of the modern Greek state in the early 1830s: one between 1890 and the 1920s, and another in the decades following the Second World War. The first wave was overwhelmingly to the United States; the second to a more diversified set of destinations, both overseas (the USA, Canada, Australia) and increasingly, after 1960, to Germany. Georgakas (1987) argues that the history of Greeks in America is best understood within the context of European transatlantic migration rather than with reference to the global Greek diaspora. This does not mean that Greeks were typical of the European transatlantic flow: there were some similarities with Italian and other Balkan migrants, but also differences. Distinctive characteristics of the Greek migrants were their humble rural or island origins, their strong ethno-national collective character (stronger, it seems, than in just about any other group), their capacity for family-based upward socio-economic mobility, and their strong connections to the homeland, including the desire to return (Laliotou 2004).

Many factors contributed to the migration of Greeks to the United States. Extreme poverty exacerbated by periodic crop failures, regional and civil wars, autocratic government and corrupt local administration were key push factors. Among pull factors were demands for Greek and other workers to contribute to reconstruction following the American Civil War, and to boost industrial production in the main manufacturing centres. Labour needs determined the regional distribution of the Greek-American population in three main belts during the first mass migration (Georgakas 1987; Moskos 1999; Saloutos 1964).

- The New England mill towns recruited Greeks to work in the textile, shoe and fur industries in New York State, Maine, New Hampshire and Massachusetts.
- Mass production in the burgeoning automobile industry and the related expansion of steel, glass, tyre, iron and coal industries opened up opportunities for Greek immigrants in the broad area from Chicago to Baltimore, with the heaviest concentration between Detroit and Pittsburgh.
- Third, smaller numbers moved farther west to work on railroad construction, in mines and quarries and in the lumber industry.

Few Greeks ventured into the Deep South, where xenophobic 'nativist' forces were hostile to immigrants, and only limited numbers followed migratory seasonal harvest work, or settled in Florida or California (Saloutos 1964).

In the absence of reliable statistics, most authors estimate that around 600,000–700,000 Greeks migrated to the USA in the first wave, including 400,000 during 1910–29 (Papademetriou 1979: 187). For the second migration wave, official Greek statistics became available in 1955, based on the definition of staying abroad for at least one year. During the period from 1955 to 1973 (the year the oil crisis halted labour migration in Europe), about 1.1 million Greeks emigrated, one in seven of the Greek population. West Germany attracted 600,000, Australia 160,000, the USA 150,000 and Canada 80,000 (Lianos 1979: 209–10).

Taking the long view, and filling in the statistical gaps with estimates, we have approximately one million Greek immigrants to the USA between 1890 and 1990 (Moskos 1999). Their patterns of settlement – overwhelmingly urban – had not changed much since the first wave: most live in, or within fifty miles of, New York City, Boston, Chicago, Detroit, Cleveland, Pittsburgh and Baltimore.

Return migration has been a constant feature of Greek migration to the United States, and the subject of an early classic study of this migration genre (Saloutos 1956). By 1931, 40 per cent had returned – for various reasons, including the US recession, the wish to find a Greek wife, nostalgia, health, climate, or simply because it was always their intention to do so. Many came back to retire or set up a small business, such as a shop or restaurant. But many also experienced problems of reintegration after so long away.

The evolving character of the diaspora

The Greek-origin population in the USA changed its character in two ways as time went by: it became more demographically balanced, and it evolved economically, leading to social stratification.

Before the turn of the twentieth century, very few Greek women entered the USA; the early migration was male-dominated, with high rates of return. The preferred way for Greek women to migrate to America was to be accompanied – if married, with her husband, otherwise in the company of brothers or other male relatives. Also, marriages were frequently arranged, so 'picture brides' did travel to America on their own. Undoubtedly, the arrival of Greek women, and the birth of the second generation, anchored the Greek community in the USA (Moskos 2002).

Until recently, most Greek women in America did not work outside the household. Exceptions to this rule occurred in family businesses such as shops and catering outlets, and in New England some were employed in the textile and shoe factories.

Soon after the start of mass migration, the Greek-American population underwent a process of social differentiation which reflected American society as a whole. Certainly, many first-generation immigrants remained in the labouring class their entire lives; but middle-class aspirations were also strong. By the 1920s, many Greeks had become owners of small businesses, mostly concentrated in certain sectors such as confectionery, food services, pool halls, florists, dry cleaners, shoe repairers and tailors, laying down the foundations for an increasing commercial and business orientation for the group over time. Many second-wave immigrants followed the path of their predecessors and went into the food-and-drink business. They became owners of restaurants, nightclubs, bars, coffee shops or, especially in New York, taxicabs. New arrivals, young and with limited education, worked for others in construction, painting and maintenance work; others became waiters or assistant cooks, hoping to become restaurant owners later on (ibid.).

Many authors have stressed the Greek-Americans' strong desire for economic advancement, social acceptance and academic achievement (for example, Christou 2001). To a certain extent this echoes the standard US-propagated rhetoric about immigrants' success through hard work; yet of course we know that others (including many immigrants) are condemned by structural obstacles to continued poverty no matter how hard they work. Extensive evidence strongly suggests, however, that, in the case of Greek immigrants, many of whom have entered the ethnic-niche small-business sector specializing in food and catering, this somewhat essentialized picture of 'struggle and success' is actually true (Constantinou 2002; Georgakas 1987; Kourvetaris 1997; Moskos 1999).

Preserving diasporic identity

If the acquisition of material goods and social mobility were the result of sustained hard work, the development and maintenance of a strong community – 'a fortress by which to protect and within which to cultivate and develop [the Greek migrant's] spiritual profile and identity' (Hatziemmanuel 1982: 182) – was the parallel strategy to preserve and enhance the ethnic heritage. For the first generations, preservation of the ethnic heritage remains undeniably linked to the spiritual well-being of the family. The strength of ethnic ancestry, ingrained in the family in many forms, is an obligation that makes the Greek Orthodox Church in the USA an institution not just of religious observance but also of ethno-cultural and linguistic preservation.

Two quotations from our recent interviews with Greek-Americans in New York are typical articulations of the strength of this family-based ethnic solidarity. In the first, Elia, who was ten years old when her parents took her to the USA in 1966, described her family's life after migration:

It was all Greek [...] all Greek. I mean [...] we lived with Greeks, we went to church [...] we participated in the festivals, we went to the Greek parades. Anything you can think of, we'd go Greek – we didn't really associate with American culture. It was all Greek [...] stay with your own kind [...]. Like my mother would have friends over and would play cards [...] but all Greeks.

Asked about language in the home:

Definitely Greek. My parents didn't speak English [...] and even when I went to high school and started to speak English, they would only speak to me in Greek at home [...]. They didn't want us to forget, my sister and I, you know, our culture, our roots, our language.

And about the possibility of returning to live in Greece:

> In a heartbeat, in a heartbeat! I mean, if I retire in a couple of years, then [...]. Because I have been travelling back and forth to Greece every year, I think the Greek-Americans [...] we seem to maintain our heritage more than the people who live in Greece [...] they really do not hold true to the values that we do here as far as wanting to marry Greeks, keeping the religion, bringing up the children.

The second excerpt is from a family interview. The speaker is sixty-eight-year-old Dora, who came to the USA via Canada in 1967.

> Have you seen that movie *My [Big Fat] Greek Wedding*? It was about our family! My kids saw it and laughed – they saw their father and me! He is from Cephalonia. His word wanted to be their command. My daughter led the same life as that girl in the movie [...] she had to be back home before dark. Now she's married to a man from Crete [...]. We have preserved our customs, the language – even our grandchildren speak Greek – and we have preserved tradition, music, festivals. Whenever new Greek folk come to town we always meet and help them [...]. We all see to it that the language and customs are preserved, and the family is kept together. We sometimes overdo it.

The Greek and Greek-American press, radio and television have also functioned as transmitters of the 'Hellenic Orthodox' ethos and national consciousness. While the post-war immigrant first generation relied heavily on newspapers and, later, satellite TV, subsequent generations are embracing the more globalized medium of the Internet. Panagakos (2003) argues that current uses of media and technology signal the creation of new dimensions of Greek diasporic identity, implying stronger ties with the ethnic homeland. This remains a hypothesis to be fully tested. Given the significant and increasing numbers of second-generation Greek-Americans who are 'returning' to Greece, often independent of their parents, this seems a reasonable supposition (Christou 2006).

Conclusion

One of the ironies of the United States' immigration scenario is that, despite a powerful national rhetoric of assimilation, diasporic and 'ethnic' identities among many immigrant groups – including those like the Greeks, long settled there – remain so strong. Part of the answer is the lack of assimilation policy in the USA: immigrants are *expected* to assimilate but not forced to do so. Indeed, the *laissez faire* stance towards immigrants, consistent with a free market economy, allows them to develop their own integration trajectory. For the Greek-Americans, this expresses itself in a generally positive outcome: they are structurally well assimilated, in terms of their access to material wealth, business and employment opportunities, housing and academic qualifications, especially for the second and subsequent generations, but they do not have to sacrifice their ethnic-Greek diasporic identity to achieve this.

Another part of the answer is to be found in Greece's own hegemonic discourse of the superiority of Greek national history and ethnic identity, which overrides all others and which must be revered at almost any cost. The strength of the Greek diasporic consciousness (as Greek first and diasporic second) feeds through to individual, family, community and national identity, with their roots in *ius sanguinis*, the Greek language and the Orthodox religion.

In the diaspora, this is reinforced by organizations geared to providing 'Greek Orthodox' education to young people, teaching Greek language, history and culture, religious beliefs and practices. A great deal of time and money (much of it coming from the working class of the diaspora, with only a little help from the Greek government) has been invested in supporting those structures and organizations which push forward 'the spiritual mission that is carried on within the community' (Hatziemmanuel 1982: 187). These organizations have multiple functions: education, religion and pastoral care; helping recently arrived compatriots to adjust to their new surroundings; and charity, humanitarian aid and scholarship funding. To this day, Greek-Americans show enormous zeal and dedication to the causes and goals of these organizations, and commitment to philanthropy (Tsemberis 1999).

Yet the Orthodox Church and Greek-American ethnic organizations have not been conflict free and have at times constituted an arena for competition and tension (Karpathakis 1994). The same holds true for family life. While early accounts underscore the significant role of the family as a source of support, guidance and comfort for the immigrants (Saloutos 1964; Scourby 1984), subsequent works have critically examined the inner complexity of families where patriarchy, intolerance, tension and emotional instability have become obstacles, especially to the aspirations of females, to interaction with other ethnicities, and to expressions of alternative sexualities (Callinicos 1991; Chock 1995; Fygetakis 1997; Tsemberis et al. 1999).

Further reading

Christou, A. (2006) *Narratives of Place, Culture and Identity: Second-Generation Greek-Americans Return 'Home'*, Amsterdam: Amsterdam University Press.

Kourvetaris, G. (1997) *Studies on Greek Americans*, New York: Columbia University Press.

Moskos, C. C. (1999) *Greek Americans: Struggle and Success*, New York: Transaction.

Orfanos, S. D. (ed.) (2002) *Reading Greek America: Studies in the Experience of Greeks in the United States*, New York: Pella.

Saloutos, T. (1964) *The Greeks in the United States*, Cambridge, MA: Harvard University Press.

32 | The Russian-Jewish diaspora at the beginning of the twenty-first century

Larissa Remennick

The Jewish communities of east-central Europe (Poland, Czechoslovakia, Romania and Hungary) were almost completely destroyed during the Holocaust; some of their remaining members moved to Israel during the post-war period, comprising altogether about 50,000 immigrants (Central Bureau of Statistics 1990). The overwhelming majority of the Jewish migrants of the last three decades, however, have left the former Soviet Union (FSU), resettling in Israel and in several Western countries, and it is upon this diaspora that this essay will focus. The movement of Soviet Jews to Israel has been part of the late-twentieth-century global flows of so-called *ethnic return migrations* (see, especially, Markowitz and Steffanson 2004; Tsuda 2009). Ideologically, this is often framed as an in-gathering of diasporas or homecoming by co-ethnics historically detached from their homelands by wars and changes to borders (Brubaker 1998). The in-gathering of the Jewish diasporas, dispersed since the destruction of the Second Temple across Europe, the Middle East and later the Americas, to the State of Israel after 1948 was the largest global project in return migration. In this case, of course, the return has been purely symbolic, given thousands of years of life in the diaspora.

Throughout the second half of the twentieth century, the condition of Jews under Soviet rule was that of a special ethnic (rather than religious) minority which experienced both social advancement and discrimination, but was always mistrusted (Brym 1994; Remennick 1998). Following an upsurge of emancipation and upward social mobility during the first three decades of Bolshevism, after the end of the Second World War Soviet Jews were subjected to covert institutional policies of exclusion from higher education and prestigious careers and lived in the shadow of anti-Jewish and anti-Israeli media campaigns, augmented by everyday social anti-Semitism. In this hostile milieu, Jewish parents aspired to educational excellence and cultivated the value of hard work in their children, which eventually earned them exceptionally high rates of higher education (over 50 per cent nationally and 70 per cent in the largest cities) and a respectable place in most professions (Remennick 1998). It can be argued that Soviet Jews excelled both despite and owing to their discrimination. This twisted need–hate relationship between Russian Jews and the Soviet power made Jewish professionals an indispensable part of the Soviet technological and cultural elite from the early 1920s, and, despite ups and downs in the waves of state anti-Semitism, they retained this special status until the end of the twentieth century (ibid.). Some were devoted loyalists of the regime, most others cynical or passive bystanders, and a few convinced dissidents; yet all carried for life a stigma of their 'ethnic disability' vis-à-vis the surrounding Slavic majority. Many Jews despised the communist regime and, after the short-lived thaw following Stalin's death, lost any hope for political and economic reforms. Wishing for a better future for themselves and their children beyond the Iron Curtain, where their efforts would be better rewarded, many Jews quietly considered the subversive option of emigration.

This dream became reality in the early 1970s, when Brezhnev's regime had to make concessions to Western pressure, and Jewish emigration became its bargaining chip in trade negotiations with the USA. Although small trickles of other ethnic migrants were allowed to leave around the same time (mainly Germans and Armenians), Soviet Jews became effectively the only ethnic group granted the exceptional privilege of mass emigration under the pretext of return to their historic homeland of Israel. Between 1971 and 1981, around 250,000 Jews left the USSR; of those, about two-thirds landed in America and one third in Israel (Gitelman 1997, 2003). During the 1980s the deteriorating Soviet regime reversed its emigration quotas to the pre-1970 level, so that only a handful of Jews could leave under exceptional clauses.

The demise of state socialism in eastern Europe in the late 1980s marked the onset of the Great New Exodus of now former-Soviet Jews, along with a few other ethnic minorities who could claim the right of return to their historic homelands or family reunification. Since 1988, over 1.6 million Jews from Russia, Ukraine and other Soviet successor states have emigrated to Israel, the USA, Canada, Germany, Australia and a few other Western countries. Some others left the FSU with job visas as research scholars and high-tech specialists, winners of the Diversity Lottery (whereby the USA makes 50,000 'Diversity Immigrant Visas' or permanent resident cards available to countries with low rates of US immigration) or via marriage. The social incorporation of these newcomers has been rather different from the experiences of their predecessors during the 1970s, reflecting multiple changes in the global economy and the geopolitical context of the late twentieth century, as well as the unprecedented scope of this exodus. Those leaving the FSU in the early to mid-1990s lived through the post-communist turmoil of a nascent 'jungle capitalism' and shaky 'drunk' democracy; some descended into poverty while others thrived in the new business milieu. Many had had a chance to travel abroad, visit relatives and friends in Israel and in the West, and generally were better informed about their potential destinations.

There were several distinct sub-waves in the course of the post-communist migrations of the late twentieth century. The first began around 1987/88 at a pivotal point of *perestroika* ('restructuring'), whereby those 'left behind' in the late 1970s (*refusniks*) were at last allowed to leave, both for Israel and for the West, although the latter destination was never openly stated. The majority of those who left the USSR with Israeli visas between 1987 and 1990 (around 85 per cent) actually arrived in the USA under Jewish refugee status (their total number is estimated at about 127,000 by Lazin 2005). At the end of 1989, however, the American government changed its refugee policy towards Soviet Jews and drastically reduced entry quotas, limiting them mainly to family reunification. At the same time, Israel opened direct flights from major Soviet cities to Tel Aviv and closed the transition camps in Europe. Thus, from the early 1990s, the bulk of Jewish émigrés were effectively redirected to Israel, reducing 'dropout' rates to 20–25 per cent. These swings in the numbers and directions of migrant flows reflected multiple political tensions and compromises between the Israeli government and the Jewish diaspora (mainly American) (Gitelman 1997; Lazin 2005). For Israel, the net results entailed adding over 950,000 newcomers to its Jewish population, significant fortification of the secular Ashkenazi majority, the economic boom of the 1990s, and the emergence of a new thriving subculture on the Israeli ethnic map. In America and Canada, about 370,000 post-1987 Soviet immigrants, although a relatively small immigrant population (vis-à-vis Hispanics and Asians), became the main source of demographic growth for North American Jewry. Germany has also experienced an upsurge in applicants for the 'special refugee' programme for Soviet Jews, and by 2004 had accommodated about 220,000 Jewish newcomers and their families (Remennick 2007).

Thus, during the early 1990s, Israel faced a mass influx of Russian-speaking Jews, whose number reached almost one million and increased the Jewish population by 20 per cent. The tide gradually subsided after 1995 and has now become a trickle. The integration of the last immigration wave posed major difficulties vis-à-vis the previous wave of 'Russians'. To begin with, the 1970s wave was much smaller and spread over a decade, compared to about half a million post-communist migrants who arrived in just three years (1990–92). The Israeli labour market of the 1970s had been ready to absorb the educated Jewish professionals from the USSR owing to shortages of skilled workers in medicine, education, technology and science; by the 1990s Israel had trained enough professionals of its own and the market was saturated. Thus, tens of thousands of Soviet-trained teachers, doctors, scientists, engineers and artists found that their former professional experience was irrelevant in Israel and had either to retrain for more in-demand, semi-skilled occupations in banking, tourism, insurance and sales, or to make a living by manual work and personal services (mainly geriatric care). Women and older professionals experienced especially harsh downward mobility (ibid.). Occupational downgrading compromised the income and living standards of Russian immigrants, causing their concentration in poorer urban neighbourhoods and social isolation from potential Israeli peers. Indirectly, it also discouraged many Russian Jews from learning Hebrew beyond the basic minimum and getting closer to Israeli culture and society. Psychologically, the failure to find professional jobs harmed immigrants' self-esteem and left them wondering whether the whole immigration venture was worthwhile. Given the gradual improvement in the economic situation in Russia and Ukraine from the mid-1990s, this also propelled some immigrants endowed with marketable skills to return to the FSU or remigrate to North America, with about 10 per cent of the 1990s wave eventually leaving Israel (Central Bureau of Statistics 2007).

Another challenge that awaited ex-Soviet immigrants in Israel was finding permanent housing, given soaring costs on the private market and the lack of public housing (especially needed for the elderly and single parents). This often caused the co-residence of three generations in small apartments, with ensuing family conflict and higher divorce rates (Lowenstein and Katz 2005). Many mixed families including partly Jewish or non-Jewish members experienced additional alienation from the host society owing to their second-class status in matters of religion, marriage, divorce, burial and visas for relatives from the FSU. Only a small fraction of non-Jews (around 3–5 per cent) could convert to Judaism via full Orthodox *giyur* (conversion) – the only form recognized by Israeli authorities. Reflecting all these pressures, many 1990s immigrants felt estranged from mainstream Hebrew society and found a solution to their needs by creating a thriving system of social and cultural institutions of their own (schools, libraries, clubs, theatres, small businesses), as well as a Russian-language media: several daily newspapers, a TV channel and radio stations (Fialkova and Yelenevskaya 2007; Elias 2008). Although the majority disliked a Russian subculture thriving side by side with the mainstream, it could hardly prevent it from emerging, giving the 'critical mass' of Russian immigrants, their high human capital, consumer potential and political clout (Al-Haj 2002; Khanin 2007).

Despite the difficulties of integration and many mistakes made in absorption policy over the last twenty years, the 1990s wave of Russian immigrants has made a deep and lasting impact on Israeli society. Indeed, community size matters in immigration: while in most other receiving countries Russian Jews comprise a small minority, in Israel they make up fully 20 per cent of its Jewish majority, in some localities forming between 30 and 60 per cent. Their presence significantly fortified the educated and secular segment of the population and added new facets to the range of Jewish identities already existing in Israel (Khanin 2007). Owing to the significant influx of skilled professionals (trained elsewhere – a pure economic gain), the Israeli economy experienced an upsurge in many sectors, such as high-tech, engineering and applied science. Russian immigrants also enriched Israeli education (both as teachers and students), culture (especially theatre), competitive sports (winning a number of Olympic medals), and encouraged many Israelis to perceive cultural diversity as good news. By introducing Russian culture to Israel, former Soviet immigrants turned Israel into a de facto multicultural society, forcing it to put aside its 'melting pot' aspirations (Al-Haj 2002).

Although the expectations and 'strings attached' in the reception of Russian Jews in the USA, Canada and Germany were not as apparent and intense, the tacit conflict between the established Jewish communities and the newcomers has also been unfolding there. The lives of Russian-speaking Jews in North America comprise a more pure case of encounter between former Soviets and Western economies and lifestyles. In contrast to the situation in Israel, with its institutional approach to absorption, in the USA and Canada they were required to dive into unfamiliar waters with relatively little public support and to learn to swim on their own. The German setting is unique in the extent and duration of welfare aid to former Soviet Jews, which partly discouraged them from labour market participation. Other salient aspects of their German immigration saga include conflicts within local Jewish organizations and historic legacies of the Great War and the Holocaust colouring host-land–immigrant relations (Remennick 2007). While *Aliya* (migration) to Israel is ideologically constructed as 'homecoming' (repatriation), and many *Olim* (migrants) internalize this view of their resettlement, with the ensuing expectations of support and social inclusion, immigration to the West is perceived by both parties as a pragmatic decision taken by the émigrés at their own risk. A comparative approach to the study of Russian-Jewish immigration illuminates the role of its ideological framing, local policies towards immigrants and their expectations from the host society as factors shaping the experiences and outcomes of integration (ibid.).

The resettlement of the majority of post-communist immigrants in Israel has reinforced its role as the demographic and social centre of an expanding Russian-Jewish diaspora, which is becoming increasingly transnational. The great exodus from the FSU over the last twenty years has split families and social networks of colleagues and friends: some stayed put while others resettled in Israel and in the West. After getting an initial foothold in the host-land countries, these dispersed individuals started to reassemble their old social networks, strongly enabled by new technologies of communication and travel. Former Soviet Jews have been moulded by Russian-Soviet culture, which they cherish and wish to preserve, as well as transfer to the next generation. Some may feel isolated from the mainstream in their new homelands and seek kindred spirits in familiar Russian social spaces, both local and global, for example in Russian Internet forums and dating websites. Many others wish to stay plugged into their old social networks despite being well integrated in the new country. Thus, Russian-speakers scattered across different locales are gradually forming an increasingly dense social space held together by physical and economic ties – mutual visits, joint business ventures and scientific projects – as well as spiritual and virtual means – cultural exchange and educational projects – fortified by the advent of the Internet and the global Russian-language media (ibid.).

Further reading

Elias, N. (2008) *Coming Home: Media and Returning Diaspora in Israel and Germany*, Albany: State University of New York Press.

Fialkova, L. and M. Yelenevskaya (2007) *Ex-Soviets in Israel: From Personal Narratives to a Group Portrait*, Detroit, MI: Wayne State University Press.

Gitelman, Z., M. Goldman and M. Glanz (eds) (2003) *Jewish Life after the USSR*, Bloomington: Indiana University Press.

Khanin, Z. (Vladmir) (2003) 'Russian-Jewish ethnicity: Israel and Russia compared', in E. Ben-Rafael, Y. Gorny and Y. Ro'I (eds), *Contemporary Jewries: Convergence and Divergence*, Leiden: Brill Academic Press.

Remennick, L. (2007) *Russian Jews on Three Continents: Identity, Integration, and Conflict*, Brunswick, NJ: Transaction.

33 | The Iranian diaspora in the West

Sanaz Raji

Historically, Persians of various ethnic and religious backgrounds, including Zoroastrians, Jews and Armenians as well as Baha'is, have migrated from their homeland for a variety of reasons. In the eighth century, for instance, Zoroastrians fled Iran in search of religious freedom after the Arab/Muslim conquest, and settled in India, becoming known as the Parsis. During the nineteenth century many Iranians left for the Russian Empire to work in the oilfields of Baku. Likewise, small-scale movements of Iranian Jews and Christians took place during the nineteenth century and after the Second World War, with many of the former emigrating to Israel. It was the tumultuous events of the 1979 Iranian Revolution and the subsequent eight-year war with Iraq, however, which produced the largest migration of Iranians to the West and beyond. During the 1960s and 1970s many Iranians – particularly from the educated elite – sought qualifications in the West with a view to improving the infrastructure of the homeland. By 1977, Iranians of all classes were studying abroad, the largest population of students being in the USA, with 36,220 enrolled in US universities, while the rest studied in the United Kingdom, West Germany, France and Austria. With many such students and professionals not returning to Iran after the revolution, a tremendous 'brain drain' was experienced at a time when the country was desperate for highly educated and talented individuals. Even today, many bright young Iranians continue to leave for the USA, Canada and Australia in search of financial security and a better life. A 2006 report from the International Monetary Fund stated that Iran had the highest rate of brain drain among ninety countries measured (Harrison 2007).

As Bozorghmehr and Sabagh (1988), Kelly (1993) and Malek (2006) have all noted, there are only estimates as to how many Iranians currently live in the diaspora. These range from over one million in the USA alone to four million worldwide. California has the largest and probably most diverse concentration of Iranians in the diaspora, Los Angeles (dubbed 'Tehrangeles') being a home abroad for non-Muslim minorities of Iranian origin, as well as dominant Shiite Muslim heritage groupings. Kathryn Spellman suggests that settlement experiences among diasporic Iranians depend upon the 'immigration policies and different historical, socio-economic and political relationships between Iran and the particular nation-state' (2004: 30). Indeed, as a result of the Iranian hostage crisis in 1981 – when fifty-two American diplomats were held for over a year by student militants – a wave of anti-Iranian discrimination occurred in the USA. For the nascent Iranian-American community this provided a deeply humiliating and terrifying moment, especially as many had fled Iran as a result of political and social persecution.

This fear of categorizing oneself as 'Iranian/Persian' (regardless of religious background) has also been reflected since 9/11, when many Middle Easterners, Muslims and South Asians encountered a 'culture of fear' inflicted by the 'war on terror' (Naber 2006). The attack on the Twin Towers led to the negative racialization of 'Middle Eastern–Muslim' diasporics, associating them with terrorism and questioning their loyalty. The much-criticized Immigration and Naturalization Service (INS) 'Special Registration Program', for example, was introduced in September 2002, gathering intelligence information on certain non-citizens, including males aged sixteen and over from Iran, Iraq, Syria, Libya and Sudan. In southern California alone, hundreds of men and teenage boys were actually arrested at INS offices as they voluntarily tried to comply with the new regulations. This prompted thousands of Iranian-Americans to rally in front of the Westwood Federal Building in Los Angeles, demanding the immediate release of their male relatives.

Another form of activism that has blossomed post-9/11 is in the form of civic and non-profit organizations such as the National Iranian American Council (NIAC), which, since its inception in 2002, has been responsible for providing the Iranian-American community with a voice on Capitol Hill. Iranian Alliances Across Borders (IAAB), established in 2004, is a non-political and non-religious organization that has staff in the USA, Europe and Iran to address issues of the Iranian diaspora community while connecting Iranians across borders. In the UK, the Iran Heritage Foundation and the Magic of Persia are both non-profit, non-political organizations designed to promote and educate Iranians and non-Iranians about Persian culture and history. With the growth of these and similar organizations, disparate groups within the Iranian diaspora have been brought closer together and non-Iranians have been informed about Iran.

For Iranians in Britain, much like their counterparts in the USA, the tense political situation of the 1980s, including mistrust between pro-royalist, pro-mujahedin, pro-Islamist and other leftist groups, meant that there was very little cohesion in the Iranian diaspora. Furthermore, because the first generation anticipated the day when the Islamic regime of the revolution would fall, there was an expectation of returning home one day. Thus, there was little effort made to transmit Iranian cultural identity to the second generation. Iranians who had left Iran during the post-revolutionary period felt that their migration to the West was *avaregi* or 'forced homelessness and vagrancy' (Naficy 1993: 11).

Nevertheless, by the 1990s many Iranians began to realize that their stay in the diaspora was unlikely to be as temporary as they had hoped. The volatile political situation in Iran after Ayatollah Khomeini's death in 1989 convinced many that it was unsafe to return. Furthermore, they were seen by the Islamic government as 'Westoxicated Iranians, members of the oppositions, and cowardly individuals who fled to escape defending the country's borders against the Iraqi aggression' (Spellman 2004: 43). Indeed, many first-generation Iranian diasporics felt acceptance neither at home nor in exile (Jaggi 1988: 164). Various scholars have noted that they still have problems accepting that they have left Iran and live in an indeterminate state of longing and reality (ibid.; Fischer and Abedi 1990; Kelly 1993; Naficy 1993; Sreberny 2001; Sullivan 2001).

The psychological restlessness faced by many first-generation diasporic Iranians is apparent in the way many identified with symbols glorifying the achievements of the ancient Persian Empire. As Hamid Naficy's (1993) seminal work on Iranian exiles and media reveals, from the 1980s until the early part of the 1990s satellite television based in Los Angeles provided a highly political voice for supporters of the late Mohammed Reza Shah in opposing the Islamic Republic. This discourse was in retaliation for the propaganda against exiles coming out of Iran, as well as an expression of the disappointment and frustration associated with feeling forced out of the homeland. Exilic Iranian satellite television also created a fetishized and nostalgic conception of Iran by incessantly circulating vintage images and television shows (with famous pop stars such as Googoosh and Vigen) prominent during the reign of the Shah. This extreme nationalism was in many ways, too, a psychological defence mechanism to counter the negative news stories being circulated after the revolution. For the decade that followed, mainstream Western media persisted in presenting an image of Iran as exclusively a country of Islamic fanatics, burning American and British flags and beating their chests in violent Shi'ite rituals. It was felt that the complexity of the situation in post-revolutionary Iran was always obscured (Morley 2000: 50).

Many of the second generation within the Iranian diaspora do not share the first generation's nostalgic idea of Iran. As Nilou Mostofi (2003) suggests in her study of Iranian-Americans, individuals who are second-generation have established 'roots' in the United States and have become too 'Americanized' to relocate to Iran. Nevertheless, what parents have transferred to their children is a reproduction of homeland class relations. In McAuliffe's (2008) study of Muslims and Baha'is living in London, Sydney and Vancouver, second-generation youth considered that many in the first generation regarded newer migrants from Iran as less socially refined, though Baha'i respondents were less elitist than their Muslim counterparts. Such differences were reinforced through language and behaviour, creating a schism within the Iranian diaspora. Class distinctions, whether among Iranian Jews, Christians, Muslims, Baha'is or Zoroastrians, also figure prominently in a study of the Los Angeles Iranian community. Kelly (1993) captures the psychological anguish among refugees who were part of Iran's upper class. Unable to transfer their personal wealth or skills, they had to re-establish themselves from the bottom of society up.

Unlike the first generation, many youth are not ashamed of proclaiming their Iranian identity, despite (or perhaps because of) their experience of post-9/11 discrimination (Mostofi 2003: 692). Through the medium of literature, particularly memoirs by Iranian second-generation women, including Gelareh Asayesh (1999), Tara Bahrampour (1999), Marjane Satrapi (2003, 2004), Firoozeh Dumas (2003) and Persis M. Karim (2006), there has been a diasporic examination of inter-generational and acculturation issues. Karim, for example, suggests that the increase in diasporic Iranian women writers has arisen as a result of 'the barrage of visual images that has simultaneously been part of the Islamic Republic's campaign to Islamicize Iranian society after 1979 and of the Western media's fixation on veiled women and women's repression' (ibid.: xx–xxi). Malek, however, views the rise of an Iranian memoir genre as part and parcel of a post-9/11 geopolitics that has positioned Iran in an 'Axis of evil' (Malek 2006: 364). Iranian women writers in the diaspora have turned to memoir writing as a means of explaining their identity and homeland to Western audiences unfamiliar with Iranian culture and history.

With the advent of the Internet in the early 1990s, diasporic Iranians, especially the youth, were able to communicate in new ways with relatives and friends back home and elsewhere. In September 1995, the launch of the web magazine *Iranian.com* also gave greater liberty in expression, as the majority of writing was in English and not in Farsi, the language of the exilic Iranian media (both satellite television and print media). Graham and Khosravi have noted that some see the Internet as an opportunity to bridge the gap between the generations (2002: 231). This is evident in such websites as *Iranian.com* but also *PersianMirror.com* and various blogs where writers are in constant dialogue over identity. Yet it would be erroneous to believe that the Internet is a haven for liberalizing views regarding taboo topics such as sex. Some men question the 'proper cultural behaviour' of women who voice their sexuality online, revealing some very crude ideas about 'authenticity'. This is one tactic by which nationalists and diasporics seek to control the cultural boundaries of dress, sexuality, marriage and family (Anthias and Yuval-Davis 1992). Within Iranian diasporic online narratives, evident in 'Photoshopped' images and home-made video clips on YouTube, one often finds a male voice critiquing and mocking diasporic women said to be transgressing boundaries in 'un-Iranian' ways.

In the aftermath of the Iranian presidential elections of June 2009, Iranians both in the homeland and in the diaspora took to online activism via Facebook and YouTube, questioning the validity of the supposed victory of President Mahmoud Ahmadinejad. They showcased protests all over Iran, spreading news about arrests and adding political commentary. The Iranian government, however, cunningly utilized European telecommunications to monitor and censor online content on a comprehensive level (Rhoads and Chao 2009). Thus, it has been able to crack down on dissent within the homeland, creating a culture of fear within the diaspora, especially for those who travel to and from Iran on a regular basis. Therefore, while the Internet can provide an open space in which to express views and ideas on a wide range of topics, for Iranians in the diaspora and the homeland, their online thoughts and views may be used against them in a repressive manner.

Further reading

Bahrampour, T. (1999) *To See and See Again: A Life in Iran and America*, New York: Farrar, Straus and Giroux.

Karim, P. (2006) *Let Me Tell You Where I've Been: New Writing by Women of the Iranian Diaspora*, Fayetteville: University of Arkansas Press.

Kelly, R. (ed.) (1993) *Irangeles: Iranians in Los Angeles*, Berkeley: University of California Press.

Naficy, H. (1993) *The Making of Exile Cultures: Iranian Television in Los Angeles*, Minneapolis: University of Minnesota Press.

Spellman, K. (2004) *Religion and Nation: Iranian Local and Transnational Networks in Britain*, New York: Berghahn.

34 | How the Japanese diaspora in Brazil became the Brazilian diaspora in Japan

Jeffrey Lesser

The big questions

Is 'diaspora' a place or a state of mind? Is it both? What are the implications of leaving a 'developed world' home for an 'underdeveloped world' diaspora? This essay analyses these questions by examining a rarely studied but extraordinary case of transnational homemaking, home-breaking and home-transforming: the migration of hundreds of thousands of Japanese to Brazil in the first half of the twentieth century and the migration of hundreds of thousands of Brazilians to Japan in the last decades of the same century.

The terms used to describe the movements to and from Brazil and Japan are highly contested. Are Brazilians who qualified for special labour visas in the 1980s and 1990s because of their ostensible Japanese descent engaging in a 'return' to Japan, a classic labour migration, or something altogether different? Does the term 'Nikkei', now in regular usage among scholars of ethnicity to refer to people of Japanese descent, have much meaning when notions of gender, class, generation, national identity and sub-ethnic identity are introduced? What ties these questions together is that some reaction to diaspora – and thus to home – is constantly in play. At one level, 'home' for Japanese-Brazilians is always Brazil, but it is related to a 'nation' that fluctuates between Japan and Brazil. Indeed, in Brazil, Japanese-Brazilians are constantly called 'Japanese' and identity often involves a failed attempt to reject the assumptions of the majority. In Japan Nikkei find themselves feeling and being treated as uncontestedly Brazilian.

This is a case where diaspora (home) and ethnicity seem to have an inverse relationship. Clearly both are constructed and thus highly mutable. Sometimes that construction is explicit and diaspora, home and ethnicity seem to be re-sources that are deployed in certain ways at certain moments. Perhaps this formulation is 'Brazilian' and has specific national-cultural dimensions. Without doubt, many readers of a volume on diasporas may be surprised to think of diaspora/home/ethnicity as currency in the marketplace of jobs, marriage partners or cultural action, but my research suggests just that, whether the subjects live in Brazil or Japan. Sometimes, however, diaspora/home/ethnicity seem less strategic in their construction, even appearing to be 'real' in that they are an emotional (and thus perhaps not explicitly strategic) way for people to comfortably think about themselves in both comfortable and awkward circumstances.

The story

When Japanese diplomat Sho Nemoto arrived in Brazil in September 1894, Brazil's planters were becoming disillusioned with European labourers who seemed more interested in protesting against labour and social conditions than in working as replacements for slaves (Holloway 1980: 36, 48). The Brazilian elite's hunt for submissive labour melded well with the Japanese government's desire to export its land-based citizens who they proposed were the 'whites' of Asia. Nemoto's visit would lead some 189,000 Japanese immigrants to settle in Brazil between 1908 and 1941 (followed by another 50,000 after the Second World War) (Saito 1961: 26–7). It is no surprise that, when the *Kasato-Maru* docked at the port of Santos with its Japanese immigrant passengers in June 1908, São Paulo's Inspector of Agriculture, J. Amândio Sobral, was impressed that almost 70 per cent of the newcomers were literate and 'in flagrant contrast [...] with our [Brazilian] workers' (Sobral 1908: 1).

The early years of immigration never lived up to the unrealistic expectations since Japanese were as unwilling to suffer bad treatment as other immigrants. Both Japanese and Brazilian officials, however, were eager to continue settlement, and with the help of the São Paulo state government, Japanese firms began to purchase large plots of land in regions where little agricultural development had taken place. By the 1920s Brazilian commercial interests in Japan had exploded. Japan became an important market for everything from rice to coffee, and Japanese immigrants and their production were seen as crucial both to the buying and selling parts of the equation. Yet the growing official ties between Brazil and Japan were challenged by a new public campaign against the large numbers of 'non-white' immigrants flowing into the country.

The twenties marked a decade of increasing Japanese visibility in Brazil. There were political movements to limit new Asian entries because 'the yellow cyst will remain in the national organism, inassimilable by blood, by language, by customs, by religion' (Reis 1931: 233–8). By the 1930s, the situation had become even more tense. In 1933, members of the Constitutional Convention, charged with producing what would become the Constitution of 1934, heavily debated Japanese immigration, conflating issues of imperialism, assimilation and nationalism. Thus, while the immigrant stream from Japan to Brazil would slow between 1933 and 1950, the discussion of the social place of Japanese and their descendants remained a national topic.

Heated debates took place in majority society as well. While Japanese entry dropped markedly between 1935 and 1942 (to a total of 15,000), discussions of immigration continued to focus on the Japanese (Crissiuma 1935; Rodrigues de Mello 1935). In a 30 May 1995 interview with the *Tokyo Nichi-Nichi Shinbun*, former minister of war Pedro Aurélio de Góis Monteiro, part of a pro-fascist contingent within the Vargas government that some years earlier had sought a ban on non-whites, claimed that 'in order to form an excellent Brazilian type, I consider it necessary to adopt the excellent Japanese element'. Such comments illustrate a number of key points that would be fundamental in the diasporic assumptions of the majority: an elite affinity for fascism, a political need to assuage the Japanese government in the years after the Constitution of 1934, and the growing sense that Japanese were 'white'. Put differently, it was just as Brazil became home for most Nikkei that the assumption of a diasporic loyalty to Japan arose among the Brazilian elite.

The imposition of the totalitarian Estado Nôvo (New State) by Getúlio Vargas in November 1937 markedly changed the ways in which ethnicity would be treated in Brazil. New decrees sought to diminish 'foreign' influence in Brazil, modifying the ways in which the Japanese and Nikkei community operated. Japanese-Brazilian newspapers were censored and then banned while the Nikkei community kept a low profile in the face of racist attacks (*Jornal do Brasil*, 19 January 1938). In 1938 a wide-ranging 'Brazilianization' campaign began. This state-driven homogenization programme sought to preserve an imagined Brazilian identity from the encroachment of ethnicity by eliminating distinctive elements of immigrant and minority culture. New legislation controlled entry and prevented foreigners from congregating in residential communities. Decrees required that all schools be directed by native-born Brazilians and that all instruction be in Portuguese and include 'Brazilian' topics. All foreign-language publications had to be accompanied by Portuguese translations and speaking foreign languages in public and private (including houses of worship) was banned (Decree Law 1.545, 25 August 1939).

The 'Brazilianization' campaign was based on an assumption that Japanese-Brazilians had diasporic Japanese rather than local Brazilian loyalties. Why, asked many Nikkei for whom Brazil was their only nation, was Brazilian citizenship not a guarantee of recognition as a non-foreigner? Was not Brazil a heterogeneous society where eugenics proved that Japanese had become Brazilians? Many Nikkei thus took Brazilian nationalist positions within the context of Japanese-Brazilian ethnicity, although this position did not resonate among the political elite, who took an increasingly bellicose stance towards resident foreigners.

Until the end of 1941 Vargas sought to maintain relations with both the Allied and Axis powers, but after the attack on Pearl Harbor in December Brazil moved firmly into the Allied camp. In March 1942, the Vargas regime ruptured diplomatic relations with Japan and compelled Japanese to move from areas defined as 'strategic'. Reports of Japanese spies (virtually all were inaccurate) were carried daily in the press (*Diário da Noite*, 30 September 1942).

The social and ethnic tension created by the anti-Japanese attitudes led members of the Japanese and Nikkei community to strike back against the public order by becoming increasingly 'Japanese'. Emperor worship, always strong among those educated in the first quarter of the century, soon began to replace ancestor worship as a form of identity preservation in Brazil (Reichl 1995: 42). Those who did not actively show their loyalty to Japan were defined as 'enemies' and the underground Japanese-language press was filled with denunciations of those judged to have lost their 'right' to be 'Japanese' (Maeyama 1979: 594). A group of secret societies emerged whose ultra-Japanese nationalism mixed with a desire to reinforce a space for Japanese-Brazilian identity. Soon the tripartite debate on hyphenated ethnicity (between Nikkei, Brazilians and Japanese) exploded into bloodshed and the destruction of property.

These movements would have been confined to historical footnotes if they had not begun to expand enormously after it became clear in 1944 that an Allied victory was assured. In July of that year Brazil sent 25,000 troops to Italy, causing immense nationalist and anti-Axis feeling in Brazil. It was during this period of intense anti-Japanese propaganda that the secret societies garnered their widest support. The idea of Japan's defeat had little resonance among immigrants and Brazilian-born rural dwellers for a number of reasons. For those educated in Japan or in Japanese-language schools in Brazil, much of the curriculum was developed with books and ideas from Japan's Education Ministry. This combined with a ban on Japanese-language newspapers and the poor circulation of Brazilian newspapers in rural areas. Newsreels of the surrender ceremonies were never seen by Japanese farmers, who had no access to cinemas, and those in rural areas often received their news about the war from hidden shortwave radios, clandestine newspapers, or orally via neighbours (Kumusaka and Saito 1970: 167–75).

The secret societies represented a counter-attack on the way Brazilian national identity was defined and thus an important redefinition of diasporic ethnicity. For example, the Shindo Renmei (Way of the Subjects of the Emperor's League) emerged after the Estado Nôvo was toppled in a 1945 coup and demanded new spaces for Japanese-Brazilian ethnicity. Its goals were to maintain a permanent Japanized space in Brazil through the preservation of language, culture and religion among Nikkei and the re-establishment of Japanese schools. What the Shindo Renmei did not promote was a return to Japan. Home was Brazil, and by December the Shindo Renmei claimed a membership of 50,000 who believed that Japan had won the war (Susumu and Yamashiro 1992; Tigner 1961). A small group of fanatical youth was recruited to assassinate those who spoke against the movement, and in early 1946 sixteen people were assassinated (*O Dia*, 6 April 1946).

By late 1947 a number of factors began to marginalize the secret societies. Efforts to raise funds for Japanese war victims, without ever declaring winners and losers, created groups that recognized defeat but, in a typical expression of minority-group politics, took the position that a 'family matter' should not be discussed with majority society. At the same time, continued Nikkei economic ascension in Brazil, and the growth of a *sansei* (third) generation, marginalized still further those who pledged loyalty to the emperor. By 1950 most Brazilian Nikkei rejected a diasporic identity even as society at large continued to define them as 'Japanese' and insist that the diaspora was the predominant identity factor in their lives. This attitude can be seen clearly in an ugly joke that even today circulates among the educated: 'Guarantee your place at the University of São Paulo tomorrow – kill a Jap today.'

The attitude that Brazilian Nikkei are 'Japanese' continues. Even today the absence of a linguistic distinction between Brazilians of Japanese descent and Japanese citizens has led some Nikkei to the conclusion that they can only become Brazilian by changing their appearance. This is most noticeable among Nikkei women, who have plastic surgery on their eyes to look more occidental. High levels of inter-ethnic marriage (almost 46 per cent overall and over 60 per cent in some regions of the country) are also a fact of life in the Nikkei community. Part of the explanation is the entry of the Japanese-Brazilian community into the middle class and above, decreasing the pool of partners for those unwilling to 'marry down'. As important is that many members of the majority have developed a model minority stereotype, making Japanese-Brazilians seem like especially good marriage partners.

The insistence by majority Brazilians that Nikkei are 'Japanese' is one important reason why some 250,000 Nikkei currently live and work in Japan. Since cultural identity is intimately tied to class status in Brazil, wage differentials play an important role in this migration. Yet oral histories with Nikkei working in Japan indicate that questions of identity are critical to the decision to leave Brazil. A thirty-seven-year-old university professor who migrated in 1991 is typical: 'In Brazil I am a stranger even though I like Brazil. I feel like I do not have Brazilian nationality and I feel like a gypsy. I wanted to make myself the perfect Brazilian but this is impossible. But here in Japan I also feel like a foreigner' (Watanabe 1995: 350–51).

In Japan many Nikkei 'feel' Brazilian for the first time; the diaspora 'home' has become the best location for non-diasporic national identity. Brazilian identity formation in Japan is based on stereotypes of Brazil most often found outside the country. A colour photo of a group of bikini-clad young Nikkei women splashed across the front page of the Tokyo-based newspaper *Jornal Tudo Bem* was a proud nod to the 'Brazilianization' of Japan: The headline reads: 'A Guide to Guarantee Your Luck this Summer' (*Jornal Tudo Bem*, 19 July 1997, p. 1).

The question of how to maintain a national identity in a national culture that insists on diaspora is as present today as it was in the 1920s and 1930s. In the early 1980s the *Diario Nippak* newspaper began publishing a biweekly Portuguese-language supplement that sought to explore the history of Japanese immigration and 'the duality of being Nipo-Brazilian'. Another Nikkei newspaper recently asked, 'Who are we? Japanese or Brazilian?' (*Japão Aqui*, April 1997, p. 63). As one nineteen-year-old interviewed during the weekly 'Nikkei night' at a dance club stated, 'Here [inside the club] we feel at home, we are all from the same nation' (*Jornal Tudo Bem*, 19 July 1997, p. 3). To which nation he was referring was not clear, but the search for home/diaspora continues today as it did 100 years ago.

Further reading

Hirabayashi, L. R., A. Kikumura and J. Hirabayashi (2002) (eds) *New Worlds, New Lives: Globalization and People of Japanese Descent in the Americas and from Latin America in Japan*, Stanford, CA: Stanford University Press.

Lesser, J. (2003) *Searching for Home Abroad: Japanese-Brazilians and Transnationalism*, Durham, NC: Duke University Press.

— (2007) *A Discontented Diaspora: Japanese-Brazilians and the Meanings of Ethnic Militancy, 1960–1980*, Durham, NC: Duke University Press.

Linger, D. (2001) *No One Home: Brazilian Selves Remade in Japan*, Stanford, CA: Stanford University Press.

Masterson, D. with S. Funada-Classen (2004) *The Japanese in Latin America*, Champaign: University of Illinois Press.

35 | Migrations within China

Flemming Christiansen

In the grand perspective of history, China's migrations assume particular importance as a dynamic that transformed disparate territories into an empire that assimilated large populations into a shared cultural universe and at the same time celebrated local and ethnic diversity. During the last 1,400 years, from the Tang (618–907 CE) dynasty, the southward migration from the North China Plain, the Lower Yangtse region and Fujian has probably been the most important frontier in China, along the coast creating settlements and trading ports like Chaozhou, Guangzhou and Haikou, and from there expanding into the South China Sea in the monsoon trade with ports in what was later to be called Luzon (Philippines), Malakka (Malaysia, Singapore), Siam (Thailand), Annam (Vietnam) and farther afield (Wang 1991), while other migrants to Lingnan (lit. 'South of the Mountain Range', mainly corresponding to today's Guangdong and Guangxi) entered through mountain passes, settling in and cultivating the huge rainforests, cohabiting and intermarrying with and assimilating local peoples to forms of agricultural production they carried with them from the north (Marks 1998).

The destruction of the rainforest and the ensuing siltation of the huge bay south of Guangzhou, caused by the great quantities of mud carried by the West, North and East Rivers, created the Pearl River and the rich mudflats and polders that gave rise to a regional affluence paralleled only in the Lower Yangtze region. It was, in particular in the Ming (1368–1644 CE) and Qing (1644–1911 CE) dynasties, large lineages (or clans) that claimed sedentary land rights over village territories who formed the local, landed power-basis of empire, submitting to Confucianist ritual and gaining recognition (Faure 1989, 2007), while less privileged groups, often jettisoned by lineage elders and joining together in gangs and brotherhoods, migrated and settled on ever more marginal lands (Leong 1997). The 100 years of unrest that began in 1840 with the Opium Wars, and continued with the Taipings, the Nian, the Red Turbans, the Fists of Righteous Harmony (Boxers) and so on, destabilized rural production with the result that millions of people were forced into migration in pursuit of a livelihood (Wakeman 1966; Skeldon 1995).

Towards the end of the nineteenth century the ailing Qing Empire, ruled by the Manchus, saw its borders threatened by the British in India and the

Russians seeking to gain control over Tibet, Xinjiang, Mongolia and Manchuria, and in response opened up these territories for immigration by land-hungry and destitute migrants from other provinces in China. The thinly populated three north-eastern provinces (together regarded as Manchuria) had already in the 1870s become a prime target for migrations, helped by sailing-ship lines from Yantai in Shandong and from Nantong in the Lower Yangtze region and the easy overland access from Zhili (now Hebei) province. In the same period, migration to Inner Mongolia took off, mainly from Shaanxi and Shanxi, rapidly populating the fertile bend of the Yellow River in Hetao, and gradually turning the forbidding soils of Chahar, Ordos and Tumed into agricultural lands. The expansion in the early twentieth century of railways from Beijing both to the north-eastern provinces, with Harbin as the new railway hub, dominated by the Russians and later the Japanese, and to the north-west, through Zhangjiakou (Kalgan), Hohhot (Guisui) and ending in Baotou, helped mass migration on its way, some routes providing settlers with free journeys (Lattimore 1947; Gottschang and Lary 2000; Tighe 2005).

The political violence of the early twentieth century surrounding the abdication of the emperor in 1911 and the establishment of the Republic of China in 1912, the warlordism of the 1910s and 1920s, intensified Japanese encroachment on Chinese territory from 1931 and the Second World War, starting in China in 1937, followed by civil war (1945–49), added further to the huge internal migrations. In the 1950s, demobilization of the large armies partly took place by building up large state farms in Xinjiang and the three north-eastern provinces of Jilin, Liaoning and Heilongjiang, i.e. what had formerly been called Manchuria (Gottschang 1987; Seymour 2000). In the late 1940s, as communist victory was imminent, many Chinese industrialists and merchants relocated to Hong Kong, while some followed the Nationalists to Taiwan.

It is probably right to say that the mass migrations of the first half of the twentieth century created the foundations for Chinese economic development. The movement of people under the Republic of China between the 1910s and the 1940s had created a sense of shared nationhood that had not existed before, and given them a sense of modern citizenship, advances in transport and communication, and the emergence of new forms of urban life, the upheavals creating the foundation for new types of industrial and economic growth. By the mid-1950s, communist rule in the mainland was channelling this new dynamic into the socialist planned economy. The industrialization, especially the large state-owned heavy industries in the north-eastern provinces, in Inner Mongolia and major cities across China, benefited from the ready availability of labour with a background in high degrees of mobility.

Even so, the planned economy, once started, locked the population into strictly separated agricultural and urban resident categories under the household registration system (Christiansen 1990; Davin 1999); only those people who were allocated as labour in urban industries (and their dependants) were urban residents, while the rest by default were members of rural people's communes, each having a share of collective land ownership in a specific production team. Between 1958 and 1986, this system, aimed at rationalizing the use of labour, consequently became a major obstacle to mobility, as people needed to obtain travel permits and would need food rationing coupons from the right jurisdiction in order to survive.

The movement of large numbers of migrants to Hong Kong, as well as the rapid land reform in Taiwan, which saw large numbers of people moving out of agriculture to small, often informal, enterprises, created new opportunities for economic growth. In Hong Kong, the continuous flow of new cheap labour enabled Chinese immigrant capital to develop new lines of mass production of plastic goods, toys and textiles, as well as electrical and electronic gadgets, taking advantage of new markets in Europe and the United States. In Taiwan, the competition for markets, investment funds and licences between large state-owned corporations and the SME (small and medium enterprises) sector forced the latter into international markets, also taking advantage of cheap, migrant labour. This led to rapid growth in these economies from the 1960s through the 1970s.

During these years, the mainland Chinese economy grew considerably, drawing on an immense productivity gain in agriculture, which allowed (with the exception of the disaster years of 1960 and 1961) the feeding of a population that doubled between 1949 and 1985 on a cultivated land area that declined in the period. Industrial output also increased to meet the greater needs of the population. In overall terms, however, more than 80 per cent of the population remained in rural areas. Life quality was, in spite of relative equality, poor and insufficient, and in per capita terms one can say that China experienced stagnation or even some decline. The economic and political reforms that started in 1978 began to set in motion a huge wave of internal migration on the mainland. The planned economy, with its all-pervasive and thorough approach to allocating the resources in the economy, allowed limited mobility into the urban areas to those whose labour was needed in the state-owned work units, policing the flow of people through a mixture of the household registration system and the rationing of essential foodstuffs and other consumer items.

The reforms opened new markets outside the planned system, and with the gradual lifting of the rationing system for more and more goods and the broadening of the activities of state-owned enterprises in the 1980s, now operating both within the planned economy and the emerging markets, increasing numbers of rural people began to seek opportunities outside their villages. Virtually all these migrants retained their rural registration, which through their household made them members of their communities and thus collective co-owners of land. This meant that their sojourn in urban areas or other parts of the countryside did not bestow any rights on them. Many obtained temporary residence permits in their destination area, while others stayed without any formal procedure; in either case, they were not entitled to formal employment in state-owned enterprises, were not included in the social, educational, health and pension provisions of the work units, and often lived on the fringes of society. Their contribution to the economy grew, and they became increasingly indispensable as the backbone of the reforms. Not only did they perform the myriad petty services that the planned economy had failed to deliver, they became the flexible (easily hired and dismissed) and cheap manufacturing workers in the increasing production outside the plan quotas, and they joined the huge construction gangs that built the motorways, railways, harbours, airports, industrial parks, urban estates and shopping centres that have characterized Chinese economic growth in the thirty years since the reforms started. Their numbers, estimated to be between 150 and 200 million, by the mid-1990s already exceeded the workforce of the state-owned enterprise sector.

The wage difference between urban workers and migrant labourers and the gulf in social provisions between the two groups must be seen in relation to the fact that migrant workers in the cities were able to earn significantly better incomes than in their home villages; their remittances helped sustain the livelihoods of their families, and their mere absence tended to be a blessing, as there were fewer mouths to feed. In return, the families and villages provided the social safety net, when non-essential migrants were on occasion forced out of the cities or when they had to return owing to illness or injury incurred in the often dangerous urban workplaces; the absence of rights to send children to school in the cities also meant that migrants' children stayed with grandparents or other family members in the villages in order to be able to go to school (Murphy 2002, 2008; Zhang 2001).

The local bond, the 'place of the ancestors' (*jiguan*), has from the time of early Chinese migration been an important vector for diasporic community-building; native place organizations (*tongxianghui*) and trade guilds (*huiguan*) formed centres of collaboration and representation both in foreign diasporas and in the Ming and Qing empires, while secret brotherhoods like the Hongmen or 'Triads' tended to mix political opposition with millenarian aspirations. These types of organization were probably so prominent because Chinese migrants were faced with environments little inclined to accommodate them: in the colonies, the Dutch, British, French, Spanish and other colonial powers 'managed' the Chinese through ghettoization in separate districts and the restriction of their economic activities, whereas in Chinese destination areas, trade guilds in particular became essential for ensuring safeguards and equal treatment of migrants and traders. The lack of social integration with local populations in terms of rights and status gained a boost with the emergence of the treaty-port working class of the late nineteenth and early twentieth centuries, whose subordinate role was made manifest in terms of dialect and 'civility', as vividly described by Emily Honig (1992) in her account of the Subei sojourners in Shanghai. The interlude of the planned economy, which restrained population mobility between the 1950s and the 1980s, was not able to deal such practices a final blow. The difficulty even today of migrant workers in gaining permanent legal residence in cities, and the fact that they must uphold vigorous links with their place of origin, means that they maintain a strong sense of 'diaspora', themselves considering their urban sojourn as temporary. Fellow-villager sentiments, real and imagined kinship relations and shared economic and social responsibilities of migrants and their rural kinsfolk on the one hand and dialect, the public discourses of 'civility' (*wenming*) and 'breeding' (*suzhi*), together with labour market fragmentations, on the other, underpin the urban diaspora of rural migrants in China (Kipnis 2006).

The internal labour migrants of the 1980s, 1990s and 2000s constituted a major driving force in China's development of a foreign-invested enterprise sector. The Special Economic Zones established in 1979 in Shenzhen, Zhuhai, Shantou and Xiamen, and in 1986 in Hainan, attracted workers from across China to work in foreign and private companies. Wider areas of Guangdong, in particular in the Pearl River delta, as well as in Fujian, Zhejiang, Jiangsu and Shandong, rapidly began to receive direct investments from Hong Kong, Taiwan and South-East Asian overseas Chinese in industries based in rural small towns, soon depleting all locally available workers and creating a huge demand for outside workers. Although the majority of the migrant workers were in manufacturing, construction and agriculture (the latter replacing local farmers entering the factories) and hailed from rural places, in fact the scale of development created needs for all skills levels in these particular growth areas along the coast. Also, urban secondary school graduates from interior provinces found their way into service sectors in, for example, the Pearl River delta, Fujian and Zhejiang. As early as the beginning of the 1980s, rural enterprises (owned by townships, villages or private entrepreneurs) began to headhunt graduates from technological colleges in the interior provinces, luring them with salaries, working conditions and living quarters vastly superior to what they could expect in state-owned enterprises at the time; this type of enterprise often involved significant de facto (not necessarily officially declared and approved) investments from Taiwan and/or Hong Kong, or production directly for the international market.

The growing affluence in China, of course, has helped emphasize the social contrasts; Deng Xiaoping's famous dictum at the outset of the reforms about allowing 'some to become rich first' has certainly come true, to the degree that China (with a Gini coefficient of 0.47) is more socially unequal than the USA (0.41), with particularly large regional disparities between inland and the coast, and between rural and urban areas. On top of this, the fact that the large migrant populations that have become permanent and indispensable in urban areas are denied basic citizenship rights where they work and live has, since the 1990s, become an increasing point of political contention. The high social costs of the pursuit of high economic growth rates were raised by foreign observers, by public intellectuals in China and within the political leadership. Although some efforts were made in the 1990s to address some of the issues, the determination to pursue policies that emphasize social justice was put on a strong footing only with the shift of leadership from Jiang Zemin to Hu Jintao in 2002. From 2003 onwards, policies, practices and in particular political discourse towards rural–urban migrants changed. The laws on enterprises (doing away with the last vestiges of the planned economy control) and on labour contracts created a significant level playing field between migrant and non-migrant workers; local rules on the household registration system began to change, and the introduction of equal treatment in terms of education, pensions, social security and health insurance also aimed to do away with disparities and labour market fragmentation.

The labour contract law of 2008 and the international economic crisis starting later in the same year have led to a serious deinvestment in coastal regions and the return of migrants to villages in large numbers. The crisis has meant, however, that foreign strategic investments in coastal areas in research and development have picked up, as highly skilled Chinese engineers and scientists can replace staff with similar skills in the UK and Europe at a fraction of the cost; this allows more graduates from good universities to migrate to Shanghai, Zhejiang, Jiangsu and Guangdong, where the main centres of such development are situated, while the workforce returning to the villages is believed by many observers to invest in informal sectors (evading the clauses of the labour contract law), which provide for both domestic and international markets at more competitive prices.

Looking at migration in China, the precarious land:labour ratio has continued to dominate, a theme of the southward migration to Guangdong and Guangxi and to Manchuria (now Liaoning, Jilin and Heilongjiang), and even more so in the internal migrations of the post-1978 reform era. In early phases, the movement of people beyond boundaries to South-East Asia created a strong recruitment base for emerging commercial and industrial sectors. In each case, the displacement and labour market fragmentation were important factors in creating a comparative advantage through exploitation of migrants. Similarly, the shifting of boundaries has allowed areas like South-East Asia, Hong Kong and Taiwan to become the investors in the coastal regions of the Chinese mainland.

It is the passing of official borders or boundaries which defines migration (of the human species); the internal migration in China is a particularly interesting case, for the official internal boundaries created differential status and rights, be it between Hong Kong and the mainland or between the rural and urban sectors. Crucial to the efficacy of labour mobility in terms of creation of growth was the perpetuation of the migrant status, enabling prolonged exploitation of the 'outsiders', and their confinement to certain sectors of the economy.

Further reading

Davin, D. (1999) *Internal Migration in Contemporary China*, Basingstoke: Macmillan.

Gottschang, T. and D. Lary (2000) *Swallows and Settlers: The Great Migration from North China to Manchuria*, Ann Arbor: Center for Chinese Studies, University of Michigan.

Leong, S. (1997) *Migration and Ethnicity in Chinese History: Hakkas, Pengmin, and Their Neighbors*, Stanford, CA: Stanford University Press.

Murphy, R. (2002) *How Migrant Labour Is Changing Rural China*, Cambridge: Cambridge University Press.

Zhang, L. (2001) *Strangers in the City: Reconfigurations of Space, Power, and Social Networks within China's Floating Population*, Stanford, CA: Stanford University Press.

36 | Beyond Tibet

Dibyesh Anand

If a worldwide survey is conducted to ascertain what people outside China have heard about Tibet, the knowledge is likely to be peppered with ingredients of the smiling Dalai Lama, illegal Chinese occupation, peaceful Tibetans, human rights, Western governments fearful of offending the economic juggernaut of China, and so on. It is an indicator of the strength of diaspora in setting the international agenda around Tibet. The Dalai Lama led the government-in-exile in Dharmasala and the 150,000-plus Tibetans living in the diaspora, mostly in India, Nepal and the West, have been instrumental in creating and nurturing the dominant narratives of Tibetanness. Thus the story of Tibet that most people are familiar with is the story narrated by the diasporic Tibetans living 'beyond Tibet'.

This sets the Tibetan diaspora apart from most other diasporas; other aspects which contribute to the uniqueness include the international media attention disproportionate to the size of diaspora, the good press which the Tibetan cause has in the West, and, most importantly, an unchallenged equation of one person with the national identity – the Dalai Lama in exile as the soul and symbol and personification of Tibet – who at the same time is a spokesperson for universal modernist Buddhism.

Where is 'beyond Tibet'?

What does 'beyond Tibet' mean? I interpret it as diaspora and not the border-land cultures infused with Tibetan Buddhism surrounding Tibet. Tibet as a distinct geopolitical entity with clearly recognizable boundaries never existed in history. It is a product of post-exilic imagination. This is not to say that Tibet as a political entity is a fiction – Tibetan empires, kingdoms, polities and societies took various forms at different points in history. But the boundaries were always blurred, very much a product of a non-modern fluid sense of state-hood (McGranahan 2003; Samuel 1982). Tibetan identity was synonymous with Tibetan Buddhism and Tibetan language, though there were a few non-Buddhist Tibetans living inside Tibet.

The adoption of the word diaspora for Tibetans needs clarification (Anand 2003; Baumann 1997). We must not read the meaning of diaspora to include those ethnic Tibetans who inhabited the contested, shifting and vague border areas of the traditional Tibetan state. Rather, the term diaspora confines itself to those Tibetans whose identity has at its core a sense of displacement from their homeland out of compulsion. The Tibetan diaspora is what started as a trickle in the 1950s with the Chinese liberation/occupation of Tibet, becoming a tide in 1959–61 when almost one hundred thousand Tibetans followed the Dalai Lama into exile. This was followed by very little outmigration while China waged a 'democratic reform' and 'cultural revolution' in Tibet, and its border relations with India were at their nadir, leading to another small but steady flow of Tibetans into South Asia since the late 1970s. This flow is now minimal and likely to remain so as the host countries, including Nepal and India, have become less indulgent. Tibetans tend to have distinct settlements in different parts of South Asia and in some Western countries; elsewhere they remain scattered among the host population.

Refugee diaspora

The Tibetan diaspora is one of refugees and their descendants. Exile and refuge is the preferred term for diasporic Tibetans for obvious reasons. These terms underline a sense of temporariness, the tragedy of exile, and hope of return. Diaspora may indicate that they have acquired a new identity that accepts their displacement as productive of their identity. While diaspora as a concept allows a scholarly and ethnographically more accurate appreciation of the key dynamics in 'beyond Tibet', it should not blind us to the self-understanding of the Tibetans which privileges a sacrifice of the certainty of citizenship in host countries through a retention of refugee status (Venturino 1997). Of course, there are differences within the diaspora itself as an acquisition of citizenship in Western countries where a considerable number of Tibetans now live is perceived as less of a betrayal than the acquisition of passports in South Asia.

Internal differentiation within the diaspora is along generational, class and regional lines (Nowak 1984; Prost 2006). Most Tibetan refugees are Buddhists belonging to one of the four sects – Gelug, Kagyu, Nyingma and Sakya – but others are Bon (which preceded Buddhism in Tibet) and still fewer are Muslims. In diaspora, however, a pan-Tibetan sense of identity has papered over these differences (Anand 2007). There is no significant fissure that has remained consistent over time. The success of the diaspora has been in creating an over-arching sense of Tibetan identity and a unity of purpose which transcends older differences. The most visible difference today is not between the older refugees and newcomers (though this is there as the new refugees are more Sinicized than the previous ones) but between the large majority who retain strong faith in the Dalai Lama's political approach, and a small minority of activists who are losing patience with it. But even the latter retain reverence for the Dalai Lama. Sectarian differences, as revealed in the Shugden issue, affect Western converts to Tibetan Buddhism more than they do the Tibetan diaspora (Lopez 1998). This is because many Western converts perceive the Dalai Lama's prohibition of the worship of a wrathful deity, Shugden, as infringing their human rights. On the other hand, most Tibetans who traditionally propitiated the deity see themselves as Tibetans first and foremost and are willing to go along with the Dalai Lama. This is a good example of Tibetans in diaspora shedding those traditional practices which encouraged sectarianism.

Preservation of culture

A close analysis of the Tibetan diaspora shows that the primary emphasis for fifty years has been on preservation of unique traditional Tibetan Buddhist culture (Bernstorff and von Welck 2003; Gyatso 1998; Michael 1985). This is understandable, for Chinese communist rule has been blamed for erasing Tibetan culture, suppressing the Buddhist religion, and destroying whatever made Tibet distinct from mainland China. The main monasteries of Lhasa were re-formed in southern India, seats of senior lamas (religious leaders) shifted to different parts of South Asia. Institutions such as Norbulingka were created explicitly for the preservation of Tibetan culture in both literary and artistic forms – including statue-making, *thangka* painting, appliqué and tailoring, woodcarving, carpentry and metal craft – that might otherwise have become extinct. The *tulku* system of reincarnate lamas – where reincarnations do not adhere to geographical boundaries – facilitates continuity. While the accent is on continuity and preservation, much research shows the innovation and constructed nature of this preserved traditional culture (Harris 1999; Klieger 2002; Korom 1997). Tibetan culture and even religion become recognizable translatable objects which can be understood within the modernist framework. The Dalai Lama is famous for his Buddhist modernism, so much so that he insists that his loyalty is first and foremost to universal human values, then to Buddhism and lastly to the Tibetan nation. This repackaged traditional Tibetan cultural identity is partly a response to the demands of imaginations in the West (Dodin and Rather 2001). It is also an inevitable product of residence in displacement. But it would be wrong to see Tibetans as merely passive, as 'prisoners of Shangri-La', for they have actively used positive exoticization to survive as a diaspora, protect their culture and keep their political agenda alive (Lopez 1998).

Nationalism in exile

Culture is an alibi for politics in the Tibetan diaspora. The formation of a pan-Tibetan culture and assertion of it as distinct from surrounding (especially Chinese) cultures is a political tool to express Tibetans as a political nation (Santianni 2003). Culture allows Tibetans to attract outside support, which is vital as the power asymmetry with China is huge. Culture allows Tibetans to foster a sense of nationhood and be politically active without an immediate crackdown by their hosts in South Asia (Kolas 1996). Culture thus is the most effective weapon in the Tibetan diaspora's struggle against Chinese rule. But this has its own limitations. For one, many young Tibetans who are more vocal and radical about Free Tibet are those who do not adhere to a purist sense of Tibetan identity. They might negotiate effortlessly with modernity in all its guises (Indian, Western, Chinese, Tibetan), are not overly religious, mix and match rock with traditional music, and yet feel proudly Tibetan. Reducing the Tibetan issue to one of cultural and religious rights in the international arena has meant that, while there is a lot of sympathy for the Tibetan cause, there are no prominent takers for Tibetan nationalism.

The Dalai Lama's middle way, which eschews independence in favour of genuine autonomy within China, insists on non-violence as a matter of principle and pragmatism. More radical Tibetans have no room to manoeuvre because of the dominance of the Dalai Lama and his culturalist paradigm restricting ethnic Tibetans to pacifist Buddhism. As protests by Tibetans since March 2008 inside China and in the diaspora show, while the reverence for the Dalai Lama is at its all-time high, people are willing to push the boundary of resistance to respond to what they see as a violent state machinery in China. Although one cannot predict the future, until now the use of violence to resist Chinese rule has been rejected as almost unpatriotic. This is despite the well-known history of Tibetan *Khampa* warriors rebelling and fighting against China in the 1950s–1970s.

Few other diasporas have the coherence of Tibetans. Few face a stronger adversary; no one has an all-powerful leader whose priority is to universal human values and not particularistic nationalist interest. The scenario of the post-Dalai Lama Tibetan diaspora is very much real and it is conjectured that the young Karmapa (third highest in the hierarchy of Tibetan Buddhism) – the most senior lama recognized by both the Dalai Lama as well as the Chinese government – who fled into exile in 2000, will take over as the main leader of the Tibetan diaspora. If this is indeed the case, it will demonstrate that Tibetans' loyalty is in fact to their national identity and not to a sectarian one for, while the Dalai Lama belongs to the Gelug sect, the Karmapa is the head of the Kagyu school. The hope of the Tibetan diaspora to one day achieve their goal in Tibet will also be kept alive.

Interactions with others

An important issue in a study of the Tibetan diaspora is its interaction with other actors. Indian political discourses (Ardley 2002), democracy and cultural influences (such as Hindi songs and movies) affect the lives of Tibetans significantly, though this is often perceived as 'alien' influence and not authentically Tibetan. The same goes for Western music or Hollywood (Diehl 2002). The interaction of the Tibetan diaspora with the West, however, is one of great importance (Anand 2007; Bishop 1989, 1993; Frechette 2007; Lopez 1998). Western conceptions of Tibet, often in positive exotic terms, affect and sometimes distort the public representation of Tibetanness in diaspora. Patronage from well-off and sympathetic Westerners is one of the most important means of social climbing and ensuring economic well-being for individuals. The strategy of the government-in-exile to internationalize the Tibetan issue through frequent foreign visits by the Dalai Lama and the activities of Tibet support groups makes the West a primary audience. As I have argued elsewhere, the West as a source of ideas and a political actor is very much integral to the Tibet question (Anand 2006). And the network of well-intentioned enthusiastic private individuals who commit themselves to the cause of Tibet ensures the continuing visibility of the Tibetan issue in the foreign relations of democratic Western states with China.

Could this diaspora have maintained its profile and unity had it not been for the leadership of the Dalai Lama (Rose and Warren 1995) or the Shangri-La-esque image of Tibet in the West (Schell 2000)? The answer is 'no'. In the face of displacement from the homeland out of fear, scattering in different parts of a vastly different landscape in alien countries, the history of sectarian and regional divisions, and the absence of a historical memory of unified statehood, unity is extremely precarious. In the case of the Tibetan diaspora, the Dalai Lama's leadership has provided the glue. He has been a visible symbol who has encapsulated different strands of Tibetan cultural identity, a spokesperson not for his sect but for the entire Tibetan nation. The government-in-exile, in its experiments with democratization since the 1990s, has gone out of its way to represent different regions of traditional Tibetan-inhabited areas in China, as it represents different sects of Buddhism and the Bon religion. The Dalai Lama's visibility, enhanced by the Nobel Peace Prize in 1989, has attracted supporters from a small but vocal group of Westerners. His status as a voice of reason and non-violence is the biggest indictment of Chinese attempts to demonize him. Western support often comes in the form of conversion to Buddhism, sponsorship of individual Tibetans, consumption of Tibetan culture, and numerous resolutions passed by legislatures in Western states to encourage China into dialogue. Even when this support is based on a misguided and distorted representation of Tibet, it at least allows Tibetans living beyond Tibet a voice in the international arena which they would not otherwise have.

The overwhelming dependence of the Tibetan diaspora on the Dalai Lama's personality and a high degree of reliance on Western support for cultural and political survival leave it vulnerable. It will have to prepare for the eventuality of the death of Tenzin Gyatso, the fourteenth Dalai Lama. China would hope that, with this, Western sympathy for Tibetans will disappear, the diaspora will scatter further and lose its unity of purpose and assimilate in various host countries. Tibetans would hope that a resolution to their political problem with China comes sooner. The Tibetan diaspora faces significant hurdles in the future and will require all its adaptability, creativity and diligence to survive and flourish.

Further reading

Anand, D. (2007) *Geopolitical Exotica: Tibet in Western Imagination*, Minneapolis: University of Minnesota Press.

Klieger, P. C. (ed.) (2002) *Tibet, Self, and the Tibetan Diaspora: Voices of Difference*, Leiden: Brill Academic Publishers.

Kolas, A. (1996) 'Tibetan nationalism: the politics of religion', *Journal of Peace Research*, 33(1): 51–66.

Korom, F. J. (ed.) (1997) *Constructing Tibetan Culture: Contemporary Perspectives*, Quebec: Heritage Press.

Lopez, D. S., Jr (1998) *Prisoners of Shangri-La: Tibetan Buddhism and the West*, Chicago, IL: University of Chicago Press.

37 | Sacred journeys, diasporic lives: sociality and the religious imagination among Filipinos in the Middle East

Mark Johnson, Claudia Liebelt, Deirdre McKay, Alicia Pingol and Pnina Werbner

The Philippines is one of the leading labour-exporting countries in the world, and Filipino migrant workers have been widely dispersed to localities in the Middle East, Europe, East and South-East Asia and North America. There is now a substantial body of work on this vast migratory movement, much of it focused on and contributing to understanding the predicament of female domestic workers (Constable 2007; Parreñas 2001; Stasiulis and Bakan 2005; Tyner 2004). This essay moves beyond the focus on inequalities associated with Filipino migrant labour, to attend to the ways in which female migrants transcend their isolation in work contexts by seeking sociality with fellow Filipinos in religious congregations. How does religion figure in the social life and imaginings of diasporic Filipinos, their moral imaginings and inscriptions of faith on sacred landscapes? This is particularly significant for Christian or Muslim migrants moving to countries that are also historically places of pilgrimage holy to Christianity or Islam. Hence, our research focused on these migrants' experiences in the Holy Land, the birthplace of Christianity, and Saudi Arabia, the birthplace of Islam. Filipinos are one of the largest groups of migrants in the Middle East (numbering some 1.5 million), making the region home to the largest population of overseas Filipinos outside North America.

Overseas Filipino workers and transnational relations of reproduction

Filipino migrants, women in particular, have popularly figured as 'maids to order': people who leave the poverty of their home country to work as domestic servants in another country in pursuit of a better standard of living for themselves and their families. Research on this topic contextualizes and complicates that popular stereotype, describing and theorizing key features of this major form of population movement in the late twentieth and early twenty-first centuries. First, this literature situates Filipino migrants within capitalist-dominated labour flows and distributions of global economic power, highlighting the growing dependence of the Philippines and other developing southern states on migrants' remittances, and arguing that the state creates and then super-exploits a feminized and unskilled migrant workforce (Parreñas 2001; Pertierra 1992; Stasiulis and Bakan 2005; Weekley 2004; Gibson et al. 2001).

Second, it explores critically the complex bureaucratic structures and discursive practices that have evolved within and across sending and receiving states to ensure the production of such compliant and self-disciplining subjects. By documenting the assemblage of discourses and bureaucracies governing domestic worker migration, this literature has explained how the circumstances of their labour migration tend to negate workers' individual rights and curtail their capacity to act collectively to change their working conditions. Though attentive to the way in which Filipinos resist their oppression through 'hidden transcripts', these critiques also emphasize how everyday acts of resistance are nonetheless circumscribed by the internalization of the regulatory ideals of the good 'foreign'/'national' worker (Constable 2007; Parreñas 2001; Tyner 2004). Third, this literature describes how broader structures of race, gender and class are reproduced in everyday working practices and intimate spaces of the employer's household, exploring how the incorporation of Filipino domestic workers into a global system of reproductive labour and care-work causes migrant women from relatively poor countries to assume the domestic and emotional labour of middle-class women in more affluent countries. Migrants' own children, in turn, are left in the care of husbands, grandmothers and other relatives at home, in the Philippines, a pattern often reproduced from one generation to another, with daughters following their mothers into overseas migration (Bakan 1995; Bakan and Stasiulis 1997; Barber 1997; Constable 2007; Parreñas 2005; Pingol 2001; McKay 2007).

This dominant focus on work and labour is undoubtedly useful for an understanding of Filipino migrants as a 'labour diaspora', but it is far from sufficient as a full account of Filipino migrant lives. Moreover, the focus on migrants' work conditions tends to ignore the fact that – despite being denied citizenship – many Filipinos become long-term residents in many countries of destination. During their extended stay they develop complex cultural practices and networks of sociality. While migrants' affective and emotional lives and motivations are no doubt inflected by highly constraining regimes of economic, institutional and disciplinary power, they are neither reducible to, nor exhausted by, them. Even when they face continuous predicaments in their work contexts, Filipinos nevertheless find ways of creating spaces for socializing and celebration that deny their image as culturally impoverished 'docile bodies'.

Beyond 'maids to order': spiritual sojourns in sacred places

Addressing these gaps in the literature, our project has explored migrants' emotional and intellectual engagement with the social and symbolic geographies of host countries. Work in the Middle East is often viewed as a stepping stone, and considered second best to working in a 'Western' country such as the USA,

Canada or the UK (Johnson 1998; Liebelt 2008a). For Muslim and Christian Filipinos, however, living and working at the holy centres or homelands of their respective faiths may mitigate the hardships of living in exile and the difficult working conditions. Filipino migrants in many parts of the world talk about the sacrifices they make in order to support their families and loved ones back home. That sacrifice may take on an altogether more religious dimension when – as some Muslim Filipino workers do – they talk about their labour in sacred places, such as Mecca or Medina, as work whose reward is deemed not only or primarily to come in this life but in the life hereafter. So, too, Christian Filipinos describe their work in Israel as enabling them to come into metonymic contact with the Holy Land and its sacred sites, and portray the challenge of caring for the elderly as part and parcel of their ministry of spreading the gospel (Liebelt 2008a).

For migrants, religion is not simply about the rewards of the afterlife. Their varied religious engagements and familiarity with a sacred landscape may increase their cultural capital at home. Undertaking the hajj or *umrah* (minor pilgrimage) exemplifies this point. Whereas before, undertaking the hajj was impossible for all but the most affluent of Muslim Filipinos, one of the positive benefits of working in the Middle East, for women as well as men, is that many have been able to fulfil this final pillar of Islam. In the process, they have also increased both their own and their families' social standing and prestige. The significance of the hajj for Muslim Filipino workers is attested to by the fact that some respondents reported walking out on employers who prevented them from going on pilgrimage. But equally, there are other examples of employers who not only allowed but positively encouraged and sometimes assisted their employees in making the hajj.

Christian Filipinos similarly can gain respect and prestige from people at home who acknowledge them as pilgrims in their journeys to 'the Holy Land'. Working as caregivers in private homes, Filipinos not only learn Hebrew, but get an intimate picture of Jewish culture and religion, especially appreciated as knowledge of Christian roots among evangelical Christians. Catholic lay groups and independent evangelical churches, formed by female Filipino domestic workers, organize Catholic Block Rosary Crusades in Tel Aviv, pilgrimages to holy sites in Galilee, Jerusalem or Bethlehem, and frequently engage in long-distance philanthropy. As with *zamzam* water from Mecca, the films and pictures taken and the devotional items acquired during pilgrimages travel back to the Philippines, supporting migrants' claims that their sacred journeys have enhanced their spiritual knowledge and potency.

Migrants, by establishing religious congregations in their places of settlement, create community away from home. This is a salient feature of migration often ignored in studies of overseas Filipinos, not all of whom are religious. For those who are, religion fills their lives with social events, from congregational meetings and prayers to the joyful celebration of ritual festivals like Christmas or Eid-al Fitr. Some of these festivals may take place in churches or mosques, others in homes where Eid celebrations, for example, bring together migrant co-workers and employers along with their extended families. This regular and recurrent sharing of religious events provides opportunities for migrant workers who may otherwise live relatively isolated lives during the week to celebrate in the company of co-religionists and fellow Filipinos, to gossip, joke and chat while providing advice and mutual aid. Importantly, these ritual events can enjoy broader social sanction in the host societies.

Filipino migrants are well known for meeting and socializing in the more secular contexts of public parks and shopping malls. One of the best-documented examples of these is the Sunday gathering of Filipino domestic workers in Hong Kong (Constable 2007; McKay 2005). Here, Filipinos, largely engaged in domestic work, routinely colonize the space of the central business district after attending church. On the streets, in the parks and along the pavements, they meet, share food and exchange news and goods with fellow migrants from the same village, town or province in the Philippines. Their village gatherings re-create and extend a sense of ethnic affiliation and village material and cultural economy in a translocal space (McKay 2005). These gatherings are also sites of political agency where migrants form 'home-town associations' that engage in philanthropy and political action at home and support internal migration within the Philippines (ibid.; McKay and Brady 2005.)

In the Middle East, Filipino migrants similarly re-create the conviviality of home and ethnicity in various ways. In Tel Aviv, they colonize the Central Bus Station for karaoke, shopping, self-decoration, clubbing and get-togethers. Elsewhere in the Middle East where public gatherings are more circumscribed, informal and mixed groups of Muslim and Christian Filipinos hire private venues and congregate in makeshift parks (designated *khamsa-khamsa* because of the five-riyal charge), re-creating 'fiestas' in desert locales. Here, religious events and congregations, like the more secular social occasions and modes of exchange in Hong Kong, may help to create and enhance a sense of a shared home place in diaspora by fostering close links with particular places in the Philippines. Thus, for example, a pilgrimage group in Tel Aviv-Jaffa donates money for building a chapel to a specific congregation in South Cotabato in the southern Philippines, while in Jeddah a group of Christian Filipino converts to Islam (referred to as 'reverts' or *balik Islam*) sends money to support the building of a mosque in their home town in Luzon.

Shared religious practice also draws in co-religionists from other countries and from other parts of the Philippines in ways that transcend ethnic and village localities. Worshipping together simultaneously creates and consolidates a wider sense of shared national affiliation and of belonging to a global community of believers. Muslim Filipinos, for example, claim what they regard as their rightful place among the universal community of the faithful, but also routinely contrast themselves as Muslim Filipinos to Arab Muslims. For Muslim Filipinos that distinction is often articulated in religious terms: Arabs may have been blessed by being the ones to whom the Prophet and the Koran were sent, and hence may have more in the way of religious knowledge and be better informed about appropriate religious conduct and ritual practice. What Muslim Filipinos lack in the way of head knowledge, however, they more than make up for in terms of purity and steadfastness of heart. Just as evangelical Christian Filipinos regarded themselves as missionaries and evangelists in the Holy Land, some Muslim Filipinos saw themselves as performing *da'wah*, calling non-believers to revert and return to Islam (*balik Islam*), and fellow believers, among them Arab Muslims, to renew their faith and examine their heart.

The idea of membership in a universal community of believers is important in establishing a language of shared ethics across divisions of status and power. This is especially so in situations for lone migrant workers who have little recourse to employment and citizen or residential rights and little or nothing in the form of collective representation. For such people, religion may be an important means of making and pressing moral claims both on fellow workers – to socialize, to exchange, to share – and on employers, even if it is only to persuade them to allow their employees to participate in, if not take time off work for, shared religious events. For some migrant workers, religion was the primary language for talking about and defending one's sense of self and personhood. Religion offered a means of expressing social agency in those diasporic situations where they might otherwise be forced to comply with and bear the everyday humiliations of subordination and difficult working conditions in exchange for a relatively small sum of money to send home.

Migrants engaged religion to express their agency in a variety of ways. Muslim Filipinos had recourse to a form of lamentation where emotional outpouring in the form of cries, tears and sobs in 'public' spaces within the home or workplace are accompanied by the pointed and vocal recitation of Koranic verses in the presence of their Arab employers. Filipino domestic workers caring for elderly Jews have learned about and drawn parallels between Jewish sufferings and experiences of exile and their own diaspora experiences. This learning enables one group to declare to state policy-makers, 'We are the Jews of today' (Liebelt 2008b).

Religion shapes the expectations and experiences of particular places and host societies for both Christian and Muslim Filipino migrants. While a religious stress on self-sacrifice, endurance and good works can, paradoxically, reinforce and consolidate dominant discourses that produce docile and disciplined bodies, religion can, at the same time, facilitate social networks and mobilization against exploitation by enabling new forms of sociality. Religion is thus an important symbolic resource for people in the struggle for recognition and rights both at home and abroad. Framing forms of sociality and social action within a moral discourse among an imagined universal community of believers not only helps migrants to make longer sojourns bearable, but also opens up ways of negotiating a sense of belonging and cultural citizenship in host nations.

Further reading

Constable, N. (2007) *Maid to Order in Hong Kong: Stories of Migrant Workers*, 2nd edn, Ithaca, NY: Cornell University Press.

Liebelt, C. (2008a) 'On sentimental Orientalists, Christian Zionists, and "working class cosmopolitans": Filipina domestic workers' journeys to Israel and beyond', *Critical Asian Studies*, 40(4): 567–85.

McKay, D. (2007) '"Sending dollars shows feeling": emotions and economies in Filipino migration', *Mobilities*, 2(2): 175–94.

Parreñas, R. S. (2001) *Servants of Globalization: Women, Migration and Domestic Work*, Stanford, CA: Stanford University Press.

Tyner, J. A. (2004) *Made in the Philippines: Gendered Discourses and the Making of Migrants*, London: Routledge.

38 | Muslim travellers: homing desire, the *umma* and British-Pakistanis

Seán McLoughlin

The 15 million people of Muslim descent now settled in western Europe represent the most significant movement of labour into the continent since the Second World War (Cesari and McLoughlin 2005). This essay explores the salience of an Islamic 'homing desire' for contemporary Muslim diasporas. It focuses on the idea of belonging to the *umma*, a synchronic and diachronic community of believers which claims membership of around one billion believers across over fifty nations worldwide. The *umma* can be said to have a clear mytho-historical and territorial orientation in terms of Mecca, the birthplace of Islam and its Prophet, as well as remaining the focus of a return there during the greater and lesser pilgrimages, the hajj and *umrah* (McLoughlin 2009). The emphasis here, however, is on more deterritorial and extraterritorial, translocal and supra-local imaginings. I begin by exploring how and why universal religions might create a homeland consciousness analogous to that of a diaspora, continue by sketching what this has meant in terms of the history of Islam as a travelling faith, and conclude by examining the extent to which global crises involving Muslims and the Islamic world since the 1990s have revealed what Werbner (2002b) calls the predicament of diaspora among British-Pakistanis.

Diaspora consciousness, homing desires and religious identity

In a highly globalized society, time and space are compressed with such increasing intensity and extensity that the experience of simultaneity across distance is becoming possible in some aspects of transnational life. Even amid the flows of people, capital, goods, information and ideas, however, social relations beyond the local remain imagined – indeed, ever more intensely so. Because of advances in communications technology, diasporas no longer struggle as they once did to maintain contact with their homelands and co-ethnics dispersed worldwide. Nevertheless, absence, loss and the fallibility of memory continue to produce fictions of home and community which, while being 'imaginatively true', inevitably remain partial and fragmented representations (Rushdie 1991: 10). For this reason postmodern and post-colonial reappropriations of diaspora theory have problematized a preoccupation with homeland origins. At the same time, such a preoccupation lends legitimacy to host-land formulations of belonging that construct racialized and ethnicized minorities as 'in' but not 'of' the nation. Instead, theorists like Hall, Gilroy and Bhabha valorize interstitial spaces between 'here' and 'there' as sites for imaginative counter-narratives which resist, reconfigure and translate home and host-land traditions anew, mapping new cartographies of identification which the conventional diasporic triad (cf. Sheffer 1986b; Safran 1991) cannot necessarily contain. This, then, is the context for scholars' consideration of more deterritorialized and metaphorical imaginings of belonging beyond place and the nation-state – for example, in terms of Brah's emphasis on 'a homing desire which is not the same thing as a desire for a "homeland"' (1996: 179–80; cf. Clifford 1997).

In this regard, Cohen's original typology (1997: x) speaks of cultural diasporas – more recently and usefully redubbed *deterritorialized* diasporas (Cohen 2008: 18). Some Caribbean peoples, for example, are said to 'have lost their conventional territorial reference points [...] [they] have become in effect mobile and multi-located' (ibid.: 124). Other examples of such atypical diasporas include the religious diaspora of Muslims, the main focus of this essay. The question of whether a particular religious tradition or religions in general can properly, or usefully, be described in terms of the concept of diaspora is, however, disputed. Vertovec, for example, draws a distinction between 'ethnic' religions such as Judaism, Sikhism and Hinduism, which seem to qualify, and 'universal' religions such as Christianity, Islam and Buddhism, about which he is more sceptical. Historically, the latter have been less obviously tied to particular peoples or places: 'It broadens the term far too much to talk – as many scholars do – about the "Muslim diaspora", "Catholic diaspora" [...] and so forth [...] [A]re Muslims in Pakistan part of a diaspora religion because Islam is derived from and broadly centred on Mecca?' (2004b: 281). For all the slipperiness of religion as a category in this regard, however, Cohen does seem to acknowledge that such issues are worthy of further exploration:

[R]eligions can provide additional cement to bind a diasporic consciousness, but they do not constitute diasporas in and of themselves [...] The myth and idealization of a homeland and a return movement are also conspicuously absent [...] their programmes are extraterritorial rather than territorial [...] On the other hand, once we admit the category of a cultural diaspora, we are also opening out the possibility that spiritual affinity may generate a bond analogous to that of a diaspora. (1997: 189)

The suggestion here is that while in different time/space combinations religions indigenize and often reinforce territorial identifications, it is the ability to trump such processes with extraterritorial imaginings which is both especially salient and peculiarly well enabled in a globalizing world. Despite 'composite origins' (Stewart and Shaw 1994: 18), the power of religions resides in their mythic, symbolic and ritual resources to narrate the idealized fictions and abstracted unities which seek to emphasize stability over flux and secure continuity through time and across space. Portable sacred texts, competitive missionary aspirations and the activities of translocal orders all point towards religion as the original globalizer (Lehmann 2001). As Turner notes, however, in the past, 'world religious systems had little opportunity to realize themselves globally' (1994: 83). Thus some key transformations associated with modernity, including advances in communications technology, have facilitated universalizing discourses seeking to better assert themselves. Rather than assimilate or liberalize, even traditions characterized as essentially resistive of singular definitions such as 'Hindu-ism' have tended to emphasize 'universalizing' religious tendencies in a pluralizing world (cf. Smart 1987; McLoughlin 2010). Indeed, self-conscious of difference – provoked by interactions with others, both with the state, wider society and a broader range of co-religionists – diasporas are notable for producing increasingly rationalized and homogenizing accounts of their traditions.

While transnational flows relativize identifications everywhere, such processes are experienced especially intensely in diaspora. Jet-setting intellectuals and artistic elites often playfully celebrate a sense of homelessness in this regard, but cultural difference and intermixture are experienced by many migrants in terms of crisis, alienation and doubt (Werbner 1997a: 12). Moreover, while multiple identities are a given, a politics that seriously challenges the inequalities and exclusions of the world's global cities has not emerged from the endless shifts of hybridity. We must all speak from somewhere, and being heard requires an act of prioritization and 're-presenting' oneself (Werbner 1997b: 228). For many migrants, then, it is in a selective return to aspects of cultural tradition that many have rediscovered the moral resources to restore certainties in the face of cultural translation and social exclusion (Hall 1991b: 52–3; Werbner 1997a: 21).

As homeland attachment, custom and language lose their valency when memories fracture, especially among those born in the diaspora, the argument here is that religious alternatives open up the possibility for a new, more mobile, 'homing desire' (Brah 1996: 179–80). Unlike assimilation, maintaining universal religious (as opposed to homeland cultural) boundaries manages the problem of cultural identity without the risk of losing all sense of a 'chain of memory' (see Hervieu-Léger 2000). New 'routes' may be imaginatively continuous with 'roots'. Of course, recalling Anthony P. Cohen (1985), the symbolic construction of community rests upon shared symbols and not unchanging meanings. Therefore, in the context of host-land exclusion of racialized and ethnicized minorities, as well as the uneven power geometry of West–Rest relations, non-Christian religions are especially well resourced to imagine moral and political orders beyond the secular nation-state and, arguably, the universal claims of Western modernity itself.

Travelling Islam and the idea of the *umma*

As Eickelman and Piscatori suggest, various forms of travel and associated 'journeys of the mind' (1990: xii) – including hajj and *ziyarah* (pilgrimage to the tombs of holy people), as well as *rihla* (travel seeking knowledge) and *da'wah* (proselytism) – have all contributed to the Islamicate religious imagination past and present. Such mobility has 'inspire[d] changes in how Muslims conceive of and experience "Islam"' (ibid.: 3) as believers have negotiated their similarities and differences in encounters with Muslim 'others' at least as much as non-Muslim 'others'. Islam's own myth of origins enshrines the symbolic significance of religiously inspired journeying in the account of early Muslims' persecution as a minority in Mecca and emigration (*hijrah*) to the oasis of Yathrib (later known as Madinat al-Nabi or Medina, the City of the Prophet). Marking the very beginning of the Muslim (*hijri*) calendar, 622 CE or 1 AH, it imagines a symbolic move from Meccan *jahiliyya* (ignorance) to a new, self-governing, social and political order. The universalizing monotheism hitherto associated with the 'higher' civilizations of the Byzantines and Sassanids became the vehicle for a broader unity among politically fragmented and polytheistic tribes. Indeed, having received God's final message from the seal of all his prophets, Muslims believe their *umma* (a term associated with both religiously inclusive and exclusive meanings in the sources) to be 'the best community' (Koran: 3.110; 4.41; 16.89 – see Dallal 1995), a new chosen people open to all humanity. Nearly 1,400 years later, Medina remains the perfect expression of Islamic purity and power for Muslims (Metcalf 1996; Mandaville 2001).

While conquest, trade and imperialism over many centuries eventually saw Islam territorialized in myriad places from Morocco in the west to Indonesia in the east, large-scale conversions were not at first encouraged among the Muslims as they burst out of the Arabian peninsula. Islam ceased to be a closed hereditary caste (a diasporic ethnic group?), becoming a cosmopolitan civilization rather than the Arab kingdom of the Umayyads (661–750) only as it travelled and universalized, a new peace economy based on trade emerging under the Abbasids (750–1258). Among the new urban elite was a class of religious scholars who confirmed a mature Sunni orthodoxy (Lapidus 2002; Rippin 2005). Indeed, some controversial revisionist historians even suggest that Islam's myth of origins is a product of this period. In any case, the emergence of Sunnism is a story of various localized Muslim knowledges, from Medina in Arabia to Kufa in Iraq, being relativized and normatively reorganized translocally in conversation with Muslims elsewhere (see Mandaville 2001). Notably, it achieved authority without a centralized structure (four schools – *madhahib* – of law being authenticated, although no others emerged after the tenth century).

In 1258 Baghdad finally fell to the Mongol invaders (who eventually became Muslim themselves), but the political/territorial decentralization and fragmentation of the Abbasid empire had been evident for some time. Certainly the institution of the caliph (deputy of God/his prophet) had lost its significance as a symbol of pan-Islamic political integration. Indeed, medieval Islam was marked by a period of worldwide diffusion and pluralization, with Muslims of Persian, Turkic and Central/South/South-East Asian origin eventually outnumbering Arabs. The religious beliefs and legal practices that Muslims shared, however, provided 'a sort of citizenship' (Dallal 1995: 269) in the homeland(ish) entity of *dar al-Islam* (the abode of Islam). Travelling scholars, Sufis and pilgrims integrated diverse populations into shared universes of meaning across tribal, agrarian and urban societies. While 'Islamizing the indigenous' necessarily involves numerous fractures and breaks, and orthodoxy's claims to universality can never be completed, the very career of Islam thus reflects the enduring power of its religious imaginary.

Perhaps because it achieved the status of a dominant ideology, Mandaville (2001) argues that it is difficult to speak of Muslims' collective effort to mobilize as a political community from its origins in Medina until the period of globalized modernity. Pan-Islamist activists such as the peripatetic Persian, Jamal al-din al-Afghani (d. 1897) and those involved in the movement to revive the Ottoman caliphate (disestablished by Mustapha Kemal in 1924), called for the *umma* to reawaken and unite in a bid to repulse European colonizers from *dar al-Islam*. With greater consciousness of the world as a single place, and their own relativized position within it at a time of growing literacy, nationalism and print capitalism, well-established patterns of religious revival in Islam became a vehicle for a new sort of identity politics among Muslim elites. While some adopted strategies of *hijrah* from and jihad against Muslim and non-Muslim 'others' in the dislocated present, more characteristic was the general desire to return – more or less imaginatively (*ijtihad* being the term for effort in interpretation) – to a sacred home and ancestors of the past, in the hope of making a better future (see Asad 1986). The emergence of Islamism in its many variants, loath to simply accept the West's attempts to copyright modernity, can be viewed as an attempt to narrate a rival universality (Sayyid 1997).

British-Pakistanis, diasporic predicaments and Islamic identities

In the post-colonial period, an identity politics with Islamic revivalism at its centre eventually gained new strength in the Muslim world from the 1960s and 1970s onwards. Often oppressive, secular nationalist regimes were struggling to deliver development equitably to growing, youthful populations with higher expectations and, as the Iranian revolution of 1979 demonstrated so iconically, Islam(ism) became more central to articulating political alternatives. Nascent Muslim diasporas such as British-Pakistanis were not at all isolated from such processes. With initial support from movements such as Jama'at-i Islami, which had a small but well-organized following among mainly urban-origin migrants (often students and professionals) in the UK, General Zia ul-Haq (1977–86) initiated a policy of Islamization in their homeland. Moreover, as the recollections of British-Pakistani writer Ziauddin Sardar (2004) begin to document, a network of activist intellectuals in London were being courted by Iran (Kalim Siddiqi's Muslim Institute) but also Saudi Arabia as the two went head to head for leadership of the putative global *umma*.

For demographic reasons, it was not until the 1980s and 1990s that such discourses impacted on significant numbers of British-born and educated Pakistanis. Educated segments of this generation especially embraced the idea of a universalizing, 'true' Islam as a serious strategy of self-identification which mapped out clear boundaries for behaviour in the testing context of cultural pluralization (J. Jacobson 1998). They distinguished a faith rediscovered anew through personal exploration and participation in study circles from the ethno-cultural and highly sectarian homeland-oriented Islam of their (often uneducated) parents (Lewis 1994). Unlike the rote Islam of the Urdu-speaking mosques, in its new, multi-ethnic and English vernacular 'true' Islam opened up a more cosmopolitical consciousness and reinvented religion as a badge of pride, a tool with which efforts could be made to transcend increasingly evident circumstances of local deprivation and racist social exclusion (Modood 1990). Even among those who were not pious or educated, and were gradually assimilating aspects of English working-class culture, Islam as identity made a lot of sense. For all their continuing pride in being Pakistani, British-born youth do not feel 'at home' when they visit Panjab or Kashmir (McLoughlin and Kalra 1999).

Grassroots British-Pakistani communities had made the case for the public recognition of Islam in an ad hoc, locally agreed fashion as part of multicultural policies since the early 1980s (Lewis 1994). The era of a truly diasporic Muslim identity politics, however, was catalysed only during the Rushdie affair of 1989, events being played out on a national and global scale. The perceived attack on Islam with the support and consent of dystopic Western powers and other conspirators produced often-to-be-repeated utopian ummatic discourse, expressed most obviously in the Ayatollah's fatwa, calling for unity and self-reliant action among Muslims as a victimized community. With the mass media relaying news of the book, protests and interventions in the debate by religious movements and leaders (Bhatt 1997), many Pakistanis, British Muslims and their co-religionists across the globe mobilized against *The Satanic Verses*, temporarily forgetting their ethnic, sectarian and other differences.

Indeed, during the last two decades, coverage of political crises involving the occupation of Islamic lands and the plight of Muslim minorities worldwide has sustained a consciousness of such issues, and the fables that surround them (Werbner 2002b), so consistently that global events now represent a key factor in being British-Pakistani. The Gulf and Bosnian wars of the early to mid-1990s, as well as the ongoing conflicts in Palestine and Kashmir, and since 9/11 the so-called 'war on terror' in Afghanistan and Iraq, have all triggered heartfelt (and increasingly publicly performed) conflicts of loyalty and co-responsibility. Most often this resulted in peaceful protest or other contributions to an increasingly transnational Muslim civil society – for example, in terms of charitable giving (McLoughlin 1996). But, for a small number, it meant taking up arms, at first overseas and then at 'home' in the host land as the events of 7/7 demonstrate (see Begg 2006). For Werbner (2002b) these are typically diasporic predicaments.

Further reading

Eickelman, D. F. and J. P. Piscatori (eds) (1990) *Muslim Travellers: Pilgrimage, Migration and the Religious Imagination*, Berkeley: University of California Press.

Mandaville, P. G. (2001) *Transnational Muslim Politics: Reimagining the Muslim Umma*, London and New York: Routledge.

McLoughlin, S. (1996) 'In the name of the umma: globalisation, "race" relations and Muslim identity politics in Bradford', in W. A. R. Shadid and P. S. van Koningsveld (eds), *Political Participation and Identities of Muslims in Non-Muslim States*, Kampen: Kok Pharos, pp. 206–28.

Metcalf, B. D. (ed.) (1996) *Making Muslim Space in North America and Europe*, Berkeley: University of California Press.

Werbner, P. (2002b) *Imagined Diasporas amongst Manchester Muslims: The Public Performance of Pakistani Transnational Identity Politics*, Oxford: James Currey.

39 | Diasporic dialogue among the British in Australia

Sara Wills

Referring potentially to tens of millions of people around the world, who on the whole moved voluntarily, can one really speak of a British diaspora and still retain any sense of a migrant community that makes a shared, active attempt to resist assimilation and maintain a sense of identity outside the 'home' country (Tölölyan 1996; cf. Tennenhouse 2007)? Especially in Australia – a colonial settlement that gained nationhood as a dominion of empire following early forced migration but mostly free settlement – what notion of diaspora might apply to inhabitants of this nation in which at least half of the population still nominate some form of British or Irish ancestry on the census, where the United Kingdom remains the largest source of all immigrants (around 20 per cent), and where, on a plain English reading of the constitution, Queen Elizabeth II is still head of state? From the beginning of the colonial era until the mid-twentieth century, migrants born in Britain or Ireland comprised the vast majority of settlers coming to Australia, and created a nation founded firmly on notions of white racial identity, British subjecthood and, notwithstanding strong Irish or Celtic identification among some, a largely English culture – an identification that remained intact even into the latter half of the twentieth century, and some might argue even later. Britishness, it is argued, is not dispersed in Australia; it is recentred there in a 'house that Jack built' (Moreton-Robinson 2005).

By way of a contribution to broader understandings of diaspora, and in particular an understanding of the specific maps and histories of the individuals who constitute groups, this essay outlines the ways in which post-Second World War British migrants to Australia have begun to develop and narrate diasporic experiences relevant to their position in a post-imperial, 'multicultural' Australia since the 1990s.

Unsettling British identities in Australia

Many scholars have argued convincingly that diasporic journeys and formations must be historicized and explained in terms of the differences between members of groups in addition to their similarities, as well as in relation to dominant social formations (Brah 1996). Any invocation of the British as a diaspora in Australia must pay attention, therefore, to the fact that during the nineteenth and much of the twentieth centuries the idea of a 'British people' – combining those of English, Scots, Welsh and even Irish origin – developed a particular currency, based on a myth of commonality reinvented and romanticized by the English themselves in the nineteenth century (Cochrane 1994; Jupp 1998). Indeed, in Australia, the argument goes, peoples from England, Scotland, Wales and even Ireland had much more in common than they did in Britain. Britishness in Australia was not the same as Britishness in Britain – it was a unique form of Britishness that underscored an emergent Australian nationalism (Meaney 2001). Thus, while it is unevenly experienced and claimed, the 'British' in Australia share a 'legitimacy' based upon a history of invasion, settlement and dispossession of Aboriginal peoples dating back to the eighteenth century, and which continued into the twentieth century; upon a history of colonialism and empire, and racially restrictive immigration policies that existed until the early 1970s; and upon British subjecthood and a sense of 'white' national identity that continued to privilege migrants from the United Kingdom and Ireland until the early 1980s (and less directly still today).

In the 1980s deliberations about the shape and nature of Australia's bicentennial celebrations provided one point of departure for the post-imperial unravelling of British identity. The period of Labour government under Paul Keating, and subsequent debates in the 1990s leading up to the referendum on a republic, also explain why Britishness in Australia has come under particular scrutiny during the last twenty years. During this period, there has been a reassessment of pre- and post-war Australia–Britain relations (Ward 2001); historians of immigration have begun to chart the specificity of regional identities within the category 'British', with questions asked also about differentiated class and gender experiences (Hammerton and Thomson 2005; Jupp 2004; Peel 1995; Wills 2004); others have analysed new and newly emergent forms of British 'whiteness', or charted its demise (Carter 2002; Brabazon 2000; Stratton 2000). At the same time, others have asserted the centrality of values figured variously as British, English or Anglo-Celtic to the well-being and affirmation of the nation (Dixson 1999).

In the last decade, however, a distinction has begun to be drawn between 'Anglo-Australia' and the identity and experience of more recent British migrants. Particular attention has been paid to the post-Second World War period. Studies have outlined, for example, how, for many post-war migrants, their movement was never a matter of simple 'transplantation' to a British settlement overseas; and how migrant Britons who arrived after the Second World War often felt distant from established 'Anglo-Australia', but were assumed to feel 'at home'. It has been recognized that for the British, also, migration has resulted in complex changes in relationships with the 'homeland', and thus in the migrant's transformed sense of self and community in Australia (Hammerton and Thomson 2005; Thomson 1999; Wills 2005).

For some, such recognition or reassessment forms part of a broader 'discourse of loss and recuperation' that has emerged as a 'response to a split and crisis within whiteness' in Australia. It has been argued that 'British migrants'' inclusion in the narrative of Australian migration history works to separate them from the history of indigenous dispossession [...] in spite of the fact that their migration is one of the benefits that accrue from that history' (Moreton-Robinson 2005: 26; see also Hage 1998). Undoubtedly some narratives do operate in this way. Yet the 'sense of declension and melancholy' emerging from new narratives also produces something more than just a 're-centring of white possession' (Moreton-Robinson 2005: 21). The notion of diaspora may be used, I believe, in order to develop an appreciation of how post-war British immigrants to Australia have begun to renegotiate multiple and conflicting histories and subject positions in contexts that have gradually required such renegotiations. Broad conditions for the emergence of these diasporic dialogues have been noted above, but greater understanding of the trends identified is provided by examining more specific 'maps and histories' (Clifford 1994: 302).

Locations and negotiations

In 2001–03 I conducted fieldwork in the outer Melbourne suburb of Frankston among self-identified 'British' migrants, whose emerging diasporic sense of self negotiated particular socio-economic outcomes and experiences of life in Australia: often (though by no means always) comprising a lack of upward social mobility (relative at least to pre-migration expectations) as a result of changes to the economy from the 1970s onwards. These changes saw the dismantling of Australia's protectionist economy – based predominantly on commodity exports, capital imports and a protected and highly regulated manufacturing sector – in favour of an 'internationally competitive structure' that 'opened' domestic capital, product and labour to global markets (Catley 1996). The profound changes that accompanied a broad macro- and microeconomic agenda had, by the late 1990s, produced what economists describe as a more 'flexible and resilient' national economy, but also saw the establishment and consolidation of disadvantage in specific locales – often in outer suburbs adjacent to declining industry (Fincher and Saunders 2001; Peel 2003). These were, in some cases, suburbs that had been identified and inhabited by British migrants in the post-war years as the locale of their migration dreams. In many respects, Frankston was one of these.

These economic conditions were coupled at the time of fieldwork with renewed discussions about the literal and metaphorical borders of the nation (these years saw a peak of asylum seekers arriving by boat in Australia largely from the Middle East and Central Asia and new legislation developed in relation to their arrival). They included the escalation of what some have described as a 'paranoid nationalism' (Hage 2003), including anti-asylum-seeker legislation pushed through by a government able to mobilize and broaden the appeal of forms of populist political nationalism that had emerged in the late 1990s. Pitched as a corrective to the excesses of a 'mushy and misguided' multiculturalism that had fostered national disunity (Wills 2002), it was a time of debate that caused some British migrants and Anglophile Australians to re-emphasize 'British culture and heritage' as a key part of Australia's 'multicultural' history and identity, and in some instances produced a form of 'self-ethnicization' in order to claim both a specific migration history and ethnic identity (Stratton 2000).

Yet to focus on these new formations only as discourses of 'loss and recuperation' of British white power in Australia is to miss significant elements of a broader picture. My fieldwork captured a set of individuals at a moment when many of them were ready to tell their stories *as* British migrants – as part of the multicultural story of Australia – but with no particular sense of their claim to now be telling *the* national story in Australia. There was certainly a sense of loss and nostalgia about this among some, which can usefully be explored as an outcome of a sense of fading 'white' power in Australia. But these are stories that also provide ways of exploring new and generative inventories and trajectories of migration. These acts of narration reveal the emerging articulation of a desire among some British migrants to redeem the silences, ellipses and unevenness that have characterized their experience as 'invisible immigrants', and of negotiating individualized inventories of identity (Wills 2005).

Memory, place and change

'Fred' is one such case in point. Fred was interviewed in 2002 as part of fieldwork conducted in the outer suburbs of Melbourne, an area that became a favoured destination for some British migrants. Fred had lived in this area since his arrival in Australia in 1960. With a Glaswegian mother and London-born father, Fred tells a story that reflects the complexities of Australian Britishness, as well as elements of the local history of seaside suburbia soured for some by recession and disadvantage. Yet it was one of the more unusual interviews conducted, not because of the details of the story relayed at interview, but because of what was communicated subsequently through the provision of a manuscript that comprised a partially completed autobiography. The manuscript details how Fred was born in Poplar, London, and came to Australia for the first time in 1960 as a thirteen-year-old with his mother and brother after his father had died. His uncle ran a boarding house in Frankston, and his mother thought that joining her brother in Australia might help them to start afresh. Over 220 pages, the unfinished but carefully written manuscript outlines a story of struggle and survival, similar to the 'battler narratives' identified by others who have charted the stories of other migrants to Australia (Hammerton and Thomson 2005).

Yet only after reading the manuscript in full did I understand that Fred did not so much want a relatively fleeting engagement over the course of an interview, but an appreciation of the ongoing, everyday meaning-making that is involved in the dialogic act of writing and creating identity in this manner – with forms of expression that for him had helped to address the question of identity in diaspora: of gathering fragments of the self into a sensible and collective whole (Papastergiadis 1998). The form of his manuscript is evocative of Fred's desire to narrate and hold this identity together. A great Beatles fan, Fred introduced each chapter with excerpts from their songs. Thus with a lyric about places remembered from the song 'In My Life' acting as a prompt for the story that follows, Fred begins Chapter 1 by locating himself firmly in the history of post-war London:

> 28th June 1947. Eros was back!
> He'd been to that place where all British treasures went during World War II. He was now back in his rightful place at the centre of Piccadilly Circus [...] home amidst the hustle and bustle that was post-war London. On the same Saturday that he returned, I arrived.

Similar gestures throughout this chapter embed Fred's childhood identity in the landscape of post-war London. Eros comes back for Fred as the desire to communicate his emergence out of such scenes, 'to go back to "square-one"', as he writes at the start of Chapter 13 when referring to a return visit to London with his wife and first child. This going back, not always a literal return, is also an act that links Fred's act of writing to his mother, who had sought to situate him before he left England. In an earlier chapter Fred describes how they walked the city and toured its sights on a series of 'magical mystery tours' to ensure that he knew about his birthplace, and could respond when people asked him where he came from.

Yet while Fred's story was constructed clearly to narrate a sense of identity in common with his mother, and their family origins in Britain – to narrate the self as a collective – it also negotiated that identity so that his children could establish their relationship to this narrative. 'Dear Sir or Madam, will you read my book?/It took me years to write, will you take a look?' Fred asks at the start of his manuscript, indicating the ongoing and everyday nature of its construction (as well as his familiarity with the Beatles' 'Paperback Writer'). This is clearly addressed to his children who 'don't appear to be interested in [...] where we, and therefore they, came from', the Foreword revealing him engaging in a process of explaining his identity to his children as part of an ongoing family concern with 'knowing where you're from'.

What I wish to underline here is not so much the story itself but the fact and mode of telling, which mark an emerging desire for wholeness among British migrants as they seek to narrate new identities for themselves in Australia. It is not an unalienated identity, and there is an acknowledgement of being dispersed at a distance from the 'centre'. What we have in Fred's manuscript is evidence of a desire to communicate how identity has been experienced in everyday life, and how this identity is marked by its journeys and placements within and between Britain and Australia. With the aid of the language of the Beatles, Fred creates for himself a poetic language to convey the moods and feelings of what constitutes belonging, placement, loss and perhaps only partial resettlement. Fred creates a vocabulary of desire through the Beatles – uses their lyrics to express *eros* in its Jungian sense – as he both 'binds' and 'loosens' what it means to be English and Scottish and British in Australia. There are places Fred remembers all his life, but he knows his place has changed.

In some respects, these findings about the British in Australia provide few original insights about migrant identity formations or diasporic activities. What is new is the conception of the British as diasporic subjects in Australia, indicating their repositioning within broader national developments and new formations of nationhood, as well as a desire to remain connected to homelands. Through personal and collective remembering, these connections are being kept alive among people now starting to articulate their experiences as migrant individuals, if not communities. Slowly, these accounts are being recorded within autobiographical narratives, memoirs and even a few novels (Kershaw 2002; Reilly 2004). Many of these underscore the embeddedness of selfhood in the *placed* histories of travel and re-establishment, weaving threads of diasporic feeling – 'forms of longing, memory, (dis)identification' (Clifford 1994: 304) – into new 'strategies of "dwelling"' (Fortier 2000: 19), both within the self and within Australia.

Further reading

Hammerton, A. J. and A. Thomson (2005) *Ten Pound Poms: Australia's Invisible Migrants*, Manchester: Manchester University Press.

Jupp, J. (2004) *The English in Australia*, Cambridge: Cambridge University Press.

Moreton-Robinson, A. (2005) 'The house that Jack built: Britishness and white possession', *Australian Critical Race and Whiteness Studies Association Journal*, 1: 21–9.

Wills, S. (2005) 'Passengers of memory: constructions of British immigrants in post-imperial Australia', *Australian Journal of Politics and History*, 51(1): 94–107.

Wills, S. and K. Darian-Smith (2003) 'Beauty contest for British bulldogs: negotiating transnational identities in suburban Melbourne', *Cultural Studies Review*, 9(2): 65–83.

40 | Diasporic creativity: refugee intellectuals, exiled poets and corporate cosmopolitanism at the BBC World Service

Marie Gillespie

The BBC World Service has received much of its intellectual and creative impetus from diasporic and displaced people. This will be illustrated in three case studies of individuals broadcasting to India and the Caribbean in the 1930s and 1940s and to the Soviet Union during the Cold War. Exiled, refugee and dissident intellectuals were assembled at Bush House, the London home of the World Service. There, they established, and historically renewed, the BBC's corporate cosmopolitanism.

The BBC World Service (BBCWS) is literally, and financially, a state broadcaster. Funded through a parliamentary 'grant-in-aid' administered by the Foreign Office, it nevertheless retains a unique 'aura of impartiality' and projects a cosmopolitan soundscape of the world, albeit limited by prevailing corporate interests and British geopolitical priorities. The Foreign and Commonwealth Office (FCO) dictates where the World Service broadcasts but editorial control rests with broadcasters, except at times of war.

Currently the BBCWS broadcasts to an estimated 185 million listeners, viewers and Web users around the world in thirty-two languages as well as in English. The number of language services changes according to geopolitical, financial and marketing imperatives. Resources are now being redirected from radio to new regional tri-platform (radio, online and TV) services in Arabic and Persian. The paradox remains: how can BBCWS as a state broadcaster maintain its aura of impartiality and its reputation as a forum for free debate? The answer proposed is: through diasporic creativity and corporate cosmopolitanism.

From Empire Service to diasporic Overseas Service

The BBC Empire Service started off as a diasporic contact zone at its foundation in 1932 (Gillespie et al. 2010). Diasporic contact zones are social and symbolic spaces and places for creativity, performance and representation (Pratt 1992). They are marked by historically forged, asymmetric power relations, in this case negotiated through the interactions between British and diasporic broadcasters based at Bush House and their audiences (interpellated by the 'London Calling!' channel signature), but also through the web of professional and personal exchanges, friendships, working relationships and rivalries among broadcasters (see Plate 3).

The first director general, Sir John Reith, announced that the Empire Service would provide 'a unique opportunity to foster bonds of understanding and friendship between the peoples of Britain's scattered dominions and the mother country, and to bring to Britons overseas the benefits already enjoyed by the British public at home' (Mansell 1982: 1). The British diaspora included administrators, soldiers, settlers, experts and assorted expatriates. The Empire Service would keep them in touch with the motherland and with each other.

The threat of war transformed the BBC's imperial mission in the English language into one of fighting fascism in foreign tongues. The first 'vernacular' language services were set up in Arabic, Spanish and Portuguese in 1938 to compete with Italian and German radio propaganda. The BBC transmuted into a polyglot Tower of Babel. From 1937 to 1941 BBC staff numbers increased threefold to 9,000 (ibid.: 104). In 1939 the Empire Service was renamed the BBC Overseas Service. The embryonic Ministry of Information asked the BBC to monitor enemy propaganda in dozens of languages. Dissident writers, artists and intellectuals who flocked to London, the epicentre of the fight against fascism in Europe, found their linguistic skills in strong demand. After a voice test and a translation exercise, 'gifted amateurs' began broadcasting to their compatriots and/or monitoring radio and press in their respective languages. By October 1941 nearly 250 bulletins in thirty languages were being monitored daily by 500 foreign language specialists who listened to the war unfold and translated its intrigues, surprises and tragedies (ibid.: 104). Among them were diasporic intellectual stars like Ernst Gombrich, George Weidenfeld, Martin Esslin and Anatol Goldberg (later the BBC's most popular voice across Russia). By 1942, the BBC was broadcasting in forty-five languages. But most of what was broadcast was scripted in English and translated.

'Talking to India'

The Eastern Services first broadcast in English and Hindustani (and later in Bengali, Gujarati and Marathi) to India. George Orwell was a talks producer (1941–43), working in close partnership with an Indian Muslim called Zulfaqar Ali Bokhari, Indian programme organizer (1940–65) for 'Talking to India', and later head of Pakistan radio. 'Talking to India' broadcast commentaries, poetry, plays and music, targeting anti-fascist propaganda at India's intellectual and cultural elites. Orwell's scripts were translated into Hindustani and read out, or 'ventriloquized', by Bokhari and other diasporic Indians (Thiranagama 2010). The aim was to secure the allegiance of Indians to Britain's war effort. This was a time of fraught Indo-British relations. The 'Quit India Movement' was taking off and prominent Indian nationalists were allying with the Axis powers. Subhas Chandra Bose's 'Free India' radio propaganda was influential among Indian audiences.

The right kind of diasporic voice emanating from the imperial metropolis was, as the BBC knew, a tool of enormous cultural and political power. Accent, tone and cadence were essential to conveying a British perspective, without compromising the BBC's reputation for impartiality (Ranasinha 2010). Diasporic Indians were courted to contribute to the programmes. Voices critical of British policy were considered particularly valuable. Mulk Raj Anand, who had arrived in Britain from the Punjab in 1924 to undertake postgraduate studies, was a key figure in London's intellectual and cultural scene. A friend of Orwell, Louis MacNeice, T. S. Eliot, E. M. Forster and Virginia Woolf, he helped shape London's literary modernism by injecting anti-imperial and cosmopolitan perspectives (ibid.). Anand was well known for his anti-imperialist Indian nationalist rhetoric. His novel *The Sword and the Sickle* (1942) raged against the exploitation as 'cannon fodder' of the 2 million Indian soldiers who fought under the British flag in the First World War. His opposition to the colonial government, and its brutal suppression of nationalists, put him in conflict with the British government. But, to the BBC, dissident diasporic voices would increase the Indian audience's confidence, and the credibility and influence of broadcasts. At first Anand refused the BBC's overtures. In 1942, however, he capitulated. He not only 'ventriloquized' Orwell's scripts but authored his own. He contributed to the 'Open Letters' series, condemning Nazism and fascism as vociferously as he did British imperialism, combining a cosmopolitan internationalism with Indian nationalism.

Many diasporic broadcasters were caught up in the contradictions posed by the war: the paradoxes of trying to fight fascism and imperialism at the same time. Some Indian dissidents and exiles aligned themselves with the British while others acted as cultural brokers. For example, Venu Chitale worked for the Indian section during the war and broadcast pioneering programmes in Hindi and Marathi comparing the situation of women in Britain and India while Princess Indira of Kapurthala was House of Commons correspondent for the BBC.

The cultural politics of Indian broadcasters during the war remains relatively little researched. The Caribbean case is better known.

Caribbean voices

The Caribbean section of the BBC's Overseas Service was launched in 1939 with the programme *Calling the West Indies* to boost the morale of the island colonies and counter nationalist sentiments. Like the Eastern Services, it relayed messages from servicemen in 'the mother country' to their families back home (Newton 2008). Una Marson, a journalist and poet, was a leading figure in the service, who believed in the power of literary expression as a tool of cultural and social development. She participated in the poetry magazine series *Voice* edited by Orwell for the Eastern Service. This poetry programme was one of the few truly cross-diasporic contact zones at the World Service. It brought together diasporic Indians and Caribbeans alongside their peers in other language services in the fight against fascism – and the shared belief in the power of the pen over the sword.

During the war, Una Marson began to receive short essays and pieces of writing and some of these were broadcast. This provided the catalyst for *Caribbean Voices*, a weekly programme in which poets, playwrights and prose writers showcased their writing. It was first broadcast in 1943 with Una Marson as the presenter, but her time at the BBC (1939–45) was difficult. She felt conflicting loyalties: supporting the war effort and campaigning for liberation from colonial rule. Living in London and moving in its transnational political, intellectual and literary networks, she became committed to pan-Africanism, and in 1945 she returned to the Caribbean. Her successor, Irishman Henry Swanzy, continued to respond to demands from audiences for cultural space and representation. *Caribbean Voices* helped launch the careers of V. S. Naipaul, George Lamming and Derek Walcott. It provided an outlet for young writers; it paid very well.

Previously unknown Caribbean voices were being selected, edited and judged by metropolitan standards. The programme's embrace of local dialect, idioms and syntax transgressed the conventions of standardized English and was often a source of conflict. *Caribbean Voices* afforded prestige and recognition, but voices legitimized by the 'mother country' and the BBC were seen as an arm of colonialism. Self-irony and distantiating devices were deployed by Caribbean writers as a means of expressing the sense of ambivalent belonging and self-consciousness they felt towards both the 'mother country' and the island colonies. *Caribbean Voices* provided a bridge between the islands and the metropolis and a creative contact zone for Caribbean writers and intellectuals, but its unique brand of corporate cosmopolitanism was marked by profound political and cultural contradictions and conflicts.

Soviet voices, literary lives

After 1945, diplomatic and World Service focus shifted to the Soviet Empire. Again, the right kinds of voices were needed and, again, diasporic intellectuals and writers provided them. Many of the staff had courageously sustained double lives as dissident poets, writers, artists and musicians at home. Those who could assemble in London found a creative 'home from home' at Bush House.

Exilic intellectuals still had an ambivalent status at Bush House and were closely monitored. The BBC employed 'switch censors' to interrupt any broadcaster who went off-script. Those preferentially hired were from their countries' educational upper echelons: brilliant linguists, many commanding five or more languages. Two demands clashed. The BBC management adopted a 'war style' of authoritative broadcasting, while the dissident intellectuals preferred a love of words that went deeper than the flat registers of World Service bulletins.

At first, the dissident hirelings were reduced to mere translators and credible ventriloquizers, and scripts were usually written by centralized editorial teams. Gradually, they won a degree of creative autonomy.

Diasporic writers often made use of their exile as a literary device – a distancing technique that plays with borders between insider and outsider, but which is also crucial to the self-distancing techniques so fundamental to the BBC World Service styles of reporting at an empathetic distance. This is a central feature of the corporate style of cosmopolitanism practised at the World Service. These tensions were experienced acutely, but also reconciled as complementary, by Ravil Bukharaev, a Tatar poet and journalist:

> There is nothing in the world less conducive to poetry than BBC journalism [...] If poetry [...] is an utterly personal and therefore highly partial medium, journalism is concerned as far as possible with objectivity in a very biased world [...] poetry puts me in touch with something imperishable and solid in a journalistic world of the ever new and quickly forgotten. Poetry shows you that with all the cultural trends and developing technologies worldwide, human beings do not change much as regards love, compassion, faith and their opposites [...] There is always hope while we try to understand one another. Even in that Babylon of languages and ethnic diversity, the BBC World Service, we can understand one another as journalists who respect the BBC Charter of fair reporting and as poets, with a need for self understanding, thereby benefiting others as well as ourselves. So journalism and poetry at the BBC have come to share the same territory and expertise. (Bukharaev 2003: 96–7)

The fate of diasporic writers was not always pleasant. In 1978 Georgi Markov, a distinguished Bulgarian novelist, was murdered by a poison-tipped umbrella while he was making his way to Bush House, where he worked for the Bulgarian Service. It is likely that he was assassinated because of his anti-communist literary rather than political activities and for fear of the impact of his dissident BBC broadcasts. This legendary tale of the deadly umbrella later found its way into a novel (written in French and translated into English) entitled *The Russian Service* by Zinovy Zinik, a broadcaster for the Russian Service since 1975. The story revolves around a Mr Narator who becomes obsessed with foreign broadcasts. He defects to the West in order to meet the faces behind the voices. In London, however, he is persuaded by émigré broadcasters that he will be the next victim of the poisoned umbrella and a political martyr. This surreal comic novel explores the often intimate and liberating relationship between émigré broadcasters and their audiences behind the Iron Curtain. In Zinik's words:

> All of us [Russian immigrants in London], especially at the time of the Iron Curtain, led a kind of ethereal existence. We existed for Russia on the air only, in a bodiless state. The very term 'foreign news' – news from a foreign i.e. another

world – has something other-worldly about it [...] The BBC canteen – that's a special case [...] All the political changes in the country were reflected in the way the BBC canteen was run! (Zinik, in Weissbort 2003: 195–205)

Zinik's writing connects past and present, being here and there. His novels, broadcasts and plays are a sustained reflection on the exile condition. The exiled writer becomes emblematic of the fate of his or her country: writing becomes a form of exile, and exile a literary device, an alternative perspective on the world. Zinik's irreverent, dissident diasporic perspective allows for an outsider's view of the English from the inside, and an insider's stance on the Russians from the outside. Ironic distances ripple through his writing.

Vibrant literary cultures blossomed in the contact zones of the bar and the canteen at Bush House, where the lights never went out. Broadcasting was always 24/7. Relative freedom of expression went hand in hand with the very peculiar 'out of body experience' that international broadcasting can be.

Conclusion

Diasporic intellectuals and journalists, poets and film directors, scriptwriters and artists from Africa, Latin America, the Middle East and the Asia-Pacific region found Bush House a fertile environment in which to develop their talents. Their talents have transformed Britain's culture of international broadcasting, literary networks and intellectual horizons, and forged a unique brand of corporate cosmopolitanism at the BBC. As writers and broadcasters, they have mediated culture, politics and identities between Britain and their (former) home countries. But balancing corporate interests and geopolitical priorities with a literary career is no easy task. Many writers experience profound political and cultural ambivalence. Diasporic contact zones are zones of conflict, where colonial, post-colonial and Cold War interests clashed, and cosmopolitan and national imaginaries and practices had either to collude or collide. The term diaspora can only be shorthand for successive displacements and complex movements. Yet these three case studies show how, examining the lives and works of diasporic individuals through the institutional prism of the BBC World Service, we can ground our analyses of the personal and political, the biographical and the literary and connect these to wider historical processes.

Further reading

Gillespie, M., A. Pinkerton, G. Baumann and S. Thiranagama (2010) 'South Asian diasporas and the BBC World Services: contacts, conflicts, and contestations', Special issue, *South Asian Diaspora*, 2(1): 3–23.

Mansell, G. (1982) *Let Truth Be Told: 50 Years of BBC External Broadcasting*, London: Weidenfeld and Nicolson.

Newton, D. (2008) 'Calling the West Indies: the BBC World Service and Caribbean Voices', in M. Gillespie, A. Webb and G. Baumann (eds), 'BBC World Service,

1932–2007: cultural exchange and public diplomacy', *Historical Journal of Film, Radio and Television*, 28(4): 475–89.

Ranasinha, R. (2010). 'South Asian broadcasters in Britain and the BBC: *Talking to India* (1941–1943)', in M. Gillespie, A. Pinkerton, G. Baumann and S. Thiranagama, *South Asian Diaspora*, 2(1): 57–71.

Thiranagama, S. (2010) 'Partitioning the BBC: from colonial to postcolonial broadcaster' in M. Gillespie, A. Pinkerton, G. Baumann and S. Thiranagama, *South Asian Diaspora*, 2(1): 39–55.

41 | Colonial space-making and hybridizing history, or 'Are the Indians of East Africa Africans or Indians?'

Ato Quayson

There are several suggestive details in the account that Salim gives of his cultural genealogy in Africa in V. S. Naipaul's *A Bend in the River* (1989 [1979]). The account, which we see in microcosm in the second chapter of the novel, but of which the entire narrative is ultimately an elaboration, turns on the idea first that East Africa has always been an area of cultural hybridity mixing Arab-Indian-Persian-Portuguese-African to the degree that, as Salim rightly puts it, 'we who lived there were really people of the Indian Ocean' (p. 10). The second suggestive detail follows subtly from the plural pronoun he uses to describe himself along with the Indian cultural community, because whereas he is at pains to show that his immediate family had been in the region for centuries, there is no doubting the fact that the communal 'we' he deploys has variant historical inflections to it. Whereas Salim's family was Gujarati, his friend Indar's grandfather had originally come from the Punjab to work as a railway labourer, remained behind after the end of his contract, and rapidly transformed himself into a highly successful merchant banker. The process of conversion from labourer to banker initially entailed lending small sums of money to indigent traders for a modest margin, but then progressively expanded into larger-scale financial arrangements until by the time of Indar's generation the family is well established as a major economic force in the region. Indeed, when we first see him, Indar is being sent off to England for post-secondary education. Both Salim and Indar use the communal 'we' to deplore the failure of the Indian community to understand the rapid changes that are taking place around them in the lead-up to independence. They don't even have a flag, the two young men lament; the mention of the word flag signalling the deep-seated communal crisis of displacement that is felt most excruciatingly by Salim, much the poorer of the two friends. Thus the communal 'we' throughout *A Bend in the River* is a deitic device that conflates and obscures two sets of complicated communal histories for the Indian community of East Africa.

But that is not all. Salim also tells us that all he knows of his people's history has been gleaned from books written by Europeans. More suggestively, even his perceptions of the environment are modulated through the framing provided by the colonial imaginary, the pertinent device here being the apparently innocuous yet incredibly evocative postage stamp. Here is how he puts it:

> Small things can start us off in new ways of thinking, and I was started off by the postage stamps of our area. The British administration gave us beautiful stamps. These stamps depicted local scenes and local things; there was one called 'Arab Dhow.' It was as though, in those stamps, a foreigner said, 'This is what is most striking about this place.' Without the stamp of the dhow I might have taken dhows for granted. As it was, I learned to look at them. Whenever I saw them tied up at the waterfront I thought of them as something peculiar to our region, quaint, something the foreigner would remark on, something not quite modern, and certainly nothing like the liners and cargo ships that berthed in our modern docks. (Ibid.: 15)

What starts off as a perspectival 'defamiliarization' of the mundane via the framing device of postage stamps escalates into a permanent state of alienation for Salim because he is in fact damned to perceive himself and his environment continually through the eyes of foreignness. The foreign perspective on the local is an apposite description of the African setting of *A Bend in the River*, which mixes wonder, bewilderment and distaste for African life in equal measure.

Naipaul's novel provides a useful entry point for linking the fields of Post-colonial and Diaspora Studies, particularly in the varied ways in which it conceptualizes complex hybrid identities and yet places them within what amounts to an obsessively rigid hierarchical grid, at least in the eyes of Salim. For it is evident that in Salim's eyes the African setting in which his life unfolds is not a 'world of accommodations', to echo a phrase by which Amitav Ghosh bewails the lost cultural hybridities of the medieval Mediterranean world in *In an Antique Land* (1992: 234–7). Ghosh also invokes for us an Indian Ocean world that produces various cultural intermixings in Africa, but in a way that is quite distinctive from Naipaul's novel. Like the earlier *A House for Mr Biswas* (1961), *A Bend in the River* tells us about a historical aspect of the Indian populations that were dispersed all over the world following the abolition of slavery in 1833 and the inception of British indentured labour policy in the 1880s. Unlike the earlier novel, however, *A Bend in the River* focalizes Indian diasporic identity through a sublimated singularity, one that takes on the force and objective of an organizing principle by which Salim the narrator seeks to establish a foundation for his own insipid and besieged sense of identity.

Despite the fact that the two fields of Post-colonial and Diaspora Studies are inextricably linked in their objects of study, not very much has been done in terms of either conceptualizing their joint interests or indeed identifying mutually illuminating research methodologies. And this is despite the influence of texts such as Paul Gilroy's *The Black Atlantic* (1993a) and James Clifford's *Routes: Travel and Translation in the Late Twentieth Century* (1997), both of which have continuing resonance for the two fields. In my view, the main reason for this lack of methodological confluence lies in the reluctance to interrogate colonial space-making through the instrumentalization of diaspora that was a central if hitherto unacknowledged aspect of colonialism. In other words it is important not to see colonialism and diasporization as separate processes, but as integral to each other. In the British Empire the deployment of diaspora as a tool of colonial space-making becomes most focused from the 1850s, speeding up decisively after the First World War (see Brown 2005 and Ray 2009). The only way to understand the process is to deploy a mutually illuminating Post-colonial and Diaspora Studies lens.

Colonial space-making

Colonial space-making does not merely designate the formation and constitution of a geographically demarcated reality, though that is definitely also important. Rather, colonial space-making is first and foremost the projection of a series of socio-political dimensions upon a geographical space. These socio-political dimensions involve not only society and politics, but also economy, culture and a wide range of symbolic practices as well (recall Salim and the postage stamps). In the specific area of politics, colonialism was not marked exclusively by the imposition of administrative and bureaucratic apparatuses upon geographical spaces. Colonial politics above all involved the alteration of already existing relations among well-constituted local groups (such as in the case of India between the Mughals and the Hindus or in Ghana between the inland Ashanti and the coastal Ga), as much as it did in the reconfiguration of the hierarchies between indigenous and diasporic populations in a variety of settings, such as was exemplified in East Africa and South-East Asia. Everywhere colonial space-making also involved the intellectual appropriation and symbolic reconfiguration of the relationship between the colonized and their natural environment. In places such as Australia, Canada and the Americas there has been a forceful and continuing attempt to convert land from a spiritual and communally held entity into an alienable commodity in the service of brute capitalist accumulation. Colonial space-making ultimately also involved the conscription of material human bodies into the schemas of colonial relations of production and the differential constitution of citizens and subjects (Mamdani 1996; Stoler 1995). Colonial space-making is thus to be understood in terms of the sets of relations that were structurally generated and contested across a series of interrelated vectors throughout the colonial encounter.

East African Asians

As already hinted at in our reading of Naipaul's novel, East Africa provides an interesting case for considering the many complications that come to the foreground when we consider matters simultaneously through a post-colonial and diaspora lens. South Asians, mainly from India, were first brought to East Africa as indentured labour from the 1880s to help build the East African Railway. The indentured labour policy was itself designed as a response to the abolition of slavery to take account of the needs of plantation owners who now felt their plantations were sure to collapse owing to the loss of slave labour. When the policy was extended to East Africa it was mainly to provide non-African labour for building the East African railway line. Of the roughly 32,000 Indian men brought in, an estimated 6,700 stayed behind to work as shopkeepers after the discontinuation of the policy in the early 1920s, with their wives and families encouraged to join them after the end of the indentured labour policy. By the end of the Second World War the Indians in East Africa were an estimated 320,000, with many of them firmly in control of the commercial trade in Uganda, Kenya and Tanzania. By the 1960s, and after the independence of Kenya, Uganda and Tanzania, the Indians had not only become a central part of the civil service administration but also considered themselves African. An effect of this was that by the 1960s the myth of return, long taken as a defining feature of diasporas, had been progressively abandoned by the East African Indians. Having come from largely rural areas in India they were also now heavily urbanized and used to negotiating with urban institutions.

The Africanization of the civil service following independence in East Africa proved deleterious for the Indian community. They were forced to take early retirement or in several cases were relieved of their jobs. Mass migration also followed the violent policies of Idi Amin in the 1970s, triggering the process of what Parminder Bhachu (1985) describes as the 'twice migrant' phenomenon. The East African Asians underwent a second process of migration, moving to the UK, Canada, the United States and India. Because of their highly urbanized and technocratic and administrative skills, these migrants were very different from Indians who had originally migrated to the Western countries directly from India itself. In the UK it did not take long for the East African Indians to enter into the higher levels of the civil service and businesses; most of them bought their own homes shortly after arrival in the UK, again distinguishing them sharply from direct migrants from India. Because of the gradual shedding of the myth of return (since they had no inclination to go back to India and could not return to East Africa) the East African Indians who moved to the West quickly consolidated their families in the new societies they had settled into. Furthermore, unlike migrants coming directly from India, the East African Indians were to rapidly replicate the community networks in their new locations, which had already evolved within the East African societies they left behind (ibid.).

There are certain questions that this brief account of the East African Indian diaspora brings to the foreground. The first is how much it allows us to see the complexity inherent in post-colonial definitions of Africa, insistently illustrating as it does different links between colonial space-making and diaspora. In the late nineteenth and early twentieth centuries the East African Indians could be described as a labour diaspora, and thus similar to the Indians who found themselves in the Trinidad of *A House for Mr Biswas* and in other parts of the Caribbean. But by the 1930s and 1940s, and after two generations of settlement, they had become a vibrant trade and administrative diaspora. The concept of trade diaspora also allows us to bring into view the long trading relations that Gujarati Indians had had with the East African coast from at least the fourteenth century onwards. After the violent dislocations of their communities following independence in the 1960s, however, the East African Indians were very much a victim diaspora, thus comparable to the Jewish, Armenian and African-American traditions.

The question remains: Are the Indians of East Africa Africans or Indians? Their case provides fascinating entry points for discussing perennial issues in African Studies (who qualifies to be called an African and how did they get to be African in the first place?), as well as wider debates in Post-colonial and Diaspora Studies in general (how do we understand the full spectrum of the after-effects of colonial space-making on state formation, cultural identification and societal affiliation?; how do we understand different forms of diasporization and what implications are to be drawn from these for understanding contemporary global identities?). Are there lessons to be drawn from the East African Asians for understanding the Lebanese of West Africa? What do we make of the identity formation of the large settlements of Hutu refugees that have been in Tanzania since the 1970s? And from the world of representation, what might the mixed-genre mockumentary/science fiction film *District 9*'s integration of Nigerians with aliens tell us about the ways in which diasporas are being situated within a South Africa still wrestling with the racial categorizations of its own recent traumatic past (see Quayson 2009)?

If we return to *A Bend in the River*, this time reading from a mutually illuminating Post-colonial and Diaspora Studies standpoint, the central lesson to be learned suddenly coalesces around the strategically (mis)translated Latin inscription on the ruined monument at the centre of the town: *Miscerique probat populos et foedera jungi*/'He approves of the mingling of the peoples and their bonds of union'. For despite the fact that every vector of Salim's identity speaks against the possibility of mixing, the history of colonial space-making that is silhouetted behind the novel's narrative suggests that the mixing and union have already taken place. The truth of history lies not so much with either victor or vanquished, colonizer or colonized, but with the hybridizing forces of history itself.

Further reading

Bhachu, P. (1985) *Twice Migrants: East African Sikh Settlers in Britain*, London: Tavistock.

Mamdani, M. (1996) *Citizen and Subject: Contemporary Africa and the Legacy of Late Colonialism*, Princeton, NJ: Princeton University Press.

Naipaul, V. S. (1989 [1979]) *A Bend in the River*, London: Vintage.

Quayson, A. (2009) 'Unthinkable Nigeriana: the social imaginary of District 9', *Johannesburg Workshop in Critical Theory*, vol. 1, www.jwtc.org.za, accessed 14 January 2010.

42 | Transnational musicians' networks across Africa and Europe

Ulrike Hanna Meinhof, Nadia Kiwan and
Marie-Pierre Gibert

African diasporas from every conceivable region are spread right across Europe, following, but also increasingly bypassing, old post-colonial trajectories. Patterns of migration are clearly linked to transnational networks, which enable movements of individuals that follow a different logic of multiple translocal and transnational flows rather than one-directional or bi-directional connections. Migrant artists are not only no exception to this, but may in fact be among the most mobile groups of transnationals, making use of their 'transcultural capital' (Meinhof and Triandafyllidou 2006) to gain a living from their art.

Artists from these 'diasporas' are active across the full range of cultural production – music, film, literature and the visual arts. Their contribution to the cultural landscape of Europe has been and continues to be so all-pervasive that their artistic presence represents a major force of creativity and innovation across the entire artistic spectrum, and any account needs by definition to be understood as highly selective. Hence, to give some flavour of the everyday life, movements and networking of African artists in Europe, we will tell the stories of three musicians originating from francophone Africa that are both representative and unique. All belong to a much larger group of North African and Malagasy artists whom we identified in our work as significant case studies, and subsequently interviewed, followed and observed. They are Justin Vali, a Malagasy singer/songwriter and the most renowned *valiha* player in Europe; Karim Dellali, an Algerian percussionist and DJ living in the United Kingdom; and Youssef El-Mejjad, a Moroccan musician based in Marrakesh. With the exception of refugees who are unable to return to their countries of origin for political reasons, artists such as these develop and uphold links between diasporas across several countries, but also have networks that link their African countries of origin or settlement with other, non-ethnically defined networks across Europe and in some cases worldwide. Such multiple networking makes their life trajectories 'transnational' rather than 'diasporic' in the classical sense of a loss of a homeland.

North African and Malagasy diasporas

Regarding North African migrants, there are two main differences to account for. One relates to their different immigration histories in European host countries; the other relates to historical, political and social differences across regions and countries of origin.

In France, North African diasporas carry a post-colonial legacy. Algeria was a *département* of France from 1830 until 1962, when it became independent. Morocco and Tunisia were both protectorates which came under French rule from 1912 until 1956 in the Moroccan case, and from 1881 until 1956 in the case of Tunisia. The vast majority of migrants in these diasporas came to France as (male) workers in the post-war period from 1945 to 1974. In 1974 non-European immigration was formally suspended, and from then on the main mode of entry for new migrants was through family reunification. In January 2005, Algerians made up the largest proportion of foreign nationals in France (679,000) and Moroccans the second-largest group (625,000) (INSEE 2004–06). These statistics do not account for the descendants of North African migrants – that is, those French nationals of North African origin.

In the UK, North African immigration is not linked to a former colonial or protectorate experience, therefore it is smaller and more recent. The Moroccan population is estimated at 50,000 members, mainly guest workers from the 1960s, and more recently highly skilled students or professionals (Cherti 2008: 73). Algerian immigration is smaller and arose largely as a result of political events that occurred in Algeria in the 1990s. Today, estimates suggest that some 30,000 Algerian-born residents live in the UK (Collyer 2004).

In comparison to the North African diasporas, the Malagasy diaspora in Europe is much smaller. There are no statistics regarding their number overall. France, the former colonial power, hosts more Malagasies than the rest of Europe put together. Their number was estimated at 41,000 in 2005 (INSEE 2004–06), excluding binational or naturalized Malagasies. In relation to the total population of Madagascar – approximately 17.8 million inhabitants – this constitutes a sizeable figure (ibid.). Most Malagasies arrived in France and other European territories after independence was gained in June 1960. Hence, at present, the majority belong to the first generation, about 70 per cent of which are professionals and 30 per cent students, while the eldest of the second generation are only starting to reach their teenage or early adult years.

Our research has adopted a strategy of following individual artists across their networks rather than focusing on preconfigured spatial diasporic communities. Whereas it is tempting to see community-based diasporas as relatively homogeneous, ethnically defined entities, an individual's networking usually links many different types of networks, ethnic and non-ethnic, religious, artistic, taste, hobby and value, just as would be the case for so-called 'native' populations. The result of such a research design for our understanding of contemporary

African diasporas can thus best be demonstrated through the examples of representative artists and their networking practices. Despite very different levels and intensities of interaction between countries of origin in the 'South' with their respective diasporas in the 'North', all three stories presented here show that the artists' self-understanding and life histories, their musical careers and their patterns of social engagement, point to the need for a reconsideration of the 'diasporic vision' in favour of a more dynamic transnational perspective.

Justin Vali

As is the case with most Malagasy musicians in the diaspora, Justin's passage to Europe was marked by a series of coincidences rather than a firm decision to migrate. Unsurprisingly, since 80 per cent of the Malagasy population live in rural rather than urban environments, Justin's life started out in a small Malagasy village on the Hauts Plateaux, and his departure for Europe had as a first major milestone the *'passage obligé'* via the capital Antananarivo. Justin Rakotondrasoa (Vali is his artistic name, taken from the instrument he plays with such virtuosity), as well as many others among his relatives from a family of artisans, specialized in the building and trading of the bamboo zither *valiha*. The *valiha* is probably the most iconic traditional instrument of Madagascar: in pre-colonial times it also played a major role as a courtly instrument. Justin's own playing was initially devoted to traditional religious and festive occasions, such as burial, reburial, circumcision and wedding ceremonies. So is he, then, a traditional Malagasy artist?

It was on one of his rare visits to the capital Antananarivo that Justin encountered a tour organizer who selected him to play in a newly formed orchestra bound for Europe. But, having arrived in France in the early 1980s, the group struggled for survival, and soon split up, with many musicians returning to Madagascar. Justin, however, fought on with a supportive diasporic network of Malagasies in France, and in the early 1990s established the Justin Vali Trio. So does this make him a diasporic or a neo-communitarian artist?

His international breakthrough came in the 1990s at the height of the 'world music' wave and established him as an international artist. Paddy Bush, a fan of Malagasy music and brother of the British star Kate Bush, produced his album *The Sunshine Within* (Paddy Bush Productions), Kate Bush recorded a single with him, Peter Gabriel supported him with the album *Ny maraina*, on his British-based Real World label, and the world music festival Womad, instigated by Peter Gabriel, established a worldwide network for Justin. These musical encounters and the production of albums in a more diversified musical style marked the beginning of his career in world music (Meinhof 2009). Hence, in contrast to most of the other Malagasy musicians in France who are signed to French indie labels such as Label Bleu, Justin's breakthrough was linked to British-based production companies and an international world music scene.

At present Justin and his family live in Lille, France, from where he embarks on worldwide tours with considerable success and critical acclaim: in 2006 he was awarded the coveted Sacem Grand Prix de la musique traditionelle in France. So has he now become a cosmopolitan, world music artist?

None of this labelling fits easily. To understand the nature of his career and that of many other so-called 'diasporic' or 'world music' artists, it would be misleading to think of it in purely ethnic terms and ignore its international dimension; just as it would be misleading to ignore the continuing strength of his intimate connection with Malagasy life and culture. Meinhof and Triandafyllidou (2006) have suggested that diaspora, neo-communitarianism and cosmopolitanism are not mutually exclusive identifiers but are best seen as registers which coexist side by side and are activated, used and performed in different life-contexts. Justin's is an excellent example of the coexistence of all three.

What underpins the continuing strength of transnational connections is the coexistence of Malagasy and global networks, and the ways in which they overlap and mutually determine one another in multiple directions: South–North and North–South. A recently formed transnational group of five solo artists, the Madagascar All Stars, in addition to Justin, comprises three Malagasy-origin artists living in France as well as one of the most famous Malagasy musicians – Dama from Mahaleo – who lives in Madagascar. The musical connections and networks of the All Stars are trans-European rather than French-based, while each individual artist in turn has different worldwide connections.

What makes Justin's career representative of that of many of his compatriots in the music industry is the multiple networking of a committed artist: someone who retains a strong connection with Madagascar and a deep involvement with and concern for its people and culture; who moves freely across diasporic networks of Malagasies all over the world. At the same time, this engagement runs side by side and occasionally overlaps with a trans-European, even in part global, network.

Karim Dellali

Born and raised in Algeria, Karim arrived in London in his early twenties, at the end of the 1980s, and remained there 'accidentally', as he puts it, driven by his studies at university, personal motives and a need to escape the political problems in Algeria, which started a few years after he arrived. Music for Karim, in contrast to Justin, was not the motivation for his relocation to Britain. Although it had been his hobby from an early age, he had never thought of earning a living from it until some years after his arrival in London. Karim is therefore more of a 'musician migrant' than a 'migrant musician'. It is by focusing on the articulation between motivation for and experience of migration that the transnational dimension of his trajectory comes to light.

From computer analyst to DJ and percussionist, the construction of Karim as a professional musician is processed through internal and external factors in which migration plays a crucial role. Particularly active as DJ at techno parties, Karim soon developed an interest in jazz and dub music, which led to what he calls 'the transition': 'At the end of my twenties, I became more interested in what I am and who I am, my culture, my music. Because before, when you are young, well, I was living in it, so I wasn't really interested.' Trying to integrate a more specifically localized music from North Africa (and to a lesser extent from other parts of the world) within his DJ mixes, he also decided to further his knowledge of the Middle Eastern and North African percussion instrument the *derbuka*. As is often the case with 'musician migrants', Karim's developing curiosity for and enjoyment of his musical heritage, as well as his desire to draw on it in a creative way, were also fed and encouraged by a growing interest from British and international audiences for so-called 'world music' and 'fusion music'. While this external positive gaze provides performance opportunities to such bands, however, it also imposes certain constraints and aesthetic norms on the musicians. In this respect, transcultural capital can become as burdensome as it is useful, as it often confines migrants in an exoticized multicultural niche.

Until this musical 'transition', Karim had only minimal interaction with other North African musicians in London. The discovery of Seddik Zebiri's 'International Jam Session' in Hackney, however, allowed him to enter a network of musicians from all over the world, which also included artists from North and sub-Saharan Africa. This jam session acted as a multilevel hub. Grounded in the local context of a multicultural north London neighbourhood and bringing together a variety of musical sources and musicians, it allowed Karim to both stimulate his artistic creation and maturity, and develop various professional opportunities and networks. Through his weekly participation in this jam he met many of the musicians with whom he is still working today in numerous bands, with musical repertoires ranging from Turko-electronic and oriental-dub to Andalous music. It is therefore the paradoxical combination of his readjustment to a very specific set of cultural practices and his appreciation and uptake of different musical influences which allowed him to establish himself as a 'freelance musician', and enter many divergent local and national musical and civil society networks in the UK.

It appears that Karim's locally grounded yet transnational encounters had provided him with the strong professional anchorage necessary for his expansion to the international level. This led to both an increasing involvement with the Algerian music industry and a commitment to humanitarian concerns in North Africa. Thus, after years of purely family-oriented trips to Algeria, Karim became involved in developing the popularity in Algeria of the London-based band Fantazia. At the same time, after having been contacted by the UK representative of a Moroccan association which advocates social work through the arts (Kif Kif), Karim began building on his double expertise as a computer specialist and musician in support of Moroccan civil society, leading workshops on electronic music for street kids and developing stronger links between local NGOs and potential sponsors in the UK.

Youssef El-Mejjad

Our research with Moroccan musicians who have migrated to Europe reveals that these diasporic individuals develop and maintain multiple transnational ties with musicians and cultural producers in their countries/regions of origin (Rabat, Agadir, Casablanca) and other locations, such as New York, Paris, Toulouse, Nancy, Montpellier and Marseilles. A key element of our research, however, also concentrates on musicians who fall into just the opposite category; that is, those musicians who have never actually migrated to Europe on a permanent basis, but who nevertheless develop and maintain complex transnational networks from their locations south of the Mediterranean. This is the case of Youssef El-Mejjad, a musician (singer, composer and player of the oud, violin, guitar, keyboard, *guembri*, *derbuka*, *bendir*, *djembe*) in his late thirties, who was born and brought up in Marrakesh. He is a French-Moroccan binational (being married to a French national) but has never lived permanently outside Morocco. In this sense, he cannot be described as part of a diaspora as such. Nevertheless, his continual circulation and collaboration with artists and producers in Europe and beyond (the USA and Japan, for example) is relevant for our study since his case quite clearly calls into question some established conceptions about what it means to be a transnational artist. Indeed, one could argue that El-Mejjad is just as transnational in his work as fellow Moroccan musicians who are based in France or the UK. El-Mejjad started his professional musical career with the Marrakesh-based group Aisha Kandisha's Jarring Effects in 1992. Aisha Kandisha was one of the early groups to marry Moroccan rhythms such as *chaâbi* and *gnawa* with Western popular music such as reggae, hip hop and electronic music, and they successfully toured internationally (Germany, Austria, the Netherlands, Belgium, Italy).

Building on his experience with Aisha Kandisha, in 1993 El-Mejjad established another band – Amira Saqati – with two musicians from the original group, and then, in 2006, set up yet another with the same two musicians under the name of Maghrebika. Maghrebika's repertoire is based on the fusion of electronic music with Moroccan rhythms. All of El-Mejjad's musical formations have been produced by the Swiss label Baraka El Fernatshi Productions, founded and run by the Swiss-based producer Pat Jabbar. What is interesting about El-Mejjad's career is the manner in which it has involved him in multiple transnational connections: his record label and main collaborator, Jabbar, is based in Basle, but he has also worked closely with New York producer Bill Laswell, and recorded Maghrebika's first album with two Algerian (Oranian) singers who are based in Switzerland. Lately he has also been working with a

Japanese musician, based in Tokyo, whom he met at a music residency organized by the Association des Musiques Innovatrices (AMI). So El-Mejjad's trajectory does not automatically link him to France, although he has had some experience of working there, particularly with the AMI organization in Marseilles. So in this sense, it is tempting to see his experience as one which bypasses established routes for the circulation of post-colonial francophone North African musicians. Furthermore, it can be argued that El-Mejjad bypasses migration itself since, owing to the nature of his music and the creative electronic and technological process associated with it, he does not need to meet his collaborators face to face in a studio on a regular basis, unlike acoustic musicians. Instead, they are able to be just as productive and creative by sending each other music files over the Internet.

So this case study throws up key questions about a kind of transnationalism which occurs *without* movement or, rather, a transnationalism which develops through transient or temporary mobility (Featherstone et al. 2007: 385). El-Mejjad is able to make his living as a musician because his music is distributed in Europe and the USA while he remains in Morocco. This suits him well, as he has no desire to migrate to Europe. Revenues from his activities with Aisha Kandisha, Maghrebika and other projects, plus his regular sets for tourists in a local Marrakesh hotel, mean that he has been able to set up his own recording studio, where he continues to make music as well as money from its hire to local emerging groups.

Conclusion

The most significant point emerging from our case studies of musicians from Africa is that their life trajectories challenge our understanding of diasporas as well as those other identifiers for transnational lifestyles such as neo-communitarianism or cosmopolitanism. Instead of a diasporic vision of African musicians having left home and resettled in Europe, or living in or between two cultures, we prefer to see their social and professional networking through a series of 'hubs' (Kiwan and Meinhof, forthcoming): as webs of spatial, human and institutional interconnections through which artists negotiate their transnational lives and careers.

Further reading

Baily, J. and M. Collyer (eds) (2006) Special issue on music and migration, *Journal of Ethnic and Migration Studies*, 32(2).

Kiwan, N. and U. H. Meinhof (forthcoming) *Cultural Globalization and Music: African Artists in Transnational Networks*, Basingstoke: Palgrave Macmillan.

Winders, J. A. (2006) *Paris Africain: Rhythms of the African Diaspora*, New York and Basingstoke: Palgrave Macmillan.

43 | Diasporic readers and the location of reception

James Procter

There is a tendency in cultural criticism and theory to think of readers (not only 'diasporic' ones) as a migratory species. According to Robert Fraser, 'readers are frequently diasporic beings whose tastes have been formed by travel, social change, disparities of social outlook and the multiple ironies springing from these ubiquitous facts' (Fraser 2008: 186). De Certeau famously argued, 'Readers are travellers; they move across lands belonging to someone else, like nomads poaching their way across fields' (De Certeau 1984: 174). Minrose Gwin (2002) has suggested that reading Toni Morrison is analogous to what she calls space travel, 'a form of dislocation, an opening of perspective, a shifting of identity' (Felski 2003: 46). More recently, in *In Defense of Reading* (2008), Daniel Schwarz proposes the notion of the 'Odyssean Reader': 'We need to think of our readings as odysseys with their own beginnings and endings or, in contemporary terms, with their own take-offs and landings, departures and arrivals. When we begin a book, we seal ourselves off from other worlds, just as when we take a trip to a different society' (ibid.: 2).

Certainly these are all productive metaphors for thinking about reading as a vicarious activity capable of taking readers outside of, or beyond, themselves. Moreover, globalization, migration and the planetary span of high-speed satellite technologies increasingly invite us to take such metaphors literally. As Arjun Appadurai has noted, there is a significant link between audiences, electronic mediation and migration: 'both viewers and images are in simultaneous circulation. Neither images nor viewers fit into circuits or audiences that are easily bound within local, national, or regional spaces' (1996: 4). Similarly, Lawrence Grossberg (1988) and Janice Radway (1988) have questioned (albeit in different ways) the existence of discrete, locatable audiences within our media-saturated world, refocusing attention on what they term 'wandering', 'dispersed' and 'nomadic' audiences.

If audiences are characteristically composed of nomadic wanderers, dislocated itinerants and dispersed travellers, does this make the 'diasporic' reader (understood here as both consumers of diaspora narratives and as migrant consumers of texts-in-general) the contemporary reader par excellence? To accept the position of the New York-based, Bombay-born anthropologist Appadurai (1996: 4), that we now live in a world where 'moving images meet deterritorialized viewers', we do not necessarily have to go along with the idea that we are all 'diasporic' audiences in the same way. This would be to neglect the uneven, unequal character of the diaspora experience: the difference between movement as choice and compulsion, for example. It would be to neglect the extent to which locale, region and nation persist as profound sites of interpretive investment for readers throughout the world, despite and because of the increased fragility of those sites. It would be to neglect responses to high-profile diasporic novels such as Salman Rushdie's *The Satanic Verses* (1988), and Monica Ali's *Brick Lane* (2003), which reveal 'divergences between various sorts of text, various protocols of reading and various constituencies of readers' (Fraser 2008: 163). It would also be to neglect the extent to which non-diasporic readers of diasporic fiction are the *consumers* of cultural *production*, a relationship which ties migrants and audiences together, certainly, but in an asymmetrical fashion whereby the migrant story is an object (not agent, even if agency might be *given* through reading acts) of enquiry, fascination, dismissal, pleasure (see Huggan 2001). Finally, it would be to neglect existing research on readers, which suggests reading itself needs to be understood as a situated rather than a straightforwardly transhistorical or translocational act (see Chartier 1992).

As Stephanie Newell notes, the logic of cosmopolitanism that underpins much of the work in globalization and diaspora studies presents a dubious opposition between the local and global which ignores how transnational objects are actively consumed, interpreted and remade locally:

> While being able to track the movement of a Coke bottle through the complex, overlapping 'scapes' in the world, globalization theorists often stop short of acknowledging the creative agency of the local who can, among other things, store kerosene in Coke bottles and decorate toy trucks with flattened bottle tops. It is important, therefore, to emphasize the diverse local uses to which even the most iconic international objects can be put [...] (Newell 2002: 352–3)

In the remainder of this essay I want to test some of these ideas about location, diaspora, readers and audiences with reference to a case study of contemporary readers and their responses to Chinua Achebe's classic post-colonial text, *Things Fall Apart* (1958). Read at the level of content, *Things Fall Apart* is not a 'diasporic' narrative at all, even if its text, from the opening allusion to Yeats to the glossary for non-Igbo readers at the close, anticipates an audience outside Africa. When viewed as a physical object within circuits of production–consumption, however, the text is remarkably Coke-like in terms of the extent it has travelled. First published in paperback within Heinemann's African Writers' Series, *Things Fall Apart* has been bought and consumed by audiences and readers throughout the world. It is currently translated into forty-five languages, and has sold over eight million copies. In 2007 and 2008 the novel's fiftieth anniversary was celebrated in a variety of public reading events across Europe, Africa and the United States.

One of these events, held on 24 July 2007, involved an online discussion of *Things Fall Apart* between readers in London, Kano, Lagos and Scotland via the British Council enCompass website (www.encompassculture.com/). This discussion, which brought together 'diasporic' and 'indigenous' readers via an Internet chat room, provides a useful, if inevitably limited and highly partial, case study in what follows. The online book group discussion in some ways embodies the kind of dislocated (disembodied) image of migrating audiences and mediated narratives anticipated in the work of Appadurai, albeit within a managed environment. Yet what is striking about the typed conversation (rendered literally below) is how the reader-participants seek to manage this dispersed, transnational environment in which they are 'meeting', through recourse to the local. Perhaps unsurprisingly, then, the opening conversation turns on questions of location and the provenance of each reader:

> Susan Tranter: Hello! Where are you chatting from?
> Susan Tranter: Hi Kim!
> Kim H: I'm at home at the moment
> Ahmed: Hi everyone
> Kim H: Hi Ahmed
> Liam: I'm sitting in Scotland, as part of the Glasgow reading group.
> Ahmed: Evening from Kano, Nigeria
> Jenny: Hi Kim, hi Ahmed
> DemocratSam: Hi people
> Jenny: I'm in Scotland, and part of the Glasgow group
> Jenny: Where is everyone else from?
> DemocratSam: Here at British council office in Ikoyi Lagos
> Ahmed: I am part of Kano Nigeria group
> Kim H: I'm from the literature team at the British Council
> Ahmed: Logged in from British Council Office Kano

The desire to reterritorialize identities within this deterritorialized environment ('Where are you from?') may seem obvious, but it is also crucial to understanding how location is prioritized here, and serves to mark, above everything else, how these readers view both their own reading identities and the reading identities of others. It forms part of a polite and 'natural' preamble that at once seems symptomatic of not being at home, a means of orienting self and others within an unfamiliar, dispersed and anonymous environment. As such it is distinct from conventional face-to-face book group conversations where questions of locale and cultural difference are either visibly evident (thus literally unremarkable) or simply immaterial, precisely because reading groups typically cluster in terms of locality (neighbourhoods, pubs, houses, libraries). In contrast, the online discussion of *Things Fall Apart* quickly turns to the weather, which, as Homi Bhabha (1990b) reminds us, is inseparable from the construction of national identity and the performance of difference:

Kim H: I bet it's not raining in Kano like it was in London earlier :-(

Susan Tranter: So glad you could all join us. So: what did you all think of Things Fall Apart? First impressions?

Ahmed: It is raining in Kano ... but certainly not like the 'floood' in London

Aside from the sense of time-space compression that theorists of diaspora and globalization might note here in the simultaneous evocation of otherwise very different weather systems, we might also note the 'time lag' that explains the disjointed and deferred dialogue between Susan and Kim in London and Ahmed in Kano. What seems clear from the discussion of the weather is the symbolic, rather than pragmatic, role it plays: a means of negotiating national and cultural alterity, and emphasizing locational difference that has little if anything to do with meteorology.

These openings and asides are arguably 'outside' the book group discussion: they do not provide interpretations of *Things Fall Apart* and so might appear to have nothing to do with reading. I would argue, however, that these readers are already establishing positions in relation to the text, positions of proximity and distance, of insider/outsider status that are crucial to both how this group constructs reading identities and to how it ultimately makes sense of the book. So, these opening comments set up a dynamic that is played out in the main body of conversation, and which sees readers in England and Scotland asking for clarification from the readers in Nigeria:

Harlesden Library2: How do Nigerians see the influence of the missionaries in the country today?

[...]

Jenny: For the readers in Nigeria, does the novel have a contemporary relevance? How do you view the novel as a modern reader from this country?

[...]

Susan Tranter: Are there any specific questions about African life or aspects of the book which British readers would like to ask African readers?

Here the UK readers (including Nigerians in London such as Harlesden Library2) make sense of *Things Fall Apart* by automatically allocating interpretive authority to the readers in Nigeria. Unlike de Certeau's reader-poacher who transgresses certain borders to take possession of the text, these UK readers seem to assert that the text does not belong to them, or rather that the text essentially belongs to Nigeria. This is a commonsense assumption that is questionable given what we have already noted is the global-diasporic context of the novel's production/reception: first published in London, *Things Fall Apart* has always carried a certain *foreignness* to Nigeria.

Again, towards the end of the online discussion all the readers 'agree' to position the novel in similar ways when an unannounced 'intruder' enters the chat room and proceeds to try to antagonize the other readers:

Brian: I thought it was [a] dreadful book

[...]

Brian: I thought it was superficial and false

Jenny: What was superficial precisely?

[...]

Harlesden Library4: Brian why don't you ask the Nigerians present how false it was?

Basira: Obviously Brian can't relate

[...]

Nom: Brian u need to come over to Africa and taste a bit of the reality which still applies today. Where are u from anyway? Have [you] read the book at all?

Harlesden Library3: Brian – why don't you ask the Nigerians present how false the story was?

The assumption here seems to be that it is Brian's outsiderness or foreignness to the text which explains his aberrant reading of *Things Fall Apart*. The novel's location is not only taken for granted: locatedness is used to explain how the text can and cannot be read. Interestingly, it is two black British or diasporic readers (Harlesden Library3 and Harlesden Library4) who are most emphatic here. Ironically, they seem to be the readers most keen to root the text within an originary Nigerian setting:

Harlesden Library4: The book [*Things Fall Apart*] really touch me as I felt that as a person of Nigerian descent I had lost the rich cultural history that displayed in the book. I really feel westernized and out of touch with my cultural roots.

Hailing from Harlesden, Brent (one of the most deprived areas of London, and home to the largest population group born outside the UK), this reader reminds us that the diaspora audience is not necessarily in thrall to the networks and routes that are the preferred tropes of diaspora studies within the academy. The diasporic audience does not necessarily read, or desire, as the post-colonial critic of diaspora studies might desire. The fantasies of detachment and uprootedness marking the work of some celebrated cosmopolitan artists are not necessarily equivalent to the everyday urges of diasporic interpretive communities beyond the text. What is striking here is the way in which Harlesden Library4 unequivocally looks to the text for a set of cultural moorings that the diaspora experience has dislocated her from. There might be an important 'distinction' (in Bourdieu's sense) to be made here between Schwarz's 'Odyssean Reader', with which we began, and the kind of reading for roots in the anonymous Nigerian Londoner's narrative: the different values and tastes they expose are not necessarily reducible to 'race' but would also appear bound up with social status and class. We might speculate, for example, whether the opportunities of transnational travel for the professional reader/critic are equally available, and affordable, to Harlesden Library4, and to what extent this fact might explain the latter's interpretive investment in home/roots rather than Odyssean flight.

Specific sites of reception, such as the one briefly explored above, have been largely elided within diaspora, post-colonial and globalization studies, where there has been a tendency to evoke 'ideal readers' in place of actual audiences. (These ideal readers are essentially nowhere, but this has not really seemed to matter; indeed, it is entirely compatible with the discursive and rhetorical logic of placelessness within diasporic literary studies since the 1990s.) Such forms of critical shorthand allow for the construction of a consoling interpretive community, an imagined audience that consciously or not serves to foreclose the local, contingent and messy work of meaning production. Thus, when critics suggest diaspora text 'x' is transgressive, or diaspora text 'y' is celebratory, we might ask 'For whom?', 'Under what conditions (of consumption)?', 'Where?' or 'When?'. While I would question the idea that there is a diasporic audience out there waiting to be discovered, or which can be delimited in terms of ethnicity, subalternity or geography, I would maintain that reading is not simply deterritorialized, or nomadic, either.

Despite the recent mainstream fascination with certain 'diasporic' texts (e.g. *White Teeth*) and authors (e.g. Zadie Smith 2000), little is yet known about actual *readers* in diaspora, or indeed of the readers of diasporic literature in general, and how they make sense of the narratives they read. Still less is known about the consumption and production of these authors and texts beyond the classic axes of migrant literary expression/consumption that Amitava Kumar (2002) brands *Bombay-London-New York*. This is partly due to a largely unexplored discrepancy in diasporic literary and cultural studies. Here the vocabularies of *dislocation* wielded by professional readers (reviewers, publishers, academics, critics) to describe or market diasporic cultural production tend to conceal the precise provenance of those vocabularies within a select series of metropolitan *locations*.

Reception study provides a productive context for thinking over this discrepancy (between the diasporic discourses of dislocation and the locations of diasporic discourse) because it is fundamentally resistant to the idea that meaning resides in one place. For instance, if London has played a hegemonic role in securing the meaning and value of certain celebrated diasporic texts, reader response criticism suggests the presence of alternative 'interpretive communities' (Fish 1980), and 'horizons of expectation' (Jauss 1982), while cultural studies insists dominant meanings are 'negotiated' (Hall 1980; Morley 1980; Fiske 1987) in different ways by different audiences. Classic ethnographies of reception (e.g. Radway 1988; Morley 1980) focusing on actual audiences have complicated these theories further, exposing contradictions *within* social groups (and even individual readers), and emphasizing the dangers of 'reading off' politics, class, ethnicity or gender as determinate factors. In short, reception study allows us to consider critically what it might mean to *relocate* and devolve the meaning production of diasporic fiction in a number of ways: outside the text, beyond 'identity', outwith the metropolitan centres of meaning production, and away from the academy.

Further reading

Fraser, R. (2008) 'The power of the consumer', in *Book History through Postcolonial Eyes: Rewriting the Script*, London: Routledge, pp. 164–86.

Innes, C. L. (2007) 'Citizens of the world: reading postcolonial literature', in *The Cambridge Introduction to Postcolonial Literatures in English*, Cambridge: Cambridge University Press, pp. 197–208.

Newell, S. (2006) *West African Literatures: Ways of Reading*, Oxford: Oxford University Press.

Procter, J. (2009) 'Reading, taste and post-colonial studies: professional and lay readers of *Things Fall Apart*', *Interventions*, 11(2): 180–98.

44 | Jews as rooted cosmopolitans: the end of diaspora?

David Shneer and Caryn Aviv

Where is the 'homeland' and where is 'diaspora' in the global spaces, communities and memories which Jews inhabit and call home? To call a place home is a statement of power. By arguing that a place is home, Jews express a sense of entitlement, control and familiarity. Home is a place where people practise identity and intimacy, where they make claims about who belongs and who doesn't. The word 'diaspora' originated in the Septuagint, one of the original Greek translations of the Bible. In its original context, it meant the divinely ordained dispersion of Jews from the Holy Land, the Land of Israel (*Erets Yisrael*), with eschatological visions of a future messianic ingathering. In the twenty-first century, Jewish policy-makers and the Jew on the street generally use the term to denote anyone or any place not within the boundaries of the modern nation-state of Israel (*Medinat Yisrael* in Hebrew). Scholars of diaspora have taken the term far beyond its original messianic and Jewish context to imply the complicated relations between place, space, power and politics that define contemporary collective identities.

Historically, Jews' understanding of home and diaspora was composed of everyday relationships to local communities and to mythic homelands, no matter where one lived. Jews needed to craft a concept of diaspora that would allow them to be at home wherever they were, while still maintaining a memory of place that connected them to Zion. In this essay, we suggest that Jews historically have lived as rooted cosmopolitans, maintaining a dynamic tension between movement and rootedness. Jews continue to express this sense of rootedness and cosmopolitanism, with complex links to one another in global communities that complicate and transcend the boundaries of nation-states.

Political Zionism, the nineteenth-century nationalist movement to establish Jewish political independence, was based on the idea that Jews needed their own territory and sovereignty in that territory to be truly safe in the modern world. Zionism, as both an ideological movement and a practical strategy of settlement 'on the ground', was predicated on ending the Jews' two-thousand-year exile in other peoples' homelands. Centuries of migration, history, politics, culture and religious yearning have layered upon Israel multiple and often conflicting meanings. For whom is Israel home, and how so? How should that home be governed and who should live there as a fully enfranchised citizen?

Political Zionism's success led to the establishment of a Jewish nation-state, *Medinat Israel*, in 1948. The state enshrined political Zionism's version of Jewish history and of the contemporary map. In this story, Israel ended 2,000 years of powerlessness and devalued displacement and claimed the right to speak for global Jewry. Ever since, Jews have wrestled with how that political fact has altered the global Jewish map. Is Israel *the* Jewish homeland, or *a* Jewish homeland? More poignantly, of course, some ask whether Israel should be a Jewish homeland and at what expense was that Jewish homeland created? Does the establishment of a political state claiming to be Jews' home render those living in other nation-states 'homeless' or at the very least living in a state of perpetual existential threat? How do Israel and many mainstream global Jewish organizations reinscribe diasporic identities for those not living in Israel? Many global Jews resist those identities and see themselves at home where they live, despite the presence of a nation-state claiming to speak for global Jewry or in some cases perhaps because of its presence.

We want to illustrate the core issues raised by these questions of rootedness and cosmopolitanism, and of reinscribing diaspora and homeland, with a recent example from global Jewish life. In the late summer of 2009, an advertisement aired in Israel began to circulate on the Internet, and immediately generated intense controversy in the Jewish world (MASA 2009). The slickly produced ad aimed to promote MASA: Israel Journeys, a 'project of the Government of Israel and Jewish communities around the world', which provides stipends for young Jews to study in Israel for a semester. MASA is just one of a host of initiatives sponsored by the Jewish Agency, the wing of the Israeli government most invested in encouraging Jews from around the world to immigrate to Israel, and most involved in propagating diaspora discourse that places Israel at the centre of the Jewish universe, and every other Jew in a different place called 'diaspora'. The advertisement begins with an image of an underground train, a headline in Hebrew that says 'The Assimilated Are Becoming Lost to Us'. Viewers see a poster with an attractive young Jewish woman, written in English – 'Lost: Julia Baer'. A sombre, melancholy flute melody plays in the background as we see more trains leaving stations and images of empty train tracks, with fluttering, lonely posters in French, English, Russian, with photos of young, smiling Jews, bearing their descriptions in terms of height, hair and eye colour.

The ad continues with anxious claims and dubious statistics as an ominous female voice intones:

> More than 50 per cent of our young people are assimilating. Know someone in the Diaspora [in Hebrew, *chutz la'aretz*, which literally means 'outside of the land']? You need to make sure he [sic] has a strong connection to Israel. Together we will strengthen his connection so that he will not be lost to us.

The video ends with the logo, a phone number and the phrase 'A year in Israel, love for a lifetime'.

The MASA ad implies quite bluntly that assimilation is the largest threat to the vitality of Jewish life and deploys not-so-subtle Holocaust imagery of trains, empty phone booths and trash to suggest a world depopulated of its Jews. In this solemn, dead and empty landscape, there are no real people, just posters of purportedly lost Jews. When we first saw this video, we asked a few questions:

- Why would such a promotional campaign define only Jews outside of Israel as somehow lost? And lost to what? Judaism? Zionism? Why does the ad assume that there are no Israelis who are 'lost' as well?
- What does this ad mean by 'assimilation'? Are the producers decrying inter-marriage rates among Jews around the world (a cause of great anxiety among Jewish communal policy-makers, but a taken-for-granted fact of life among most ordinary Jews)? Is 'diasporic' a code word for a Jew always in danger of assimilating?
- What are some of the core assumptions about contemporary Jewish identity here that both conflate Jewishness with nationalism, and simultaneously and indirectly disparage the choices and identities of those who do not live in Israel?

Perhaps not surprisingly, the MASA ad generated global outrage from many different quarters of the Jewish world. For example, the editor of *Forward*, the leading American Jewish newspaper, J. J. Goldberg, wrote:

> The reality is that a major proportion of self-identified Jews under 25 today have only one Jewish parent. Huge numbers of these children [...] grow up to become active, identifying Jews. From a practical point of view, the issue in America is no longer how to fight intermarriage [...]. The question now is how to draw the new Jews to Judaism. If the Masa folks are looking for young Jews who could use some outreach, these are the ones they're after. And nobody is going to win their hearts with commercials implying that their parents' marriage was a form of genocide. (Goldberg 2009)

The recent debacle over the MASA ad, which was shelved rather quickly given the uproar it created, revealed a profound misunderstanding among Israelis about Jews in the rest of the world. Israeli policy-makers tend to reinscribe a 'Jewish homeland = Israel' and 'diaspora = everywhere else Jewish' map that implies the inferiority of Jews outside Israel, even when most Jews around the world reject that categorization and don't see themselves as 'a problem' to be solved. The ad shows how dominant discourses within the Jewish world attempt to reinscribe diasporic relations into the language of global Jews. At the same time, the global response to the ad shows how many global Jews actively resist the idea of diaspora. There is a simultaneous and understandable pull towards relying on that established, if problematic, discourse, but there is also pushback – in the form of a growing global recognition among Jews that this discourse no longer describes Jewish realities effectively or fairly.

Our argument is that the very terms of the conversation – diaspora and Israel – are outmoded in that they reinscribe discarded models of centres and peripheries. Diaspora theory has done much to complicate our understanding of home and collective identity, but the theoretical work has not changed the discursive or political reality among Jews. Rather than refer to Jews as 'in Israel' or 'in (the) diaspora' (or, as modern Hebrew reinscribes the hierarchy, inside or outside of 'the land') we refer to contemporary Jews as 'global', whether they are in Israel, Russia or the United States (or many other places). This breaks down the inherent dichotomy and hierarchy that the Israel/diaspora metaphor maintains. (The hierarchy looks different if one is an Israeli government minister or a self-proclaimed leftist anti-Zionist Jewish diasporist, but both operate in the same hierarchy that privileges national allegiances in contemporary Jewish discourse around identity.)

Such labelling privileges the nation-state as the locus of global Jews' identity and has the homogenizing effect of suggesting that everyone not in Israel has something in common that implies a deficiency or inadequacy, the fact of not living in a Jewish nation-state. For us, the question is how Jews could change their collective identity and self-perception if we recognized that the Jewish world is more complex than the simple diaspora–Israel dichotomy suggests. Abandoning the language of diaspora to describe global Jewry allows us to see the real, and sometimes multiple, diasporas *within* the Jewish world – whether of Russians to Israel, Germany, the USA and Canada, of Israelis to those same places, or of Argentinians, Russians, Americans and French Jews in Israel. Larissa Remennick's work in this volume shows what diaspora theory has to say to these internal Jewish diasporas, in her case post-Soviet Jewish migrants, who complicate notions of home when they speak Russian in Israel, maintain multiple passports and have Internet relationships with Russian-speakers around the world, even as they disengage from Israeli neighbours. One could examine Chabad Lubavitch Hasids, the black-hatted internal Jewish missionaries, with headquarters in New York and origins in eastern Europe, but who are at home anywhere, from the farthest reaches of Siberia and Nepal to the hilltops overlooking Jerusalem. In both of these cases diaspora means dispersion from some common place (the former Soviet Union or Brooklyn), and that those in these diasporas share some common experience (secular, racialized Jewish identity or messianic, missionary-driven Judaism). But in a global world, these diasporic groups are also much more than dispersed from their originary home. They complicate the very idea of home.

If the Israel–diaspora binary framework no longer works, then why continue to rely on 'diaspora' at all to describe contemporary Jewish identities? The term has become a catch-all phrase to describe complex spatial and cultural formations in a fragmented world. In our book *New Jews* (Aviv and Shneer 2005), we showed that many Jews, as individuals and collectives, do not operate in this diasporic map and reject the notion of Israel as their homeland. We question whether diaspora best articulates this kind of group and individual identity in the modern world, and whether it has discounted or overshadowed the extent to which people – as individuals and as groups – are creating new forms of home in a more mobile world. Seeing all Jews as global eliminates hierarchies of value and allows new forms of affiliations and identities – defined by culture, class, sexual identity, language group and common political experience – to emerge. It does not privilege the Israeli national experience over the American pluralistic liberal one, or the ultra-Orthodox religiously observant one over the post-Soviet secular one. Many scholars of other diasporas have shown the problems of presuming that 'imagined communities' – groups that identify as a collective without each person knowing every member of the group – have centres and peripheries. And as James Clifford (1994: 303) points out, global people do not live 'in diaspora', because global people do not live either 'at home' or 'in exile'. For global people, home is constantly shifting.

Jews, as a collective group of people, define themselves beyond the parameters of the nation. One might say that we are arguing for a return to a pre-nationalist, pre-Zionist notion of collective identity across time and space. We are not, as that argument depends on a sense of collective identity defined by religious affiliation and adherence to a set of social practices as well as kinship networks and bloodlines. Jewishness at this point is far more complex than religiosity, and does not necessarily involve blood ties. But from our vantage point, a consistent historical thread that ties pre-nationalism to post-Zionism is the constantly changing boundaries of this community that has *always* been global. Perhaps a global Jewish collective identity should simply be called peoplehood. In the contemporary Jewish world, peoplehood is more flexible, slippery and complicated, and therefore more interesting to analyse. And at the same time, whether anti-Zionists and diaspora theoreticians like it or not, there is a self-proclaimed Jewish nation-state that claims to represent the voice of global Jewry, even though most global Jews do not trace their pasts (or their present) to that place. Moving away from the binary of diaspora–homeland towards a vision of a global people should be celebrated as evidence of Jews' ability to set down roots, to build houses and live in them. It is evidence that Jews are a group of diverse peoples with many cultures, many homes, and infinitely creative ways of expressing what it means to be at home, as Jews.

Further reading

Aviv, C. and D. Shneer (2005) *New Jews: The End of the Jewish Diaspora*, New York and London: New York University Press.

Gitelman, Z. (1998) 'The decline of the diaspora Jewish nation: boundaries, content and Jewish identity', *Jewish Social Studies*, 4(2): 112–32.

Goldberg, J. J. (2009) '"Lost" in plain sight: an Israeli plan to rescue American Jews', *Forward*, blogs.forward.com/jj-goldberg/113535/, accessed 28 December 2009.

Conclusion: new directions

Seán McLoughlin and Kim Knott

Concluding *Diasporas*

The aim of this volume has been to add something significantly different in a scholarly market of publications on diasporas that has relied heavily on classic books by key authors and on a multitude of ethnographies and edited collections on particular diasporas in context. The collected essays chart the history of scholarship on diasporas through its principal concepts, disciplinary intersections and exemplary global movements. Whether in the popular imagination or the classroom, 'diasporas' are more than empirical distributions of scattered people, their networks, artefacts and consciousness (Vertovec 1997); they are what scholars, diasporic interlocutors and other commentators have made of them: their representations, descriptions and analyses. How they are studied, conceptualized and theorized, by whom, in relation to what questions and problems, in which disciplines, and according to which frameworks and processes, are all important for understanding the subject of diasporas. This book is an attempt to bring some clarity to these issues, and, by engaging with the many perspectives of its contributors, to position diaspora studies within the academy while also recognizing its dynamism.

All fields of study change over time, and this one is no exception. As Part One showed, scholars writing about population movements and their social and cultural entailments have at various times favoured differing concepts, linking them in different ways, and devising or importing new ones. Over the last twenty years, the focus on 'diaspora', in association with 'transnationalism' and 'globalization', provided substantial theoretical and methodological resources for mounting a critique of those bounded conceptions, such as 'nation', 'community' and 'ethnicity', once central to the discussion of social groups and identities. Of the three critical terms, 'diaspora', in particular, was the one that allowed culture back into a scholarly debate that had become dominated by ideas about structure and society. With attention given to agency, to subjectivity as well as the identity of groups, to consciousness and imagination of home and away as well as migration, to representations as well as reality, and to things as well as people, 'diaspora' allowed for multidisciplinary participation, interdisciplinary engagement and, unsurprisingly, vocal debate about the application, definition and elasticity of the term.

At various moments in the last twenty years 'diaspora' has been used in the following ways: as a circumscribed reference to a particular people; an inclusive notion incorporating a multitude of different types of groups, things and ideas; a term that signals a minority identity politics; a label with political purchase; an insider term to convey particular sentiments, history and identity; a novel, transgressive category; a tired and exhausted one; and as a concept that brings into question its own end. When is a diaspora no longer diasporic? When does the conviction of 'staying put' make the notion of 'diaspora' no longer appropriate? As Shneer and Aviv enquire at the end of Part Three, can we conceive of the end of (a) diaspora? And, shifting the question from diasporas themselves to their study, when does the concept of 'diaspora' stop being useful? Ultimately it will be for future scholars to adjudicate on this, but the answer will depend on the continuing capacity of the term to have broad spatial, temporal, social and cultural application, to satisfy the theoretical instincts of academics in a range of disciplines, and to be resilient in the face of criticism.

Many disciplines and fields of enquiry within the humanities, arts and social sciences have treated the subject matter of diasporas, and we have sought to illustrate such engagements in Part Two. The authors writing in this part have brought an enormous range of concepts, models, perspectives, problems and possibilities to the scholarly table. A careful reading of the essays on intersections reveals the way in which certain disciplines and fields have built on the intervention of particular theorists, such as Bhabha and Hall in cultural studies or Glick Schiller and Levitt in sociology, with others – particularly Gilroy, Clifford, Cohen and Appadurai – used by scholars irrespective of their disciplinary niche. Of immense value has been the way in which each essayist has also brought to light more specialized research from their own field; so we leave the multidisciplinary feast with references to work on diasporas by economists, political scientists, development and security specialists, by linguists, cultural critics, and scholars of religion, film and performance, among others.

As we suggested in the Introduction, the global movements, networks, circulations and exchanges illustrated in Part Three criss-cross the globe, linking places in the South, East, West and North, sometimes becoming well trodden and familiar, but also facilitating new connections, identities and possibilities. In the third part of the book the authors have charted experiences of return as well as setting out, of circulation and networking as well as travel and settlement. Different historical, political and economic circumstances have been foregrounded, and questions posed about the relationships between religion and diaspora, and colonialism and diaspora, and whether the transnational movements of artists and intellectuals are really diasporic. The significance of space and movement for understanding diasporas becomes clear when we consider not only the variety of geographical movements represented by the essays in Part Three but the different diasporic spatialities reflected in them.

Some populations have maintained dynamic relations with places of origin, with repeated movements back and forth; others have experienced exile or permanent resettlement. Some diasporas have been sustained by religious sentiments rather than or in addition to a consciousness of national origins. Some have exhibited complex identities based on multiple historical movements and local positioning. Some formally settled, indigenous people have participated in diasporic contact zones and sought to unsettle their own seemingly stable identities, while others, labelled diasporic, have desired only to be settled and accepted as citizens with full rights and opportunities.

Leaving 'diaspora' for 'diaspora space'

At the end of Part One the importance of location for diasporas was stressed, in terms of multi-locality as well as the conventional pairing of here and there, but also in the context of being *in situ* as well as in transit. As James Procter noted, the term 'diaspora' signifies 'to deposit' as well as 'to scatter' and 'to sow' (2003: 14), thus anticipating the 'burden of dwelling' (ibid.: 209). Those diaspora spaces (Brah 1996), where people – whether they see themselves as new diasporans, established settlers or indigenous natives – must learn to dwell and to rub along together, have themselves become key sites for an analysis of the complex entailments and impacts of diasporas. Arguably, it is in the practical, political and intellectual challenges that arise when such spaces are foregrounded that the future of diaspora studies lies.

Leaving 'diaspora' for 'diaspora space' means occupying an arena in which locations and their complex populations are taken seriously, one that necessarily constitutes a challenge for policy-makers, makes intellectual and political demands of scholars and other engaged commentators, and is a public and civic responsibility. As Avtar Brah suggested,

> Diaspora space as a conceptual category is 'inhabited' not only by those who have migrated and their descendants but equally by those who are constructed and represented as indigenous. In other words, the concept of *diaspora space* (as opposed to that of diaspora) includes the entanglement of genealogies of dispersion with those of 'staying put'. (1996: 181)

Indeed, such entanglements led to over a decade of extensive engagement with the ideas and ideals of both 'multiculturalism' and 'cosmopolitanism', as scholars and other commentators sought to make sense of and respond to ethnic difference, urban plurality and the challenges of people living together rather than apart. Failed policies, unfulfilled dreams and melancholic malaise led Paul Gilroy (2006: 2) to write in 'unorthodox defense of this twentieth-century utopia of tolerance, peace and mutual regard' that is multicultural society. As a cultural theorist, he argued against revisionist accounts and for the need to locate contemporary multicultures in their imperial and colonial histories, suggesting that 'multicultural ethics and politics could be premised upon an agonistic, planetary humanism' (ibid.: 4) in which it is possible to celebrate difference with conviviality.

From a very different perspective in social anthropology, and with new directions in migration studies in mind, Steven Vertovec (2007) faced the issue of the complex entanglements of diaspora space by proposing the notion of super-diversity. He identified the factors associated with the complex diversity of contemporary cities as 'country of origin (comprising a variety of possible subset traits such as ethnicity, language[s], religious tradition, regional and local identities, cultural values and practices)', migration channel, legal status, migrants' human capital, access to employment, locality, transnationalism, and the responses by local government, service providers and other local people (ibid.: 1049). He noted also the challenges posed for policy-makers by such an environment and set of conditions, suggesting that scholars have a role to play with their knowledge and expertise in the various aspects that contribute to super-diversity (ibid.: 1047). New contact zones and types of engagement, new expressions of cosmopolitanism and creolization, but also new patterns of segregation and prejudice, all present possibilities for future research and analysis (ibid.: 1045–6).

Looking back at the history of diaspora studies, we suggest that the widening of public as well as scholarly interest in diasporas in the last decade led to a shift in the theoretical agenda from a focus on the poetics and politics of diasporic location associated with a fragmented black Atlantic and post-colonial context (e.g. Gilroy 1993a; Bhabha 1994), to one grounded in the urban multicultures of the South and North, informed by globalization and super-diversity (e.g. Glick Schiller and Caglar 2009; Vertovec 2007), and contextualized by public debates and government and multinational priorities. As Kalra et al. (2005) argued, the overwhelming emphasis on culture in diaspora studies had previously distracted scholars from the material realities of political economy and the continuing power of the security-conscious state to regulate citizenship, 'de-diasporize' and 'undo' hyphenated identities, especially since 9/11. Notably, some more recent publications are by political scientists (e.g. Sheffer 2003; Esman 2009) who are concerned with the problem and implications of diasporas for nation-states, whether in terms of loyalty and international relations, ethnic conflict and adaptation, or public policy.

Nation-states, hardly touched by theoretical claims that they would face erasure as a result of repeated transnational circuits by diasporic world citizens, have reasserted themselves to mark, secure and protect their borders and once more to classify and control their – increasingly fluid and complex – populations. Joining the debate about the importance and impact of diasporas, they have refocused their energies by managing and capitalizing upon both their diasporas abroad and migrants within through a range of discursive and policy mechanisms, focused particularly in areas such as aid and development, security and community. The nature of diasporas scholarship is changing to reflect such shifts and interventions, while continuing to connect with an ideological legacy critical of the nation-state, immigration policy and political discourse on multiculturalism and integration. Within diaspora studies, as in other fields in the social sciences and increasingly the arts and humanities, scholars face a tension between a critical politics of resistance and an opportunity to make a difference through engaged research. The two are not incommensurable, but the path to combine them with integrity may indeed be demanding and thorny.

About the contributors

Nadje Al-Ali is chair of the Centre for Gender Studies at the School of Oriental and African Studies, University of London.

Claire Alexander is reader in sociology at the London School of Economics.

Dibyesh Anand is an associate professor in international relations at Westminster University in London.

Caryn Aviv is Posen Lecturer in Secular Jewish Culture at the University of Denver, and director of research with Jewish Mosaic: the National Center for Sexual and Gender Diversity.

Gerd Baumann works at the University of Amsterdam and the Dutch Research College of Social Sciences.

Martin Baumann is professor of the study of religions at the University of Lucerne (Switzerland).

Daniela Berghahn is reader in film studies at Royal Holloway, University of London.

Victoria Bernal is associate professor of anthropology at the University of California, Irvine.

Jaine Beswick is programme leader for Portuguese studies and lecturer in linguistics at the University of Southampton.

Flemming Christiansen is professor of Chinese studies at the University of Leeds and director of the National Institute of Chinese Studies, White Rose East Asia Centre UK.

Anastasia Christou is research fellow in the Sussex Centre for Migration Research at the University of Sussex.

Robin Cohen is professor of development studies and director of the International Migration Institute, James Martin 21st Century School, University of Oxford.

Philip Crang is professor of cultural geography at Royal Holloway, University of London.

Claire Dwyer is a senior lecturer in geography at University College London, where she is deputy director of the Migration Research Unit.

John Eade is professor of sociology and anthropology at Roehampton University and executive director of the Centre for Research on Nationalism, Ethnicity and Multiculturalism.

Marie-Pierre Gibert is lecturer in social anthropology at the Université Lyon 2, France.

Helen Gilbert is professor of theatre at Royal Holloway, University of London.

Marie Gillespie is professor of sociology at the Open University and director of the Centre for Research on Socio-Cultural Change.

Graham Huggan is chair of Commonwealth and Postcolonial Literatures, and director of the Institute for Colonial and Postcolonial Studies (ICPS) and the Centre for Canadian Studies (CCS) at the University of Leeds.

John Hutnyk is professor of cultural studies at Goldsmiths, University of London.

Mark Johnson is senior lecturer in social anthropology at the University of Hull.

Ananya Jahanara Kabir is senior lecturer at the School of English, University of Leeds.

Karim H. Karim is presently co-director and professor at the Institute of Ismaili Studies in London. He was previously director of Carleton University's School of Journalism and Communication in Ottawa.

Russell King is professor of geography at the University of Sussex, co-director of the Sussex Centre for Migration Research, and editor of the *Journal of Ethnic and Migration Studies*.

Nadia Kiwan is lecturer in French and Francophone studies at the University of Aberdeen.

Kim Knott is professor of religious studies at the University of Leeds. She directed 'Diasporas, migration and identities', a research programme funded by the UK Arts and Humanities Research Council.

Kira Kosnick is junior professor of cultural anthropology and European ethnology at Goethe University Frankfurt.

Jeffrey Lesser is Samuel Candler Dobbs Professor of Latin American History at Emory University, Atlanta, Georgia.

Peggy Levitt is a professor of sociology at Wellesley College and a research fellow at Harvard University.

Claudia Liebelt completed her doctorate in social anthropology in Halle

(Germany). She was research assistant at the Research Institute of Law, Politics and Justice, Keele University, UK, and is currently at the University of Bayreuth.

Jacqueline Lo is head of the School of Humanities at the Australian National University.

Terrence Lyons is an associate professor of conflict resolution at the Institute for Conflict Analysis and Resolution, George Mason University, and co-director of the Center for Global Studies' project on Global Migration and Transnational Politics.

Peter Mandaville is an associate professor in the Department of Public and International Affairs, and co-director of the Center for Global Studies at George Mason University.

Deirdre McKay is senior lecturer in geography at Keele University.

Seán McLoughlin is senior lecturer in religious studies and Islamic studies at the University of Leeds.

Ulrike Hanna Meinhof is professor of German and cultural studies and director of the Centre for Transnational Studies, University of Southampton.

Claire Mercer is lecturer in human geography at the London School of Economics.

Tariq Modood is professor of sociology, politics and public policy and director of the Centre for the Study of Ethnicity and Citizenship at the University of Bristol, and editor of the international journal *Ethnicities*.

Ben Page is reader in geography at University College London.

Alicia Pingol earned her doctorate in sociology from the University of the Philippines, and is a research fellow at the University of Hull.

James Procter is a reader in modern English and postcolonial studies at Newcastle University.

Ato Quayson is professor of English and director of the Centre for Diaspora and Transnational Studies at the University of Toronto.

Sanaz Raji is a doctoral candidate in communication studies at the University of Leeds.

Larissa Remennick is professor of sociology and director of the Sociological Institute for Jewish Community Studies at Bar-Ilan University in Israel.

David Richardson is professor of economic history and director of the Wilberforce Institute for the Study of Slavery and Emancipation at the University of Hull.

David Shneer is associate professor of history and director of Jewish studies at the University of Colorado at Boulder.

Alex Stepick is professor of global and socio-cultural studies at Florida International University and professor of sociology at Portland State University.

Carol Dutton Stepick is research coordinator for the Center for Labor Research and Studies at Florida International University, Miami.

Femke Stock is a doctoral candidate at the University of Groningen, the Netherlands.

Simon Turner is senior researcher at the Danish Institute for International Studies.

Patricia Vanderkooy is a doctoral candidate at Florida International University.

Nicholas Van Hear is deputy director of the Centre on Migration, Policy and Society (COMPAS) at the University of Oxford.

Manuel A. Vásquez is associate professor of religion at the University of Florida, Gainesville.

Steven Vertovec is managing director of the Max Planck Institute for the Study of Religious and Ethnic Diversity, based in Göttingen, Germany.

Pnina Werbner is professor of social anthropology at Keele University.

Sara Wills is director of the Australian Centre in the School of Historical Studies at the University of Melbourne, Australia.

Bibliography

Achebe, C. (1958) *Things Fall Apart*, London: Heinemann.

— (2000) *Home and Exile*, Oxford: Oxford University Press.

Adams, R. and J. Page (2005) 'Do international migration and remittances reduce poverty in developing countries?', *World Development*, 33(10): 1645–69.

Adamson, F. (2005) 'Globalisation, transnational political mobilisation and networks of violence', *Cambridge Review of International Affairs*, 18(1): 31–49.

Al-Ali, N. (2007) 'Gender, diasporas and post-Cold War conflict', in H. Smith and P. Stares (eds), *Diasporas and Post-Cold War Conflict*, Washington, DC: United States Institute for Peace and United Nations University, pp. 39–62.

Al-Ali, N. and K. Koser (eds) (2002) *New Approaches to Migration? Transnational Communities and the Transformation of Home*, London: Routledge.

Al-Ali, N. and N. Pratt (eds) (2009) *Women and War in the Middle East: Transnational Perspectives*, London and New York: Zed Books.

Al-Ali, N., R. Black and K. Koser (2001) 'Refugees and transnationalism: the experience of Bosnians and Eritreans in Europe', *Journal of Ethnic and Migration Studies*, 27(4): 615–34.

Alexander, C. (2010) 'Diaspora and hybridity', in P. H. Collins and J. Solomos (eds), *Handbook of Race and Ethnic Studies*, London: Sage.

Alexander, J. M. (2005) *Pedagogies of Crossing: Meditations on Feminism, Sexual Politics, Memory, and the Sacred*, Durham, NC, and London: Duke University Press.

Al-Haj, M. (2002) 'Ethnic mobilization in an ethno-national state: the case of immigrants from the former Soviet Union in Israel', *Ethnic and Racial Studies*, 25(2): 238–57.

Ali, M. (2003) *Brick Lane*, London: Doubleday.

Ambrosio, T. (2002) *Ethnic Identity Groups and U.S. Foreign Policy*, Greenport, NY: Praeger.

Ammassari, S. (2004) 'From nation-building to entrepreneurship: the impact of elite return migrants in Côte d'Ivoire and Ghana', *Population, Space and Place*, 10(2): 133–54.

Anagnostou, Y. (2003) 'Model Americans, quintessential Greeks: ethnic success and assimilation in diaspora', *Diaspora*, 12(3): 279–327.

— (2008) *Contours of White Ethnicity: Popular Ethnography and the Making of Usable Pasts in Greek America*, Athens: Ohio University Press.

Anand, D. (2003) 'A contemporary story of "diaspora": the Tibetan version', *Diaspora: A Journal of Transnational Studies*, 12(3): 211–29.

— (2006) 'The West and the Tibetan issue', in B. Sautman and J. T. Dreyer (eds), *Contemporary Tibet: Politics, Development and Society in a Disputed Region*, Armonk, NY: M. E. Sharpe, pp. 285–304.

— (2007) *Geopolitical Exotica: Tibet in Western Imagination*, Minneapolis: University of Minnesota Press.

Anderson, B. (1983) *Imagined Communities: Reflections on the Origin and Spread of Nationalism*, London: Verso.

— (1991) *Imagined Communities: Reflections on the Origin and Spread of Nationalism*, 2nd edn, London: Verso.

— (1992) 'The new world disorder', *New Left Review*, I(193): 3–13.

— (1994) 'Exodus', *Critical Inquiry*, 20(2): 314–27.

Anderson, N. and Council of Social Agencies of Chicago (1923) *The Hobo: The Sociology of the Homeless Man*, Council of Social Agencies of Chicago.

Ang, I. (2001) *On Not Speaking Chinese: Living between Asia and the West*, London: Routledge.

Ang, I., J. E. Brand, G. Noble and D. Wilding (2002) *Living Diversity: Australia's Multicultural Future*, Artamon: Special Broadcasting Service Corporation.

Anthias, F. (1998) 'Evaluating diaspora: beyond ethnicity?', *Sociology*, 32(3): 557–80.

— (2001) 'New hybridities, old concepts: the limits of culture', *Ethnic and Racial Studies*, 24(4): 619–41.

— (2008) 'Where do I belong? Narrating collective identity and translocational positionality', *Ethnicities*, 2(4): 491–514.

Anthias, F. and G. Lazaridis (2000) (eds) *Gender and Migration in Southern Europe: Women on the Move*, Oxford and New York: Berg.

Anthias, F. and N. Yuval-Davis (1989) (eds) *Woman, Nation, State*, London, New Delhi and New York: Sage.

— (1992) *Racialised Boundaries: Race, Nation, Gender, Colour and Class and the Anti-Racist Struggle*, London: Routledge.

Appadurai, A. (ed.) (1986) *The Social Life of Things: Commodities in Cultural Perspective*, Cambridge: Cambridge University Press.

— (1996) *Modernity at Large: Cultural Dimensions of Globalization*, Minneapolis: University of Minnesota Press.

— (2003) 'Disjuncture and difference in the global cultural economy', in J. A. Braziel and A. Mannur (eds), *Theorizing Diaspora*, Oxford: Blackwell, pp. 25–48.

— (2006) *Fear of Small Numbers: An Essay on the Geography of Anger*, Durham, NC: Duke University Press.

Ardley, J. (2002) *The Tibetan Independence Movement: Political, Religious and Gandhian Perspectives*, London: Routledge Curzon.

Armbruster, H. (2002) 'Homes in crisis: Syrian Orthodox Christians in Turkey and Germany', in N. Al-Ali and K. Koser (eds), *New Approaches to Migration? Transnational Communities and the Transformation of Home*, London: Routledge, pp. 17–33.

Armstrong, J. A. (1976) 'Mobilized and proletarian diasporas', *American Political Science Review*, 70(2): 393–408.

Arowele, A. P. J. (1977) 'Diaspora-concept in the New Testament. Studies on the idea of Christian sojourn, pilgrimage and dispersion according to the New Testament', Unpublished PhD thesis, University of Würzburg.

Asad, T. (1986) *The Idea of an Anthropology of Islam*, Washington, DC: Georgetown University.

Asayesh, G. (1999) *Saffron Sky: A Life between Iran and America*, Boston, MA: Beacon Press.

Ashcroft, B., G. Griffiths and H. Tiffin (eds) (1998) *Key Concepts in Post-Colonial Studies*, London: Routledge.

Assayag, J. and V. Benei (ed.) (2003) *At Home in Diaspora: South Asian Scholars and the West*, New Delhi: Permanent Black.

Aviv, C. and D. Shneer (2005) *New Jews: The End of the Jewish Diaspora*, New York and London: New York University Press.

Back, L., M. Keith, A. Khan and J. Solomos (2009) 'Islam and the new political landscape: faith communities, political participation and social change', *Theory, Culture and Society*, 26(4): 1–23.

Baghdiantz-McCabe, I., G. Harlaftis and I. P. Minoglou (eds) (2005) *Diaspora Entrepreneurial Networks*, Oxford: Berg.

Bahrampour, T. (1999) *To See and See Again: A Life in Iran and America*, New York: Farrar, Straus and Giroux.

Bailey, O. G., M. Georgiou and R. Harindranath (eds) (2007) *Transnational Lives and the Media: Re-imagining Diasporas*, Basingstoke: Palgrave Macmillan.

Baines, D. (1991) *Emigration from Europe 1815–1930*, London: Macmillan, London.

Bakan, A. (1995) 'Making the match: domestic placement agencies and the racialization of women's household work', *Signs*, 20(2): 303–35.

Bakan, A. and D. Stasiulis (1997) *Not One of the Family: Foreign Domestic Workers in Canada*, Toronto: University of Toronto Press.

Balinska, M. (2008) *The Bagel: The Surprising History of a Modest Bread*, New Haven, CT, and London: Yale University Press.

Ballard, R. (1994) 'Introduction: the emergence of *Desh Pardesh*', in R. Ballard (ed.), *Desh Pardesh: The South Asian Presence in Britain*, London: C. Hurst, pp. 1–34.

Barber, P. G. (1997) 'Transnationalism and the politics of "home" for Philippine domestic workers', *Anthropologica*, 39: 1–14.

Barclay, J. M. G. (1996) *Jews in the Mediterranean Diaspora. From Alexander to Trajan, 323 BCE–117 CE*, Edinburgh: T. & T. Clark.

Barrett, G. and D. McEvoy (2006) 'The evolution of Manchester's Curry Mile: from suburban shopping street to ethnic destination', in D. Kaplan and W. Li (eds), *Landscapes of the Ethnic Economy*, Lanham, MD: Rowman and Littlefield.

Barringer, T. and T. Flynn (eds) (1998) *Colonialism and the Object: Empire, Material Culture and the Museum*, London: Routledge.

Basch, L. G., N. G. Schiller and C. Szanton Blanc (eds) (1994) *Nations Unbound: Transnational Projects, Postcolonial Predicaments, and Deterritorialized Nation States*, Langhorne, PA: Gordon and Breach.

Bauböck, R. (2003) 'Towards a political theory of migrant transnationalism', *International Migration Review*, 37(3): 700–23.

Baumann, G. (1996) *Contesting Culture: Discourses of Identity in Multi-Ethnic London*, Cambridge: Cambridge University Press.

— (1999) *The Multicultural Riddle: Rethinking National, Ethnic and Religious Identities*, New York: Routledge.

Baumann, G. and A. Gingrich (eds) (2004) *Grammars of Identity/Alterity: A Structural Approach*, Oxford: Berghahn.

Baumann, M. (1997) 'Shangri-La in exile: portraying Tibetan diaspora studies and reconsidering diaspora(s)', *Diaspora*, 6(3): 377–404.

— (2000) 'Diaspora: genealogy of semantics and transcultural comparison', *Numen: International Review for the History of Religions*, 47(3): 313–37.

— (2003) *Alte Götter in neuer Heimat. Religionswissenschaftliche Analyse zu Diaspora am Beispiel von Hindus auf Trinidad*, Marburg: diagonal.

Beckles, H. M. (1982) 'The 200 Years War: slave resistance in the British West Indies', *Jamaican Historical Review*, 13: 1–10.

Bedolla, L. G. (2005) *Fluid Borders: Latino Power, Identity, and Politics in Los Angeles*, Berkeley and Los Angeles: University of California Press.

Begg, M. (2006) *Enemy Combatant: A British Muslim's Journey to Guantanamo and Back*, London: Free Press.

Beine, M., F. Docquier and C. Özden (2009) 'Diasporas', World Bank Policy Research Working Paper 4984.

Bell, D. (ed.) (2006) *Cybercultures*, London and New York: Routledge.

Benhabib, S. (1992) *Situating the Self: Gender, Community and Postmodernism in Contemporary Ethics*, Cambridge: Polity Press.

— (ed.) (1996) *Democracy and Difference*, Princeton, NJ: Princeton University Press.

Benitez-Rojo, A. (1996) *The Repeating Island: The Caribbean and the Postmodern Perspective*, 2nd edn, Durham, NC: Duke University Press.

Bennett, Louise (1964) *Poems*, London: Arnold.

Berger, P. and T. Luckmann (1967) *The Social Construction of Reality: A Treatise in the Sociology of Knowledge*, New York: Anchor.

Berghahn, D. and C. Sternberg (eds) (2010) *European Cinema in Motion: Migrant and Diasporic Film in Contemporary Europe*, Basingstoke: Palgrave Macmillan.

Berlin, I. (2003) *Generations of Captivity: A History of African-American Slaves*, Cambridge, MA: Harvard University Press.

Bernal, V. (2005) 'Eritrea on-line: diaspora, cyberspace, and the public sphere', *American Ethnologist*, 32(4): 661–76.

Bernstorff, D. and H. von Welck (eds) (2003) *Exile as Challenge: The Tibetan Diaspora*, New Delhi: Orient Longman.

Beswick, J. (2005) 'The Portuguese diaspora in Jersey', in B. Preisler, A. Fabricius, H. Haberland, S. Kjaerbeck and K. Risager (eds), *The Consequences of Mobility. Linguistic and Sociocultural Contact Zones*, Denmark: Roskilde University Press.

— (2007) *Regional Nationalism in Spain: Language Use and Ethnic Identity in Galicia*, Clevedon: Multilingual Matters.

— (2010a) 'English at school, Portuguese at home: identity practices in the Portuguese-speaking community of Bournemouth', *Portuguese Studies*, London: MHRA.

— (2010b) 'Galician-Spanish-British? Migrant identity in Guildford, UK', in K. Hooper and M. Puga Moruxa (eds), *Galician Cultural Studies: Between the Local and the Global*, New York: MLA.

Bhabha, H. (1990a) 'The third space', in J. Rutherford (ed.), *Identity: Community, Culture, Difference*, London: Lawrence and Wishart, pp. 207–21.

— (1990b) *Nation and Narration*, London: Routledge.

— (1994) *The Location of Culture*, London and New York: Routledge.

— (1996) 'Unsatisfied: notes on vernacular cosmopolitanism', in L. Garcia-Morena and P. C. Pfeifer (eds), *Text and Nation*, London: Cambden House, pp. 191–207.

Bhachu, P. (1985) *Twice Migrants: East African Sikh Settlers in Britain*, London: Tavistock.

— (2004) *Dangerous Design: Asian Women Fashion the Diaspora Economies*, London: Routledge.

Bhatt, C. (1997) *Liberation and Purity*, London: University College London Press.

Bigo, D. (2002) 'Security and immigration: towards a critique of the governmentality of unease', *Alternatives*, 27: 63–92.

Bishop, P. (1989) *The Myth of Shangri-La: Tibet, Travel Writing and the Western Creation of a Sacred Landscape*, Berkeley: University of California Press.

— (1993) *Dreams of Power: Tibetan Buddhism and the Western Imagination*, London: Athlone Press.

Blunt, A. and R. Dowling (2006) *Home*, London: Routledge.

Bolt, P. (1996) 'Looking to the diaspora: the overseas Chinese and China's economic development, 1978–1994', *Diaspora*, 5(3): 25–36.

Bommes, M. and F. O. Radtke (1996) 'Migration into big cities and small towns: an uneven process with limited need for multiculturalism', *Innovation: The European Journal of Social Sciences*, 9(1): 75–86.

Boyarin, D. and J. Boyarin (1993) 'Diaspora: generation and the ground of Jewish identity', *Critical Inquiry*, 19: 693–725.

Boyarin, J. and D. Boyarin (2002) *The Powers of Diaspora: Two Essays on the Relevance of Jewish Culture*, Berkeley: University of California Press.

Bozorghmehr, M. and G. Sabagh (1988) 'High status immigrants: a statistical study of Iranians in the United States', *Iranian Studies*, 23(3): 3–33.

Brabazon, T. (2000) *Tracking the Jack: A Retracing of the Antipodes*, Sydney: University of New South Wales Press.

Brah, A. (1996) *Cartographies of Diaspora: Contesting Identities*, London: Routledge.

Brah, A. and A. Coombs (2000) *Hybridity and Its Discontents*, London: Routledge.

Branover, H., I. Berlin and Z. Wagner (1998) *The Encyclopedia of Russian Jewry, Biographies*, Northvale, NJ, and Jerusalem: Jason Aronson.

Braziel, J. E. (2008) *Diaspora: An Introduction*, Oxford: Wiley-Blackwell.

Braziel, J. E. and A. Mannur (2003) (eds) *Theorizing Diaspora: A Reader*, Oxford and Malden, MA: Blackwell.

Brettell, C. (2005) 'The spatial, social, and

political incorporation of Asian Indian immigrants in Dallas', *Urban Anthropology*, 34(2/3): 247–80.

Brinkerhoff, J. (2009) *Digital Diasporas: Identity and Transnational Engagement*, Cambridge: Cambridge University Press.

Brockmeier, J. (2000) 'Autobiographical time', *Narrative Inquiry*, 10(1): 51–73.

Brown, J. N. (2005) *Dropping Anchor, Setting Sail: Geographies of Race in Black Liverpool*, Princeton, NJ: Princeton University Press.

Brown, K. (1999) 'Staying grounded in a high-rise building: ecological dissonance and ritual accommodation in Haitian Vodou', in R. Orsi (ed.), *Gods of the City: Religion and the American Urban Landscape*, Bloomington: Indiana University Press, pp. 79–102.

Browne, D. R. (2005) *Ethnic Minorities, Ethnic Media and the Public Sphere: A Comparative Study*, Cresskill, NJ: Hampton Press.

Brubaker, R. (1998) 'Migrations of ethnic un-mixing in the "New Europe"', *International Migration Review*, 3(4): 1047–65.

— (2005) 'The "diaspora" diaspora', *Ethnic and Racial Studies*, 28(1): 1–19.

Brydon, D. (2004) 'Post-colonialism now: autonomy, cosmopolitanism, and diaspora', *University of Toronto Quarterly*, 73(2): 691–706.

Brym, R. J. (with R. Ryvkina) (1994) *The Jews of Moscow, Kiev and Minsk: Identity, Antisemitism, Emigration*, New York: New York University Press.

Bugarski, R. (2001) 'Language, nationalism and war in Yugoslavia', *International Journal of the Sociology of Language*, 151: 69–87.

Buijs, G. (1993) (ed.) *Migrant Women: Crossing Boundaries and Changing Identities*, Oxford and Providence, RI: Berg.

Bukharaev, R. (2003) 'The BBC and poetry', in D. Weissbort (ed.), 'Poets at Bush House: the BBC World Service', *Modern Poetry in Translation*, 22: 96–7.

Bunt, G. (2000) *Virtually Islamic: Computer Mediated Communication and Cyber Islamic Environment*, Cardiff: University of Wales Lampeter Press.

— (2009) *iMuslims: Rewiring the House of Islam*, London: C. Hurst and Co.

Burchell, G. et al. (eds) (1991) *The Foucault Effect. Studies in Governmentality*, Chicago, IL: University of Chicago Press.

Burke, P. (2009) *Cultural Hybridity*, Cambridge and Malden, MA: Polity Press.

Burnard, T. (2007) 'The Atlantic slave trade and African ethnicities in seventeenth century Jamaica', in D. Richardson, S. Schwarz and A. Tibbles (eds), *Liverpool and Transatlantic Slavery*, Liverpool: Liverpool University Press, pp. 139–64.

Burrell, J. and K. Anderson (2008) '"I have great desires to look beyond my world": trajectories of information and communication technology use among Ghanaians living abroad', *New Media and Society*, 10(2): 269–90.

Butler, J. (1993) *Bodies that Matter: On the Discursive Limits of 'Sex'*, New York and London: Routledge.

Byrd, A. (2008) *Captives and Voyagers: Black Migrants across the Eighteenth-century British Atlantic World*, Baton Rouge: Louisiana State University.

Caglar, A. (1994) 'German Turks in Berlin: migration and their quest for social mobility', Unpublished PhD thesis, McGill University.

Calhoun, C. (ed.) (1992) *Habermas and the Public Sphere*, Cambridge, MA: MIT Press.

Callinicos, C. (1991) *American Aphrodite: Becoming Female in Greek America*, New York: Pella.

Campt, T. and D. Thomas (eds) (2008) 'gendering diasporas', *Feminist Review*, 90.

Carney, J. (2001) *Black Rice: The African Origins of Rice Cultivation in the Americas*, Cambridge, MA: Harvard University Press.

Carretta, V. (1998) (ed.) *Letters of the Late Ignatius Sancho: An African*, London: Penguin.

— (1999) *Thoughts and Sentiments on the Evil of Slavery and Other Writings by*

Quobna Ottobah Cugoano, London: Penguin.

— (2003) *The Interesting Narrative and Other Writings by Olaudah Equiano*, London: Penguin.

— (2005) *Equiano the African: Biography of a Self-Made Man*, Athens: University of Georgia Press.

Carter, D. (2002) 'Going, going, gone? Britishness and Englishness in contemporary Australian culture', *Overland*, 169: 81–6.

Carter, D. M. (2010) *Navigating the African Diaspora: The Anthropology of Invisibility*, Minneapolis: University of Minnesota Press.

Castells, M. (1996) *The Information Age: Economy, Society and Culture*, Cambridge, MA: Blackwell.

— (2001) *The Internet Galaxy*, Oxford and New York: Oxford University Press.

Castles, S. and M. Miller (2009 [1993]) *The Age of Migration: International Population Movements in the Modern World*, New York: Palgrave Macmillan.

Catley, R. (1996) *Globalising Australian Capitalism*, Melbourne: Cambridge University Press.

Central Bureau of Statistics (1990–2007) *Statistical Yearbooks*, Jerusalem: Government Press Office.

Cesari, J. and S. McLoughlin (2005) (eds) *European Muslims and the Secular State*, Aldershot: Ashgate.

Chambers, I. (1994) *Migrancy, Culture, Identity*, London: Routledge.

— (1996) 'Signs of silence, lines of listening', in I. Chambers and L. Curtis (eds), *The Post-Colonial Question*, London: Routledge, pp. 47–62.

Chariandy, D. (2006) 'Postcolonial diasporas', *Postcolonial Text*, 2(1), journals.sfu.ca/pocol/index.php/pct/article/viewArticle/440/159, accessed 28 December 2009.

Chartier, R. (1992) 'Labourers and voyagers: from the text to the reader', *Diacritics*, 22(2): 49–61.

Chatterji, J. (2009) 'Dispositions and destinations: towards a model of migration, displacement and diaspora for the Bengal Delta', Unpublished paper presented at 'Diaspora, migration and identities: crossing boundaries, new directions', University of Surrey, June.

Cherti, M. (2008) *Paradoxes of Social Capital: A Multi-generational Study of Moroccans in London*, Amsterdam: Amsterdam University Press.

Chock, P. P. (1995) 'The self-made woman: gender and the success story in Greek-American family histories', in S. J. Yanagisako and C. Delaney (eds), *Naturalizing Power: Essays in Feminist Cultural Analysis*, London: Routledge, pp. 239–55.

Christiansen, F. (1990) 'Social division and peasant mobility in mainland China: the implications of the Hu-k'ou system', *Issues and Studies*, 26(4): 32–3.

Christou, A. (2001) 'The struggle, success and national consciousness of the Greek diaspora in America', in L. Koski and K. Pajala (eds), *American Studies at the Millennium: Ethnicity, Culture and Literature*, Turku: University of Turku, pp. 125–35.

— (2006) *Narratives of Place, Culture and Identity: Second-Generation Greek-Americans Return 'Home'*, Amsterdam: Amsterdam University Press.

Clarke, A. J. (2001) 'The aesthetics of social aspiration', in D. Miller (ed.), *Home Possessions. Material Culture behind Closed Doors*, Oxford: Berg, pp. 23–45.

Clifford, J. (1994) 'Diasporas', *Cultural Anthropology*, 9(3): 302–38.

— (1997) *Routes: Travel and Translation in the Late Twentieth Century*, Cambridge, MA: Harvard University Press.

— (2000) 'Taking identity politics seriously: "the contradictory stony ground ..."', in P. Gilroy, L. Grossberg and A. McRobbie (eds), *Without Guarantees: In Honour of Stuart Hall*, London: Verso, pp. 94–112.

Clyne, M. (1991) *Community Languages: The Australian Experience*, Cambridge: Cambridge University Press.

— (2003) *Dynamics of Language Contact: English and Immigrant Languages*, Cambridge: Cambridge University Press.

Cochrane, P. (1994) 'Anglo-Saxonness: ancestors and identity', *Communal/ Plural*, 4: 1–16.

Cockburn, C. (1999) 'Background paper: gender, armed conflict and political violence', World Bank Conference on Gender, Armed Conflict and Political Development, Washington, DC.

Cohen, A. P. (1985) *The Symbolic Construction of Community*, London: Routledge.

Cohen, R. (ed.) (1995) *The Cambridge Survey of World Migration*, Cambridge: Cambridge University Press.

— (1997) *Global Diasporas: An Introduction*, London: Routledge.

— (2007) 'Creolization and cultural globalization: the soft sounds of fugitive power', *Globalizations*, 4(3): 369–84.

— (2008) *Global Diasporas: An Introduction*, 2nd edn, London and New York: Routledge.

Cohen, S. J. D. (1999) *The Beginning of Jewishness: Boundaries, Varieties, Uncertainties*, Berkeley: University of California Press.

Cohen, S. J. D. and E. S. Frerichs (eds) (1993) *Diasporas in Antiquity*, Atlanta, GA: Scholars Press.

Collier, P. and A. Hoeffler (2004) 'Greed and grievance in civil war', *Oxford Economic Papers*, 56(4): 563–95.

Collins, F. L. (2008) 'Of Kimchi and coffee: globalisation, transnationalism and familiarity in culinary consumption', *Social and Cultural Geography*, 9(2): 151–69.

Collins, J. (2006) 'Ethnic diversity and ethnic economy in cosmopolitan Sydney', in D. Kaplan and W. Li (eds), *Landscapes of the Ethnic Economy*, Lanham, MD: Rowman and Littlefield, pp. 135–48.

Collyer, M. (2004) 'Profile of the Algerian population in the UK', Information Centre about Asylum and Refugees in the UK, www.icar.org.uk/9512/media/services.html, accessed 9 January 2010.

Constable, N. (2007) *Maid to Order in Hong Kong: Stories of Migrant Workers*, 2nd edn, Ithaca, NY: Cornell University Press.

Constantinou, S. T. (2002) 'Profiles of Greek-Americans', in K. L. Berry and M. L. Henderson (eds), *Geographical Identities of Ethnic America: Race, Space and Place*, Reno and Las Vegas: University of Nevada Press, pp. 92–115.

Cook, I. (2004) 'Follow the thing: papaya', *Antipode*, 36(4): 642–64.

— (2008) 'Geographies of food: mixing', *Progress in Human Geography*, 32(6): 821–33.

Cook, I., P. Crang and M. Thorpe (1999) 'Eating into Britishness: multicultural imaginaries and the identity politics of food', in S. Roseneil and J. Seymour (eds), *Practising Identities: Power and Resistance*, London: Macmillan, pp. 223–48.

Coombe, R. and P. Stoller (1994) 'X marks the spot: the ambiguities of African trading in the commerce of the black public sphere', *Public Culture*, 7(1): 249–74.

Coulmas, F. (2005) *Sociolinguistics: The Study of Speakers' Choices*, Cambridge: Cambridge University Press.

Crang, P. and S. Ashmore (2009) 'The transnational spaces of things: South Asian textiles in Britain and *The Grammar of Ornament*', *European Review of History – Revue Européene d'Histoire*, 16(5): 655–78.

Crang, P., C. Dwyer and P. Jackson (2003) 'Transnationalism and the spaces of commodity culture', *Progress in Human Geography*, 27(4): 438–56.

Crissiuma, E. de F. (1935) 'Concentração Japonesa em São Paulo', *Geografia*, 1(1): 110–14.

Cruz-Malavé, A. and M. Manalansan IV (eds) (2002) *Queer Globalizations: Citizenship and the Afterlife of Colonialism*, New York and London: New York University Press.

Cunningham, S. and J. Sinclair (eds) (2002) *Floating Lives: The Media and Asian Diasporas*, Lanham, MD: Rowman and Littlefield.

Curtin, P. (1967) *Africa Remembered: Narratives of West Africa from the Era of the Slave Trade*, Madison: University of Wisconsin Press.

Dahan, M. and G. Sheffer (2001) 'Ethnic groups and distance shrinking communication technologies', *Nationalism and Ethnic Politics*, 7(1): 85–107.

Dahlberg, L. (2005) 'The Habermasian public sphere: taking difference seriously?', *Theory and Society*, 34(2): 111–36.

Dallal, A. S. (1995) '*Ummah*', in J. Esposito (ed.), *Oxford Encyclopaedia of the Modern Islamic World*, Oxford: Oxford University Press, pp. 267–70.

Davidson, A. P. (2008) 'The play of identity, memory and belonging: Chinese migrants in Sydney', in K. E. Kuah-Pearce and A. P. Davidson (eds), *At Home in the Chinese Diaspora: Memories, Identities and Belongings*, Basingstoke: Palgrave MacMillan, pp. 12–32.

Davies, R. (2007) 'Reconceptualising the migration – development nexus: diasporas, globalisation and the politics of exclusion', *Third World Quarterly*, 28(1): 59–76.

Dávila, A. (2001) *Latinos Inc.: The Marketing and Making of a People*, Berkeley: University of California Press.

Davin, D. (1999) *Internal Migration in Contemporary China*, Basingstoke: Macmillan.

Davis, D. (2006) *Inhuman Bondage: The Rise and Fall of Slavery in the New World*, Oxford: Oxford University Press.

De Certeau, M. (1984) *The Practice of Everyday Life*, Berkeley: University of California Press.

De Haas, H. (2005) 'International migration, remittances and development: myths and facts', *Third World Quarterly*, 26(8): 1269–84.

— (2007) *Migration, Remittances and Social Development*, Geneva: United Nations Research Department for Social Development.

Delaney, C. (1991) *The Seed and the Soil: Gender and Cosmology in Turkish Village Society*, Berkeley: University of California Press.

Dembour, M. (2006) *Who Believes in Human Rights?*, Cambridge: Cambridge University Press.

Desai, J. (2004) *Beyond Bollywood: The Cultural Politics of South Asian Diasporic Film*, London and New York: Routledge.

Diasporas, Migration and Identities (2005) *Programme Specification*, www.diasporas.ac.uk/assets/programme%20specification.pdf, accessed 10 January 2010.

Diehl, K. (2002) *Echoes from Dharamsala: Music in the Life of a Tibetan Refugee Community*, Berkeley: University of California Press.

Diouf, S. (2003) (ed.) *Fighting the Slave Trade: West African Strategies*, London: James Currey.

Dixson, M. (1999) *The Imaginary Australian: Anglo-Celts and Identity – 1788 to the Present*, Sydney: University of New South Wales Press.

Dodin, T. and H. Rather (eds) (2001) *Imagining Tibet: Perceptions, Projections, and Fantasies*, Boston, MA: Wisdom Publications.

Dolan, J. (2005) *Utopia in Performance: Finding Hope at the Theatre*, Ann Arbor: University of Michigan Press.

Donald, J. and A. Rattansi (eds) (1992) *'Race', Culture and Difference*, London: Sage.

Drieskens, B., F. Mermier and H. Wimmen (eds) (2007) *Cities of the South: Citizenship and Exclusion in the 21st Century*, London: Saqi.

Dubois, L. (2004) *A Colony of Citizens: Revolution and Slave Emancipation in the French Caribbean, 1789–1804*, Chapel Hill: University of North Carolina Press.

Duffield, M. (2001) *Global Governance and the New Wars: The Merging of Development and Security*, London: Zed Books.

DuFoix, S. (2008) *Diasporas*, Berkeley: University of California Press.

Dumas, F. (2003) *Funny in Farsi: A Memoir of Growing Up Iranian in America*, New York: Villard.

Durkheim, Emile (1971 [1915]) *The Elementary Forms of the Religious Life*, London: George Allen and Unwin.

Durrant, S. (2004) *Postcolonial Narrative and the Work of Mourning*, New York: State University of New York.

Duruz, J. (2005) 'Eating at the borders: culinary journeys', *Environment and Planning D: Society and Space*, 23(1): 51–69.

Dwyer, C. (2004) 'Tracing transnationalities through commodity culture: a case study of British-South Asian fashion', in P. Jackson et al., *Transnational Spaces*, London: Routledge, pp. 60–77.

Dwyer, C. and P. Crang (2002) 'Fashioning ethnicities: the commercial spaces of multiculture', *Ethnicities*, 2(3): 410–30.

Dwyer, C. and P. Jackson (2003) 'Commodifying difference: selling Eastern fashion', *Environment and Planning D: Society and Space*, 21(3): 269–91.

Eade, J. (ed.) (1997) *Living the Global City: Globalization as a Local Process*, London and New York: Routledge.

Edwards, E., C. Gosden and R. B. Phillips (eds) (2006) *Sensible Objects: Colonialism, Museums and Material Culture*, Oxford: Berg.

Eickelman, D. F. and J. P. Piscatori (1990) (eds) *Muslim Travellers: Pilgrimage, Migration and the Religious Imagination*, Berkeley: University of California Press.

Eisenstadt, S. N. (1992) *Jewish Civilization: The Jewish Historical Experience in a Comparative Perspective*, Albany: State University of New York Press.

Eliade, M. (1982) *Ordeal by Labyrinth*, Chicago, IL: University of Chicago Press.

Elias, N. (2008) *Coming Home: Media and Returning Diaspora in Israel and Germany*, Albany: State University of New York Press.

Elsaesser, T. (1999) 'Ethnicity, authenticity and exile: a counterfeit trade? German filmmakers and Hollywood', in H. Naficy (ed.), *Home, Exile, Homeland: Film, Media, and the Politics of Place*, London and New York: Routledge, pp. 97–123.

— (2005) *European Cinema: Face to Face with Hollywood*, Amsterdam: Amsterdam University Press.

Eltis, D. (1983) 'Free and coerced transatlantic migrations: some comparisons', *American Historical Review*, 88(2): 251–80.

Eltis, D. and S. Engerman (1993) 'Fluctuations in sex and age ratios in the transatlantic slave trade, 1663–1864', *Economic History Review*, new series, 46(2): 308–23.

Eltis, D. and P. Lachance (2008) 'The demographic decline of Caribbean slave populations: new evidence from the transatlantic and intra-American slave trades', in D. Eltis and D. Richardson (eds), *Extending the Frontiers: Essays on the New Transatlantic Slave Trade Database*, New Haven, CT: Yale University Press, pp. 335–63.

Eltis, D. and D. Richardson (1997) 'The "numbers game" and routes to slavery', *Slavery and Abolition*, 18(1): 1–15.

— (2008) 'A new assessment of the transatlantic slave trade', in D. Eltis and D. Richardson (eds), *Extending the Frontiers: Essays on the New Transatlantic Slave Trade Database*, New Haven, CT: Yale University Press, pp. 1–60.

— (2010) *Atlas of Transatlantic Slavery*, New Haven, CT: Yale University Press.

Eltis, D., F. Lewis and D. Richardson (2005) 'Slave prices, the African Slave trade and productivity in the Caribbean, 1674–1807', *Economic History Review*, 58(4): 673–700.

Eltis, D., P. Morgan and D. Richardson (2007) 'Agency and diaspora in Atlantic history: reassessing the African contribution to rice cultivation in the Americas', *American Historical Review*, 112(5): 1329–58.

Erikson, E. (1963 [1950]) *Childhood and Society*, New York: W. W. Norton.

Esman, M. (2009) *Diasporas in the Contemporary World*, Cambridge: Polity Press.

Ezra, E. and T. Rowden (eds) (2006) *Transnational Cinema: The Film Reader*, London and New York: Routledge.

Fabos, A. (2002) 'Sudanese identity in diaspora and the meaning of home: the transformative role of Sudanese NGOs in Cairo', in N. Al-Ali and K. Koser (eds), *New Approaches to Migration? Transnational Communities and the Transformation of Home*, London and New York: Routledge.

Fabricant, C. (1998) 'Riding the waves of (post)colonial migrancy: are we really in the same boat?', *Diaspora*, 7(1): 25–51.

Faist, T. (2004) 'The border-crossing expansion of social space: concepts, questions and topics', in T. Faist and E. Ozveren (eds), *Transnational Social Spaces: Agents, Networks and Institutions*, Aldershot: Ashgate, pp. 1–34.

— (2005) *The Migration–Security Nexus: International Migration and Security before and after 9/11*, Bielefeld: Centre on Migration, Citizenship and Development.

— (2008) 'Migrants as transnational development agents: an inquiry into the newest round of the migration-development nexus', *Population, Space and Place*, 14(1): 21–42.

Faist, T. and P. Kivisto (eds) (2008) *Dual Citizenship in Global Perspective: From Unitary to Multiple Citizenship*, Basingstoke: Palgrave.

Farmer, P. (1990) *Aids and Accusation: Haiti and the Geography of Blame*, Cambridge, MA: Harvard University Press.

Faure, David (1989) 'The lineage as a cultural invention – the case of the Pearl River delta', *Modern China*, 15(1): 4–6.

— (2007) *Emperor and Ancestor: State and Lineage in South China*, Stanford, CA: Stanford University Press.

Favell, A. (2003) 'Games without frontiers? Questioning the transnational social power of migrants', *European Journal of Sociology*, 44(3): 397–427.

Featherstone, D., R. Phillips and J. Waters (2007) 'Spatialities of transnational networks', *Global Networks*, 7(4): 383–91.

Felski, R. (2003) *Literature after Feminism* Chicago, IL: Chicago University Press.

Fialkova, L. and M. N. Yelenevskaya (2007) *Ex-Soviets in Israel: From Personal Narratives to a Group Portrait*, Detroit, MI: Wayne State University Press.

Fikes, K. (2008) 'Diasporic governmentality: on the gendered limits of migrant wage labour in Portugal', in T. Campt and D. Thomas (eds), special edition on gendering diasporas, *Feminist Review*, 90.

Fincher, R. and J. Jacobs (eds) (2000) *Cities of Difference*, New York: Guilford Press.

Fincher, R. and P. Saunders (eds) (2001) *Creating Unequal Futures? Rethinking Poverty, Inequality and Disadvantage*, Crows Nest, NSW: Allen and Unwin.

Fischer, M. J. and M. Abedi (1990) 'Diasporas: re-membering and re-creating', *Debating Muslims: Cultural Dialogues in Postmodernity and Tradition*, Madison: University of Wisconsin Press.

Fish, S. (1980) *Is There a Text in This Class? The Authority of Interpretive Communities*, Cambridge, MA: Harvard University Press.

Fishman, J. (1964) 'Language maintenance and language shift as a field of inquiry', *Linguistics*, 9: 32–70.

Fiske, J. (1987) *Television Culture*, London: Methuen.

Fitzgerald, D. (2006) 'Rethinking emigrant citizenship', *New York University Law Review*, 81(1): 90–116.

Foner, N. (1997) 'What's new about transnationalism? New York immigrants today and at the turn of the century', *Diaspora*, 6(3): 355–75.

Fortier, A. (2000) *Migrant Belongings: Memory, Space, Identity*, Oxford: Berg.

— (2002) 'Queer diasporas', in D. Richardson and S. Seidman (eds), *Handbook of Lesbian and Gay Studies*, London: Sage, pp. 183–97.

Foucault, M. (1978) *The History of Sexuality*, vol. 1: *An Introduction*, New York: Pantheon.

— (1986) 'Of other spaces', *Diacritics*, 16(1): 22–27.

Fraser, N. (1992) 'Rethinking the public sphere: a contribution to the critique of actually existing democracy,' in C. Calhoun (ed.), *Habermas and the Public Sphere*, Cambridge, MA: MIT Press, pp. 109–42.

Fraser, R. (2008) *Book History through Postcolonial Eyes: Rewriting the Script*, London: Routledge.

Frechette, A. (2007) 'Democracy and democratization among Tibetans in exile', *Journal of Asian Studies*, 66(1): 97–127.

Freitag, S. (1989) *Collective Action and Community: Public Arenas and the Emergence of Communalism in North India*, Berkeley: University of California Press.

Fuglerud, Ø. (1999) *Life on the Outside: The Tamil Diaspora and Long Distance Nationalism*, London: Pluto Press.

Fygetakis, L. H. (1997) 'Greek American lesbians: identity odysseys of honorable good girls', in B. Greene (ed.), *Ethnic and Cultural Diversity among Lesbians and Gay Men*, Thousand Oaks, CA: Sage, pp. 152–90.

Gabaccia, D. R. (1998) *We Are What We Eat: Ethnic Food and the Making of Americans*, Cambridge, MA: Harvard University Press.

— (2000) *Italy's Many Diasporas*, London: UCL Press.

Georgakas, D. (1987) 'The Greeks in America', *Journal of the Hellenic Diaspora*, 14(1/2): 5–53.

George, S. M. (2005) *When Women Come First: Gender and Class in Transnational Migration*, Berkeley: University of California Press.

Georgiou, M. (2006) 'Diasporic communities online', in K. Sarkakis and D. Thussu (eds), *Ideologies of the Internet*, Cresskill, NJ: Hampton Press, pp. 131–46.

Germenji, E. and I. Gedeshi (2008) *Highly Skilled Migration from Albania: An Assessment of Current Trends and the Ways Ahead*, Working Paper T-25, Development Research Centre on Migration, Globalization and Poverty, University of Sussex.

Ghorashi, H. (2003) *Ways to Survive, Battles to Win: Iranian Women Exiles in the Netherlands and United States*, New York: Nova Science Publishers.

Ghosh, A. (1989) 'The diaspora in Indian culture', *Public Culture*, 1: 73–8.

— (1992) *In an Antique Land*, London: Granta.

— (2008) *The Sea of Poppies*, London: John Murray.

Ghosh, B. and B. Sarkar (1995/96) 'The cinema of displacement: towards a politically motivated poetics', *Film Criticism*, 20(1/2): 102–13.

Gibson, K., L. Law and D. McKay (2001) 'Beyond heroes and victims: Filipina contract migrants, activism and class transformations', *International Feminist Journal of Politics*, 3(3): 365–86.

Giddens, A. (2006) *Europe in the Global Age*, London: Polity Press.

Gilbert, H. and J. Lo (2007) *Performance and Cosmopolitics: Cross Cultural Transactions in Australasia*, London: Palgrave Macmillan.

Gillespie, M. (1995) *Television, Ethnicity and Cultural Change*, London: Routledge.

Gillespie, M., A. Pinkerton, G. Baumann and S. Thiranagama (2010) 'South Asian diasporas and the BBC World Services: contacts, conflicts, and contestations', Special issue, *South Asian Diaspora*, 2(1): 3–23.

Gilroy, P. (1993a) *The Black Atlantic: Modernity and Double Consciousness*, Cambridge, MA/London: Harvard University Press/Verso.

— (1993b) *Small Acts: Thoughts on the Politics of Black Cultures*, London: Serpent's Tail.

— (1994) 'Black cultural politics: an interview with Paul Gilroy by Timmy Lott', *Found Object*, 4: 46–81.

— (1997) 'Diaspora and the detours of identity', in K. Woodward (ed.), *Identity and Difference*, London: Sage, pp. 299–346.

— (2000) *Between Camps*, Harmondsworth: Penguin.

— (2002 [1987]) *There Ain't No Black in the Union Jack: The Cultural Politics of Race and Nation*, London and New York: Routledge.

— (2004a) *After Empire: Melancholia or Convivial Culture?*, London: Routledge.

— (2004b) 'It's a family affair', in M. Forman and M. A. Neal (eds), *That's the Joint! The Hip-Hop Studies Reader*, London: Routledge, pp. 87–94.

— (2006) *Postcolonial Melancholia*, New York: Columbia University Press.

Gimenez, M. E. (1998) 'Latinos/Hispanics

... What Next! Some Reflections on the Politics of Identity in the US', *Cultural Logic: An Electronic Journal of Marxist Theory and Practice*, 1(2), clogic.eserver.org/1–2/gimenez.html.

Gingrich, A. and M. Banks (eds) (2006) *Neo-Nationalism in Western Europe and Beyond: Perspectives from Social Anthropology*, London: Berghahn.

Gitelman, Z. (1997) '"From a northern country": Russian and Soviet Jewish immigration to America and Israel in historical perspective', in N. Lewin-Epstein et al. (eds), *Russian Jews on Three Continents: Migration and Resettlement*, London: Frank Cass, pp. 21–44.

— (1998) 'The decline of the diaspora Jewish nation: boundaries, content and Jewish identity', *Jewish Social Studies*, 4(2): 112–32.

— (2003) 'Thinking about being Jewish in Russia and Ukraine', in Z. Gitelman, M. Goldman and M. Glanz (eds), *Jewish Life after the USSR*, Bloomington: Indiana University Press.

Glick Schiller, N. (2005) 'Long-distance nationalism', in M. Ember et al. (eds), *Encyclopedia of Diasporas: Immigrant and Refugee Cultures around the World*, New York: Springer, pp. 570–80.

Glick Schiller, N. and A. Caglar (2008) 'Beyond methodological ethnicity and towards city scale: an alternative approach to local and transnational pathways of migrant incorporation', in L. Pries (ed.), *Rethinking Transnationalism*, London and New York: Routledge.

— (2009) 'Towards a comparative theory of locality in migration studies: migrant incorporation and city scale', *Journal of Ethnic and Migration Studies*, 35(2): 177–202.

Glick Schiller, N., L. Basch and C. Szanton Blanc (1992) 'Transnationalism: a new analytic framework for understanding migration', *Annals of the New York Academy of Sciences*, 645: 1–24.

Glissant, É. (1997) *The Poetics of Relation*, Ann Arbor: University of Michigan Press.

Global Commission on International Migration (2005) *Migration in an Interconnected World: New Directions for Action*, Switzerland: Global Commission on International Migration.

Goldberg, D. T. (ed.) (1994) *Multiculturalism: A Critical Reader*, Oxford and Malden, MA: Blackwell.

Goldberg, J. J. (2009) '"Lost" in plain sight: an Israeli plan to rescue American Jews', *Forward*, blogs.forward.com/jj-goldberg/113535/, accessed 28December 2009.

Goldsmith, E. S. (1976) *Architects of Yiddishism at the Beginning of the Twentieth Century: A Study in Jewish Cultural History*, London: Associated University Press.

Gomez, M. (2004) *Reversing Sail: A History of the African Diaspora*, Cambridge: Cambridge University Press.

Goonewardena, K. (2004) 'Post-colonialism and diaspora: a contribution to the critique of nationalist ideology and historiography in the age of globalization and neoliberalism', *University of Toronto Quarterly*, 73(2): 657–90.

Gopinath, G. (1995) '"Bombay, UK, Yuba City": bhangra music and the engendering of diaspora', *Diaspora*, 4(3): 303–22.

— (2003) 'Nostalgia, desire, diaspora: South Asian sexualities in motion', in J. E. Braziel and A. Mannur (eds), *Theorizing Diaspora: A Reader*, Oxford: Blackwell, pp. 261–79.

— (2005) *Impossible Desires: Queer Diasporas and South Asian Popular Cultures*, Durham, NC: Duke University Press.

Gottschang, T. R. (1987) 'Economic change, disasters, and migration: the historical case of Manchuria', *Economic Development and Cultural Change*, 35(3): 461–90.

Gottschang, T. and D. Lary (2000) *Swallows and Settlers: The Great Migration from North China to Manchuria*, Ann Arbor: Center for Chinese Studies, University of Michigan.

Gourgouris, S. (2004) 'The concept of diaspora in the contemporary world',

in I. B. McCabe, G. Harlaftis and
I. Pepelasis Minoglou (eds), *Diaspora Entrepreneurial Networks: Four Centuries of History*, Oxford: Berg, pp. 383–90.

Grabbe, L. L. (2008) *A History of the Jews and Judaism in the Second Temple Period*, London: T & T Clark.

Graham, M. and S. Khosravi (2002) 'Reordering public and private in Iranian cyberspace: identity, politics, and mobilization', *Identities: Global Studies in Culture and Power*, 9(2): 219–46.

Grossberg, L. (1988) 'Wandering audiences, nomadic critics', *Cultural Studies*, 2(3): 377–92.

Gruen, E. S. (2002) *Diaspora: Jews amidst Greeks and Romans*, Cambridge, MA: Harvard University Press.

Guarnizo, L. (2003) 'The economics of transnational living', *International Migration Review*, 37(3): 242–81.

Guarnizo, L. and M. Smith (eds) (1998) *Transnationalism from Below*, New Brunswick, NJ, and London: Transaction Publishers.

Gudmestad, R. (2003) *A Troublesome Commerce: The Transformation of the Interstate Slave Trade*, Baton Rouge: Louisiana University Press.

Gupta, A. and J. Ferguson (1992) 'Beyond "culture": space, identity, and the politics of difference', *Cultural Anthropology*, 7(1): 6–23.

Gutmann, A. (ed.) (1993) *Multiculturalism: Examining the Politics of Recognition*, Princeton, NJ: Princeton University Press.

Gwin, M. (2002) *The Woman in Red Dress: Gender, Space, and Reading*, Urbana: University of Illinois Press.

Gyatso, T. (1998) *Freedom in Exile: The Autobiography of the Dalai Lama of Tibet*, 2nd edn, London: Abacus.

Hage, G. (1998) *White Nation: Fantasies of White Supremacy in a Multicultural Society*, Sydney: Pluto Press.

— (2003) *Against Paranoid Nationalism: Searching for Hope in a Shrinking Society*, Sydney: Pluto Press.

Halberstam, J. (2005) *In a Queer Time and Place: Transgender Bodies, Subcultural Lives*, New York: New York University Press.

Hall, G. M. (2005) *Slavery and African Ethnicities in the Americas: Restoring the Links*, Chapel Hill: University of North Carolina Press.

Hall, S. (1980) 'Encoding/decoding', in D. Hobson, A. Lowe and P. Willis (eds), *Culture, Media, Language*, London: Hutchinson, pp. 123–38.

— (1990) 'Cultural identity and diaspora', in J. Rutherford (ed.), *Identity: Community, Culture, Difference*, London: Lawrence and Wishart, pp. 222–37.

— (1991a) 'The local and the global: globalization and ethnicity', in A. D. King (ed.), *Culture, Globalization and the World-System*, London: Macmillan, pp. 19–39.

— (1991b) 'Old and new identities, old and new ethnicities', in A. D. King (ed.), *Culture, Globalization and the World-System*, London: Macmillan, pp. 41–68.

— (1992) 'New ethnicities', in J. Donald and A. Rattansi (eds), *'Race', Culture and Difference*, London: Sage.

— (1993) 'Cultural identity and diaspora', in P. Williams and L. Chrisman (eds), *Colonial Discourse and Post-Colonial Theory*, New York: Harvester Wheatsheaf, pp. 392–401.

— (1994 [1990]) 'Cultural identity and diaspora', in P. Williams and L. Chrisman (eds), *Colonial Discourse and Post-Colonial Theory: A Reader*, New York: Columbia University Press, pp. 392–403.

— (1995) 'Black and white television', in J. Givanni (ed.), *Remote Control: Dilemmas of Black Intervention in British Film and TV*, London: British Film Institute, pp. 13–28.

— (1996) 'When was the postcolonial: thinking about the limit', in I. Chambers and L. Curtis (eds), *The Post-Colonial Question*, London: Routledge, pp. 242–60.

Hall, S., B. Anderson, T. Modood and R. Berthoud (1999) 'Thinking the diaspora: home-thoughts from abroad', *Small Axe*, 3(6): 1–18.

Halter, M. (2000) *Shopping for Identity: The Marketing of Ethnicity*, New York: Schocken.

Hammerton, A. J. and A. Thomson (2005) *Ten Pound Poms: Australia's Invisible Migrants*, Manchester: Manchester University Press.

Haney, P. J. and W. Vanderbush (1999) 'The role of ethnic interest groups in US foreign policy: the case of the Cuban American National Foundation', *International Studies Quarterly*, 43: 341–61.

Hannerz, U. (1987) 'The world in creolization', *Africa*, 57(4): 546–59.

— (1990) 'Cosmopolitans and locals in world culture', in M. Featherstone (ed.), *Global Culture*, London: Sage, pp. 237–51.

— (1996) *Transnational Connections: Culture, People, Places*, London: Routledge.

Hansen, R. and P. Weil (eds) (2002) *Dual Nationality, Social Rights and Federal Citizenship in the US and Europe: The Reinvention of Citizenship*, New York: Berghahn.

Haraway, D. (1991) 'A cyborg manifesto: science, technology, and socialist-feminism in the late twentieth century', in D. Haraway, *Simians, Cyborgs and Women: The Reinvention of Nature*, New York: Routledge.

— (1997) *Modest_Witness@Second_Millennium.FemaleMan©_Meets_OncoMouse™*, New York: Routledge.

Hargreaves, A. G. and M. McKinney (eds) (1997) *Post-Colonial Cultures in France*, London: Routledge.

Hargreaves, A. G. and D. Mahdjoub (1997) 'Satellite television viewing among ethnic minorities in France', *European Journal of Communication*, 12(4): 459–77.

Harris, C. (1999) *In the Image of Tibet: Tibetan Painting after 1959*, London: Reaktion Books.

Harris, J. E. (ed.) (1993) *Global Dimensions of the African Diaspora*, 2nd edn, Washington, DC: Howard University Press.

Harrison, F. (2007) 'Huge cost of Iranian brain drain', news.bbc.co.uk/2/hi/middle_east/6240287.stm, accessed 28 April 2009.

Harvey, D. (2006) 'Space as a keyword', in N. Castree and D. Gregory (eds), *David Harvey: A Critical Reader*, Oxford: Blackwell.

Hatziemmanuel, E. (1982) 'Hellenic Orthodox education in America', in H. Psomiades and A. Scourby (eds), *The Greek American Community in Transition*, New York: Pella, pp. 181–9.

Hendrowski, M. and M. Hendrowski (1997) 'Yiddish cinema in Europe', in G. Nowell-Smith (ed.), *The Oxford History of World Cinema*, Oxford: Oxford University Press, pp. 174–6.

Herbert, J., J. May, J. Wills, K. Datta, Y. Evans and C. McIlwaine (2008) 'Multicultural living? Experiences of everyday racism amongst Ghanaian migrants in London', *European Urban and Regional Studies*, 15(2): 103–17.

Hervieu-Léger, D. (2000) *Religion as a Chain of Memory*, Cambridge: Polity Press.

Higman, B. (1995) *Slave Populations of the British Caribbean 1807–1834*, Kingston: University Press of the West Indies.

Higson, A. (2000) 'The limiting imagination of national cinema', in M. Hjort and S. McKenzie (eds), *Cinema and Nation*, London and New York: Routledge, pp. 63–74.

Hine, D. C., T. D. Keaton and S. Small (eds) (2009) *Black Europe and the African Diaspora*, Champaign: University of Illinois Press.

Hirji, F. (forthcoming) *Beyond Resistance: Canadian Youth, Indian Cinema, and Identity Construction*, Vancouver: University of British Columbia Press.

Hirsch, M. (1997) *Family Frames: Photography, Narrative and Postmemory*, Cambridge, MA, and London: Harvard University Press.

Hoberman, J. (1991) *Bridge of Light: Yiddish Film between Two Worlds*, New York: Schocken.

Hockenos, P. (2003) *Homeland Calling: Exile Patriotism and the Balkan Wars*, Ithaca, NY: Cornell University Press.

Holloway, T. (1980) *Immigrants on the Land*, Chapel Hill: University of North Carolina Press.

Hondagneu-Sotelo, P. (2008) *God's Heart Has No Borders: How Religious Activists Are Working for Immigrant Rights*, Berkeley: University of California Press.

Honig, E. (1992) *Creating Chinese Ethnicity: Subei People in Shanghai, 1850–1980*, New Haven, CT: Yale University Press.

hooks, b. (1992) 'Eating the other', in b. hooks, *Black Looks: Race and Representation*, Cambridge, MA: South End Press, pp. 21–39.

Hoskin, M. (1991) *New Immigrants and Democratic Society: Minority Integration in Western Democracies*, Greenport, NY: Praeger.

Huggan, G. (2001) *The Postcolonial Exotic: Marketing the Margins*, London: Routledge.

Huntington, S. (1996) *The Clash of Civilisations and the Remaking of World Order*, New York: Simon and Schuster.

— (2005) *Who Are We? The Challenges to America's National Identity*, New York: Simon and Schuster.

Husband, C. (ed.) (1994) *A Richer Vision: The Development of Ethnic Minority Media in Western Democracies*, Paris/ London: UNESCO/John Libbey.

Hutnyk, J. (2000) *Critique of Exotica: Music, Politics and the Culture Industry*, London: Pluto Press.

Hüwelmeier, G. and K. Krause (eds) (2009) *Traveling Spirits: Migrants, Markets and Mobilities*, London and New York: Routledge.

INSEE (2004–06) 'Enquêtes annuelles de recensement', www.insee.fr, accessed 31 December 2009.

IOM (International Migration Organization) (2008) *World Migration Report 2008: Managing Labour Mobility in the Evolving Global Economy*, London: IOM Publications.

— (2010) 'Facts and figures', www.iom. int/jahia/Jahia/about-migration/facts-and-figures/lang/en, accessed 6 January 2010.

Iordanova, D. (2007) 'Transnational film studies', in P. Cook (ed.), *The Cinema Book*, London: British Film Institute, pp. 508–9.

Jackson, P. (1999) 'Commodity cultures: the traffic in things', *Transactions of the Institute of British Geographers*, 24(1): 95–108.

— (2000) 'Rematerialising social and cultural geography', *Social and Cultural Geography*, 1(1): 9–14.

Jackson, P., P. Crang and C. Dwyer (eds) (2004) *Transnational Spaces*, London and New York: Routledge.

Jacobson, J. (1998) *Islam in Transition: Religion and Identity among British Pakistani Youth*, London: Routledge.

Jacobson, R. (1998) 'Conveying a broader message through bilingual discourse: an attempt at contrastive code-switching research', in R. Jacobson (ed.), *Codeswitching Worldwide*, Berlin and New York: Mouton de Gruyter, pp. 51–76.

Jaggi, M. (1988) 'The politics of exile: introduction', *Third World Affairs 1988*, pp. 161–6.

James, C. L. R. (1980 [1938]) *The Black Jacobins*, London: Allison and Busby.

Jauss, H. R. (1982) *Aesthetic Experience and Literary Hermeneutics*, Minneapolis: University of Minnesota Press.

Johnson, M. (1998) 'At home and abroad: inalienable wealth, personal consumption and formulations of femininity in the southern Philippines', in D. Miller (ed.), *Material Cultures: Why Some Things Matter*, Chicago, IL: University of Chicago Press.

Johnson, P. (2007) *Diaspora Conversions: Black Carib Religion and the Recovery of Africa*, Berkeley: University of California Press.

Jones, G. (2000) *Merchants to Multinationals: British Trading Companies in the Nineteenth and Twentieth Centuries*, Oxford: Oxford University Press.

Jupp, J. (1998) *Immigration*, Melbourne: Oxford University Press.

— (2004) *The English in Australia*, Cambridge: Cambridge University Press.

Jusdanis, G. (1991) 'Greek Americans and the diaspora', *Diaspora*, 1(2): 209–23.

Kaldor, M. (2001) *New and Old Wars: Organized Violence in a Globalized Era*, Cambridge, MA: Polity Press.

Kalra, V. S., R. Kaur and J. Hutnyk (2005) *Diaspora and Hybridity*, London: Sage.

Kaplan, D. and W. Li (2006) *Landscapes of the Ethnic Economy*, Lanham, MD: Rowman and Littlefield.

Karim, K. H. (ed.) (2003) *The Media of Diaspora*, London: Routledge.

— (2007) 'Nation and diaspora: rethinking multiculturalism in a transnational context', *International Journal of Media and Cultural Politics*, 2(3): 267–82.

Karim, P. (2006) *Let Me Tell You Where I've Been: New Writing by Women of the Iranian Diaspora*, Fayetteville: University of Arkansas Press.

Karpathakis, A. (1994) 'Whose church is it anyway? Greek Immigrants of Astoria, New York, and their church', *Journal of the Hellenic Diaspora*, 21(1): 97–122.

Keaton, T. D. (2006) *Muslim Girls and the Other France: Race, Identity Politics and Social Exclusion*, Indianapolis: University of Indiana Press.

Keith, M. (2005) *After the Cosmopolitan? Multicultural Cities and the Future of Racism*, London: Routledge.

Kelly, R. (ed.) (1993) *Irangeles: Iranians in Los Angeles*, Berkeley: University of California Press.

Kershaw, G. (2002) *The Home Crowd*, Fremantle: Fremantle Arts Centre Press.

Khagram, S. and P. Levitt (eds) (2007) *The Transnational Studies Reader*, New York: Routledge.

Khanin, Z. (Vladimir) (2003) 'Russian-Jewish ethnicity: Israel and Russia compared', in E. Ben-Rafael, Y. Gorny and Y. Ro'I (eds), *Contemporary Jewries: Convergence and Divergence*, Leiden: Brill Academic Press.

— (2007) '"Revival" of Russian politics in Israel: the case of 2006 elections', *Israel Affairs*, 13(2): 346–67.

Khondker, H. H. (2008) 'Sociological reflections on the diasporic Bangladeshis in Singapore and USA', in R. Rai and P. Reeves (eds), *The South Asian Diaspora: Transnational Networks and Changing Identities*, Oxford: Taylor and Francis, pp. 124–40.

King, R. (1996) 'Migration in a world historical perspective', in J. van den Broeck (ed.), *The Economics of Labour Migration*, Cheltenham: Edward Elgar, pp. 7–75.

Kipnis, A. (2006) 'Suzhi: a keyword approach', *China Quarterly*, 186: 295–313.

Kiwan, N. and U. H. Meinhof (forthcoming) *Cultural Globalization and Music: African Artists in Transnational Networks*, Basingstoke: Palgrave Macmillan.

Kleist, N. (2008) 'Mobilising "the diaspora": Somali transnational political engagement', *Journal of Ethnic and Migration Studies*, 34(2): 307–23.

Klieger, P. C. (ed.) (2002) *Tibet, Self, and the Tibetan Diaspora: Voices of Difference*, Leiden: Brill Academic Publishers.

Knott, K. (2005a) 'Towards a history and politics of diasporas and migration: a grounded spatial approach', Diasporas, Migration and Identities Working Paper 1, www.diasporas.ac.uk, accessed 9 January 2010.

— (2005b) *The Location of Religion: A Spatial Analysis*, London and Oakville: Equinox.

— (2009) 'From locality to location and back again: a spatial journey in the study of religion', *Religion*, 39(2): 154–60.

Knowles, C. (2004) *Race and Social Analysis*, London: Sage.

Koehn, P. H. and J. N. Rosenau (2002) 'Transnational competence in an emerging epoch', *International Studies Perspectives*, 3: 105–27.

Kofman, E., A. Phizacklea, P. Raghuram and R. Sales (2000) *Gender and International Migration in Europe: Employment, Welfare and Politics*, London and New York: Routledge.

Kolas, A. (1996) 'Tibetan nationalism: the politics of religion', *Journal of Peace Research*, 33(1): 51–66.

Korom, F. J. (ed.) (1997) *Constructing*

Tibetan Culture: Contemporary Perspectives, Quebec: Heritage Press.

— (1999) 'Tibetans in exile: a Euro-American perspective', *Passages: Journal of Transnational and Transcultural Studies*, 1(1): 1–23.

Korte, B. and C. Sternberg (2004) *Bidding for the Mainstream? Black and Asian British Film since the 1990s*, Amsterdam and New York: Rodopi.

Koser, K. (2001) *War and Peace in Eritrea: The Role of the Diaspora*, Copenhagen: Centre for Development Research.

Kothari, U. (2008) 'Global peddlers and local networks: migrant cosmopolitanisms', *Environment and Planning D: Society and Space*, 26: 500–16.

Kourvetaris, G. (1997) *Studies on Greek Americans*, New York: Columbia University Press.

Kraidy, M. M. (2005) *Hybridity or the Cultural Logic of Globalization*, Philadephia, PA: Temple University Press.

Krohn, C. D. (ed.) (1998) *Handbuch der deutschsprachigen Emigration 1933–1945*, Darmstadt: Wiss. Buchgesellschaft.

Kuah-Pearce, K. E. and A. P. Davidson (2008) *At Home in the Chinese Diaspora: Memories, Identities and Belongings*, Basingstoke: Palgrave Macmillan.

Kumar (2009) *Pelicula de Barrio*, Barcelona: Bigfish Productions.

Kumar, A. (2002) *Bombay-London-New York*, London: Routledge.

Kumusaka, Y. and H. Saito (1970) 'Kachigumi: a collective delusion among the Japanese and their descendants in Brazil', *Canadian Psychiatric Association Journal*, 15(2): 167–75.

Kymlicka, W. (1996) *Multicultural Citizenship: A Liberal Theory of Minority Rights*, Oxford: Oxford University Press.

Laguerre, M. S. (1998) *Diasporic Citizenship: Haitians in Transnational America*, New York: St Martin's Press.

Laliotou, I. (2004) *Transatlantic Subjects: Acts of Migration and Cultures of Transnationalism between Greece and America*, Chicago, IL: University of Chicago Press.

Lambropoulos, V. (1997) 'Building diasporas', *Crossings*, 1(2): 19–26.

Landau, L. (2006) 'Transplants and transients: idioms of belonging and dislocation in inner-city Johannesburg', *African Studies Review*, 49(2): 125–45.

Landau, L. B. and I. S. M. Haupt (2007) 'Tactical cosmopolitanism and idioms of belonging: insertion and self-exclusion in Johannesburg', Migration Studies Working Paper Series 32, University of Witwatersrand, Johannesburg.

Landsberg, A. (2003) 'Prosthetic memory: the ethics and politics of memory in an age of mass culture', in P. Grainge (ed.), *Memory and Popular Film*, Manchester: Manchester University Press, pp. 144–61.

Lang, D. M. (1989) *Armenians in Exile*, London: Unwin.

Lapidus, I. (2002) *A History of Islamic Societies*, 2nd edn, Cambridge: Cambridge University Press.

Lattimore, O. (1947) 'Inner Asian frontiers: Chinese and Russian margins of expansion', *Journal of Economic History*, 7(1): 24–52.

Law, L. (2001) 'Home cooking: Filipino women and geographies of the senses in Hong Kong', *Cultural Geographies*, 8(3): 264–83.

Lazin, F. A. (2005) *The Struggle of Soviet Jewry in American Politics: Israel versus the American Jewish Establishment*, New York: Lexington Books.

Le Page, R. B. and A. Tabouret-Keller (1985) *Acts of Identity: Creole-based Approaches to Language and Ethnicity*, Cambridge: Cambridge University Press.

Lefebvre, H. (1991 [1974]) *The Production of Space*, Oxford and Cambridge, MA: Blackwell.

Lehiste, I. (1988) *Lectures on Language Contact*, Cambridge, MA: MIT Press.

Lehmann, D. (2001) 'Religion and globalization', in L. Woodhead, P. Fletcher, H. Kawanami and D. Smith (eds), *Religions in the Modern World*, London: Routledge, pp. 299–315.

Leong, S. (1997) *Migration and Ethnicity in Chinese History: Hakkas, Pengmin, and Their Neighbors*, Stanford, CA: Stanford University Press.

Leontis, A. (1997) 'Mediterranean topographies before Balkanization: on Greek diaspora, emporium and revolution', *Diaspora*, 6(2): 179–94.

Lesser, J. (2003) *Searching for Home Abroad: Japanese-Brazilians and Transnationalism*, Durham, NC: Duke University Press.

— (2007) *A Discontented Diaspora: Japanese-Brazilians and the Meanings of Ethnic Militancy, 1960–1980*, Durham, NC: Duke University Press.

Leung, M. W. H. (2008) 'Memories, belonging and homemaking: Chinese migrants in Germany', in K. E. Kuah-Pearce and A. P. Davidson (eds), *At Home in the Chinese Diaspora: Memories, Identities and Belongings*, Basingstoke: Palgrave Macmillan, pp. 164–86.

Levitt, P. (2001) *The Transnational Villagers*, Berkeley: University of California Press.

— (2007) *God Needs No Passport: Immigrants and the Changing American Religious Landscape*, New York: New Press.

Levitt, P. and N. Glick Schiller (2004) 'Transnational perspectives on migration: conceptualizing simultaneity', *International Migration Review*, 38(145): 595–629.

Levitt, P. and M. C. Waters (eds) (2002) *The Changing Face of Home: The Transnational Lives of the Second Generation*, New York: Russell Sage Foundation.

Lewis, P. (1994) *Islamic Britain*, London: I. B. Tauris.

Ley, D. (1995) 'Between Europe and Asia: the case of the missing sequoias', *Ecumene*, 2(2): 185–210.

— (2010) *Millionaire Migrants*, Oxford: Blackwell.

Li, W. (1998) 'The "why" and "how" questions in the analysis of conversational code-switching', in P. Auer (ed.), *Code-switching in Conversation, Language,*

Interaction and Identity, London and New York: Routledge, pp. 156–76.

Lianos, T. P. (1979) 'Greece', in D. Kubat (ed.), *The Politics of Migration Policies*, New York: Center for Migration Studies, pp. 209–18.

Liebelt, C. (2008a) 'On sentimental Orientalists, Christian Zionists, and "working class cosmopolitans"": Filipina domestic workers' journeys to Israel and beyond', *Critical Asian Studies*, 40(4): 567–85.

— (2008b) '"We are the Jews of today": Filipino domestic workers in Israel and the language of diaspora', *Hagar: Studies in Culture, Polity and Identities*, 8(1).

Light, I. and P. Bhachu (eds) (1993) *Immigration and Entrepreneurship: Culture, Capital and Ethnic Networks*, New Brunswick, NJ: Transaction.

Lin, J. (1998) *Reconstructing Chinatown, Ethnic Enclave, Global Change*, Minneapolis: University of Minnesota Press.

Linger, D. (2001) *No One Home: Brazilian Selves Remade in Japan*, Stanford, CA: Stanford University Press.

Lopez, D. S., Jr (1998) *Prisoners of Shangri-La: Tibetan Buddhism and the West*, Chicago, IL: University of Chicago Press.

Lowenstein, A. and R. Katz (2005) 'Living arrangements, family solidarity and life satisfaction of two generations of immigrants', *Aging and Society*, 25(5): 749–67.

Luibhéid, E. and L. Cantú, Jr (eds) (2005) *Queer Migrations: Sexuality, US Citizenship, and Border Crossings*, Minneapolis: University of Minnesota Press.

Lyons, T. (2006) 'Diasporas and homeland conflict', in M. Kahler and B. Walter (eds), *Globalization, Territoriality, and Conflict in an Era of Globalization*, Cambridge: Cambridge University Press, pp. 111–32.

— (2007) 'Conflict-generated diasporas and transnational politics in Ethiopia', *Conflict, Security and Development*, 7: 529–49.

Ma, L. J. C. (2003) 'Space, place and transnationalism in the Chinese diaspora', in L. J. C. Ma and C. Cartier (eds), *The Chinese Diaspora: Space, Place, Mobility and Identity*, Lanham, MD, and Oxford: Rowman and Littlefield, pp. 1–50.

Ma, L. J. C. and C. Cartier (eds) (2003) *The Chinese Diaspora: Space, Place, Mobility and Identity*, Lanham, MD, and Oxford: Rowman and Littlefield.

Maeyama, T. (1979) 'Ethnicity, secret societies, and associations: the Japanese in Brazil', *Comparative Studies in Society and History*, 21(4): 589–610.

Malek, A. (2006) 'Memoir as Iranian exile production: a case study of Marjane Satrapi's *Persepolis* series', *Journal of the International Society for Iranian Studies*, 39(3): 353–80.

Malkki, L. (1992) 'National geographic: the rooting of peoples and the territorialization of national identity among scholars and refugees', *Cultural Anthropology*, 7: 24–44.

Mallett, S. (2004) 'Understanding home: a critical review of the literature', *Sociological Review*, 52(1): 62–89.

Mamdani, M. (1996) *Citizen and Subject: Contemporary Africa and the Legacy of Late Colonialism*, Princeton, NJ: Princeton University Press.

Manalansan, M. (2006) 'Queer intersections: sexuality and gender in migration studies', *International Migration Review*, 40(1): 224–49.

Mandaville, P. G. (2001) *Transnational Muslim Politics: Reimagining the Umma*, London and New York: Routledge.

Mander, J. and E. Goldsmith (eds) (2003) *The Case against the Global Economy and for a Turn towards Localization*, London: Earthscan.

Mankekar, P. (2005 [2002]) 'India shopping: Indian grocery stores and transnational configurations of belonging', in J. L. Watson and M. L. Caldwell (eds), *The Cultural Politics of Food and Eating: A Reader*, Oxford: Blackwell, pp. 197–214.

Mannan, N. and B. J. Boucher (2002) 'The Bangladeshi diaspora and its dietary profile in East London, 1990–2000', in A. J. Kershen (ed.), *Food in the Migrant Experience*, Aldershot: Ashgate, pp. 229–43.

Manning, P. (2005) *Migration in World History*, London and New York: Routledge.

Mansell, G. (1982) *Let Truth Be Told: 50 Years of BBC External Broadcasting*, London: Weidenfeld and Nicolson.

Marchetti, G. (2006) *From Tian'anmen to Times Square: Transnational China and the Chinese Diaspora on Global Screens, 1989–1997*, Philadelphia, PA: Temple University Press.

Marcuse, P. and R. Van Kampen (eds) (2000) *Globalizing Cities: A New Spatial Order?*, Oxford: Blackwell.

Marienstras, R. (1989) 'On the notion of diaspora', in G. Chaliand (ed.), *Minority Peoples in the Age of Nation States*, London: Pluto Press, pp. 119–25.

Markowitz, F. and A. H. Steffanson (eds) (2004) *Homecomings: Unsettling Paths of Return*, Lanham, MD: Lexington Books.

Marks, R. B. (1998) *Tigers, Rice, Silk, and Silt: Environment and Economy in Late Imperial South China*, Cambridge: Cambridge University Press.

Martin, M. T. (ed.) (1995) *Cinemas of the Black Diaspora: Diversity, Dependence and Oppositionality*, Detroit, MI: Wayne State University Press.

MASA (2009) *Israel Journeys*, www.masaisrael.org/masa/english, accessed 28 December 2009.

Massey, D. (1994) *Space, Place and Gender*, Minneapolis: University of Minnesota Press.

— (2005) *For Space*, London: Sage.

— (2007) *World City*, Cambridge and Malden, MA: Polity Press.

Massey, D., J. Arango, G. Hugo, A. Kouaouci, A. Pellegrino and J. Taylor (1998) *Worlds in Motion: Understanding International Migration at the End of the Millennium*, Oxford: Clarendon Press.

Mathur, S. (2007) *India by Design: Colonial History and Cultural Display*, Berkeley: University of California Press.

Matory, J. L. (2005) *Black Atlantic Religion: Tradition, Transnationalism, and Matriarchy in Afro-Brazilian Candomblé*,

Princeton, NJ: Princeton University Press.

Matras, Y. and P. Bakker (eds) (2003) *The Mixed Language Debate: Theoretical and Empirical Advances*, Berlin: Mouton de Gruyter.

Matthews, G. (2006) *Caribbean Slave Revolts and the British Abolitionist Movement*, Baton Rouge: Louisiana University Press.

Mau, S., J. Mewes and A. Zimmermann (2008) 'Cosmopolitan attitudes through transnational social practices?', *Global Networks*, 8(1): 1–24.

Mavrommatis, G. (2006) 'The new creative Brick Lane: a narrative study of local multicultural encounters', *Ethnicities*, 6(4): 498–517.

Mazzucato V., M. Kabki and L. Smith (2006) 'Transnational migration and the economy of funerals: changing practices in Ghana', *Development and Change*, 37(5): 1047–72.

McAuliffe, C. (2008) 'Transnationalism within: internal diversity in the Iranian diaspora', *Australian Geographer*, 39(1): 63–80.

McEwan, C., J. Pollard and N. Henry (2005) 'The "global" in the city economy: multicultural economic development in Birmingham', *International Journal of Urban and Regional Research*, 29(4): 916–33.

McGranahan, C. (2003) 'Empire and the status of Tibet: British, Chinese and Tibetan negotiations, 1913–1934', in A. McKay (ed.), *The History of Tibet*, vol. III, London: Routledge Curzon.

McKay, D. (2005) 'Translocal circulation: place and subjectivity in an extended Filipino community', *Asia Pacific Journal of Anthropology*, 7(3): 265–78.

— (2007) '"Sending dollars shows feeling": emotions and economies in Filipino migration', *Mobilities*, 2(2): 175–94.

McKay, D. and C. Brady (2005) 'Practices of place-making: globalisation and locality in the Philippines', *Asia Pacific Viewpoint*, 46(2): 89–103.

McKittrick, K. and C. Woods (eds) (2007)

Black Geographies and the Politics of Place, Toronto/Cambridge, MA: Between the Lines/South End Press.

McLeod, J. (2000) *Beginning Postcolonialism*, Manchester: Manchester University Press.

McLoughlin, S. (1996) 'In the name of the Umma: globalisation, "race" relations and Muslim identity politics in Bradford', in W. A. R. Shadid and P. S. van Koningsveld (eds), *Political Participation and Identities of Muslims in Non-Muslim States*, Kampen: Kok Pharos, pp. 206–28.

— (2009) 'Contesting Muslim pilgrimage: British-Pakistani identities, sacred journeys to Makkah and Madinah and the global postmodern', in V. S. Kalra (ed.), *The Pakistani Diaspora*, Karachi and Oxford: Oxford University Press, pp. 233–56.

— (2010) 'Religion and diaspora', in J. Hinnells (ed.), *Routledge Companion to the Study of Religion*, 2nd edn, London and New York: Routledge, pp. 558–80.

McLoughlin, S. and V. S. Kalra (1999) 'Wish you were(n't) here: discrepant representations of Mirpur in narratives of migration, diaspora and tourism', in J. Hutnyk and R. Kaur (eds), *Travel-Worlds: Journeys in Contemporary Cultural Politics*, London: Zed Books, pp. 120–36.

McLoughlin, S., W. Gould, A. J. Kabir and E. Tomalin (eds) (forthcoming) *Diaspora and Multilocality in British Asian Cities*, London and New York: Routledge.

Meaney, N. (2001) 'Britishness and Australian identity: the problem of nationalism in Australian history and historiography', *Australian Historical Studies*, 32(116): 76–90.

Meinhof, U. H. (2009) 'Transnational flows, networks and "transcultural capital": reflections on researching migrant networks through linguistic ethnography', in S. Slembrouck, J. Collins and M. Baynham (eds), *Globalization and Languages in Contact: Scale,*

Migration, and Communicative Practices, London: Continuum.

Meinhof, U. H. and A. Triandafyllidou (2006) 'Beyond the diaspora: transnational practices as transcultural capital', in U. Meinhof and A. Triandafyllidou (eds), *Transcultural Europe: Cultural Policy in a Changing Europe*, Basingstoke: Palgrave Macmillan.

Melucci, A. (1997) 'Identity and difference in a globalized world', in P. Werbner and T. Modood (eds), *Debating Cultural Hybridity: Multi-cultural Identities and the Politics of Anti-Racism*, London: Zed Books, pp. 58–69.

Mercer, C., B. Page and M. Evans (2009) *Development and the African Diaspora: Place and the Politics of Home*, London: Zed Books.

Mercer, K. (1988) *Black Film, British Cinema*, London: ICA.

— (1994) *Welcome to the Jungle: New Positions in Black Cultural Studies*, London: Routledge.

— (ed.) (2008) *Exiles, Diasporas and Strangers*, London/Cambridge, MA: Iniva/MIT Press.

Metcalf, B. D. (ed.) (1996) *Making Muslim Space in North America and Europe*, Berkeley: University of California Press.

Michael, F. (1985) 'Survival of a culture: Tibetan refugees in India', *Asian Survey*, 25(7): 737–44.

Miller, D. (ed.) (2005) *Materiality*, London: Duke University Press.

Miller, D. and D. Slater (2006) 'Being Trini and representing Trinidad', in D. Bell (ed.), *Cybercultures*, London and New York: Routledge, pp. 106–37.

Miller, J. (1988) *Way of Death: Merchant Capitalism and the Angolan Slave Trade 1730–1830*, Madison: University of Wisconsin Press.

Mintz, S. and R. Price (1992) *The Birth of African-American Culture: An Anthropological Perspective*, Boston, MA: Beacon Press.

Mirzoeff, N. (ed.) (1999) *Diaspora and Visual Culture: Representing Africans and Jews*, London: Routledge.

Mishra, S. (2006) *Diaspora Criticism*, Edinburgh: Edinburgh University Press.

Mishra, V. (1996) 'The diasporic imaginary: theorising the Indian diaspora', *Textual Practice*, 10: 421–7.

— (2007) *The Literature of the Indian Diaspora: Theorizing the Diasporic Imaginary*, London and New York: Routledge.

Modood, T. (1990) 'British Asian Muslims and the Rushdie Affair', *Political Quarterly*, 61: 143–60.

— (2007) *Multiculturalism: A Civic Idea*, Cambridge: Polity Press.

Mohan, G. (2002) 'Diaspora and development', in J. Robinson (ed.), *Development and Displacement*, Oxford: Oxford University Press, pp. 77–140.

— (2006) 'Community, cloth and other travelling objects', in N. Clark, D. Massey and P. Sarre (eds), *A World in the Making*, Milton Keynes: Open University, pp. 267–309.

Mohanty, C. T. and M. J. Alexander (eds) (1997) *Feminist Genealogies, Colonial Legacies, Democratic Futures*, New York: Routledge.

Mojab, S. and R. Gorman (2007) 'Dispersed nationalism: war, diaspora and Kurdish women's organizing', *Journal of Middle East Women's Studies*, 1(3): 59–85.

Moorti, S. (2003) 'Desperately seeking an identity: diasporic cinema and the articulation of transnational kinship', *International Journal of Cultural Studies*, 6(3): 355–76.

Moreton-Robinson, A. (2005) 'The house that Jack built: Britishness and white possession', *Australian Critical Race and Whiteness Studies Association Journal*, 1: 21–9.

Morgan, P. (1998) *Slave Counterpoint: Black Culture in the Eighteenth Century Chesapeake and Lowcountry*, Chapel Hill: University of North Carolina Press.

Morley, D. (1980) *The 'Nationwide' Audience: Structure and Decoding*, London: BFI.

— (2000) *Home Territories: Media, Mobility and Identity*, London: Routledge.

Moskos, C. C. (1999) *Greek Americans:*

Struggle and Success, New York: Transaction.

— (2002) 'Greek American studies', in S. D. Orfanos (ed.), *Reading Greek America: Studies in the Experience of Greeks in the United States*, New York: Pella.

Mosse, G. (1985) *Nationalism and Sexuality: Middle-Class Morality and Sexual Norms in Modern Europe*, Madison: University of Wisconsin Press.

Mostofi, N. (2003) 'Who we are? The perplexity of Iranian-American identity', *Sociological Quarterly*, 44(4): 681–703.

Murphy, R. (2002) *How Migrant Labour Is Changing Rural China*, Cambridge: Cambridge University Press.

— (ed.) (2008) *Labour Migration and Social Development in Contemporary China*, London and New York: Routledge.

Naber, N. (2006) 'The rules of forced engagement: race, gender, and the culture of fear among Arab immigrants in San Francisco post 9/11', *Cultural Dynamics*, 18(3): 235–67.

Naficy, H. (1993) *The Making of Exile Cultures: Iranian Television in Los Angeles*, Minneapolis: University of Minnesota Press.

— (2001) *An Accented Cinema: Exilic and Diasporic Filmmaking*, Princeton, NJ, and Oxford: Princeton University Press.

Naipaul, V. S. (1961) *A House for Mr Biswas*, New York: Knopf.

— (1989 [1979]) *A Bend in the River*, London: Vintage.

Nallatamby, P. (1995) *Mille mots du français mauricien: réalités lexicales et francophonie à l'île Maurice*, Paris: Conseil international de la langue française.

Natarajan, N. (ed.) (1993) *Writers of the Indian Diaspora*, Westport, CT: Greenwood Press.

Ndangam, L. (2008) 'Free lunch? Cameroon's diaspora and online news publishing', *New Media and Society*, 10(4): 585–604.

Neusner, J. (1965–70) *A History of the Jews in Babylonia*, 5 vols, Leiden: Brill.

Newell, S. (2002) 'Paracolonial networks: some speculations on local readerships in colonial West Africa', *Interventions*, 3(3): 336–54.

Newland, K. and E. Patrick (2004) *Beyond Remittances: The Role of Diaspora in Poverty Reduction in Their Countries of Origin*, Report for the Department for International Development, Migration Policy Institute, Washington, DC.

Newman, D. (1999) 'Real spaces, symbolic space: interrelated notions of territory in the Arab–Israeli conflict', in P. F. Diehl (ed.), *A Road Map to War: Territorial Dimensions of International Conflict*, Nashville, TN: Vanderbilt University Press, pp. 3–34.

Newton, D. (2008) 'Calling the West Indies: the BBC World Service and Caribbean Voices', in M. Gillespie, A. Webb and G. Baumann (eds), 'BBC World Service, 1932–2007: cultural exchange and public diplomacy', *Historical Journal of Film, Radio and Television*, 28(4): 475–89.

Nichols, G. (2003) *The Fat Black Woman's Poems*, London: Virago.

Nield, S. (2008) 'The Proteus Cabinet, or "we are here but not here"', *Research in Drama Education*, 13(2): 137–45.

Niranjana, T. (2006) *Mobilizing India: Women, Music, and Migration between India and Trinidad*, Durham, NC: Duke University Press.

Northrup, D. (2000) 'Igbo and Myth Igbo: culture and ethnicity in the Atlantic world 1600–1850', *Slavery and Abolition*, 21(3): 1–20.

Nowak, M. (1984) *Tibetan Refugees: Youth and the New Generation of Meaning*, New Brunswick, NJ: Rutgers University Press.

O'Brien, E. (2008) *The Racial Middle: Latinos and Asian Americans Living beyond the Racial Divide*, New York: New York University Press.

Office for National Statistics (n.d.) 'Population and migration', www.statistics. gov.uk/CCI/nscl.asp?ID=7588&x=9&y=8, accessed 6 January 2010.

Olwig, K. F. (1993) *Global Culture, Island Identity: Continuity and Change in the*

Afro-Caribbean Community of Nevis, Philadelphia, PA: Harwood Academic Publishers.

Ong, A. (1999) *Flexible Citizenship: The Cultural Logics of Transnationality*, Durham, NC: Duke University Press.

Ong, A. and D. Nonimi (eds) (1997) *Ungrounded Empires: The Cultural Politics of Modern Chinese Transnationalism*, New York: Routledge.

Oonk, G. (ed.) (2007) *Global Indian Diasporas: Exploring Trajectories of Migration and Theory*, Amsterdam: Amsterdam University Press.

Orozco, M. (2002) 'Globalization and migration: the impact of family remittances in Latin America', *Latin American Politics and Society*, 44(2): 41–66.

— (2004) 'Mexican hometown associations and development opportunities', *Journal of International Affairs*, 57(2): 31–51.

— (2009) 'Understanding the continuing effect of the economic crisis on remittances to Latin America and the Caribbean', Inter-American Dialogue (IDB), www.thedialogue.org/PublicationFiles/FINAL%20OROZCO.pdf, accessed 9 January 2009.

Ossman, S. (2004) 'Studies in serial migration', *International Migration*, 42(4): 111–21.

Østergaard-Nielsen, E. (2002) 'Working for a solution through Europe: Kurdish political lobbying in Germany', in N. S. Al-Ali and K. Koser (eds), *New Approaches to Migration? Transnational Communities and the Transformation of Home*, London: Routledge, pp. 186–201.

— (2003a) 'The politics of migrants' transnational political practices', *International Migration Review*, 37(3): 760–86.

— (2003b) *Transnational Politics: Turks and Kurds in Germany*, London: Routledge.

Pahl, K. and A. Pollard (2008) 'Bling – the Asians introduced that to the country. Gold and its value within a group of families of South Asian origin in Yorkshire', *Visual Communication*, 7(2): 170–92.

Palmary, I., J. Rauch and G. Simpson (2003) 'Violent crime in Johannesburg', in R. Tomlinson (ed.), *Emerging Johannesburg: Perspectives on the Post-Apartheid City*, New York and London: Routledge, pp. 101–22.

Palmer, C. (2006) *Eric Williams and the Making of the Modern Caribbean*, Chapel Hill: University of North Carolina Press.

Panagakos, A. N. (2003) 'Downloading new identities: ethnicity, technology and media in the global Greek village', *Identities: Global Studies in Culture and Power*, 10(2): 201–19.

Panagakos, A. and H. Horst (2006) 'Return to Cyberia: technology and the social worlds of transnational migrants', *Global Networks*, 6(2): 109–24.

Panayi, P. (2008) *Spicing Up Britain: The Multicultural History of British Food*, London: Reaktion Books.

Papademetriou, D. (1979) 'Greece', in R. E. Krane (ed.), *International Labor Migration in Europe*, New York: Praeger, pp. 187–200.

Papastergiadis, N. (1998) *Dialogues in the Diasporas*, London: Rivers Oram.

— (2000) *The Turbulence of Migration*, Cambridge: Polity Press.

Parekh, B. (2000) *Rethinking Multiculturalism: Cultural Diversity and Political Theory*, London/Cambridge, MA: Macmillan/Harvard University Press.

Park, R. (1922) *The Immigrant Press and Its Control*, New York: Harper and Brothers.

— (1950) *Race and Culture*, Glencoe, IL: Free Press.

Parker, D. (2000) 'The Chinese takeaway and the diasporic habitus: space, time and power geometries', in B. Hesse (ed.), *Un/settled Multiculturalisms: Diasporas, Entanglements, Transruptions*, London: Zed Books, pp. 73–95.

Parreñas, R. S. (2001) *Servants of Globalization: Women, Migration and Domestic Work*, Stanford, CA: Stanford University Press.

— (2005) *Children of Global Migration:*

Transnational Families and Gendered Woes, Stanford, CA: Stanford University Press.

Parry, B. (2004) *Postcolonial Studies: A Materialist Critique*, London: Routledge.

Patterson, O. (1982) *Slavery and Social Death: A Comparative Study*, Cambridge, MA: Harvard University Press.

Pavlenko, A. (2006) *Emotions and Multilingualism*, Cambridge: Cambridge University Press.

Pavlinic, A. (1993) 'Croatian or Serbian as a diaspora language in western Europe', in G. Extra and L. Verhoeven (eds), *Immigrant Languages in Europe*, Clevedon: Multilingual Matters, pp. 101–16.

Peel, M. (1995) *Good Times, Hard Times: The Past and the Future in Elizabeth*, Melbourne: Melbourne University Press.

— (2003) *The Lowest Rung: Voices of Australian Poverty*, Cambridge: Cambridge University Press.

Pertierra, R. (ed.) (1992) *Remittances and Returnees: The Cultural Economy of Migration in Ilocos*, Quezon City: New Day.

Petridou, E. (2001) 'The taste of home', in D. Miller (ed.), *Home Possessions: Material Culture behind Closed Doors*, Oxford: Berg, pp. 87–104.

Phillips, A. and G. Vincendeau (eds) (2006) *Journeys of Desire: European Artists in Hollywood*, London: BFI.

Phizacklea, A. (1983) *One Way Ticket*, London: Routledge and Kegan Paul.

Pines, J. (1991) *Representation and Blacks in British Cinema*, London: BFI Education.

Pingol, A. (2001) *Remaking Masculinities*, Quezon City: University of the Philippines.

Pollard, J. and M. Sammers (2007) 'Islamic banking and finance: postcolonial political economy and the decentring of economic geography', *Transactions of the Institute of British Geography*, 32(3): 313–33.

Poovaya-Smith, N. (1998) 'Keys to the Magic Kingdom: the new transcultural collections of Bradford art galleries and museums', in T. Barringer and T. Flynn (eds), *Colonialism and the Object: Empire, Material Culture and the Museum*, London: Routledge, pp. 111–25.

Poplack, S. and M. Meechan (1998) 'Introduction: how languages fit together in codemixing', *International Journal of Bilingualism*, 2(2): 127–38.

Portes, A. (1996) 'Transnational communities: their emergence and significance in the contemporary world system', Program in Comparative and International Development Working Papers Series 16, Department of Sociology, John Hopkins University, Baltimore, MA.

Portes, A. and P. Landholt (1999) 'The study of transnationalism: promises and pitfalls of an emergent research field', *Ethnic and Racial Studies*, 22(2): 217–37.

Portes, A., C. Escobar and A. Walton Radford (2007) 'Immigrant transnational organisations and development: a comparative study', *International Migration Review*, 41(1): 242–81.

Portes, A., L. Guarnizo and W. Haller (2003) 'Assimilation and transnationalism: determinants of transnational political action among contemporary migrants', *American Journal of Sociology*, 8(6): 1211–48.

Postero, N. G. and L. Zamosc (eds) (2004) *The Struggle for Indigenous Rights in Latin America*, Brighton: Sussex Academic Press.

Pratt, M. L. (1992) *Imperial Eyes: Travel Writing and Transculturation*, London: Routledge.

Price, R. (ed.) (1996) *Maroon Societies: Rebel Slave Communities in the Americas*, Baltimore, MA: Johns Hopkins University Press.

Price, S. and R. Price (2000) *Maroon Arts: Cultural Vitality in the African Diaspora*, Boston, MA: Beacon Press.

Pries, L. (ed.) (2008) *Rethinking Transnationalism*, London and New York: Routledge.

Procter, J. (2003) *Dwelling Places: Postwar*

Black British Writing, Manchester and New York: Manchester University Press.

— (2009) 'Reading, taste and postcolonial studies: professional and lay readers of *Things Fall Apart*', *Interventions*, 11(2): 180–98.

Prost, A. (2006) 'The problem with "rich refugees": sponsorship, capital, and the informal economy of Tibetan refugees', *Modern Asian Studies*, 40(1): 233–53.

Quayson, A. (2009) 'Unthinkable Nigeriana: the social imaginary of District 9', *Johannesburg Workshop in Critical Theory*, vol. 1, www.jwtc.org.za, accessed 14 January 2010.

— (2010) 'Oxford Street, Accra: spatial logics, street life, and the transnational imaginary', in S. Watson and G. Hart (eds), *Blackwell Companion to Urban Studies*, Oxford: Blackwell.

Quirk, J. (2009) *Unfinished Business: A Comparative Survey of Historical and Contemporary Slavery*, Paris: UNESCO Publications.

Rabine, L. (2002) *The Global Circulation of African Fashion*, Oxford: Berg.

Radway, J. (1988) 'Reception study: ethnography and the problems of dispersed audiences and nomadic subjects', *Cultural Studies*, 2(3): 359–76.

Raghuram, P. (2009a) 'Caring about "brain drain" migration in a postcolonial world', *Geoforum*, 40(1): 25–33.

— (2009b) 'Which migration, what development? Unsettling the edifice of migration and development', *Population, Place and Space*, 15(2): 103–17.

Rai, R. and P. Reeves (eds) (2008) *The South Asian Diaspora: Transnational Networks and Changing Identities*, Oxford: Taylor and Francis.

Ram, M. and G. Hillin (1994) 'Achieving "break-out": developing mainstream ethnic minority business', *Small Business Enterprise and Development*, 1(1): 5–21.

Rampton, B. (1995) *Crossing: Language and Ethnicity among Adolescents*, London: Longman.

Ranasinha, R. (2010) 'South Asian broad-casters in Britain and the BBC: *Talking to India* (1941–1943)', in M. Gillespie, A. Pinkerton, G. Baumann and S. Thiranagama, *South Asian Diaspora*, 2(1): 51–71.

Rapport, N. and A. Dawson (eds) (1998) *Migrants of Identity: Perceptions of Home in a World of Movement*, Oxford: Berg.

Rath, J. (2000) *Immigrant Business: The Economic, Political and Social Environment*, Basingstoke: Macmillan.

— (2001) *Unravelling the Rag Trade: Immigrant Entrepreneurship in Seven World Cities*, Oxford: Berg.

Ratha, D., S. Mohapatra, K. M. Vijayalak-shmi and Z. Xu (2008) 'Revisions to remittance trends 2007', Migration and Development Brief 5, World Bank, Washington, DC.

Ray, C. (2009) '"The white wife problem": sex, race, and the contested politics of repatriation to interwar British West Africa', *Gender and History*, 21(3): 628–46.

Reichl, C. A. (1995) 'Stages in the historical process of ethnicity: the Japanese in Brazil, 1908–1988', *Ethnohistory*, 42(1): 31–62.

Reilly, G. (2004) *Sweet Time*, Sydney: Hodder Headline.

Reis, F. (1931) *Paiz a Organizar*, Rio de Janeiro: A. Coelho Branco.

Remennick, L. (1998) 'Identity quest among Russian Jews of the 1990s: before and after emigration', in E. Krausz and G. Tulea (eds), *Jewish Survival: The Identity Problem at the Close of the 20th Century*, New Brunswick, NJ: Transaction, pp. 241–58.

— (2007) *Russian Jews on Three Continents: Identity, Integration, and Conflict*, Brunswick, NJ: Transaction.

Rex, J. and R. Moore (1967) *Race, Community and Conflict*, London: Oxford University Press.

Rex, J. and S. Tomlinson (1979) *Colonial Immigrants in a British City*, Oxford: Hutchinson.

Rhoads, C. and L. Chao (2009) 'Iran's web spying aided by Western technology', *Wall Street Journal*, online.wsj.com/

article/SB124562668777335653.html, accessed 22 June 2009.

Richardson, D. (2001) 'Shipboard slave revolts, African authority and the Atlantic slave trade', *William and Mary Quarterly*, 58(1): 69–92.

Richmond, A. (1994) *Global Apartheid: Refugees, Racism and the New World Order*, Oxford: Oxford University Press.

Riggins, S. H. (ed.) (1992) *Ethnic Minority Media: An International Perspective*, Newbury Park, CA: Sage.

Rippin, A. (2005) *Muslims: Their Religious Beliefs and Practices*, London: Routledge.

Robbins, B. (1998) 'Introduction part I: actually existing cosmopolitanism', in P. Cheah and B. Robbins (eds), *Cosmopolitics*, Minneapolis: University of Minnesota Press, pp. 1–19.

Robertson, R. (1995) 'Glocalization: time-space and homogeneity-heterogeneity', in M. Featherstone, S. Lash and R. Robertson (eds), *Global Modernities*, London: Sage, pp. 25–44.

Rodrigues de Mello, A. (1935) 'Immigração e colonização', *Geografia*, 1(4): 25–49.

Rogoff, I. (2000) *Terra Infirma: Geography's Visual Culture*, London and New York: Routledge.

Root, D. (1996) *Cannibal Culture: Art, Appropriation, and the Commodification of Difference*, Boulder, CO: Westview Press.

Rose, N. H. and B. Warren (1995) *Living Tibet: The Dalai Lama in Dharamsala*, New Delhi: Paljor Publications.

Rushdie, S. (1988) *The Satanic Verses*, New York: Viking.

— (1991) 'Imaginary homelands', in S. Rushdie, *Imaginary Homelands: Essays and Criticism 1981–1991*, London: Granta, pp. 9–21.

Safran, W. (1991) 'Diasporas in modern societies: myths of homeland and return', *Diaspora: A Journal of Transnational Studies*, 1(1): 83–99.

— (1999) 'Comparing diasporas: a review essay', *Diaspora*, 8(3): 255–91.

— (2007) 'Concepts, theories and challenges of diaspora: a panoptic ap-proach', Società Italiana per lo Studio della Storia Contemporanea, www.sissco.it/index.php?id=1311, accessed 11 January 2010.

Said, E. W. (1998) *Where Do the Birds Fly after the Last Sky: Palestinian Lives*, New York: Columbia University Press.

— (2001) *Reflections on Exile and Other Essays*, 2nd edn, Cambridge, MA: Harvard University Press.

Saito, H. (1961) *O Japonês no Brasil: Estudo de Mobilidade e Fixação*, São Paulo: Editora Sociologia e Política.

Salih, R. (2003) *Gender in Transnationalism: Home, Longing and Belonging among Moroccan Migrant Women*, London and New York: Routledge.

Saloutos, T. (1956) *They Remember America: The Story of the Repatriated Greek-Americans*, Berkeley: University of California Press.

— (1964) *The Greeks in the United States*, Cambridge, MA: Harvard University Press.

Samuel, G. (1982) 'Tibet as a stateless society and some Islamic parallels', *Journal of Asian Studies*, 41(2): 215–29.

Santianni, M. (2003) 'The movement for a free Tibet: cyberspace and the ambivalence of cultural translation', in H. K. Karim (ed.), *The Media of Diaspora*, London: Routledge, pp. 189–202.

Sardar, Z. (2004) *Desperately Seeking Paradise: Journeys of a Sceptical Muslim*, London: Granta.

Sassen, S. (1991) *The Global City: New York, London, Tokyo*, Princeton, NJ: Princeton University Press.

Satrapi, M. (2003) *Persepolis: Story of a Childhood*, New York: Pantheon.

— (2004) *Persepolis 2: Story of a Return*, New York: Pantheon.

Sayyid, B. S. (1997) *A Fundamental Fear: Eurocentrism and the Emergence of Islamism*, London: Zed Books.

Schank, R. C. and R. P. Abelson (1977) *Scripts, Plans, Goals and Understanding: An Inquiry into Human Knowledge Structures*, Hillsdale, NJ: Lawrence Erlbaum.

Schell, O. (2000) *Virtual Tibet: Searching*

for Shangri-La from the Himalayas to Hollywood, New York: Metropolitan Books/Henry Holt.

Schiff, A. I. (2002) 'Hebrew in New York', in O. Garcia and J. A. Fishman (eds), *The Multilingual Apple: Languages in New York City*, 2nd edn, New York: Mouton de Gruyter, pp. 203–27.

Schiffauer, W., G. Baumann, R. Kastoryano and S. Vertovec (eds) (2004) *Civil Enculturation: Nation-State, School and Ethnic Difference in Four European Countries*, Oxford: Berghahn.

Scholte, J. (2000) *Globalization: A Critical Introduction*, London: Macmillan.

Schwarz, D. (2008) *In Defense of Reading: Teaching Literature in the Twenty-first Century*, Oxford: Blackwell.

Scourby, A. S. (1984) *The Greek Americans*, Boston, MA: Twayne.

Sensbach, J. (2005) *Rebecca's Revival: Creating Black Christianity in the Atlantic World*, Cambridge, MA: Harvard University Press.

Seymour, J. D. (2000) 'Xinjiang's production and construction corps, and the sinification of Eastern Turkestan', *Inner Asia*, 2(2): 171–93.

Shaffer, L. (2002 [1994]) *Southernization*, Washington, DC: American Historical Association.

Shain, Y. (2008) *Kinship and Diasporas in International Affairs*, Ann Arbor: University of Michigan Press.

Sharma, S., J. Hutnyk and A. Sharma (eds) (1996) *Dis-Orienting Rhythms: The Politics of the New Asian Dance Music*, London and New Jersey: Zed Books.

Sheffer, G. (ed.) (1986a) *Modern Diasporas in International Politics*, London: Croom Helm.

— (1986b) 'A new field of study: modern diasporas in international politics', in G. Sheffer (ed.), *Modern Diasporas in International Politics*, London: Croom Helm, pp. 1–15.

— (2003) *Diaspora Politics: At Home Abroad*, Cambridge: Cambridge University Press.

Sheppard, E. R. (2006) *Leo Strauss and the Politics of Exile: The Making of a Political Philosopher*, Waltham, MA: Brandeis University Press.

Shepperson, G. (1993) 'African diaspora: concept and context', in J. E. Harris (ed.), *Global Dimensions of the African Diaspora*, 2nd edn, Washington, DC: Howard University Press, pp. 41–9.

Shohat, E. (1999) 'By the bitstream of Babylon: cyberfrontiers and diasporic vistas', in H. Naficy (ed.), *Home, Exile, Homeland*, London: Routledge, pp. 213–32.

— (2006) 'Taboo memories, diasporic visions', in E. Shohat, *Taboo Memories, Diasporic Visions*, Durham, NC: Duke University Press, pp. 201–32.

Sivanandan, A. (1990) *Communities of Resistance: Writings on Black Struggles for Socialism*, London: Verso.

Skeldon, R. (1995) *Emigration from Hong Kong: Tendencies and impacts*, Hong Kong: Chinese University Press.

Sklair, L. (2001) *The Transnational Capitalist Class*, Oxford: Blackwell.

Skrbis, Z. (1999) *Long-distance Nationalism: Diasporas, Homelands and Identities*, Aldershot: Ashgate.

Smallwood, S. E. (2007) *Saltwater Slavery: A Middle Passage from Africa to American Diaspora*, Cambridge, MA, and London: Harvard University Press.

Smart, N. (1987) 'The importance of diasporas', in S. Shaked, R. Y. Werblovsky, D. D. Shulman and G. A. G. Strounka (eds), *Gilgul: Essays on Transformation, Revolution and Permanence in the History of Religions*, Leiden: Brill, pp. 288–95.

Smelser, N. J. and J. C. Alexander (eds) (1999) *Diversity and Its Discontents: Cultural Conflict and Common Ground in Contemporary American Society*, Princeton, NJ: Princeton University Press.

Smith, H. and P. Stares (eds) (2007) *Diasporas in Conflict: Peace-makers or Peace-wreckers?*, Tokyo, New York, Paris: United Nations University Press.

Smith, M. P. (2001) *Transnational Urbanism*, Oxford: Blackwell.

Smith, M. P. and L. Guarnizo (eds) (1998) *Transnationalism from Below: Cities,*

Migrations and Identities, New Brunswick, NJ: Transaction.

Smith, N. and C. Katz (1993) 'Grounding metaphor: towards a spatialised politics', in M. Keith and S. Pile (eds), *Place and the Politics of Identity*, London: Routledge.

Smith, R. C. (2006) *Mexican New York: Transnational Lives of New Immigrants*, Berkeley: University of California Press.

Smith, Z. (2000) *White Teeth*, London: Hamish Hamilton.

Snel, E., G. Engberson and A. Leerkes (2006) 'Transnational involvement and social integration', *Global Networks*, 6(3): 285–308.

Sobral, J. A. (1908) 'Os japonezes em S. Paulo', *Correio Paulistano*, 25 June, p. 1.

Sökefeld, M. (2000) 'Religion or culture? Concepts of identity in the Alevi diaspora', Paper presented at conference on 'Locality, identity, diaspora', University of Hamburg.

Solomos, J. and J. Wrench (eds) (1995) *Racism and Migration in Western Europe*, Oxford and New York: Berg.

Spellman, K. (2004) *Religion and Nation: Iranian Local and Transnational Networks in Britain*, New York: Berghahn.

Spivak, G. C. (1999) *Critique of Postcolonial Reason: Towards a History of the Vanishing Present*, Cambridge, MA: Harvard University Press.

Spooner, B. (1986) 'Weavers and dealers: the authenticity of an oriental carpet', in A. Appadurai (ed.), *The Social Life of Things: Commodities in Cultural Perspective*, Cambridge: Cambridge University Press, pp. 195–235.

Sreberny, A. (2001) 'Media and diasporic consciousness: an exploration among Iranians in London', in S. Cottle (ed.), *Ethnic Minorities and the Media: Changing Cultural Boundaries*, Buckingham: Open University Press, pp. 179–96.

Stam, R. (2003) 'Beyond Third Cinema: the aesthetics of hybridity', in A. Guneratne and W. Dissanayake (eds), *Rethinking Third Cinema*, London and New York: Routledge, pp. 31–48.

Stasiulis, D. K. and A. B. Bakan (2005)

Negotiating Citizenship: Migrant Women in Canada and the Global System, Toronto: University of Toronto Press.

Stephen, L. (2007) *Transborder Lives: Indigenous Oaxacans in Mexico, California, and Oregon*, Durham, NC: Duke University Press.

Stepick, A. (1998) *Pride against Prejudice: Haitians in the United States*, Boston, MA: Allyn and Bacon.

Stepick, A. and C. Dutton Stepick (2009) 'Diverse contexts of reception and feelings of belonging', *FQS, Forum: Qualitative Social Research, Sozialforschung*, 10: 1–17, www.qualitative-research.net/index.php/fqs/article/view/1366/2863, accessed 14 January 2010.

Stepick, A. and G. Grenier (1993) 'Cubans in Miami', in J. Moore and R. Rivera (eds), *In the Barrios: Latinos and the Underclass Debate*, New York: Russell Sage Foundation, pp. 79–100.

Stepick, A., G. Grenier, M. Castro and M. Dunn (2003) *This Land Is Our Land: Immigrants and Power in Miami*, Berkeley: University of California Press.

Stewart, C. and R. Shaw (eds) (1994) *Syncretism/Anti-syncretism: The Politics of Religious Synthesis*, London: Routledge.

Stewart, J. (2010) (ed.) *Venture Smith and the Business of Slavery and Freedom*, Boston, MA: University of Massachusetts Press.

Stiglitz, J. E. (2002) *Globalization and Its Discontents*, New York: Norton.

Stoler, A. L. (1995) *Race and the Education of Desire: Foucault's History of Sexuality and the Colonial Order of Things*, Durham, NC: Duke University Press.

Stratton, J. (2000) 'Not just another multicultural story: the English from "fitting in" to self-ethnicisation', *Journal of Australian Studies*, 24(66): 23–47.

Sullivan, Z. T. (2001) *Exiled Memories: Stories of the Iranian Diaspora*, Philadelphia, PA: Temple University Press.

Sun, W. (2002) *Leaving China: Media, Migration and Transnational Imagination*, Lanham, MD: Rowman and Littlefield.

Susumu, M. and J. Yamashiro (1992)

'A Comunidade Enfrenta um Caos sem Precedentes', in Comissão de Elaboração da História dos 80 Anos da Imigração Japonesa no Brasil, *Uma Epopéia Moderna: 80 Anos da Imigração Japonesa no Brasil*, São Paulo: Editora Hucitec, pp. 265–360.

Sutton, D. E. (2001) *Remembrance of Repasts: An Anthropology of Food and Memory*, Oxford: Berg.

Sweet, J. (1996) *Recreating Africa: Culture, Kinship and Religion in the African-Portuguese World*, Chapel Hill: University of North Carolina Press, Chapel Hill.

Sweetman, C. (1998) *Gender and Migration: Oxfam Focus on Gender*, Oxford: Oxfam.

Swidler, A. (1986) 'Culture in action: symbols and strategies', *American Sociological Review*, 51(2): 273–86.

Tadman, M. (1989) *Speculators and Slaves: Masters, Traders, and Slaves in the Old South*, Madison: University of Wisconsin Press.

Tarr, C. (2005) *Reframing Difference:* Beur *and* banlieue *Filmmaking in France*, Manchester: Manchester University Press.

Taylor, C. (1994) 'Multiculturalism and "the politics of recognition"', in A. Gutmann (ed.), *Multiculturalism and the Politics of Recognition*, Princeton, NJ: Princeton University Press.

Taylor, D. (2003) *The Archive and the Repertoire: Performing Cultural Memory in the Americas*, Durham, NC, and London: Duke University Press.

Tennenhouse, L. (2007) *The Importance of Feeling English: American Literature and the British Diaspora, 1750–1850*, Princeton, NJ: Princeton University Press.

Thieme, J. (1999) *Derek Walcott*, Manchester: Manchester University Press.

Thiranagama, S. (2010) 'Partitioning the BBC: from colonial to postcolonial broadcaster', in M. Gillespie, A. Pinkerton, G. Baumann and S. Thiranagama, *South Asian Diaspora*, 2(1): 39–55.

Thomas, D. (2008) 'Wal-Mart, "Katrina" and other ideological tricks: Jamaican hotel workers in Michigan', in T. Campt and D. Thomas (eds), *Gender-*

ing Diasporas, special issue of *Feminist Review*, 90.

Thomason, S. and T. Kaufman (1988) *Language Contact, Creolization, and Genetic Linguistics*, Berkeley: University of California Press.

Thomson, A. (1999) 'Moving stories: oral history and migration studies', *Oral History*, 27(1): 24–37.

Thornton, J. (1998) *Africa and Africans in the Making of the Atlantic World, 1400–1800*, Cambridge: Cambridge University Press.

Thrasher, F. (1927) *The Gang*, Chicago, IL: University of Chicago Press.

Tighe, J. (2005) *Constructing Suiyuan. The Politics of Northwestern Territory and Development in Early Twentieth-century China*, Leiden: Brill.

Tigner, J. L. (1961) 'Shindo Remmei: Japanese nationalism in Brazil', *Hispanic American Historical Review*, 41(4): 515–32.

Tolia-Kelly, D. (2004) 'Locating processes of identification: studying the precipitates of re-memory through artefacts in the British Asian home', *Transactions of the Institute of British Geographers*, New Series, 29(3): 314–29.

Tölölyan, K. (1991) 'The nation state and its others: in lieu of a preface', *Diaspora*, 1(1): 3–7.

— (1996) 'Rethinking *diaspora*(s): stateless power in the transnational moment', *Diaspora*, 5(1): 3–36.

— (2007) 'The Armenian diaspora and the Karabagh conflict since 1988', in H. Smith and P. Stares (eds), *Diasporas in Conflict: Peace-makers or Peace-wreckers?*, Tokyo, New York, Paris: United Nations University Press, pp. 106–28.

Tolts, M. (2004) 'The post-Soviet Jewish population in Russia and the world', *Jews in Russia and Eastern Europe*, 1(52): 37–63.

Tönnies, F. (1912) *Gemeinschaft und Gesellschaft*, Berlin: Karl Curtius.

Torabully, K. and M. Carter (2002) *Coolitude: An Anthology of the Indian Labour Diaspora*, London: Anthem Press.

Trivellato, F. (2009) *The Familiarity of Strangers: The Sephardic Diaspora, Livorno, and Cross-Cultural Trade in the Early Modern Period*, New Haven, CT: Yale University Press.

Tromp, J. (1998) 'The ancient Jewish diaspora: some linguistic and socio-logical observations', in G. ter Haar (ed.), *Strangers and Sojourners: Religious Communities in the Diaspora*, Leuven: Uitgeverij Peeters, pp. 13–35.

Tsemberis, S. J. (1999) 'Greek American families: immigration, acculturation and psychological well-being', in S. J. Tsemberis, A. Karpathakis and H. J. Psomiades (eds), *Greek American Families: Traditions and Transforma-tions*, New York: Pella, pp. 197–222.

Tsemberis, S. J., A. Karpathakis and H. J. Psomiades (eds) (1999) *Greek American Families: Traditions and Transformations*, New York: Pella.

Tsuda, T. (2009) *Diasporic Homecomings: Ethnic Return Migration in Comparative Perspective*, Stanford, CA: Stanford University Press.

Turner, B. S. (1994) *Orientalism, Post-modernism and Globalism*, London: Routledge.

Turner, S. (2008a) 'The waxing and waning of the political field in Burundi and its diaspora', *Ethnic and Racial Studies*, 31(4): 742–65.

— (2008b) 'Cyberwars of words: express-ing the unspeakable in Burundi's dias-pora', *Journal of Ethnic and Migration Studies*, 34(7): 1161–80.

Tweed, T. A. (1997) *Our Lady of the Exile: Diasporic Religion at a Cuban Catholic Shrine in Miami*, New York: Oxford University Press.

— (2006) *Crossing and Dwelling: A Theory of Religion*, Cambridge, MA: Harvard University Press.

Tyner, J. A. (2004) *Made in the Philippines: Gendered Discourses and the Making of Migrants*, New York: Routledge.

Um, H. (ed.) (2005) *Diasporas and Inter-culturalism in Asian Performing Arts*, Oxford: Routledge.

United Nations (2008) 'Trends in total migrant stock: 2008 revision', esa.un.org/migration, accessed 6 January 2010.

UNPA (2007) 'State of the world popula-tion 2007: unleashing the potential of human growth', www.unfpa.org/swp/2007/english/introduction.html, accessed 25 August 2009.

Urry, J. (2000) *Sociology beyond Societies: Mobilities for the Twenty-first Century*, London: Routledge.

Van Hear, N. (1998) *New Diasporas: The Mass Exodus, Dispersal and Regroup-ing of Migrant Communities*, London: Routledge.

— (2002) 'Sustaining societies under strain: remittances as a form of transnational exchange in Sri Lanka and Ghana', in K. Koser and N. Al-Ali (eds), *New Approaches to Migration: Transnational Communities and the Transformation of Home*, London and New York: Routledge, pp. 202–23.

— (2006) '"I went as far as my money would take me": conflict, forced migration and class', in F. Crepeau et al. (eds), *Forced Migration and Global Processes: A View from Forced Migration Studies*, Lanham, MD: Lexington/Row-man and Littlefield.

— (2009a) 'The rise of refugee diasporas', *Current History*, 108(717): 180–85.

— (with R. Brubaker and T. Bessa) (2009b) *Managing Mobility for Human Develop-ment: The Growing Salience of Mixed Migration*, UNDP Human Development Research Paper 2009/20, UNDP, New York.

Van Munster, R. (2009) *Securitizing Im-migration: The Politics of Risk in the EU*, London: Palgrave Macmillan.

Van Unnik, W. C. (1993) *Das Selbstver-ständnis der jüdischen Diaspora der hellenistisch-römischen Zeit*, ed. P. W. van der Horst, Leiden: Brill.

Vásquez, M. A. and M. F. Marquardt (2003) *Globalizing the Sacred: Religion across the Americas*, New Brunswick, NJ: Rut-gers University Press.

Velasco Ortiz, L. (2005) *Mixtec Trans-national Identity*, Tucson: University of Arizona Press.

Venturino, S. (1997) 'Reading negotiations in the Tibetan diaspora', in F. J. Korom (ed.), *Constructing Tibetan Culture: Contemporary Perspectives*, Quebec: Heritage Press, pp. 98–121.

Vertovec, S. (1997) 'Three meanings of "diaspora" exemplified among South Asian religions', *Diaspora: A Journal of Transnational Studies*, 6(3): 277–99.

— (1999) 'Conceiving and researching transnationalism', *Ethnic and Racial Studies*, 22(2): 447–62.

— (2004a) 'Migrant transnationalism and modes of transformation', *International Migration Review*, 38(3): 970–1001.

— (2004b) 'Religion and diaspora', in P. Antes, A. W. Geertz and R. Warne (eds), *New Approaches to the Study of Religion: Textual, Comparative, Sociological, and Cognitive Approaches*, Berlin and New York: Verlag de Gruyter, pp. 275–303.

— (2006) 'Diasporas good, diasporas bad', *Metropolis World Bulletin*, 6.

— (2007) 'Super-diversity and its implications', *Ethnic and Racial Studies*, 30(6): 1024–54.

Vertovec, S. and R. Cohen (eds) (1999) *Migration, Diasporas and Transnationalism*, Cheltenham: Edward Elgar.

Vickerman, M. (1998) *West Indian Immigrants and Race*, Oxford: Oxford University Press.

Wakeman, F., Jr (1966) *Strangers at the Gate: Social Disorder in South China, 1839–1861*, Berkeley: University of California Press.

Waldinger, R. (1986) *Through the Eye of the Needle: Immigrants and Enterprise in New York's Garment Trades*, New York: New York University Press.

Walsh, K. (2006) 'British expatriate belongings: mobile homes and transnational homing', *Home Cultures*, 3(2): 123–44.

Wang, G. (1991) *China and the Chinese Overseas*, Singapore: Times Academic Press.

Ward, S. (2001) *Australia and the British Embrace: The Demise of the Imperial Ideal*, Melbourne: Melbourne University Press.

Warner, M. (ed.) (1993) *Fear of a Queer Planet: Queer Politics and Social Theory*, Minneapolis and London: University of Minnesota Press.

Warner, S. R. and J. G. Wittner (1998) *Gatherings in Diaspora: Religious Communities and the New Migration*, Philadelphia, PA: Temple University Press.

Watanabe, M. (ed.) (1995) *Kyôdôkenkyû dekassegui-nikkei-baurajiru-jin: shiryô-hen* [Group study – Brazilian Dekaseguis], vol. 2, Tokyo: Akashi Shoten.

Waters, J. (2006) 'Geographies of cultural capital: education, international migration and family strategies between Hong Kong and Canada', *Transactions of the Institute of British Geographers*, 31(2): 179–92.

Wayland, S. (2004) 'Ethnonationalist networks and transnational opportunities: the Sri Lankan Tamil diaspora', *Review of International Studies*, 30(3): 405–26.

Weber, E. (1976) *Peasants into Frenchmen: The Modernization of Rural France 1870–1914*, Stanford, CA: Stanford University Press.

Weekley, K. (2004) 'Saving pennies for the state? A new role for Filipino migrant workers', *Journal of Contemporary Asia*, 34(3): 349–64.

Weiner, M. (1986) 'Labour migrants as incipient diasporas', in G. Sheffer (ed.), *Modern Diasporas in International Politics*, London: Croom Helm.

Weinreich, U. (1966 [1953]) *Languages in Contact*, 2nd edn, The Hague: Mouton de Gruyter.

Weissbort, D. (ed.) (2003) 'Poets at Bush House: the BBC World Service', Special issue of *Modern Poetry in Translation*, 22.

Werbner, P. (1984) 'Business on trust: Pakistani entrepreneurship in the Manchester garment trade', in R. Ward and F. Reeves (eds), *Ethnic Communities in Business*, Cambridge: Cambridge University Press, pp. 166–88.

— (1996) 'Public spaces, political voices: gender, feminism and aspects of British Muslim participation in the public sphere', in W. A. R. Shadid and

P. S. van Koningsveld (eds), *Political Participation and Identities of Muslims in Non-Muslim States*, Kampen: Kok Pharos, pp. 53–70.

— (1997a) 'Introduction', in P. Werbner and T. Modood (eds), *Debating Cultural Hybridity*, London: Zed Books, pp. 1–26.

— (1997b) 'Essentialising essentialism, essentialising silence', in P. Werbner and T. Modood (eds), *Debating Cultural Hybridity*, London: Zed Books, pp. 226–54.

— (1999a) 'Global pathways: working class cosmopolitans and the creation of transnational ethnic worlds', *Social Anthropology*, 7(1): 17–35.

— (1999b) 'Political motherhood and the feminisation of citizenship: women's activism and the transformation of the public sphere', in N. Yuval-Davis and P. Werbner (eds), *Women, Citizenship and Difference*, London: Zed Books, pp. 221–45.

— (2000) 'Introduction', *Diaspora*, 9(1): 83–106.

— (2002a) 'The place which is diaspora: citizenship, religion and gender in the making of chaordic transnationalism', *Journal of Ethnic and Migration Studies*, 28(1): 119–33.

— (2002b) *Imagined Diasporas amongst Manchester Muslims: The Public Performance of Pakistani Transnational Identity Politics*, Oxford: James Currey.

— (2004) 'Theorising complex diasporas: purity and hybridity in the diasporic public sphere', *Journal of Ethnic and Migration Studies*, 30(5): 895–911.

Werbner, P. and M. Anwar (eds) (1991) *Black and Ethnic Leaderships in Britain: The Cultural Dimensions of Political Action*, London: Routledge.

Wesling, M. (2008) 'Why queer diaspora?', in T. Campt and D. Thomas (eds), *Gendering Diasporas*, special issue of *Feminist Review*, 90: 30–47.

Westwood, S. and P. Bhachu (eds) (1988) *Enterprising Women: Ethnicity, Economy and Gender Relations*, London: Routledge.

Whitaker, M. (2004) 'Tamilnet.com: some reflections on popular anthropology, nationalism, and the Internet', *Anthropological Quarterly*, 77(3): 469–98.

Williams, E. (1944) *Capitalism and Slavery*, Chapel Hill: University of North Carolina Press.

Wills, S. (2002) 'Unstitching the lips of a migrant nation', *Australian Historical Studies*, 33(118): 71–89.

— (2004) 'When good neighbours become good friends: Australia's possession of its millionth migrant', *Australian Historical Studies*, 35(124): 332–54.

— (2005) 'Passengers of memory: constructions of British immigrants in post-imperial Australia', *Australian Journal of Politics and History*, 51(1): 94–107.

Wills, S. and K. Darian-Smith (2003) 'Beauty contest for British bulldogs: negotiating transnational identities in suburban Melbourne', *Cultural Studies Review*, 9(2): 65–83.

Wilson, R. and W. Dissanayake (eds) (1996) *Global/Local: Dimensions of the Transnational Imaginary*, Durham, NC: Duke University Press.

Wimmer, A. and N. Glick Schiller (2003) 'Methodological nationalism and the study of migration', *International Migration Review*, 37(3): 576–610.

Winch, J. (2002) *A Gentleman of Color: The Life of James Forten*, Oxford and New York: Oxford University Press.

Wirth, L. (1928) *The Ghetto*, Chicago, IL: University of Chicago Press.

Wolf, E. R. (1982) *Europe and the People without History*, Berkeley: University of California Press.

Wong, L. (2003) 'Chinese business migration to Australia, Canada and the United States: state policy and the global immigration marketplace', *Asia and Pacific Migration Journal*, 12(3): 301–36.

Yan Haiping (2005) 'Other transnationals: an introductory essay', *Modern Drama*, 48(2): 225–48.

Young, I. M. (1987) 'Impartiality and the civic public: some implications of feminist critiques of moral and political theory', in S. Benhabib and D. Cornell (eds), *Feminism as Critique: Essays on the Politics of Gender in Late-Capitalist Societies*, Cambridge: Polity Press, pp. 56–76.

— (1990) *Justice and the Politics of Difference*, Princeton, NJ: Princeton University Press.

Young, R. (1995) *Colonial Desire: Hybridity in Theory, Culture and Race*, London: Routledge.

Yuval-Davis, N. (1997) *Gender and Nation*, London, New Delhi and New York: Sage.

Zentella, A. C. (2002) 'Spanish in New York', in O. Garcia and J. A. Fishman (eds), *The Multilingual Apple: Languages in New York City*, 2nd edn, New York: Mouton de Gruyter, pp. 167–201.

Zhang, L. (2001) *Strangers in the City: Reconfigurations of Space, Power, and Social Networks within China's Floating Population*, Stanford, CA: Stanford University Press.

Zorbaugh, H. (1929) *Gold Coast and Slum: A Sociological Study of Chicago's Near North Side*, Chicago, IL: University of Chicago Press.

Zukin, S. (1995) *The Cultures of Cities*, Oxford: Blackwell.

Index

cyborg, 60

Dalai Lama, 15, 211, 212, 214, 215
Dama, a musician, 252
deindustrialization of cities, 108
Dellali, Karim, 249, 252–4
democracy, 77; liberal, as hegemonic culture, 50
Deng Xiaoping, 208
deterritorialization, 167, 224, 258
development, in relation to diasporas, 102–6
development studies: and diaspora studies, 104–6; decolonization of, 105
diaspeírein, 129
diaspora: and creolization, 73; as a category of practice, 116; as biological term, 79; as exhausted concept, 2; as generator of cultural newness, 147–9; as 'group of migrants', 104; as mobile seed, 123; as neologism, 20–1; as opportunity, 26; as part of soteriological scheme, 21–2; classic, 114; concept of, 70, 81, 112 (limits of, 11, 74–5; overloaded, 70); contingency of, 116; definition of, 112, 198; durability of, 37–8; empirical, 112; empowering paradox of, 26; end of, 263–8; individualization of, 135; multidisciplinary approach to, 269; origin of term, 263; use of term, 55, 102, 129, 270, 271 (in Christianity, 22)
Diaspora: A Journal of Transnational Studies, 9
diaspora entrepreneurial networks, 87–8
diaspora–homeland binary, 267
diaspora space, 11, 82–3, 89, 90, 113, 116, 152, 160, 270, 271–3
diaspora studies, 1–5, 35, 46, 83, 104–6, 244–5, 257, 269; breadth of, 7; consolidation phase in, 116–17; emphasis on culture, 272; genealogy of, 9; spatial theory in, 79–80
diaspora theory, critique of, 112–17
diasporas: analysis of, 58; as enabling contexts, 119; as essence of globalization, 97; as historical formations, 74; as peacemakers/peacebreakers, 12, 99; bad, 57; complex, 74–8; empirical, 113–16; formation of, 34–7; good, 56–7; metaphorical, 113–16; of

casualization, 55; of settlement, 55; or privilege, 113; pluralized, 2, 126; political volatility of, 58; segmented, 76; social heterogeneity of, 74; statistics for, 5–7; typology of *see* typology of diasporas; working-class, 176
diasporic consciousness, 223
diasporic identities: hybridity of, 136; preservation of, 184–5; production of, 56; recasting of, 72
diasporic journeys, historicization of, 230
difference, 50, 51, 112–17; categorizations of, 12; in category of women, 119–20
dignity, 52
dislocation, vocabularies of, 261
diversity: in cyberspace, 168; penchant for, 64
Diversity Lottery (USA), 188
Dolan, Jill, 155
double consciousness, 160
dual loyalty of migrants, 37, 98
DuFoix, S., 114
Durkheim, Emile, 128
Dutch East India Company, 87

East African railway line, building of, 246
East West Players, 151
Economic and Social Research Council (ESRC), 3
economies, in relation to diasporas, 87–90
Egypt, ancient, 20
El Salvador, refugees from, 176
El-Mejjad, Youssef, 249, 254–5
electronic communications, 75, 109, 162, 165, 177; in music, 255
Eliade, Mircea, 128
Elmina Castle (Ghana), 1, 18
emperor worship among Japanese, 201
Epicurus, 20
Equiano, Olaudah, 33
Erikson, Erik, 69
Eritrean diaspora, 167, 168, 169
essentialization of groupings, 51, 61
Esslin, Martin, 237
ethnic economies, 88
ethnic labels, meaning of, 32
ethnic lobbies, 92, 95
ethnic-niche businesses, 184
ethnicity, 10, 45–9, 50–1, 109, 120–1, 198, 200, 269; commodification of, 89; methodological, 42